San Representation

The San or Bushmen of southern Africa have exerted a fascination over generations of writers and scholars, from novelists and anarchists to ethnologists and geneticists, and also occupy a special place in the popular imagination as the First People and the contemporary remnant of spiritual and natural man. The ways in which particular groups of people from southern Africa have been traditionally categorised as San or Bushman and positioned as objects of scrutiny by a range of academic disciplines is increasingly being contested and questioned. There is also a growing awareness of the cultural, economic and genetic entanglement of the peoples of the region.

This book examines how San and Khoe people are represented, by others, as well as by those who themselves identify as San or Khoe. The book interrogates the ways in which disciplines, through their methodologies and ways of authorising knowledge, not only 'discover' or 'reveal' knowledge but produce it in ways that involve complex and often ambiguous relationships with power structures and forms of intellectual, symbolic and cultural capital. One major trend that emerges from the different essays is that the San and Khoe can no longer be seen as people of the past but have to be acknowledged as contemporary and socially situated individuals and communities who are increasingly contesting the representations which others have imposed on them.

This book was originally published as two special issues of *Critical Arts: South-North Cultural and Media Studies*.

Keyan G. Tomaselli is distinguished professor, University of Johannesburg, and was previously director of the Centre for Communication Media and Society, University of KwaZulu-Natal, Durban, South Africa. His books on the topic include *Cultural Tourism: Rethinking Indigeneity* (2012), *Writing in the San/d* (2007), and *Where Global Contradictions are Sharpest* (2005).

Michael Wessels is an associate professor in the Department of English at the University of the Western Cape, Cape Town, South Africa. He has written extensively about San narrative and the theory and politics of interpreting folklore and mythology. He is the author of *Bushman Letters* (2010).

San Representation

Politics, practice and possibilities

Edited by

Keyan G. Tomaselli and Michael Wessels

Routledge
Taylor & Francis Group

LONDON AND NEW YORK

First published 2015
by Routledge

2 Park Square, Milton Park, Abingdon, Oxon OX14 4RN
711 Third Avenue, New York, NY 10017, USA

Routledge is an imprint of the Taylor & Francis Group, an informa business

First issued in paperback 2017

Copyright © 2015 Critical Arts Projects & Unisa Press

All rights reserved. No part of this book may be reprinted or reproduced or
utilised in any form or by any electronic, mechanical, or other means, now
known or hereafter invented, including photocopying and recording, or in
any information storage or retrieval system, without permission in writing
from the publishers.

Notice:
Product or corporate names may be trademarks or registered trademarks,
and are used only for identification and explanation without intent to
infringe.

British Library Cataloguing in Publication Data
A catalogue record for this book is available from the British Library

ISBN 13: 978-1-138-89844-8 (hbk)
ISBN 13: 978-1-138-08295-3 (pbk)

Typeset in Times New Roman
by RefineCatch Limited, Bungay, Suffolk

Publisher's Note
The publisher accepts responsibility for any inconsistencies that may have
arisen during the conversion of this book from journal articles to book chapters,
namely the possible inclusion of journal terminology.

Disclaimer
Every effort has been made to contact copyright holders for their permission to
reprint material in this book. The publishers would be grateful to hear from any
copyright holder who is not here acknowledged and will undertake to rectify
any errors or omissions in future editions of this book.

Contents

CONTENTS

Citation Information

The chapters in this book were originally published in the journal *Critical Arts: South-North Cultural and Media Studies*. When citing this material, please use the original journal volume and issue number, and page numbering for each article, as follows:

Chapter 1

San representation: an overview of the field
Michael Wessels
Critical Arts: South-North Cultural and Media Studies, volume 28, issue 3 (2014)
pp. 465–471

Chapter 2

To exhibit or be exhibited: the visual art of Vetkat Regopstaan Boesman Kruiper
Nyasha Mboti
Critical Arts: South-North Cultural and Media Studies, volume 28, issue 3 (2014)
pp. 472–492

Chapter 3

Simulacral, genealogical, auratic and representational failure: Bushman authenticity as methodological collapse
William Ellis
Critical Arts: South-North Cultural and Media Studies, volume 28, issue 3 (2014)
pp. 493–520

Chapter 4

Development narratives: the value of multiple voices and ontologies in Kalahari research
Lauren Dyll-Myklebust
Critical Arts: South-North Cultural and Media Studies, volume 28, issue 3 (2014)
pp. 521–538

CITATION INFORMATION

Chapter 5

The music of dead sisters: a feminist comparison of two folktales about singing bones and reeds
Cheryl Stobie
Critical Arts: South-North Cultural and Media Studies, volume 28, issue 3 (2014)
pp. 539–554

Chapter 6

The creation of the eland: a close reading of a Drakensberg San narrative
Michael Wessels
Critical Arts: South-North Cultural and Media Studies, volume 28, issue 3 (2014)
pp. 555–568

Chapter 7

The damaging effects of romantic mythopoeia on Khoesan linguistics
Menán du Plessis
Critical Arts: South-North Cultural and Media Studies, volume 28, issue 3 (2014)
pp. 569–592

Chapter 8

The boer and the jackal: satire and resistance in Khoi orature
Hermann Wittenberg
Critical Arts: South-North Cultural and Media Studies, volume 28, issue 4 (2014)
pp. 593–609

Chapter 9

'Di-xɛrretən and the lioness': text and landscape of a |Xam narrative
José Manuel de Prada-Samper
Critical Arts: South-North Cultural and Media Studies, volume 28, issue 4 (2014)
pp. 610–630

Chapter 10

Who owns what? Indigenous knowledge and struggles over representation
Keyan G. Tomaselli
Critical Arts: South-North Cultural and Media Studies, volume 28, issue 4 (2014)
pp. 631–647

Chapter 11

Narrating Biesje Poort: negotiating absence of storyline, vagueness and multivocality in the representation of Southern Kalahari rock engravings
David Morris
Critical Arts: South-North Cultural and Media Studies, volume 28, issue 4 (2014)
pp. 648–669

Please direct any queries you may have about the citations to
clsuk.permissions@cengage.com

Permissions

Chapter 11

Narrating Biesje Poort: negotiating absence of storyline, vagueness and multivocality in the representation of Southern Kalahari rock engravings

David Morris

Notes on Contributors

José Manuel de Prada-Samper is a postdoctoral researcher in English Studies at the University of KwaZulu-Natal, Pietermaritzburg, South Africa.

Menán du Plessis is a research associate in the Department of Linguistics at Stellenbosch University, South Africa.

Lauren Dyll-Myklebust is a lecturer at the Centre for Communication, Media and Society (CCMS) at the University of KwaZulu-Natal, South Africa.

William Ellis is a lecturer at the University of the Western Cape, South Africa.

Nyasha Mboti is a senior lecturer in the Department of Communication Studies at the University of Johannesburg, South Africa.

Mark McGranaghan is a postdoctoral researcher at the Rock Art Research Institute, University of the Witwatersrand, South Africa.

David Morris is affiliated to the Department of Archaeology at the McGregor Museum in Kimberley and the Department of Heritage Studies, Sol Plaatje University, South Africa.

Anne Solomon is an archaeologist whose principal research interest is the rock arts of San-speaking peoples.

Cheryl Stobie is an associate professor in English Studies at the University of KwaZulu-Natal, Pietermaritzburg, South Africa.

Keyan G. Tomaselli is distinguished professor, University of Johannesburg, and was previously director of the Centre for Communication, Media and Society at the University of KwaZulu-Natal, South Africa.

Michael Wessels is an associate professor in the Department of English at the University of the Western Cape, Cape Town, South Africa.

Justine Wintjes is a lecturer in History of Art, Wits School of Arts, University of the Witwatersrand, South Africa.

Hermann Wittenberg is an associate professor at the Department of English, University of the Western Cape, South Africa.

San representation: an overview of the field

Michael Wessels

The title of the special issues on 'San representation', published in two parts, is deliberately ambiguous. It seeks to capture both the representation of the San in various media, including academic publications, popular culture, literature, film and advertising, and also representation of various sorts by people who have been identified as San in the past, or who themselves claim such an identity today. The phrase includes 'traditional' and contemporary narrative, art, dance, music, political writing and autobiography as well as forms of self-representation that are linked to different kinds of political activism and economic activity. The title also seeks to enlist the sense of the word 'representation' as participation and representivity, in order to encourage discussion of forms of inclusion and exclusion in relation to the broader political and economic life of the region of people who identify as San, Khoe or Khoesan, and also in the ways that knowledge is produced and authorised.

The 1980s saw the beginning of a critical and self-reflexive turn in the study of San ethnography, culture and representation. In 1995 the ground-breaking issue of the journal *Critical Arts*, 'Recuperating the San' appeared and was followed a year later by the set of essays in Pippa Skotnes' *Miscast: negotiating the presence of the Bushmen*. Twenty years on, it is striking to see how current most of the debates and concerns that ran through the essays in the two volumes still are. At the same time there have been many new developments within the disciplines that comprise the broader research field, as well as in the arena of San and Khoi identity politics, in addition to a growing awareness of the historical, cultural, economic and genetic entanglement of the peoples of the region and of the ideological basis of much of the research related to the San. Researchers are also increasingly being challenged from outside the academy. What they see as a contribution to the universal knowledge base of mankind can be regarded as the appropriation of cultural capital by others, the contemporary manifestation of old colonial relationships.

Critical Arts, though drawing much of its early conceptual framework from European social theory and, later, British cultural and media studies, from the very first number (see Van Zyl 1980) attempted to position the journal's work in a south–north, and, more recently, an east–west axis. In pursuing these inter-hemispherical links with regard to global aboriginal studies, the journal has opened sustained spaces for comparative studies that link theories and case studies, rather than publishing only on *one* geographically located group. In this vein, work published on and by Australian Aboriginals has shaped debates in, and on, the publication itself (see, e.g., Mudrodroo 1996; Trees and Turk 1998) and on issues of governmentality, comparing, for example, the Sami (Norwegian) and Botswanan approaches to ethical political organisation and economic development (Mikalsen 2008). Steve Mickler (1998) examines pathologies of othering of Aboriginals, an analysis that is relevant to studies of the San also (see Webster [2000] for an analysis of anthropomorphic photographs commissioned by Wilhelm Bleek, whose work features extensively in this volume). Finally, there is the article by Megan Biesele (2000) that examines processes of discourse development amongst the Ju|'hoansi in post-independence Namibia. These are just a few of the studies carried by the journal on the topic.

It is hoped that the articles in the current issues, drawn as they are from a number of disciplines and approaches to research, will in the future lead to more cross-pollination and further comparative analysis with regard to ideas and methodologies. Also, we hope that a greater interrogation will occur of the ways in which disciplines, through their methodologies and ways of sanctioning knowledge, not only 'discover' or 'reveal' knowledge but produce it in ways that involve complex and often ambiguous relationships with power structures.

The different disciplines offer different bodies of knowledge and modes of discourse in relation to the Khoe and the San; at the same time they also impose limits on the sorts of thinking, research and modes of interpretation that are possible (see Mboti, this issue). The broader corpus of *Critical Arts*' work is neither solely anthropological, nor solely cultural studies, but like the conference from which these issues arose is multi-disciplinary. It is this mixture that provides broader conceptual and methodological traction with regard to what might be termed 'aboriginal studies'. Taken together, the articles featured here provide a context in which these limits can be identified, interrogated and transgressed. The debates in the summing up section are particularly important in this regard.

One common thread, it seems to me, that emerges in all the articles despite their different and sometimes antithetical approaches, is that categories such as 'San' and 'Khoe' cannot be used uncritically to refer to essentialised, unhistoricised and pure identities. The San and Khoe are not people of the past but have to be acknowledged as contemporary and socially situated individuals and communities, whose histories, cultures, languages and genes are interwoven in complex and contested ways with those of others in the region. The contributions in this issue examine not only the implications this has for current academic practice and knowledge production, but also for the re-appraisal of past work, by earlier generations of scholars.

The disciplines that together constitute something that might be called 'Khoesan studies' often have surprisingly little in common beyond perhaps their origins in colonialism and their apparently common object of study. Indeed, the San, and people like them, were central to the formation of several of these disciplines, and in some way a necessary invention for their existence in the 19th century (see Wright and Weinthroub, Part II). It is not too far-fetched to claim that we are often talking about a belief in something rather than a tangible, historical presence.

It is true that the San (and people categorised with them, such as native Americans and Aboriginals) as an object of study have generated an enormous amount of knowledge of various sorts. One has only to think of rock art studies, anthropology, linguistics and archaeology. The idea of the San has philosophical, political and even spiritual potency. But many of the articles in these two issues raise a critical question: what happens when an object of knowledge becomes the subject and agent of history, especially in the inflammatory historical context of genocide, colonisation, racism and competing nationalisms? What happens, too, when historical work problematises a category, such as 'San', at the same time as it is being claimed by contemporary actors? There is a speaking back today, from contemporary people and also from the archives of rock art and narrative, as they are approached in new ways. The researched might manipulate the researchers for different purposes, reverse the anthropological gaze, or respond in the voice of anger or beauty or the everyday. The binary of knower and the source of knowledge is breaking down. As Tomaselli writes: 'The other is now within the academy' (see Part II).

Areas of dissonance emerged in the discussions during the conference on San representation from which the articles in these two issues resulted. These are cogently presented in Keyan Tomaselli's position paper on the fissures that were in evidence. His observations are supported or challenged in some of the other responses to the conference and also to his paper, which was circulated for comment among the delegates. This level of meta-analysis about the general area of Khoesan studies, its aims, pitfalls and ethics, is replicated in several of the articles, particularly in the pieces by Anne Solomon (Part II) and William Ellis (Part I), and again in Tomaselli's own contribution. But the spirit of critical reflexivity and conscious revisionism is present in different ways in almost all the articles. While the contours of the field are contested, and even its reality outside of bad history and ideology is questioned, a revitalisation, reconfiguration and reconceptualisation is in evidence, and has consequences not only for the individual disciplines and their methodologies, but also for the ideological and political economies of the region more broadly. Tomaselli (Part II) again describes the situation trenchantly: 'In post-apartheid South Africa the indigenous are no longer considered indigenous and the new indigenous (i.e., those in power) now control what "indigenous" means.'

Tomaselli, in his comments on the conference, reads the divisions that emerged during the discussions in terms of a split between the messy realities of research involving real agents in the present, and the more clearly delineated and more easily manageable materials that linguists, folklorists and rock art specialists analyse and interpret, even when these are shadowed by a history of genocide and displacement. This division emerged in the responses of people from different disciplines to the self-reflexive anthropological video, *I Am, You Are?* (Sætre 2003). These responses lead Tomaselli to reflect on the possibilities offered by different disciplinary approaches, but even more on their limitations and their openness or suspicion towards the scope and methodologies of other disciplines.

In her article Solomon explores these issues on a theoretical level, discussing the degree to which disciplines represent rather than produce 'authentic' knowledge; without ever claiming that such a knowledge is possible or desirable the article proposes different directions in which Khoesan studies could develop so as to become 'more than purely representational'. Ellis addresses the question of representation and authenticity in a way that is simultaneously theoretical and situated in real-life encounters. San research, however well-intentioned, is inextricably complicit in a history of epistemic violence that has correspondences with other forms of dispossession and genocide. Contemporary people employ various strategies to resist this violence or to exploit their position as informants. They might stage San-ness in various ways, for example, in order to elicit capital from researchers and seldom conform to the type posited by traditional scholarship. They also often refuse to become anthropological subjects and 'authentic' others, or turn the anthropological gaze back on the researcher.

The dynamics and ethics of San research are examined by Tomaselli on a more practical and legal level, in terms of indigenous knowledge and struggles over representation. Who actually owns the research records that result from research projects, and what happens when legalistic notions of intellectual property come into contact with indigenous notions of knowledge and aesthetic production? The article also asks questions about the flow of largesse to the researcher and the subject of research more generally, and examines the role of the publishing industry and other vested interests. The idea of pure research is a naive impossibility in such an environment.

The other articles are primarily concerned with areas of disciplinary specialisation, such as rock art, narrative, tourism and linguistics. Each contribution, in its own way, represents new challenges for its area of research, and is likely to provoke debate and stimulate new work, within the confines of the traditionally demarcated disciplines and beyond.

Menán du Plessis poses a challenge to scholars of Khoe and San languages, arguing that ideas about the primeval nature of the Khoe and San and their location as the first people of the region have interfered with the application of sound linguistic principles when it comes to studying language groups. This has resulted in the construction of linguistic layers that have more to do with ideology than with linguistic realities.

Rock art copies in the 19th century are examined by Justine Wintjes (Part II), who points out that they are not only copies in a literal sense, but representations and interpretations. This leads her to consider questions of authenticity when interrogating the relationship between rock art reproductions and original in situ paintings in a landscape. This approach enables new questions to emerge about both the rock art and its reproduction – ones in which form is not subordinate to content, as is often the case in rock art studies.

Nyasha Mboti brings the discussion of San art into the realm of contemporary artistic practice and the politics of representation in his discussion of the work of the late Vetkat Kruiper. Kruiper's work, he argues, shows that San art cannot be confined to the past, to the rock wall or to the glass case in the museum, where it becomes the possession of the voyeuristic viewer. It is a contemporary form that constitutes 'an active authoring of citizenship and belonging in contemporary South Africa'.

A |Xam story is brought 'back to earth' by José de Prada (Part II), who situates it in a particular place in the northern Cape and also links the 19th narrative to stories told by the present-day inhabitants of the area. Intriguingly, he posits a relationship between the rock engravings in the area and narrative. He argues, too, for an arrangement of the narrative on the page in short lines. This captures the spirit and rhythm of the spoken narrative better than the commonly used prose arrangement of the translated |Xam materials in the Bleek and Lloyd collection.

Mark McGranaghan's exploration of the construction of alterity in |Xam narrative (Part II) shows that narrative can provide a conceptual framework and a language for engaging with and comprehending the violent political milieu of the northern Cape in the 19th century. Categories derived from the characteristics of animals can be transposed to the human sphere. Examining the language of the stories in this way allows for the emergence of representations of self and other, including the colonial relation, that provide a counter-weight to dominant representations.

Both Cheryl Stobie's and Michael Wessels' articles provide readings of San narratives that emphasise their aesthetic and literary qualities, but in very different ways. Stobie produces a feminist reading of a Nama story. She shows in the course of a comparison with an Irish story that the narrative can be linked to a universal story with recurring motifs. The universal story, though, is always reinterpreted in terms of local cultural and social patterns, especially with regard to relations of power and gender. Wessels seeks to restore a sense of aesthetic and conceptual depth to a story from the famous set of narratives Joseph Orpen collected from Qing in the early 1870s in the Malotis. He emphasises the multivocality of the text when it is subjected to the close reading techniques of literary studies, arguing that the story would have elicited a similarly rich and varied (if impossible to recapture) hermeneutic response from an indigenous audience. The stories, the article maintains, have to be considered as literature and not just as ethnographic evidence if their full historical and cultural importance is to be reclaimed for the present.

In Part II, Hermann Wittenberg reminds us of the selective nature of scholarship whose interests give an inaccurate idea of the relative weight of the cultures and literatures of the region. The focus on San narrative over the last half a century has resulted in a neglect of the rich body of Khoe materials that were collected. Wittenberg provides a timely discussion of Wilhelm Bleek's *Reynard the Fox in South Africa; or Hottentot fables and tales*, showing how Khoe orature differs in significant ways from that of the |Xam. Its satirical characteristics have enabled it to become a potent site of cultural, social and psychological resistance to the social and economic order imposed by colonialism.

Lauren Dyll-Myklebust discusses very different sorts of narratives, those used by participants in development projects to describe and analyse their experiences. The critical indigenous qualitative approach that she employs allows for the emergence of a discourse about development that draws on San and Khoe storytelling traditions and categories of thought. Paying attention to these narratives is an essential way of enabling local participants to guide development initiatives, such as the !Xaus Lodge development project in the Kgalagadi Transfrontier Park.

This quick summary of the articles only gives some idea of their rich and varied nature, and of the complex relationships and tensions between them. They will give rise to further debate, some of which will undoubtedly be played out in the future in *Critical Arts*. It is planned that special issues of *Critical Arts* on the Khoe and San, and aboriginality more generally, will become a regular feature.

References

Biesele, M. 2000. To whom it may concern: or, is anyone concerned? The Nyae Nyae Ju|'hoan tape archive, 1987–1993. *Critical Arts: A South-North Journal of Cultural and Media Studies* 14(2): 145–174.

Mickler, S. 1998. News, governmentality and aboriginality: beyond pathologies of othering in media studies. *Critical Arts: A South-North Journal of Cultural and Media Studies* 12(1-2): 45–77.

Mikalsen, O. 2008. Development communication and the paradox of choice: imposition and dictatorship in comparing Sami and San Bushmen experiences of cultural autonomy. *Critical Arts: South–North Cultural and Media Studies* 22(2): 295–332.

Mudrodroo. 1996. Maban reality and shape-shifting the past: strategies to sing the past our way. *Critical Arts: South-North Cultural and Media Studies* 10(2): 1–20.

Sætre, M. 2003. The Bushmen and the others. *Current Writing: Text and Reception in Southern Africa* 15(3): 118–134.

Skotnes, P., ed. 1996. *Miscast: negotiating the presence of the Bushmen.* Cape Town: University of Cape Town.

Trees, K. and A. Turk. 1998. Community, participation and cultural heritage: the Ieramugadu Cultural Heritage Information System (ICIS). *Critical Arts: South-North Cultural and Media Studies* 12(1-2): 78–91.

Van Zyl, J. 1980. 'No God, no morality, no history': South African ethnographic film. *Critical Arts: South-North Cultural and Media Studies* 1(1): 32–37.

Webster, C. 2000. The portrait cabinet of Dr Bleek: anthropometric photographs by early Cape photographers. *Critical Arts: South-North Cultural and Media Studies* 14(1): 1–15.

To exhibit or be exhibited: the visual art of Vetkat Regopstaan Boesman Kruiper

Nyasha Mboti

Abstract

This article examines the visual art of the late San 'Bushman' artist Vetkat Regopstaan Kruiper. The significance of Kruiper's artistic work is explored in order to call into question two problematic assumptions: first, that visual art amongst the San ended with rock art, turning the 'Bushman' artist into a vanished specimen, and, second, that what is found amongst the San today is not, strictly speaking, art. Anchoring these assumptions is the pigeon-holing of 'Bushmen' as objects to be gazed at. Taking its theoretical departure from Lee and Hitchcock's call for an 'expanded anthropology', the article views Vetkat's art as both an act of authoring citizenship and belonging in contemporary South Africa, and as a form of exhibition-resisting exhibition.

Introduction

It is not often that one sees or hears minoritised subjects such as the San representing themselves to themselves, or to the world, on their own terms. Rather, they are talked *about* and represented both by their supporters and detractors. They are the *exhibited* rather than *exhibitors.* The conference that resulted in these two special issues is a case in point. Though the gathering was made up of intellectuals largely sympathetic to the San, not a single 'Bushman' was present to give his/her side of the story. The absence may have been due to logistical or other issues, but it tended to underline the fact that the 'Bushmen' remain the *told* and the talked about.

The *tellers* of San stories remain mainly white intellectuals, and the telling continues to happen with or without the San people's presence. It is as if these 'small relic people' (Lee and De Vore 1976: xvi) were never *necessary* to their own discourse and to discourses *about* them. An infamous instance of this specific 'they-are-not-themselves-needed' discourse is the so-called 'Great Kalahari debate' (Hitchcock 1985; Lee and De Vore 1976; Lewis-Williams and Biesele 1978; Wilmsen 1989). The debate was not 'great' because the San called it great. Rather, it was a great debate because two rival groups of white intellectuals chose to pitch their theoretical camps in an imaginary Kalahari. The Kalahari of the debate was imaginary in the sense that the debate largely took place in the minds of the interlocutors. It was not a debate in which Bushmen themselves debated about their origins and identities.

Why are Bushman *thinking* and *presence* in debates about the Bushman seemingly *unthinkable*? An historical aporia, with its roots in colonial cultures and imperial forgetfulness, seems to prevent Bushmen from being seen as thinkers, artists, philosophers and knowers. Lee and Hitchcock (2001: 273), in calling for an 'expanded anthropology', rightly celebrate the fact that 'perhaps the most significant development of the last two decades has been indigenous peoples speaking to us in their own voices'. This is an extremely important point. But why should this 'significant development' be reduced to a question of *them* speaking to *us*? Which group is encompassed by the term 'us'? Why do we assume that their voice *should* be used to speak to us? Who are we to be spoken to? None of the issues should be about 'us' at all. The prevalence of 'us' in the discourse about Bushmen exemplifies what this articles refers to as the 'glass case' problem within which Bushmen continue to be exhibited – even by those who appear to fight in the Bushmen's 'corner'.

The 'Bushman' historically has been located in the place of the exhibition. When Clicko (real name Franz Taibosh), the so-called 'wild dancing Bushman' (Parsons 2009) died in 1940, the *New York Times* referred to him as 'the only African bushman ever exhibited in this country'. It appears that the only top billing Bushmen and other 'exotics' could be expected to achieve was via the trope of exhibition, as objects being displayed, enjoyed, fought over, fought for, fought against, used or pitied. From 19th-century colonial exhibitions, to Clicko, to *The Gods Must be Crazy* (1980), the Bushman has been constantly subjected to the traumas and absences of exhibition. The expectation that the Bushman is there *to be had*, as exhibition material, is what this article refers to as the glass-case effect. The glass case, a *container* housing exhibited objects, is a central feature of the macro-environments of museums and galleries. Its purpose in relation to the Bushman is its ability to fix, control and manage meanings centring on the Bushman's identity. The view that the Bushman artist has vanished, for instance, is possible only in the context of the historical surveillance and panoptical capabilities of the glass case. This article explores Vetkat's (2014) work in terms of resistance to the glass case, with his visual art being regarded as refracting and critiquing the notions of *display* and *container*.

A people (and an art) presumed extinct

The display and the container are core motifs in a discourse that, wittingly or unwittingly, reduces the San (and the Khoekhoe, among others) to a people presumed extinct. Many writers and scholars, some of them bestselling authors, have suggested that the San are extinct. Alistair Sparks (1997: 12), for instance, claims that there are no San people alive in South Africa today. The same assertion about San extinction is made by Laurens van der Post in *The lost world of the Kalahari* (1977). As one of the first accounts to introduce the (myth of) San to Westerners,[1] *The lost world of the Kalahari* is significant for its myths, the most important of which, as directly implied in the book's title, is that the Kalahari culture of the San represents a lost world.[2] One question that could be asked of Van der Post's thesis is: lost to whom?

The racist marking of the San as belonging to a 'lost world' puts them on the same zoological scale as dinosaurs.[3] As the self-designated last eye-witness of the lost world, Van der Post imagined that he had (re)discovered the lost San in the same way that the fictional Professor Challenger discovered dinosaurs in Venezuela in Arthur Conan Doyle's *The lost world* (1912). In fact, there has never been a point in the history of the San when they needed to be discovered or rediscovered. The San, like other Africans, have always been conscious actors in history, and have never been 'lost'.[4] The myth of lost worlds, expressing the notions of pre-history and irretrievable loss, is itself hinged on displays and containers that have the supposed ability to arrest loss and disintegration.

The myth of discovery, as such, was entirely colonial in origin, in the same way that David Livingstone's discovery of Mosioa Tunya or Robert Fagg's discovery of the so-called Nok culture (Fagg and Plass 1964) were patent colonial myths. Linked to the discovery of the San was the fiction that they were remnants of the Stone Age, and that Van der Post had located the 'last bushman'. This myth dehumanised living Bushmen by suggesting they were a 'vanishing people', soon to be extinct. The myth fed patronising gestures (see Gordon 1985) aimed at the 'conservation' (see Miller [1993] and Kent [1996]) of the Bushman.[5] Ed Wilmsen (1995), Gordon (1993) and a few others have, however, largely debunked the Van der Post-style romanticisation of the San.

The 'discourse on the extinction of primitive races' (Brantlinger 2003) extends to some commentators who sympathise with the cause of the San, with many of them still subscribing to the view that the San 'perished' or, at least, were destined to do so. For instance, Nigel Penn (1996: 83), in discussing the 'destruction of the Cape San', appears to conclude that the San 'perished' through no fault of their own. Robert Thornton (1983), Saul Dubow (1995) and Albert Moran (2009) suggest that well-known archivist of |Xam oral material, Wilhelm Bleek, also viewed Bushmen as a race destined for extinction. Despite his vastly cited /Xam collection, Bleek was a pioneer of the 'discourse of dying races' (Thornton 1983). Former South African president, Thabo Mbeki (in Barnard 2004: 10) – the political figure who presided over the return of parts of ‡Khomani land in the Northern Cape – is also on record as describing the |Xam as a people who 'have perished and even ceased to exist'. Patricia Vinnicombe (1976) makes reference to 'the last' Bushmen of the Maloti-Drakensberg mountains.

The glass case effect

The glass case effect occurs when the object of an exhibition is locked away behind safety glass for purposes of preservation, storage, and, most importantly, display. Glass cases are made to order for artworks, specimens, collectibles, trophies and memorabilia. They are airtight, sealed and climate-controlled. They represent an environment where things can be displayed and, by being displayed, disciplined. This metaphor arises out of my previous work for the National Art Gallery in Zimbabwe, where I assisted with visual art education, curation and preservation. It is during this tenure that I became aware of how the display case interacts with, and shapes, art objects. Display cases are special visual and semiotic objects in their own right, in addition to being permanent and important fixtures of museums and galleries.

The glass case incorporates several features, such as a sturdy wooden pedestal and locks to keep the contents safe. The case may also come with wheels to enable movement from site to site within the protected and protective walls of the exhibition space. Because objects that belong in a glass case are sensitive to damage, the art gallery and the museum are designed to be inert internal dust-proof environments, with minimal sunlight and air circulation. Within the silent and isolated micro-environment of the glass case, climate, humidity and temperature are carefully monitored and managed. All objects meant for display have a display lifespan, and the glass is meant to *prolong* the life of the displayed object. In this way the object continues to be available to paying or invited audiences for as long as possible.

Easily the most important feature of the display case is the glass; often tempered and shatter-resistant, it is the feature that invites the voyeuristic gaze. It is transparent so that whatever is being exhibited is available to the panoptical gaze of the viewer. Whether wall-mounted, table-display, freestanding, hanging-from-the-ceiling or custom-made, all glass cases are *containers*. This is an important feature. As containers, they function to *contain* in the sense not only of *keeping inside* and *having within*, but also *holding back*, *limiting* and *regulating*. A contained thing is simultaneously lessened, fetishised and objectified. This is due to the fact that the contained object takes the shape of its container, or, at the very least, exists within its limits.

11

Displayed things are preserved in tempered safety glass not only so that they are *available* to be seen, but also because of the objects' permanent and perpetual inertness, fragility and assumed defencelessness. Displayed objects are protected from fading, damage, embrittlement, corrosion, shrinking, accretions, discolouration, dust and deterioration, because they cannot protect themselves. Yet, they have no control over the way in which they are positioned as items in the glass case. Rather, the curator, collector, seller or museum director chooses how the objects should be placed in order to obtain the maximum exhibition effect.

The glass case belongs within the macro-environment of display and exhibition, i.e., the entire display area. The exhibited objects, however, belong only within the micro-environment of the display case – an enclosed space which, from one point of view, represents *arrested movement* and *arrested history*. This sense and reality of arrest or fossilisation is at the heart of so-called conservation. It is a fixation in place and time, and retains power in the hands of the arrestor. Objects that retain both movement and history are ill-suited for the macro-environment of the museum and the micro-environment of the vitrine. To have movement and history is to cease to be an object. It is, rather, to expand into a *doing* and *speaking* subject. Exhibition is hence a form of prevention, in that it prevents both doing and speaking, and is a careful replacing of the subject with an unprotesting object or fetish.

Figure 1: Typical glass display case

The displayed object, which depends on the transparent glass for effect, is a fetish that draws its power from being gazed at. The displayed object pulls crowds and draws gazes towards it. However, the power of the fetish-object is always already limited: it is one-dimensional, dependent and *accidental* because the object cannot transcend the trauma-based *isolation* into which it has been condemned. The truth of this point is asserted in the Aesopian fable of the fox and the theatrical mask:

> A Fox had by some means got into the store-room of a theatre. Suddenly he observed a face glaring down on him and began to be very frightened; but looking more closely he found it was only a Mask such as actors use to put over their face. 'Ah,' said the Fox, 'you look very fine; it is a pity you have not got any brains.' (Aesop n.d.: 23)

The mask only has *accidental* power over the fox. As the fox observes, the object has no brains, no agency. Real power lies with the exhibitor, i.e., the one arranging the display and asserting his/her preferences for how and where to place the display. As Kent Brockman, the newsman in *The Simpsons*, says: 'There is an eclipse when I say there is an eclipse.'[6] The power of the exhibition glass case is out-bound communication. It is, fairly and squarely, the power of vitrification. Exhibition works by ultra-saturating the micro-environment with isolation, and dispensing frames with which the displayed object is seen into the macro-environment.

This paradox of exhibition as frame-dispenser and echo chamber is observed in Pippa Skotnes' 'Miscast' exhibition. Despite in large part exposing the racist and dehumanising ways in which the San were exhibited, 'Miscast' remained an exhibition which failed to free the San from the vitrine effect. In fact, it freed them from one set of exhibitions, only to lead them into another. The word 'exhibition' occurs 77 times in the 'Miscast' catalogue, where not once is it enclosed in quotes. The colonial exhibitions that degraded the San and the 'Miscast' exhibition which sought to disrupt them both shared and used the same term to refer to what they were doing. 'Miscast' as an exhibition failed to draw attention to this anomalous relationship, and the word 'exhibition' retained all of its centuries-old privilege and traumatic-institutional power over the San. 'Miscast' can thus be said to have failed to achieve its goals, because it was never going to be anything but an exhibition[7] – it simply exchanged one kind of echo for another, and managed to leave everything as it had found it. The environment of the exhibition is always a manufacture of some sort – specifically one within which it is impossible to exhibit as if one were *not* exhibiting. It is impossible to exhibit in such a way that the result is not an exhibition. What else is the glass case outfitted for?

Vetkat Kruiper

Born at Twee Rivieren, a rest camp in the then Kalahari Gemsbok Park on 1 April 1969, Vetkat was the youngest son of the late Ou Regopstaan Kruiper, the well-known Kalahari ǂKhomani leader. Vetkat died on 11 April 2007, aged 38. Vetkat had his 'studio' on a farm called Blinkwater, just outside the reserve now known as the Kgalagadi Transfrontier Park, where he lived with his poet wife, Belinda. Vetkat's works are in private collections at the Natal Museum Services, the McGregor Museum at Kimberley and the University of Pretoria. From 2002 to 2005 his art was displayed at the United Nations (UN) as part of an exhibition of indigenous art, while his 2004 tour of the United States of America culminated in his addressing the UN. Vetkat's visual art is remembered and celebrated in the first edition of *Mooi loop*, launched at the Bergtheil Museum in Durban in 2011.[8]

Figure 2: Vetkat Kruiper (Source: SouthAfricanArtists.com)

'They make no rock art and have no tradition of rock art'

Kalahari San rock engravings and rock paintings are regarded as an irretrievably lost culture. The Kalahari San artist is thought of as an absent and vanished museum specimen, hence:

> A more visible part of the archaeology of the Bushmen, and one which more people know about, is the rock art found throughout the mountains of southern Africa. Initial attempts to understand these paintings were fraught with problems, because the painters *had all died* before anyone thought to try to find out why they had painted. (Smith, Malherbe and Guenther et al. 2000: 18, emphasis added)

The context of a people who had 'all died' continues to inform questions of dating and authorship. David Lewis-Williams and Thomas Dowson (1989: 4), for instance, ask '[w]ho were the artists?', noting that 'there was heated controversy over the identity of the artists'. Their conclusion is that

> [t]oday remnants of the Bushmen survive only in the Kalahari Desert. Contrary to popular belief, *these survivors are not descendants of the southern painters* who were driven into inhospitable areas by more powerful peoples; *they make no rock art and have no tradition of rock art*. Some of them are aware of paintings in the Tsodilo hills, but, as Megan Biesele found, they say god put them there. *The groups who lived farther to the south and made the art spoke different languages. They became extinct about a century ago* as a result of white colonisation. (ibid: 11, emphasis added)

The conclusion is that artists such as Vetkat are not related in any sense to the rock artists who are said to have been extinct for a century.[9] Rock art researchers generally note that 'there are no recorded interviews with the painters themselves',[10] thus no one is around to shed light on the codes and meanings of the rock paintings.[11]

Lewis-Williams' 'shamanistic model' attains its framing power in the context of extinct artists. His commitment to refuting one form of exhibition – that the San were 'primitive people who had no sensitivity and certainly no spiritual experiences' (Lewis-Williams 2002: 143) – leads him to propose a more severe form of exhibition: Bushmen as shamanistic freaks. Lewis-Williams' generally accepted theory[12] explains all Bushman art as having been inspired by 'altered states of consciousness'.

He therefore constructs what he calls a 'shamanistic cosmos' composed of 'tiers' generated in these altered states (ibid: 145).[13]

Chimamanda Adichie (2010) succinctly warns of 'the dangers of the single story'. Lewis-Williams' oeuvre on San rock art, beginning in the late 1970s, has sought to assert 'how San cosmos and art are inseparable' (2002: 148), but what if they *are* separable? This imposition of inseparability is not only troubling for the way it denies the San agency, but also for the way it continues to glass-case Bushmen. Lewis-Williams, for instance, uses the words 'San' and 'shaman' interchangeably, arbitrarily sealing the two together. The so-called 'trance hypothesis', which seems to have been developed not from asking the Bushmen themselves what they thought and knew about their world, but more or less from hypothetical speculation, is in many ways an aspect of the glass-casing of Bushmen. This totalising of Bushmen into shamans through interpretations of rock art that allows only single readings is related to the present-day exhibiting of Bushmen.

The postulations of supposed vanishings and disappearances[14] are resisted by Richard Lee and Bob Hitchcock (2001), who call for 'an expanded anthropology, by celebrating the birth of new ethnicities and not just mourning the passing of the old'. Part of this study of Vetkat Kruiper's art is a response to their call for an 'expanded anthropology' (ibid: 273).

Vetkat's art

Titles

Since Vetkat did not give any of his paintings titles, it is difficult to refer specifically to individual paintings. It is not possible to reference specific paintings by page number either, because the 2011 edition of *Mooi loop* has none. It is quite possible that Vetkat never intended his pieces to be separated and individualised. I have therefore distinguished the anonymous paintings simply by labelling them as Figures 3 to 9. I photographed all the artworks used here, from the originals.

Fragments

One way of analysing Vetkat's visual art is to literally fragment and examine it piece by piece, as with a magnifying glass. This 'fragmentation method' is informed by the art itself. Vetkat often literally crams many fragments of representation onto a single A4 canvas (see Figures 3 and 8). I hence present some artworks as wholes and others as photographed fragments of wholes. This method of visual analysis shows both the detail and the several layers of meaning that Vetkat built into his pieces.

The three pieces in Figure 3 show the density of detail that the artist preferred. Several stories or bits of action co-exist in a single frame. The space around the other-worldly monochromatic swaggering figures is either occupied by free-form plants, huts, tunnels, snakes or flowers, or is simply left empty. The technique of layering objects horizontally, shown in the three panels in Figure 3, manifests in the majority of Vetkat's pieces. This 'layer motif' indicates the existence of repeatedly and densely overlapping worlds and planes of reality, giving unity to Vetkat's work. No parts are dominant or subordinate; rather, each fragment represents an authentic world. The human figures seem to be the primary focal point initially, but this perspective changes when one looks more closely at the hut, eland, snake or mantis.[15]

Technique

Vetkat's chosen technique is drawing, but he does more than just draw. Rather, he crosshatches and squirkles his 'canvases' with the tip of his pencil or brush. The effect is that his line-drawn figures seem like kinetic gesture sketches (Figure 4). The three worlds divided by the red and black barbed wire fences are full of the life and activity of humans, therianthropes, animals, reptiles and birds. Even the trees appear to be gesturing to the side and towards the skies. The landscape is unfinished; each 'scene' appears to have an individual identity linked to the others through kinaesthetic, animated gestures. There is rarely a smooth finish. Rather, Vetkat continually mixes blunt short strokes, curved short strokes, dashed lines, and strange and familiar shapes. In drawing this way, Vetkat seems to have found the simplest and most efficient way to communicate visual ideas.

Figure 3: Untitled. Ink on paper. (Source: Author)

The pigment used in Vetkat's work is often very simple. Rock painters used red ochre (with some paintings in maroon, yellow, black and white pigments) to represent subjects ranging from animals (mainly eland) to humans, therianthropes and even ox-wagons and mounted men with rifles (Lewis-Williams 1981). Vetkat also works with splashes of colour (Figures 3 and 4), as well as in monochrome and bichrome. Representations of humans and therianthropes, however, are mostly in monochrome. Many of the 'painted' objects in *Mooi loop* are monochrome images with the colour blocked in.

Vetkat brings together a number of varied techniques: fine-line paintings where he traces the outline of an image, filling the interior with lines of the same colour; tracing the outline in one colour, with the image filled in with another slightly different colour (Figure 6); two or three blocks of colour in the same image (Figure 5) sometimes creating strong contrasts; polychrome where he uses three or more colours in the same image; outlining the image with a single line; 'pecking' out in a chopping motion; inky scratching; shaded polychrome in which several colours blend to create depth effects and shading; large areas of colour and tone (Figure 5), and so on. Figure 5, for instance, shows the expressive use of brown and white inks. Partially wet media appear to have been used to create the flowing softness, transitions and organic quality of the flocks of birds. None of Vetkat's paintings seem to have been done with a finger or a very broad brush/applicator, suggesting an interest in detail. There are a few bold designs, although most are highly stylised, regardless of the subject matter. The style ranges from energetic to subtle (Figures 4 and 9).

Some paintings are plain, while others are furiously decorated with gestural strokes, down to the 'calligraphy' of Vetkat's signature and date. Some of Vetkat's artworks are 'engravings' on paper, characterised by careful detail in depicting plants and a delicate portrayal of emotion and postures. Regular patterns compete with asymmetrical patterns. This blending has more than a simple mimetic function; it also shows how Vetkat imagined his social world.

There is a personal touch to Vetkat's visuality that suggests innovation and originality. I observed that the 'chaos' in his paintings is actually unity – a result of his mastering a new technical harmony which the artists who engraved in the open on igneous rocks and painted in caves on granite, limestone, sandstone and quartzite did not (and perhaps could never) negotiate. The distribution of the two techniques of rock art (engravings and rock paintings) was largely governed by geology, with engravings associated with igneous rocks such as dolerite and occurring out in the open, while rock paintings were most common in areas where there are caves or rock shelters in outcrops of granite and in sedimentary rock formations of limestone, sandstone and quartzite. Basically, it is rare, though not unknown, to find both rock paintings and engravings together at the same site. Vetkat seems to have found a way to blend and represent both engravings and rock paintings as composites, on the same canvases, thus doing away with the limitations that faced the Kalahari 'old masters'. His medium simultaneously allowed immediacy, ex/change and a sense of movement.

Vetkat's polyptych

The word 'polyptych', which comes from the Greek *polu* which means 'many' and *ptyche* for 'fold', refers to a painting that is separated into sections or panels.[16] Polyptychs often display a 'main' panel (usually the largest) and several 'side' panels or 'wings' which can be varied to show different 'views' or 'openings' in the artwork. Vetkat's representation of several worlds-in-one in nearly all his paintings suggests he adopted a polyptych-style representation of Bushman social worlds. For instance, Figures 6 and 8 can easily be broken down into panels depicting various objects and happenings. Figure 6 shows animated human figures, eland, plants and huts in the central panel flanked by 30 other 'wings', all carrying various messages. The relationship between the centre and its margins is ambiguous. The side panels seem to strengthen the message of the central panels, while simultaneously retaining their own independent identities. The central panel itself is far from a unified whole, but rather contains several other fragments. There are even three panels with text in Afrikaans, showing the fluid interaction between the text and the visual. The central panel of Figure 6, in shaded polychrome, has its own centre depicting what seem to be translucent human beings bathed in light along with several other fragments. To see the amount of 'code' hidden and compressed in this polyptych, one might need to zoom in on the artwork or use a magnifying glass.

Where the polyptych ordinarily refers to multi-panel paintings, Vetkat's polyptych style is a multi-world staging of encounters. Figure 8, for instance, can be divided into representations of sex, war, dancing, child's or horse-play, religious worship, celebration, quarrel, division, friendship and community. The viewer can choose to see this as a single or as many artworks. Vetkat's polyptych also facilitates transport and mobility, which rock art cannot do in its original locations. Finally, Vetkat's polyptych vision is not merely visual but also tactile, not only 2D but 3D and 4D, stereoscopic rather than just monocular – an effect of weaving and interlacing objects and the use of perspective that allows the viewer to see many worlds unfolding at once.

The placement of objects and choice of themes

Vetkat's depictions are fragments of different impulses that are impossible to sew into a univocal whole. Nevertheless, the placement of objects in most of his pieces is seldom random. An example is the use of the understated symbols/features of the hut and the fence (Figure 6). The repeated placement of the hut suggests a conscious preoccupation with and celebration of 'home' and shelter. Incidentally, 'home' is a real and grounded need amongst the ǂKhomani – just as is the impulse to heal and be healed. Their history of dispossession, dispersal and displacement makes the hut a powerful metaphor of return. The fence, on the other hand, underlies the division of private space (marked by 'trespassers will be prosecuted' signs), and Bushman space and desire paths in the Kalahari (Mboti, forthcoming). Whereas the hut gives a sense of place and celebrates Bushman 'rurality', the fence suggests division, alienation and the violence of 'modernisation'. In several of Vetkat's works, objects and things separated by fences are twisted and bent out of shape.

Vetkat has a seemingly inexhaustible store of images to draw from. Apart from the hut and the fence, he explores a range of other themes such as violence, love, modernity, change, beauty, nature, sex, humanity, music, work, fertility, nation, space(s), time, place, boundaries and silence(s). Ecology, movement, stasis, ex/change and family are also a conscious preoccupation.[17] Vetkat Kruiper's polyptych, layered vision does not limit itself to any specific expressive mode, nor is it limited by taboo topics.

Interpretation[18]

One possible definition of Vetkat's Kalahari visuality is to represent it as *art brut* or 'outsider-art', a 'rough' or 'unofficial' art that is defined as the work of artists who demonstrate little influence from the mainstream art world. Vetkat's oeuvre is certainly boundary-crossing, boundary-smashing and boundary-refusing. I do not believe, however, that Vetkat's art is really outsider art at all. The outside-ness of the

Figure 4: Untitled. Ink on paper (Source: Author)

Figure 5: Untitled. Ink on paper (Source: Author)

19

Kalahari San as a people has been exaggerated, partly as a result of the romanticising myth of the ultra-remote lost/vanished world. In fact, I think of Vetkat's drawings as representing a thematic refutation of enforced outsideness. The discourse of *art brut*, possibly emancipatory, still returns us to the unproductive meme of primitive, idle doodlings or to the outside/inside that, pursued to its (il)logical conclusion, takes us back to apartheid. To define Vetkat's work as 'outsider art' is, in one sense, to falsely insist on the Kalahari San's separateness, especially at a time when no one has done anything substantial to prepare the ground for a culturally sensitive understanding of the many histories that account for how the San came to be labelled as 'outside'.[19] Ultimately, affirmation/refutation of outsideness can only be pronounced on the Kalahari's San's own terms, by the Kalahari San themselves.

Nhamo Mhiripiri (2008) defines Vetkat's art as postmodernist because of the artist's thematic focus on identity and 'sensitivity to moral ecology', his 'cryptic' style and polysemic meanings. Mhiripiri draws on notions of simulacra and hyperreality, as well as Jungian psychoanalysis, to strengthen this view. However, Vetkat's art fits postmodernism uneasily, as noted with the examples of the fence and the hut. Mhiripiri's latest intimations to me (2012) suggest that he has begun to question his earlier postmodernist-art thesis; he emphasised that Vetkat's visual art is best appreciated as intellectual production, with a conscious aesthetics and

a socio-political awareness. It is not instinctive 'trance' art. It is never merely 'ethnic' art. I would go further to say Vetkat's work evidences not only intellectual production but also advances a future-solving intellectual proposition: to exhibit or to be exhibited.

To the extent that art is a part of the world from which it emerges, Vetkat's work is 'Kalahari style' in the sense of Kalahari visuality; to the extent that art is about other art, Vetkat's art is in conversation with rock art. In *Mooi loop* (2011), the first published collection of Vetkat's visual art, the history of Bushman visual art, previously separated generically as engraving/painting,

Figure 6: Untitled. Ink on paper (Source: Author)

Figure 7: Untitled. Ink on paper (Source: Author)

 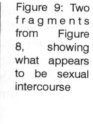

Figure 9: Two fragments from Figure 8, showing what appears to be sexual intercourse

Figure 8:.Untitled. Ink on paper (Source: Author)

re-emerges for the first time as a new 21st-century hybrid. The cave and the open site have been united powerfully in Vetkat's works, which hence symbolise e/mergence (emerging/merging). Most of the motifs used in his paintings show objects and characters emerging out of, and merging into, each other. Twenty years after the 'end' of apartheid in South Africa the so-called rainbow nation has not been able to make its colours merge into a humanising harmony. E/mergence is a complex cultural technique that Vetkat has already mastered.

Vetkat's work is a number of things simultaneously: a demonstration, a refutation and an affirmation, a breaking and a joining, and a movement within stasis. Part of the reason his work assumes these functions can be attributed to the existence of gaps and aporias that serve to structure collective memory (and forgetting) about the Bushman. Vetkat's visual art, in fact, has two clear cultural uses (though it is not limited to these): ref(m)utation and affirm(n)ation. What is refuted is the Cartesian mutilation (colonial and postcolonial) and collapsing of being-Bushman into being-exhibited. Mutilation (and its absences) is replaced by a radical and productive (trans)mutation and newness that Vetkat found possible in the silences and openness of Blinkwater and the Kalahari. What is affirmed is the voluntary citizenship of the Bushman in the modern nation of South Africa, born in 1994, with all the attendant curses, consequences, losses, gains, rights, obligations and responsibilities that citizenship entails.

Refutation and affirmation are tied to the fact that identity cannot be forced. It is at once a birthright and a conscious choice. Vetkat's polyptych vision, a function of being grounded, refutes many incorrect notions about the Kalahari San: that they were and are outcasts and remnants of the Stone Age, that they were a child-like, vanishing/vanished people, or that rock visual art was a collection of naïve daubings by primitive doodlers. It replaces all these absences with citizenship. Above all, however, it affirms radical cultural ex/change: the ability to exhibit and not just be exhibited.

Conclusion

There is a lacuna, a hiatus of sorts, around the reality of *being* San. The hiatal reality is this: the 'Bushman', though living, is actually meant for the glass case. This fissure (really an absence) takes many forms which collectively play the same sort of role: to fissure and separate the Bushman from his reality, and to hyphenate his identity. S/he is not actual, but only a signification, a type. This article has explored the visual art of San 'Bushman' artist Vetkat 'Regopstaan' Kruiper and how it diffracts and refracts the glass case effect and represents a breaking out of the glass case. A factor in the glass display effect is the *availability* of a thing to be seen, looked at and gazed at. Vetkat's art resists availability. He does not paint simply to be displayed. Rather, he seems to deliberately retain an opaqueness, a density and a layeredness of visual style, symbolism and theme that frustrate expectations of transparent themes, patterns and motifs. His art is, in a sense, invitrifiable art. It actively resists the micro-climate of the glass case. It is neither dependent on glass, nor on what the glass-makers say.

Notes

1   Ironically, less than a quarter of the book is about the San, much of it is about Van der Post the desert explorer and 'last eye-witness', and the process and details of his expedition. Van der Post barely spent two weeks with the Bushmen.

2   The myth of 'lost worlds' goes back as far as 1912 with Conan Doyle's novel, *The lost world*, which describes a journey to the Amazon where dinosaurs and other extinct 'prehistoric' creatures are to be found. Other than dinosaurs, carnivorous plants and giant spiders, there are also cannibalistic natives to be found in this 'lost world'. Irwin Allen's *The Lost World* (1960) took the myth to the screen.

3   Though extinct, dinosaurs are re-made for display, for instance, in Stephen Spielberg's cinematic classics, *Jurassic Park* (1993) and *The Lost World* (1997).

4   As Mklós Szalay (1995) notes, the Bushmen did not become extinct at all. Rather, their history is replete with evidence of varieties of resistance against colonial expansion (Elphick 1977; Marks 1972; Wright 1971) as well as incorporation and absorption into farm labour populations, rural proletariat and the military (Marshall 1980; Szalay 1995; Volkman 1985). In fact, the San have proven remarkably suited to surviving one existential threat after another (Guenther 1997, 1999; Hitchcock 1985; Lee and Hitchcock 2001; Tomaselli 2005).

5   It was also implied that there used to be untouched, truly-wild, authentic and 'real' Bushmen who are – unfortunately – gone forever. This untouched Bushman could do no wrong, was lovable, child-like, innocent and pure, and could only be corrupted by external influence. This myth, which is a corollary of the 'noble savage', is found at its starkest in cinematic form in Jamie Uys' popular 1981 film, *The Gods Must be Crazy*, where the Bushmen have no law and are incapable of anger or crime. The untouched Bushmen – a symbol of 'the primitive in ourselves' according to Van der Post – were also the first inhabitants of South Africa, before being driven into the Kalahari by hostile blacks and whites.

6   *The Simpsons* S20/E13 'Gone Maggie Gone'.

7   For different perspectives on 'Miscast' see Skotnes (2002) and Jackson and Robins (1999).

8   Important pioneering questions in contemporary San art have been raised by Skotnes (1991, 1994), Guenther (1997, 2003), Barnabas (2010) and Mhiripiri (2010). Skotnes' (1994: 316) paper marks the first attempt in critical literature to depart from the 'previous insistence that the painting itself is unable to offer any information as to its meaning'.

9   The cultural meanings of this 'lost world' of the Kalahari are supposedly tucked away in ancient code, needing Rosetta stone-type code to allow decoding (Lewis-Williams 1981, 1984). The continued natural deterioration, as rock faces slowly crumble, of the petroglyphs and pictographs compounds the sense of irretrievable loss.

10 Bradshaw Foundation 'Cracking the code of San rock art' http://www. bradshawfoundation.com/bushman/san_bushmen_south_africa.php. Brentjies (1965: 1)

refers to rock art as 'galleries of primeval art' which 'bear witness to otherwise forgotten centuries of African life'.

11 Ironically, it is not logical or expressly necessary to have Picasso's physical presence to sense the chaos of 'Guernica', Munch to feel the choking panic of 'Scream', or Van Gogh to sense the earthiness of 'The Potato Eaters'.

12 That Lewis-Williams' shaman model is widely accepted is clear, when even Mathias Guenther (1997: 121), whose pioneering study of contemporary Bushman art is among the soundest, refers to Qwaa Mangana as a 'shamanistically inclined artist'. The theory has not been uncontested, though (see, e.g., Solomon 1997, 2006, 2009).

13 Thanks to the important work of scholars such as Lewis-Williams (1978, 1981a and b, 1983a and b, 1984, 1989, 2002) and Megan Biesele (1978, 1993), it cannot now be denied that the San are *not* religious. However, the 'discovery' of San religiousness appears to have become a ready tool to subsume and explain everything to do with the San.

14 It has been asserted that '[t]he dating of rock art is perhaps the most important empirical issue' (Dowson and Lewis-Williams 1994: 5). The early concern with issues of dating and authorship in rock art research (*cf.* Beaumont and Morris 1990; Dowson 1988; Dowson and Lewis-Williams 1994; Lewis-Williams 1983; Morris 1988; Morris and Beaumont 1991; Schoonraad 1971; Steel 1988) reflects precisely the assumption that the rock artists may have vanished. This is illustrated, for instance, at the beginning of Eastwood and Eastwood's (2006) book about rock art where they state: 'We have set out to take you with us on a tracking expedition, showing you tantalising signs of the spoor of *vanished or vanishing cultures* (2006: 17, emphasis added).

15 Key features of the Bushman worldview, according to Guenther (1999: 13), are 'flexibility, adaptability and diversity, fluidity and amorphousness, ambivalence and ambiguity'. These attributes are suggested in the dense composition and layering of objects.

16 'Diptych' describes a two-part/panel work of art; 'triptych' three; tetraptych or quadriptych four; pentaptych five; hexaptych six; heptaptych seven; and octaptych eight.

17 Just as in the art of Qwaa Mangana which fuses 'traditional scenes' ('veld animals and plants, and leather-clad men and women out a-hunting and a-gathering, as well as other elements of traditional culture, including mystical and ecological ones') with 'modern scenes' ('horses and cattle, radios and guitars, jeans, shirts, belts or shoes, angels and peace doves') (Guenther 1997: 125).

18 These interpretations of Vetkat's work are not to be deemed in any sense exhaustive, but are only meant to open up a dialogue about the artist's oeuvre.

19 Guenther (2003) succinctly illustrates how Westerners tend to view contemporary San art from Botswana and Namibia as 'primordial' art when, in fact, such art challenges and decolonises those notions. Fortunately, the Eurocentrism behind notions of 'tribal' or 'primitive' art has been the subject of previous discussion and critical exposition (Anderson 1989; Guenther 1997; Price 2001). Guenther (1997: 121), in his study of the art of Qwaa Mangana, has bemoaned

the Western art critics and collector's inclination to treat such art as the anonymous, collective, cultural product of some iconic, primitive or primordialist "Other", cloaked with the mystique of pristinism, rather than of a living, breathing man or woman, with idiosyncrasies in style, vision, subject matter or aesthetic approach.

Ironically, despite bemoaning the Eurocentrism of art criticism which names non-Western art as 'tribal' or 'primitive', Guenther inexplicably persists in calling Bushman art 'tribal art' and Bushman artists such as Qwaa Mangana 'tribal artists'. Barnabas (2010) lucidly argues against attempts to see San art selectively as if it were not 'real' art. In particular, Barnabas questions the selective use of such art 'merely as a tool of development, a tourism endeavour and an income generator' (ibid: 427). Fitting Bushman art into preselected categories continues the traditions of exhibition.

References

Adichie, C. 2009. The danger of a single story. http://www.ted.com/talks/chimamanda_ adichie_the_danger_of_a_single_story (accessed 3 March 2011).

Aesop. n.d. *Aesop's fables*: 'The fox and the mask'. www.planetebooks.com (accessed 12 July 2010).

Anderson, R.L. 1989. *Art in small scale societies*. Englewood Cliffs: Prentice Hall.

Bank, A. 2006. *Bushmen in a Victorian world: the remarkable story of the Bleek–Lloyd collection of Bushman folklore*. Cape Town: Double Storey.

Barnabas, S.B. 2010. Picking at the paint: viewing contemporary Bushman art as art. *Visual Anthropology* 23(5): 427–442.

Barnard, A. 2004. Coat of arms and the body politic: Khoisan imagery and South African national identity. *Ethnos* 69(1): 5–22.

Beaumont P.B. and D. Morris. 1990. *Guide to archaeological sites in the Northern Cape*. Kimberley: McGregor Museum.

Brantlinger, P. 2003. *Dark vanishings: discourse on the extinction of primitive races, 1800–1930*. Ithaca, NY: Cornell University Press.

Brentjies, B. 1965. *African rock art*. London: JM Dent & Sons Limited.

Conan Doyle, A. 1912. *The lost world*. London: Hodder and Stoughton.

Deacon, J. 1988. Rock engravings of the flat and grass Bushmen: some recent discoveries. In *The state of the art: advances in world rock art research*, ed. T.A. Dowson. Johannesburg: University of Witwatersrand Rock Art Research Unit.

Dickens, C. 1996[1884]. *Great expectations*. London: Penguin Classics.

Dowson, T.A., ed. 1988. *The state of the art: advances in world rock art research*. Johannesburg: University of Witwatersrand Rock Art Research Unit.

Dubow, S. 1995. *Illicit union: scientific racism in modern South Africa*. Cambridge: Cambridge University Press.

Eastwood, E. and C. Eastwood. 2006. *Capturing the spoor: an exploration of southern African rock art*. Claremont, SA: New Africa Books.

Elphick, R. 1977. *Kraal and castle: the birth of South African society*. New Haven: Yale University Press.

Fagg, W. and M. Plass. 1964. *African sculpture*. London: Dutton.

Gordon, R.J. 1985. Conserving Bushmen to extinction in southern Africa: the metaphysics of Bushman hating and empire building. In *An end to laughter? Tribal peoples and economic development*, ed. M. Colchester, 28–42. London: Survival International.

Gordon, R.J. 1993. *The Bushman myth: the making of a Namibian underclass*. Oxford: Westview Press.

Guenther, M. 1997. 'Farm labourer, trance dancer, artist: the life and works of Qwaa Mangana.' *Proceedings of Khoisan Identities and Cultural Heritage Conference*, Cape Town, 12–16 July. Cape Town: InfoSource, pp. 121–134.

Guenther, M. 2003. Contemporary Bushman art, identity politics and the primitivism discourse. *Anthropologica* 45(1): 95–110.

Guenther, M.G. 1997. Lords of the desert land: politics and resistance of the Ghanzi Basarwa in the nineteenth century. *Botswana Notes and Records* 29(1): 121–140.

Guenther, M.G. 1999. *Tricksters and trancers: Bushman religion and society*. Bloomington: Indiana University Press.

Hitchcock, R.K. 1985. Foragers on the move: San survival strategies in Botswana parks and reserves. *Cultural Survival Quarterly* 9(1): 31–36.

Jackson, S. and S. Robins. 1999. Miscast: the place of the museum in negotiating the Bushman past and present. *Critical Arts* 13(1): 69–101.

Kent, S., ed. 1996. *Cultural diversity among twentieth-century foragers: an African perspective*. Cambridge: Cambridge University Press.

Kruiper, V.R. 2011. *Mooi loop: the sacred art of Vetkat Regopstaan Kruiper*. Pretoria: Unisa Press (2014 edition).

Lee, R.B. 2003. Indigenous rights and the politics of identity in post-apartheid South Africa. In *At the risk of being heard: identity, indigenous rights and post-colonial states*, ed. B. Dean and J.S. Levi, 80–111. Ann Arbor, Michigan: University of Michigan Press.

Lee, R.B and I. de Vore, eds. 1976. *Kalahari hunter-gatherers: studies of the !Kung San and their neighbours*. Massachusetts: Harvard University Press.

Lee, R.B. and R.K. Hitchcock. 2001. African hunter-gatherers: survival, history and the politics of identity. *African Study Monographs* Suppl. 26(1) : 257–280.

Lewis-Williams, D.J. and J. Clottes. 1998. *The shamans of prehistory: trance magic and the painted caves*. New York: Abrams.

Lewis-Williams, J.D. 1981a. *Believing and seeing: symbolic meanings in southern San paintings*. London: Academic Press.

Lewis-Williams, J.D. 1981b. The thin red line: southern San notions and rock paintings of supernatural potency. *South African Archaeological Bulletin* 36(1): 5–13.

Lewis-Williams, J.D. 1983a. *The rock art of southern Africa*. Cambridge: Cambridge University Press.

Lewis-Williams, J.D. 1983b. Science and rock art: introductory essay. South African Archaeological Society, *Goodwin Series* 4(1): 3–13.

Lewis-Williams, J.D. 1984. The empiricist impasse in southern African rock art studies. *South African Archaeological Bulletin* 39(1): 58–66.

Lewis-Williams, J.D. 2002. *The mind in the cave: consciousness and the origin of art*. London: Thames and Hudson.

Lewis-Williams, J.D. and M. Biesele. 1978. Eland hunting rituals among Northern and Southern San groups: striking similarities. *Africa* 48(1): 117–134.

Marks, S. 1972. Khoisan resistance to the Dutch in the seventeenth and eighteenth centuries. *Journal of African History* 8(1): 55–80.

Mhiripiri, N. 2008. The tourist viewer, the Bushmen and the Zulu: imaging and (re)invention of identities through contemporary visual cultural productions. Ph.D. thesis, University of KwaZulu-Natal.

Mhiripiri, N. 2012. Re: *Mooi loop* republication. Email to the author, 17 November.

Miller, M. 1993. *State of the peoples: a global human rights report on societies in danger.* Boston: Beacon Press.

Morris, D. 1988. Engraved in place and time: a review of variability in the rock art of northern Cape and Karoo. *South African Archaeological Bulletin* 43(2): 109–121.

Morris, D. and P.B. Beaumont. 1991. !Nawabdanas: archaeological sites at Renosterkop, Kakamas District, Northern Cape. *South African Archaeological Bulletin* 46(1): 115–124.

Parson, N. 2009. *Clicko: the wild dancing Bushman.* Chicago: University of Chicago Press.

Penn, N.G. 1996. 'Fated to perish': the destruction of the Cape San. In *Miscast: negotiating the presence of the Bushmen*, ed. P. Skotnes, 81–91. Cape Town: University of Cape Town Press.

Price, S. 2001. *Primitive art in civilized places*, 2nd edition. Chicago: University of Chicago Press.

Schoonraad, M., ed. 1971. *Rock paintings of southern Africa.* Johannesburg: South African Association for the Advancement of Science.

Skotnes, P. 1991. Is there life after trance? *de arte* 44(1): 16–24.

Skotnes, P. 1994. The visual as a site of meaning. In *Contested images: diversity in southern African rock art research*, ed. T.A. Dowson and D. Lewis-Williams. Johannesburg: Witwatersrand University Press.

Skotnes, P., ed. 1996. *Miscast: negotiating the presence of the Bushmen.* Cape Town: University of Cape Town Press.

Skotnes, P. 2002. The politics of Bushman representations. In *Images and empires: visuality in colonial and postcolonial Africa*, ed. P.S. Landau and D.D. Kaspin, 253–274. California: University of California Press.

Smith, A., C. Malherbe, M. Guenther and P. Berens. 2000. *The Bushmen of southern Africa: a foraging society in transition.* Cape Town: David Philip.

Solomon, A. 1997. The myth of ritual origins? Ethnography, mythology and interpretation of San rock art. *South African Archaeological Bulletin* 52(1): 3–13.

Solomon, A. 2006. San spirituality and human evolution: eight questions for Lewis-Williams and Pearce. *South African Archaeological Bulletin* 61(1): 209–212.

Solomon, A. 2009. Broken strings: interdisciplinarity and |Xam oral literature. *Critical Arts* 23(1): 26–41.

Sparks, A. 1997. *The mind of South Africa: the story of the rise and fall of apartheid.* London: Arrow Books.

Steel, R. 1988. *Rock engravings of the Magaliesberg Valley.* Johannesburg: Broederstroom Press.

Szalay, M. 1995. *The San and the colonization of the Cape, 1770–1879: conflict, colonization and acculturation.* Köln: R. Köppe.

Thornton, R.J. 1983. 'This dying out race': W.H.I. Bleek's approach to the languages of southern Africa. *Social Dynamics* 9(2): 1–10.

Tomaselli K.G., ed. 2007. *Writing in the San/d: autoethnography among indigenous southern Africans.* Lanham, MD: AltaMira.

Van der Post, L. 1977. *The lost world of the Kalahari.* London: Harvest/HBJ.

Volkman, T.A. 1985. *Study guide: N!ai: the story of a !Kung woman.* Watertown, Mass.: Documentary Educational Resources.

Wilmsen, E. 1995. First peoples? Images and imaginations in South African iconography. *Critical Arts* 9(2): 1–27.

Wilmsen, E.N. 1989. *Land filled with flies: a political economy of the Kalahari.* Chicago: University of Chicago Press.

Wright, J. 1971. *Bushman raiders of the Drakensberg, 1840–1870.* Pietermaritzburg: University of Natal Press.

Films

N!ai: the story of a !Kung woman. 1980. Dir. Jon Marshall. Documentary Educational Resources, 59 mins.

The Gods Must be Crazy. 1981. Dir. Jamie Uys. Ster Kinekor & 20th Century Fox, 109 mins.

The Lost World. 1960. Dir. Irwin Allen. 20th Century, 97 mins.

Jurassic Park. 1993. Dir. Stephen Spielberg. Universal Pictures, 126 mins.

The Lost World: Jurassic Park. 1997. Dir. Stephen Spielberg. Universal Pictures, 129 mins.

The Simpsons S20/E13 'Gone Maggie Gone'. 2009. Dir. Chris Clements. Fox Broadcasting Corporation, 21 mins.

Artworks

Edvard Munch, *The Scream.* 1910. Oil, tempera, and pastel on cardboard, 91 cm × 73.5 cm. National Gallery, Oslo.

Pablo Picasso, *Les Demoiselles d'Avignon* (The Young Ladies of Avignon, originally titled The Brothel of Avignon). 1907. Oil on canvas, 243.9 cm × 233.7 cm. Museum of Modern Art, New York.

Pablo Picasso, *Guernica.* 1937. Oil on canvas, 349 cm × 776 cm. Museo Reina Sofia, Madrid.

Vincent van Gogh, *The Potato Eaters.* 1885. Oil on canvas, 82 cm × 114 cm. Van Gogh Museum, Amsterdam.

Simulacral, genealogical, auratic and representational failure: Bushman authenticity as methodological collapse

William Ellis*

Abstract

This article engages with the concept of authenticity as deployed in anthropology. The first section critiques authenticity as a simple reference to cultural purity, a traditional isomorphism or historical verisimilitude or as an 'ethnographic authenticity'. Demarcation of authenticity must take into account philosophical literature that argues that authenticity is an existential question of the 'modern' era. Thus, authenticity is offered to us as individuals as a remedy for the maladies of modernity: alienation, anomie and alterity. Authenticity is then discussed as a question of value within an economy of cultural politics that often draws on simulacra, creating cultural relics of dubious origin. The final section discusses various methodological failures and *problematiques* that are highlighted by the concern for, and scrutiny of, authenticity. The first is the simulacral failure. The subjects of anthropology are mostly real flesh-and-blood people-on-the-ground with real needs. In contrast is the simulacral subject, the brand, the tourist image, the media image or the ever-familiar hyper-real bushmen. Lastly, the article considers what Spivak calls 'withholding' – a resistance to authentic representation by the Other. Resistance suggests a need for a radically altered engagement with the Other that includes both a deepening, and an awareness, of anthropology as a process of common ontological unfolding.

Prelude

What are the ends of authenticity? Where does a discourse of authenticity lead? As Walter Benjamin (1969) and Theodor Adorno (1964) watched the world plunge into

*I acknowledge the Centre for Humanities Research of the University of the Western Cape for the fellowship award that facilitated the writing of the present chapter. All credit for the article is attributed to the CHR at UWC.

World War II, they viewed the very 'modern' angst that is authenticity as pathology of power and capital. Benjamin (in Jay 2006) saw in talk of authenticity the growth of fascism (as a political arm of capital) and eventually war. Adorno (1964, 1987, 2003) saw the extermination of the inauthentic and migrants by those who perceived themselves and their kin as autochthonous. Authenticity suggests: 'All arrivals are to be excluded and if they do not move they will be made to do so.' Think Nazi Germany, apartheid, Israel/Palestine, Rwanda, Bosnia and Serbia, Mbotu's Zaire, Idi Amin's Uganda, India and Pakistan after independence, and now Zimbabwe.

This prelude reveals my awareness of authenticity as an ideological device, one that has been used in the past and continues to be used as a means of exclusion, especially in the service of ethno-nationalistic agendas. Heidegger (1927) focuses on authenticity as being an individualistic attribute to a conception based in groups (Jay 2006). Authenticity presented as an attribute of a group is at its most dangerous, because it is at precisely this moment that authenticity expresses its antagonism to the inauthentic most violently. The use of authenticity is a double-edged sword that can do as much harm to the authenticated as to the authenticator (Feuser 1988).

Introduction

Contemporary anthropologists seemingly cannot find the authentic 'Other' anywhere! When first encountering the authentic I doubted this claimed and performed status. The concomitant searches for *cultural purity, existential veridicality, the commodity price of cultural life* as well the *search for methodologies* that locate, verify and author(ise) these authenticities, all fall short. Some are at pains to find the methods, theories, new insights, nuances and even to engage in perspectival experiments to help us describe the 'Other' more authentically. These searches and devices are clearly a 'nostalgia for lost origins' (Derrida 1972). This nostalgia has also characterised anthropology as an epistemic endeavour. Having taken many forms, anthropology has not been resolved nor completely abandoned – it has simply transformed from one form to another, especially within the Western episteme.

Anthropology and Western philosophy cannot and have not been able to locate the prelapsarian, the true authentic human, the person at the moment after animal thought ceases. Both disciplines have searched for the ethnological representative of Adam and Eve. The prelapsarian 'Other', the authentic and the right methods to represent them, elude us all the time and, if we do not find the authentic, then anthropology seems pointless. This search for the essence of humanity, the true form – in short, its authenticity – has been most avidly sought among 'Stone Age peoples' – those apparently perfect models of early human life. However, most contemporary anthropologists agree that what were once considered to be paragons of authentic humanity, foragers and other non-Western societies, cannot deliver the West from its alienated and de-natured problematic selves. Anthropology has had a unique engagement with the search for the authentic that needs to be unpacked – the gist of my objective here.

The first section moves beyond the use of authenticity as a simple reference to cultural purity, a kind of traditional isomorphism or historical verisimilitude (Bruner 1994, 2001; Handler and Saxton 1988) or as an 'ethnographic authenticity' (Carrier 2009). This refusal to simply use authenticity as a cultural purity may seem a familiar criticism of essentialism and the idea of bounded 'cultures'. As a critique of authenticity, however, it is not sufficient to focus on authenticity as a 'cultural' attribute or process. Reframing outmoded concepts such as tribe or recuperating ethnic monikers as being about authenticity or authentication do not wholly capture the nuances of authenticity. Attempts to examine and demarcate authenticity must take into account a body of philosophical literature that argues that authenticity is an existential question of the 'modern' era. In other words, authenticity is about an individual's aspirations to live the best possible life despite the limitations and contingencies of the human condition. Authenticity is thus offered as a remedy for the maladies of modernity. Claims are made that with authenticity we can overcome alienation by claiming back the fruits of our labour; we rid ourselves of anomie by finding our identity and belonging; we transcend alterity by embracing it and staking equal claim to the world and its resources. This take has been duly called the 'search for authenticity', because adherents are engaged in attempts to recover lost presence. These are false hopes; 'recovery' is not possible because those who cling to this type of authenticity risk being 'paralyzed by the melancholy of their nostalgia for a lost past' (Ghosh 1998).

Those who 'buy' into authenticity view it as part of an economy of cultural politics in which signs, as measures of value, circulate for the production of commodities. Authenticity in this economy often draws on simulacra and creates cultural relics of dubious origin.

The final section discusses various methodological failures and *problematiques*. The first is simulacral failure. As regards authenticity and simulacra, a distinction needs to be made between two phenomena. The subjects of anthropology are, for the most part, real people-on-the-ground with real needs. In contrast is the simulacral subject (the lower case *b* for *bushman* (after Rasool and Hayes 1998), the brand, the tourist image, the media image or the ever-familiar hyper-real bushmen. In South American contexts, the creation of a hyper-real Indian (in the South African case a hyper-real bushman) conveniently served the need for bureaucratic efficiency of various Indian organisations and non-governmental organisations (NGOs) (Ramos 1992). This representation is easily made into an image that can be conveniently marketed. The simulacral subject, that is bushman, is created to serve the need for bureaucratic efficiency and is good for court cases, films, books, marketing, land claims, NGO reports, policy and the like, but does not always deliver for those caricatured, parodied or simplified as simulacra.

The breakdown of the genealogical method in the examination of the 'Other' is now examined. When it concerns the 'Other', genealogy, as a method, can only make reference to what Benjamin (1969) terms an aura of authenticity. This aura is that semblance of the original state that copies retain; hence anthropology can only recover fragments of the original. As an engagement with Western thought, genealogy seems sufficient; however as an attempt at revelation of the 'Other' it is often simply an auratic critique, a standpoint that refers to an insufficiently mourned past (Mufti 2000). An auratic reading laments the loss of a loosely described past bathed in a glow of romanticism and, although the original object is gone, the aura remains. Lastly, I consider what Gayatri Spivak (1990: 16) calls 'withholding' – a resistance to authentic representation by the 'Other'. This resistance to representation suggests the need for a radically altered engagement with the 'Other'.

The problem of Bushman authenticity in South Africa[1]

Many terms are used here (San, Bushmen, southern Kalahari San, ǂKhomani San, *Boesman* and bushman) to indicate the people who were the participants or subjects in the study. 'San' is used to denote those former foragers claiming 'first nation' status; it is preferred as an umbrella category although it is actually a derogatory term employed by Nama speakers (see Biesele and Hitchcock 2010, Wilmsen 1989). 'Bushman', and the Afrikaans *Boesman*, are used either as a self-referent or when employed by sources, texts or authors to describe the group under study. While this may be the convention employed here, the terms San and Bushman are so intricately interwoven that they are impossible to separate (Douglas 1995; Voss 1990). When bushman is used it denotes a representational category, a simulacrum not an actual 'people'. The regional–geographical referent, southern Kalahari San, is used when indicating the ethno-linguistic community of that region of South Africa, and also when speaking about this specific group historically. The predominant term ǂKhomani San, rather than meaning an ethnic unit, refers to a specific collective that was formed during the land claims process (Crawhall n.d.; Ellis 2010).

Absence and presence in the landscape

On his journey to find the San, Rupert Isaacson (2000, 2001) was told that none exist in South Africa. Popular and academic perceptions were that the last 'pure' remnants, who roamed much of the subcontinent prior to the arrival of the Bantu-speaking groups (circa 400AD) and the European colonists (17th century), were only to be found in Botswana and Namibia (see, e.g., Humphreys 1985; Marshall 1976; Tobias 1956). Besides South Africa, San descendants continued to live in parts of

Malawi, Angola, Zimbabwe, Zambia, and until the last one was murdered in 1988, in Swaziland (Suzman 2001).

It is only with extensive academic work and paradigmatic review that the continued San presence outside Namibia and Botswana became 'known'. This review is not a matter of challenging the previous revisions by means of the 'Kalahari Debates' (see Barnard 1990; Solway and Lee 1990; Wilmsen and Denbow 1990), or those that had earlier proposed a placement of the Khoi-San on a spectrum where they could oscillate from hunter to herder or vice versa (Bredenkamp 1991; Smith 1990), but is also a matter of political and communal reorientations.

With the exception of Botswana, new legal frameworks for access to land and natural resources have recently emerged, which allowed for a quest to revive Khoi-San culture based on privileged access to land and ecology (see Ellis 2010). This entitlement is not solely linked to the land but also to the emergence of cultural systems through this resource, for example, the hunting and gathering cultural formation as a function of land claims and ecology. That is, in the present bushman, identity emerges or re-emerges because of the renewed access to land and natural resources.

Khoi-San descendants have in the political present begun to think it possible that they might revive and reclaim Khoi-San identity despite the obvious lack of perceptible markers of ethnographic authenticity, such as language, 'cultural practices', dress and the like. It is within these shifts in regional policy on land and natural resources that the regional revival of Khoi-San identity occurs.

This begs the question: Where do the San people who lodged a land claim in the South African Parliament and the other two groups living inside its boundaries come from; how and why did they 'reappear'? Officially, three decades ago, no San lived in South Africa, yet by the mid-1990s three distinct groups had re-emerged onto the political landscape. The first are the so-called 'Bushmen Battalions' – the !Xu or Khwe, late of Schmidtsdrift in the Northern Cape. Second is the ‡Khomani, a group reconstituted as a result of the initiation of a land claim lodged in the mid-1990s. Last is the so called 'Secret San', a group of individuals who were unwilling to 'reveal' their status and openly identify themselves as San. They include groups of scattered individuals living in areas of South Africa that are traditionally considered to be occupied by Nguni-speaking farmers (Prins 2009).

The 'Bushmen Battalions' initially lived at Schmidtsdrift in the Northern Cape, but moved as part of the land redistribution programme (Robins 2001). Linguistically distinct, the !Xu are from Namibia and the Khwe from southern Angola. Both groups served with the South African Defence Force (SADF) in conflicts with the South West African People's Organisation (SWAPO) and against the *Movimento Popular de Libertação de Angola*[2] (MPLA). The SADF recruited and trained them. It was perceived that they had a natural hatred for 'blacks' who hunted them on both sides of the border; and that their exceptional skills in tracking and *veld*-craft made them good soldiers (Erasmus 1997).

The end of the war in 1989 saw the SADF withdraw from the region. The San feared retribution[3] from their fellow Namibians and Angolans, and were transferred to a resettlement camp near Kimberley and granted South African citizenship (Sharp and Douglas 1996). After a rocky start characterised by internal conflicts, uncertainty about continued employment in the army, contesting land claims and a myriad social problems, the groups entered into discussions with the now South African National Defence Force (SANDF) and the Department of Land Affairs (DLA) that made the future seem a bit more certain (Douglas n.d.). The two groups later moved onto land received through the redistribution programme, at Platfontein (see Robbins 2006). This, in brief, is how the !Xu and the Khwe re-emerged on the South African landscape. More accurately, the story of the !Xu and the Khwe is one that should be characterised as a series of relocations, not necessarily a re-emergence. The two distinct groups were relocated in 2004, yet they continue to experience various problems characterised as issues of coherence, largely the result of 'forced togetherness of the past' (Den Hertog 2013: 356).[4]

The re-emergence of the ǂKhomani appears more complex as they are from South Africa and were not brought from 'elsewhere'. In order to understand their re-emergence, I will briefly examine the conditions that led to their disappearance. In the 1930s, the so-called 'Wits expedition' led by Raymond Dart sought to seek out the 'purest' San people. They went, on the advice of Dorothea Bleek, into the southern Kalahari to 'the furthest end of the Union' (Maingard 1937). Once the fieldwork had been completed some members of the expedition tried to establish a reserve for the San people of the southern Kalahari, but the response of the government and local farmers was negative. A government report labelled the San of this region as 'fakes' (Gordon 1999). In this particular instance, the argument put forward was that the San group in question was completely 'bastardized', that they had 'lost their culture', that many spoke Afrikaans and were employed on the farms of Europeans as domestic workers or farmhands (Gordon 1995: 282). Government and farmers claimed that these people were no longer Bushmen and therefore not entitled to have land set aside for their sole use, for example, as a native reserve for the preservation[5] of their 'traditional' lifestyle (Boydell 1948). This was the first important instance where the 'authenticity' construct/debate concerning specifically the southern Kalahari San, arose. Several decades passed and the descendants of this group continued to live in the Mier and wider Gordonia region. Some were still considered to be 'Bushmen' by the local farmers and the authorities within the Kalahari Gemsbok National Park.

The final death knell for the San of South Africa came when, in terms of the *Population Registration Act*, 30 of 1950, most of the San were registered, and thus reinscribed onto the South African political landscape and legislation, as coloured (Steyn 1984). With the implementation of the act, the San officially ceased to exist.

One of the reasons was that the former category, 'Bushmen', was seen to represent the very lowest point in the hierarchy of 'races'. In this regard the San were originally classified as a 'native race'[6] (Carstens 1966). Their reclassification as coloureds was perceived to be a 'step up' in the racial hierarchy of South Africa at the time. For example, one participant, the late Ouma |unnas, proudly told me how they lived and worked as coloureds in the Kalahari Gemsbok National Park and on farms in the region, and how they were prevented from interacting with Dawid Kruiper and other 'Bushmen'. It was only after 1994, when the political landscape in South Africa changed, and with a new constitution in the making, that many San again began to refer to themselves as San or 'Bushmen'. Boonzaier and Sharp (1993), who found similar processes at work in the revival of Nama identity, argued that under apartheid it was better to be known as coloured than as Nama. This was similarly the case for the 'Bushmen' (see also Robins 1997, 2000, 2001).

The process of re-emergence is a fundamental part of government strategies to manage these groups, and authenticity is the main tool used to validate or dispute claims. Thus, both in the present and in the past there have been active processes of authentication and de-authentication, contingent on the particular political aims of those in power. The process of authentication was apparent in the 1930s, with attempts to establish a San homeland in the Kalahari.[7] Such managed re-emergence and authentication resurface again in racial reclassification during the formative years of apartheid, and once more in the present with regard to the ‡Khomani land claim and that of the Schmidtsdrift Bushmen. In the postapartheid period authenticity has become vital in the construction of citizenship, claims to citizenship and the subsequent resource distribution that may result. It is as if successive regimes have had to allow for a rediscovery and re-emergence of the San, and to re-script the story of these representations into their foundation myths. At each point of shift in the political landscape, bushman, Bushman, San and whatever other name used, needed to be reinvented to establish the notion of a nation. The San must be let into and included in the nationalist narratives, because one cannot tell the story of southern Africa without them.

Two key developments set the stage for San identity and people to re-emerge in South Africa post-1994. The first was the new political dispensation; the second, land reform legislation. Steven Robins (2000) comments that political changes facilitated the reclaiming of these identities without the stigmas associated with them during apartheid. Land reform legislation, and especially the *Restitution of Land Rights Act*, 1994, enabled the ‡Khomani to lodge the claim. The process played a key role in the reconstitution and construction of the group known as the ‡Khomani San. Within this context it is apparent that the San never really 'disappeared', but rather had been renamed and stripped of representation and representativeness by policies and perceptions of the past.

Once these policies and perspectives had been removed, those who considered themselves San[8] reasserted their position and identity. It is within this context that groups like the 'secret' San reappeared, albeit warily (see Prins 2009). In other words, it is in the 'new South Africa' that many new identities could be asserted, exercised and claimed (see Comaroff and Comaroff 1999, 2009).

The perception that the San had 'vanished', were bastardised through miscegenation or were at least 'culturally extinct' in South Africa would come back to haunt the ǂKhomani after they had lodged their land claim. Many who encountered the ǂKhomani – from tourists, farmers, and former neighbours to researchers and the media – expressed surprise that the San still existed. Others, like the government and farmers in the 1930s, were sceptical about the 'authenticity' of people claiming to be San. In fact, Mier residents who claimed either coloured or *Baster*[9] identity, reacted with astonishment and questioned how their neighbours, friends and colleagues, whom they had known as coloureds or *Basters*, were suddenly calling themselves San.

The following sections consider the question of ǂKhomani authenticity. The etymology deals with some issues of translation and I attempt to operationalise the term 'authenticity'.

A note on etymology, definition, translation and operationalisation

Let us consider *authenticity* as mere word, first in terms of etymology. Second, a brief 'definition in the negative' is offered. Lastly, it is necessary to offer a brief note on translations of the concept of authenticity from cited texts.

Etymology

'Authenticity' has two Greek roots: *auto* = self and *hentes* = made, hence authenticity is about being self-made. This particular definition reveals the flaws in the concept, particularly as it relates to authenticity as cultural purity. The entity in question, say a painting,[10] is an object that is authored by its own hand, has its own authority and is given a primal, chthonic origin, if not a simple and pure divine derivation. An entity that drafts its own destiny is just too convenient for primordialist, essentialist, racist and ethnic exclusionary agendas.

Most dictionaries point to three aspects of the word: particularity, lack of artifice and some kind of conformity to a pre-existing form or item. Authenticity as particularity suggests that an object is unique, singular, primal and, in a sense, never before seen. In the second sense (lack of artifice) a phenomenon is not some echo or reproduction of a pre-existing form. If not made by god(s), and if human hands had a role in its production, then it is assumed to be divinely inspired (here the links to autochthony are suggested). Lastly, if reproduction is uncontestable then authenticity means that the phenomenon in question has to conform to, or at least illustrate, a verisimilitude or isomorphism with that of which it is a reproduction or copy.

The real is something radically different from the authentic. Jean Lyotard (1991) asks: Can thought continue without the body? He asks the reader to consider the solar holocaust (coming in a few billion years), and whether any human thought or reflection on the universe can outlast this cataclysm. With this apocalypse what we know and think about the world will disappear, yet some 'things' will escape and survive this event. Those that remain are the 'real', they continue to exist regardless of our ability to conceptualise and theorise about them. In this view the authentic is a product of the human brain and only therein lies its genesis. All that is 'real' lies within the realm of the pre-discursive and the pre-social. The discussion below relies on this simple point of departure, namely that the authentic is a socio-cultural product.

Translation

Let us begin with the response by Adorno to Heidegger (my point is limited to single terms and not the general debate) and German existentialism in general through the text entitled 'The jargon of authenticity'. I am fairly confident that in the English translations the terms are congruent and that they exhibit a degree of fidelity to the original.

In the case the San of the southern Kalahari, another set of translation issues arises. Most of the informants use Afrikaans as mother tongue, and the words I include as referring to or indicating authenticity are as follows: *Regte* = real, *egte* = genuine, *ware* = true, *werklik* = real, *opregte* = upright, real, true. While the terms *outentiek* or *outentiteit* (authenticity) exist in Afrikaans, they are Anglicisms that were not frequently (if ever) employed by anyone in the field. These terms are often used in Afrikaans as alliterations or rhyming idioms, e.g., *regte egte* = really genuine or *werklik waar* = really true. These reduplications were regularly used by my respondents for emphasis.

Operationalisation: inauthentic/authentic

'Authenticity is born out of fakery' (Lindholm 2002).
' ... it is Disneyland that is authentic here!' Jean Baudrillard (1989: 104) states, implying that authenticity is the artifice, while cinema and television are the reality of America. The 'real' America is to be discovered underneath all that veneer. Authenticity is a gloss of a the nation that is really about ghettoes, trailer parks, pink

flamingos and middle-class lawns covered with Christmas décor. Slavoj Žižek (1991) contends that the search for the 'authenticity' of objects, and I suppose subjects, is actually a pseudo-problem. If these social and cultural artefacts are fabrications, why bother to investigate their authenticity? This view, which suggests that authenticity is simply a by-product of the constructed-ness of the world, is echoed by others. For Benjamin (1969), the exactness of artifice is what endows many of the objects in the present era of 'mechanical reproduction' with their authenticity. Authenticity is only possible, he argues, once the technologies that allow art to be mechanically and exactly reproduced have been invented. This line of argument, which associates authenticity with an event (for Benjamin, the invention of particular technologies), places authenticity within the historical (Shiner 1994). Authenticity can only be spoken of within a context that recognises its artificiality and the historicality of its emergence, and it is within this frame that it should be read throughout the article.

Adorno (1964) suggests that 'the authentic', as asserted by the existentialists of his day, was not a desirable position. He therefore avoids the essentialist, autochthonous and purist tendency that authenticity suggests (Paddison 2004). If these are the trends and ends of authenticity (referring to Heidegger; fascism, racism, Auschwitz), they are inauthentic as a matter of principle and as a reflection of 'actual humanity' (Adorno 2003; Paddison 2004). This reference to 'actual humanity' is key for the study of the San, because this is what many philosophers sought to arrive at, and what I refer to as prelapsarian.

What about the copy that is more real than the thing it copied? This is a copy so exact as to defy any attempt to de-authenticate it. A question I continually asked myself was how portrayals of the San (of themselves by themselves, as well as the portrayals tourists want to see) can be so completely textbook? How is it possible that the acts, stories, tools, materials and objects that I saw during the first few years of the 21st century were the exact same as those I had seen in my school textbooks and in popular (and, I may add, discredited) portrayals of the San? We have to return to Žižek's (1991) point about the nature of the problem. It seems that authenticating is not the real problem here, but rather an investigation of the conditions (discursive, historical and so forth) in which authenticities are produced.

Authenticity as cultural purity

Most of my research participants realise that their 'culture' is less than 'pure'. They know and acknowledge that some of their cultural rituals and performances are recreations. Many admit that they have 'lost their culture' or 'forgotten the old ways'. While many realise that claiming an original bushman-ness which has a perfect congruence with groups that once existed is futile, the action space that is the land claim requires that they make some declaration of such an ethnic identity, even if the identity is simply 'approximate'. Few ǂKhomani assert an authenticity based on what I call 'cultural purity', which is here taken to mean traditional isomorphism, historical similitude, mimetic credibility (Bruner 1994; Gable and Handler 1996; Handler and Saxton 1988) or ethnographic authenticity (Carrier 2009).

If few ǂKhomani San can claim that their lifestyle matches that of a people who were in the past differently referred to as San, *Boesman* or Bushman, how do they claim such an identity in the present? It would seem they selectively draw on a few easily reproducible traditional, historical, mimetic or ethnographic traits. No one individual can, however, draw on these traits in an all-inclusive manner: perfect equivalence is only possible for the simulacra (see later). Let me illustrate this awareness of the limits of authenticity as cultural purity through a brief ethnographic interlude.

Oom Hans Tieties had been a municipal worker all his life, before taking early retirement and investing his pension in a herd of sheep and a few goats. He became a member of the ǂKhomani San Communal Property Association (hereinafter CPA)[11] and grazed his animals on CPA land, the same that the ǂKhomani had won in the land claim. As a livestock farmer his lifestyle was seen as antithetical to a way of life thought of as 'San'. I was often told, in reference to Hans, that 'real San people hunt, they do not farm'. In addition to his livelihood strategies, salaried work and farming, Hans spoke neither Nama nor N|u – the two languages that fewer than 40 individuals of the ǂKhomani San claim to speak. Dawid Kruiper spoke a smattering of Nama (widely considered to be a language of the Khoi pastoralists of Namaqualand and southern parts of Namibia). Other individuals who spoke N|u were regarded as San, because theirs was understood to be the lost language of the San of the region. That Kruiper spoke Nama led many to question his legitimacy as a bushman, and some even suggested that he did not hail from this part of southern Africa. These commentators noted that Kruiper's ancestors had arrived in the southern Kalahari around the early 20th century as refugees from the German wars in Namibia (Grant 2011). Nama or N|u is thus used to determine whether or not an individual is autochthonous to the region.

Oom Hans did not participate in any cultural performances for tourists because of his relative wealth[12] (inter alia and in contrast to other CPA members he owned a vehicle and lived in a formal brick home at Klein Mier). He was considered by many other ǂKhomani as less authentically San. He would often tell me he was aware that his lifestyle did not reflect actual San characteristics. He was not alone in this: many other ǂKhomani were unable to base their claims to San-ness on any of the constitutive mimetic characteristics that many argued constituted 'true bushmen-ness'. Many who did not display or perform a mimetically credible bushman script were called *westerse Boesmans* (western Bushmen), because their way of life reflected what was considered to be a 'modern Westernised' lifestyle, and did not adequately mirror that of the bushmen (see also Simões 2001). San livestock farmers faced a very particular dilemma: they had to show that they were *regte Boesmans* and that they had as much claim to San-ness and the available resources as those ǂKhomani who could claim ethnographic authenticity.

How did these San farmers show that they were *regte* (real) or *ware* (true) San? They could not claim to follow the traditions of San people; after all, their workaday lives did not match up with those who were considered bushmen. These farmers could make reference to being San through an appeal to authenticity as existential veridicality. They could claim they had in fact been 'marred by modernity'. Several suggested to me that they may have had a true bushman story, had their lives not been interrupted by modernity/modernisation. Oom Hans and others like him claimed they were '*regte Boesmans*' because of a shared history of dispossession and violence experienced at the hands of Europeans and other groups. Thus, the claim was that the 'modernising' project of colonialism (and subsequently, apartheid) had alienated, made anomic, and burgeoned their alterity.

Oom Hans reported that they 'have lost the names and the way of life and the land and its resources and for years lived on the bottom of the heap'. For these farmers, participating in the land claim was not an ordinary reclamation of some 'auratic' identity (Mufti 2000) – in fact, they had never known such an identity. They were, however, seeking redress for the alienation, anomie and alterity of modernity. They were asking us to believe that they were San farmers, even though the notion of being both a farmer and a San seemed antithetical. Moreover, since they had no recourse to cultural purity or tradition in order to define themselves as San, these farmers made claims to their San-ness through appeals to the common dispossession, domination and destruction of their traditional culture by 'forces of westernisation'.

Authenticity as an existential question

The example above shows that authenticity as cultural purity is closed off to some people who need recourse to a different type of authenticity. Authenticity is not so much a matter of showing that their life conforms to some perceived form, but that it at least reflects a 'rightly guided' life, especially within the 'modern age'. First, authenticity becomes a moral question; second we are reminded of authenticity as a modern phenomenon; and lastly as an attempt to make this version of authenticity seem critical, occidental claims are deployed to validate these accounts. In addition, when authenticity is described as existential veridicality it helps us understand why the San and the Kalahari are visited by what I broadly refer to as 'new age seekers'.

Claims to, and assertions of, authenticity are sometimes made on moral grounds. Here the human agents appeal to a sense of a rightly guided, ethically informed, self-aware life. The research participants, who are often characterised as less culturally pure (i.e., less authentic) most commonly use these normative statements to construct the authenticity or inauthenticity of the more 'culturally pure'. Let us see how this plays out in the field.

One small extended family group who are in key leadership positions in the CPA, the Eamons, are regularly de-authenticated by the *tradisie Boesmans*. The latter, under the leadership of the late Dawid Kruiper, would regularly claim the Eamons were not real San because they refused to participate in cultural tourist activities where participants were in states of undress. The Eamons wore Western clothes, went to church, spoke Afrikaans, drove modern vehicles and, above all, engaged in economic activities that were not 'San' (like farming, wage labour and other business). The Eamons countered these de-authenticating claims with a similar set of declarations, arguing that Oom Dawid and the *tradisie Boesmans* were unfairly at the forefront of community activities, despite the fact that they were allegedly often drunk, unruly, smoked marijuana or had relaxed morals, etc. For both 'camps' authenticity was not simply about being culturally correct: both the *tradisie Boesmans* and the *westerse Boesmans* held the notion that being San was also about a set of normative principles.

Tradisie Boesmans argue that *westerse Boesmans* have betrayed the idea of what it means to be San, and that their resistance to this ideal (even if we recognise it as the simulacral bushman) serves as evidence of their lesser bushman-ness. The de-authentication is thus an admonition for their perceived betrayal of their culture by the *westerse Boesmans* and thus a moral issue. Conversely, since the authenticity of the *tradisie Boesmans* is established through a hegemonic mimetic credibility, the *westerse Boesmans* mostly de-authenticate with references to normative sanction and claims of unethical and un-Christian behaviour.

One of the single most influential principles in earlier literature about the San (especially that produced after the 1950s) is the idea that egalitarian principles lie at the foundation of all San societies. Some argue that this manner of representing San society largely resulted from a critique of Western industrialised capitalist society of the post WWII era (Wilmsen 1995). The values found in San societies represented the way life should, and could, be and also what the Western world had 'lost' (Wilmsen 1989). The construction of San identity through the 'critique of the modern' persists today, albeit outside of academic circles. My argument is that authenticity in San culture is constructed by 'outsiders' through the lens of Occidentalism (Chanock 2000; Rabinow 1986). Others have characterised this concern for authenticity as a characteristically 'modernist anxiety' (Gable and Handler 1996).

Authenticity and its anxieties emerge in a particular historical context. While not all theorists have as confidently attributed its emergence as a concern to a particular moment as does Benjamin (1969), most agree that the trope of authenticity is modern (Baugh 1988; Berman 1970; Gaugnion 2004; McCannell 1973; Tomaselli 2001; Trilling and Trilling 2009). This does, however, suggest something very specific about the 'presence' of authenticity in what I heard spoken about in the field. If these thinkers are correct, and authenticity is a phenomenon resulting from a particular set of social and cultural markers of this stage in the development of capitalist culture, what then of the ‡Khomani among whom these concerns are constantly expressed and addressed? Well, it places the ‡Khomani firmly in the culture of the present! Their attempts to assert an authenticity can now be read as efforts to participate in the local and global political economy as astute players who are an actual part of the here and now, and not simply temporal misfits.

Elsewhere I documented extensively authenticity as a concern with the maladies of modernity (Ellis 2010). It may suffice to note one or two brief examples. The first idea is that the practices of the San somehow reflect sound conservation strategies. My PhD thesis extensively discusses how the harvesting of firewood by the ‡Khomani San was used a means of drawing a distinction between *tradisie Boesmans* and *westerse Boesmans*. Further, this split between the two groups is framed by discourses of good and bad environmental management strategies linked to their degree of westernisation.

The *tradisie Boesmans* repeatedly raised concerns about sound environmental management and living in harmony with nature. For them, a major factor that ensured entitlement to resources (the land) hinged on the continued ability of the individual to seat themselves within nature. Those who claimed San identity but had little interaction with nature were seen as suffering from so-called 'cosmological autism' (Kohn 2007: 9). In this view, a person can easily lose the ability to interact with or live within a particular domain and have aspects of that domain completely closed off to them. Some ‡Khomani felt it was not enough to be able simply to call oneself San or *Boesman*. Rather, the individual had to retain a way of being, in order to be San, that firmly seats them within nature. The so-called westernised San were often categorised in this way by 'traditional San', who saw their westernised 'cousins' as outside their own eco-cosmos, because they had lost the ability to live in or with nature, the plants and animals found in their world of objects and subjects.

Another example of efforts to use Bushmen authenticity as a remedy for the maladies of modernity is the hope of recovery, a nostalgia for the past, and the varied calls for a return to source, i.e., 'auratic critique' (Mufti 2000: 88). Auratic critiques pertain to an object that is only accessible as an aura as a glimmer from the past. This epitomises the postcolonial moment, the rueful longing for an unrecoverable past, and the postcolonial as that which has been insufficiently mourned (Spivak 1999). These hopes of recovery are especially evident in attempts by the ‡Khomani to recreate the way of life of the 'real Bushmen'. My fieldwork was filled with one lament after another about the lost way of life. Such laments recall these auratic elements, those supposed aspects of San life that made it such a 'wondrous thing'. These elements of an imagined San past are offered to the ‡Khomani as an apparent treasure trove of development and livelihoods by government and NGOs. The challenges of authenticity and the failure of plans to use auratic cultural models as a means of making a living are typical of postcolonial subjects.

Authenticity as circulating value

Where authenticity operates as a question of value it is viewed by those who buy into it as part of an economy of cultural politics in which signs, as measures of value, circulate for the production of cultural commodities. Authenticity in this economy often draws on simulacra and cultural relics of dubious origin, and represents some of the clearest examples of Spivakian post-coloniality. This is a state of being where the colonial past paralyses the agents and keeps them living in a moment after the end of the anti-colonial struggle. The ‡Khomani reminisce and their recollections are ripe with nostalgic imagery. The simulacral bushman is offered to the outsider and to the world as a commodity, but the world is suspicious (see Dyll-Myklebust 2007). Some tourists, journalists, farmers, neighbours demand to know: Is this a 'real' Bushman, am I not buying a fake experience or thing?

It is telling of what the Other is aware of. Dawid learned over the years of interaction with researchers, information gatherers, tourists and the like, what kinds of information would be interesting to them – something like a beetle picking lice out of a child's hair – and he was able to offer this information on the spur of the moment. This is an intuitive ability to offer up types of stories to researchers. There are no vestiges of ancient traditions here, except those that are drawn from the simulacra to please global audiences. People travelled great distances to consult Dawid on matters herbal, medicinal and magical.[13] He and his father and those around him shaped and sustained a micro-political economy – one that plays with nature, ecology, culture, magic, myth, fantasy and reality. Ersatz political economy or not, there is at least the germ of a small market in bushman-ness in the southern Kalahari that the ‡Khomani have tried to grow.

The ‡Khomani have turned bushman-ness into work, they have tried to make it pay, and they have tried to sell it on the open market. A key point in this genealogical reading is that attempts to commoditise bushmen-ness have almost always been mediated by outsiders like philanthropists, entrepreneurs, tour operators and NGOs. Such mediation has drawn on readily available stereotyping and racist iconography of the San, which include popularly held perceptions about San bodies, culture, habits and language. The commoditisation of bushman-ness in this mediated form is seldom questioned, and its authenticity seldom interrogated. However, when the ‡Khomani obtained their own land and began to replicate mediated ventures like those that used to be managed by outsiders, consumers consistently questioned the authenticity of the enterprise.

Why do consumers question the San in their production of bushman-ness, but not the mediated undertaking? First, the desire for authentic experience is exactly what tourism delivers (Cohen 1988; McCannel 1973). McCannel (1973) argues the tourist is actually satisfied to purchase a 'performed experience' and may be completely aware of the contrivance. S/he is fine with experiencing an essentially fictional (can we say inauthentic?) encounter, as long as they know it is staged. Instead of focusing on establishing authenticity, anthropologists should be examining the processes through which 'authenticity is made' (Cohen 1988). In Erik Cohen's view authenticity is established through the imposition of subject distance between the tourist and commoditised culture; the greater the distance, the more authentic the experience even if it is an obvious contrivance. The example offered is of the conspicuousness of cash transactions. Exchange is usually handled through booking offices or administrators, thus tourists do not feel they have paid for something. The unmediated ǂKhomani tourist interactions often involved direct exchanges of money between the San and visitors. Tourists and outsiders on occasion felt that the ǂKhomani were begging or were somewhat forceful when they suggested payment for photographs or offered crafts for sale on the roadside. In these encounters very little subjective distance is placed between the San person and the tourists, who are confronted with very real human realities: money, food and poverty.

Another connection can be made to the existential take on authenticity, namely that of scripting one's own story or narrative employment (Baugh 1988). The imposition of 'subject distance' in the touristic encounter allows tourists to produce their own narrative, to have their own reading and thus create their own particular sense of authenticity. It is as if the production of authenticity is a carefully choreographed interaction that should not be forced onto the tourist but rather offered tentatively, in snippets, so as to not spook him/her.

A crude formula can be proposed from Cohen's argument; the more subjective distance the more authentic the experience seems (note experience). Conversely, the fewer attempts or the less successful the attempts at creating subjective distance are, the more the tourists see the people, their needs, their poverty, their misery and their humanity, and this mars the touristic experience. After all, tourism is about an exotic experience that allows tourists to escape the realities of everyday life that they leave behind in Europe and elsewhere. During these unmediated tourist encounters, observers confront the inauthentic directly. The inauthentic reminds us of the rawness of the lives of the rural poor. Visitors who question the authenticity of the encounter are not querying the cultural purity of the San, but rather the people-ness. They do not see bushman but they see the rural poor,[14] they see the sick elderly, they see single mothers living with grandparents who have to support their great grandchildren. I ask the readers to ignore the simple aesthetic perfection of the bushman and spend a moment considering the raw life of the various rural poor who inhabit and have moved to Witdraai and other farms in the Mier area, hoping for relief from their hardships and poverty.

Struggle for the real: the methodological problem of authenticity

Clifford Geertz (1971) raises a concern about the efficacy of anthropological methods in studying religion. Participants know that we are concerned with a subject like Islam, and whenever they encounter us as researchers, they don their Islamic identity. Geertz's question is the following: When are we as anthropologists watching a performance and when are the actions of the 'Other' 'real' or authentic? For Geertz it is not merely the interference of capital and modernity in the lives of the non-Western world which leaves us as anthropologists with mere remnants of former cultural glories to study in our far-off research sites. In the end, our ethnographies produce nothing more than accounts that reflect only what Benjamin (1969) terms an aura of authenticity, where every time an object is reproduced it only retains some minor semblance or aura of the original object. Nor is it simply a question of witnessing and capturing an uncorrupted, pure portrayal of non-Western culture, a sort of fossilisation and museumisation of 'people'. Rather, authenticity should be a central methodological concern for anthropologists. In part, Geertz suggests that it is useful to know how deep these identities penetrate into the 'being' of humanity. The 'struggle for the real' or for authenticity, in the Geertzian sense, means being able to penetrate this methodological veil and to decode the cultural.

In addition, it should be acknowledged that the presence of anthropologists impacts on the roles research participants choose to play. Put differently, our presence as anthropologists force participants to constantly wear their 'anthropological subject' hats. When do these real people emerge without their subject hats, or does our presence always keep our subjects in character? The ethnographic method suggested by Geertz has to be able to see beyond this character that the Other acts out in the research encounter.

In this last instance I offer a scene from Arundhati Roy's (2002) text, *God of small things*, to further illuminate what Geertz might have been after. In the passage two of the main protagonists, Rahel and her twin brother Estha, approach a temple to watch a performance of the *kathakali*.[15] The narrator tells us that this particular temple is off the usual tourist routes and holds no significance other than its lack of audience. The performers come to placate their gods and ask forgiveness for encashing (*sic*) their religion/culture. The sense one gets from this scene is of a group who wish to practise their religious and cultural rituals earnestly, not for the voyeuristic touristic performances they have become. 'On these occasions, a human audience was welcome, but entirely incidental' (Roy 2002: 229). Geertz, in my view, wants *this* culture to be revealed; he wants these 'audience incidental' moments to be made clear by the ethnographic endeavour. I wonder whether the San ever wait for occasions where human audiences are incidental. Below I recount an incident that reveals the aversion to the audience and the Other's engagement with it.

In the last two decades the San, and more so the ǂKhomani, have been overrun with researchers from a variety of disciplinary backgrounds: natural, agricultural, nutritional, social sciences and humanities. The ǂKhomani often told stories of, and described, the research encounters they had with researchers. On occasion some of these stories were told so as to ridicule researchers and the type of activities their research included. Kruiper often tells about various controls involved in experiments like only eating this or that bread, or only eating a particular maize meal, or of having to collect stool samples from his grandchildren. The San's accounts of researchers offer an unusual lens into how our efforts as researchers were interpreted and perceived by participants. What was related to me usually suggested that there may be problems with the data that were collected, that the participants were deceptive or may have been actively misleading. For me, the issue was the authenticity of the data. There is another way of reading it, however; the participants are actively scripting the ethnographies of their lives.

Abraham, in those days Dawid's frequent companion, occasionally asked me to interpret for him on guided walks through the San farms. One such tour ended at Dawid's house. I was sitting in his yard, where one of his grandchildren was playing nearby. I saw a *tok-tokkie* (darkling beetle/Tenebrid beetle) crawling across the sand and Dawid saw me watching it. He said: '*This beetle, you know, we use it to get rid of lice in children's heads.*' He scooped up the beetle, put in the hair of the child, and walked off to a nearby fence in his limping gait. At first the child did not realise that a beetle was in her hair, but as soon as she felt it crawling she was startled by the sensation (she became suddenly wide eyed) and frantically brushed it off. Dawid laughed, looked away, the child ran off to find her mother.

Is the beetle really used to pick lice from children's hair? I seriously doubt it! Tenebrid beetles only eat detritus, they are not active predators that hunt, they are scavengers. I know Dawid to be rather mischievous and his reaction to the scene that played out suggested that he was making it up, his tell-tale laugh and his aloofness after the child had run off, left the impression that he had been caught out.

Several aspects of this story are significant to the arguments about authenticity. First, the story points to the way in which authenticity is constructed out of extraordinary elements – a beetle becomes a medium though which to read bushman-ness, it feeds into the simulacral bushmen. Second, the methodological aspects of doing work among these heavily researched communities are highlighted; these communities have been extensively researched by the Centre for Communication, Media and Society (CCMS), and I will not attempt to cover those methodological strategies and debates. The argument here focuses on two particular processes: that of withholding (Spivak 1990) and that of 'common ontological unfolding', which often happens in the anthropological research process (Ramos 1992).

Deepening anthropologies: hyper-reflexivity and research intimacies

As a point of departure and because it speaks to some of the issues I want to offer as a conclusion, let us briefly mention some of the work by done by CCMS in the southern Kalahari. The research done by a long succession of students since the early 1990s highlights two invaluable sets of contributions: the first results from attempts by CCMS to develop 'a hyper-reflexive ethnographic methodology' (Kapoor 2004). Hyper-reflexivity is a method of engagement derived from Spivak's 'problem of the native informant'.[16] The resolution of the 'problem' is to be found in an 'obsessive interest in self reflexivity' in which anthropologists are aware that they are 'intimately inhabiting and negotiating discourse' in order to 'produce a non-hierarchical encounter with the other', and ultimately to make anthropological and all research 'engagement more accountable to the subaltern' (ibid). Examples of the methods used by the CCMS include auto-ethnographic work (see Tomaselli 2003, 2005, 2012; Tomaselli et al. 2013), 'campfire ethnography' (McLennan-Dodd 2003), and fieldwork friendships (Dyll 2003; Mhiripiri 2012).

The second set of methodologies can be classed as a series of ethnographic experiments that include not just a 'classic ethnographic approach' (here rather crudely understood as extended field stays and mixed methods), but also a range of other ethnographic elements linked to methodological concerns. The research efforts by CCMS are diverse and appear haphazardly organised or based on students' whims and preferences. These include: the production of ethnographic film, multi-vocal epistemologies (Dyll-Myklebust 2013), narrative analysis, semiotics (Tomaselli 2001a), tourist analyses (Barnabas 2010; Peters 2013; Tomaselli 2011; Wang 2001), art studies (Barnabas 2010, Finlay and Barnabas 2012; Lange et al. 2013), and rock art studies (Tomaselli 2001b). I mention here also that the work of Shane Moran (2009) and Michael Wessels (2010) has equally attempted to shift the boundaries of San scholarship, albeit through the deployment of different literary, textual, translation and theoretical strategies. The aforementioned falls under a Derridadean critique that attempts to re-read the San archive in relation to the nostalgia for the lost origin (Wessels 2010). Overall, the mainstay of San studies is, for the most part these days, grounded firmly within a tradition of critique that aims to transcend what has been problematic in this body of scholarship.

In short, cumulative CCMS accounts have produced a meta-anthropology (an anthropology of anthropology) and a range of other techniques I call 'research intimacies', i.e., attempts at closing the subjective, epistemological and other gaps between researcher and researched (see Jeursen and Tomaselli 2002; McLennan-Dodd 2004). For all its seeming arbitrariness these diverse engagements have responded to an epistemological problem of studying the San and the range of representations as well as engagements and how these encounters have produced particular 'knowledges'. Moreover, the research has also responded to issues beyond epistemology. I argue that epistemology does not adequately capture the *problematique* of anthropology. What the work of some of these researchers contends with, is that they operate in a common dialogic process of revealing each other's most basic being. The question of a deeper anthropology is not simply: How do I get to know who you are? The more fundamental question of anthropology is: Who are you and who am I? (see Tomaselli 2013, in response to a critique of CCMS's reflective/reflexive position offered by Hitchcock and Biesele 2008).

Anthropologising the self and common ontological unfolding

The longitudinal aspect of the CCMS ethnographic encounter, together with its very serious consideration of the 'epistemic violence' (Ayotte and Husain 2005) the San have been subjected to through years of being studied and talked about in the West, creates a unique opportunity (read ethnological database/archive) that will allow us to 'anthropologise' not just the Other, but also Western epistemic travellers (researchers, journalists, media, tourists, government agents, NGO workers, etc.). For Rabinow (1986) the call to 'anthropologise the West' is an attempt to turn the gaze of the West and to use anthropology to problematise and interrogate the role of the West in constructing a non-Western subject. However, anthropologising the West does not mean the simple production of an Occidentalism; it is rather a dialogue. Agamben (2004) speaks of the 'anthropological machine' – a particularly Western epistemic undertaking that creates an ethnological subject by granting it an externally imposed ontological status. The CCMS engagement offers a meta-anthropology that anthropologises bushman studies, the San and bushman students, by turning gazes and asking how the ethnographic subject is, in turn, created by the gazes.

I conclude with a question, a line of inquiry, a *problematique*. Why is the abovementioned methodological and meta-anthropological work necessary? Two aspects of my own ethnographic encounter and search for an authenticity stand out. The first is what I can best describe as following a process of 'withholding' on the part of the Other. Such withholding is the retreat of the other, our anthropological subject is withdrawing and our efforts to represent it clearly and even in a critically deconstructed state seem increasingly unlikely. Baudrillard (1998) alludes to the self-same resistance to representation by the Other or to a retreating Other.

Is this the now-familiar crisis of representation? Not quite, but this crisis does figure in the resistance/withholding. Withholding is not the simple catachresis, the continued use of concepts without real-world referents, as highlighted in the work of

Spivak in her engagement with postcolonial theory. This is not the Western knower misjudging the exact identity of the Other through the misapplication of concepts and ideas. No, what I am conceptualising here is an active process undertaken by the Other, and its victim is not the Third-World postcolonial subject, but rather the Western European self. What I am dealing with here is the refusal to be represented, noted in literary characters such as Friday in J.M. Coetzee's *Foe* (1986). In Coetzee's text Friday eludes all attempts to represent him, the best that those who encounter him can do is hazard a guess.

In the field I often encounter people unwilling to speak to me or other researchers. Various 'strategies' are employed to resist or withhold participation, for instance, Pooi, the grandson of one of the last N|u speakers, would often shout loudly at journalists and filmmakers and threaten to lock the gates of the farms and not let anybody in. When I asked him about this he complained that '*everyone keeps coming in and taking their knowledge but bringing nothing back*', and for this reason he refuses to participate in research and dislikes it when his mother or grandmother participate. On other occasions I noticed some San 'pretending to be drunk' in order to avoid researchers. Some are rude to researchers, others ask for large sums of money. Attempts were also made by organisations and legal representatives to limit and shape the contours of interaction with the San. The South African San Institute (SASI) drafted legal contracts that set out the terms of contact between the San and journalists, media, film makers, researchers, farmers, tour operators and the like. In an effort to enforce these contracts and their terms, the San people were asked to not participate in any research, nor to allow anyone to photograph them. Literally, this meant there was sometimes an actual silence, a reluctance to speak, but in addition to this the San and SASI thought it useful to also impose a visual absence or silence.

One of the most telling entanglements in this regard was the suicide of Dals in late 1999. Dals took his own life by jumping in front of a bus filled with tourists. I read this event as an attempt on his part to remove himself from the equation of representation. His suicide was a last-ditch attempt to place himself outside the grasp of an externally imposed representation. He took his own life, he placed himself in the path of the tourist bus; in my view he took back his voice and in the final act represented himself and wrote his own story in a classic existentialist move.

Withholding on the part of the Other is a process that complicates the production of an authentic ethnological subject. Anthropology among the San in the southern Kalahari is not experiencing the limits of a paradigm or a scientific consensus that can no longer explain what it is observing without creating a new, conceptual technical toolbox. Rather, we are witnessing a shift in the agency of the Other, who no longer behaves like a willing and docile research subject. We are now confronted with a self-asserting, sometimes silent, sometimes hostile, retreating other.

Let me return to a point made in passing at the beginning of this text, where I noted that the prelapsarian 'Other' eludes us all the time and if we do not find the authentic, then anthropology seems pointless. Barriers (theoretical or methodological) do not seem to offer a ready way out. I have suggested a deepening anthropology (e.g., work done by CCMS), but I intuitively sense I may need to offer a different solution. The reason for this is that the problematic is not simply a theoretical issue of how the Western episteme interrogates or constructs an authentic view of the other. Far beyond this, the retreat and withholding by the research subject shows that the challenge for bushman scholars is located in both worlds, that of a Self and an Other. Once this realisation sinks in, then the parties involved can begin to tackle the problem not as a characteristic of this world or that world, but rather as an issue of 'common ontological unveiling' (Ramos 1992). Some of this is suggested from the field by research activities that are hyper-reflexive and intimate of the CCMS, and also by other ethnographic tidbits like 'lice-eating beetles', by withholding. In the end these suggest that any failed attempt at locating the authentic is a failure to locate not just the Other, but the Self as well.

Notes

1   The discussion that follows is based on ethnographic fieldwork I conducted between 1999 and 2003.

2   People's Movement for the Liberation of Angola.

3   My supervisor notes that the 'fear', as much as it was real, was also drummed into the heads of the soldiers in these battalions by the SADF.

4   The communities, now living in Platfontein, 15km from Kimberly, have recently become the focus of extensive research by students from the University of KwaZulu-Natal. See Barnabas (2010) on art-making; Mhlanga (2006) and Hart (2011) on radio, and Dockney (2011) on storytelling via video.

5   Here preservation is employed as it was used by members of the 'Preservation Committee' that is to have measures in place to preserve the culture, ways and lifestyle of 'a people'.

6   The reclassification of Bushmen as coloureds and no longer native means they do not need to be catered for as with other 'native' groups. Importantly, the state need not cater for their land needs; in terms of the policies of separate development the native must ideally be provided a homeland. From sources we see that the successive governments did not view a San-tustan as a possibility.

7   For more on the San homeland proposed in the 1930s, see Gordon (1995) and Boydell (1948).

8   I am not suggesting that the mere assertion of San identity is enough to cause its re-emergence: the identity is not simply voluntaristic, rather 'authenticity' is at once volunteered but needs other elements which are not solely the body (race elements), nor are they simply ethnic (culture elements).

9   The Afrikaans term 'Baster' literally translates as a bastard, but when applied to animals it can denote a cross breed, or when applied to dogs, a mutt. In earlier uses of this word, it referred to people who were first-generation offspring of a white male and a slave/ indigenous woman. These persons occasionally enjoyed greater privileges than other slaves, but the laws of the colony became increasingly oppressive and many Basters left to farm beyond the frontier. Today the term is not widely used and seems to be confined to regions of the Northern Cape and the southern parts of Namibia. In the context of present-day Mier, it has gained more currency as an economic status category than a racial one. Bredenkamp (1991) suggests that the term 'Khoisan' be applied even to those who are historically termed Basters or Bastaards.

10   The example of painting is one also by Benjamin in his 'Mechanical reproduction'.

11   The CPA is a common property institution that allows groups (in the South African case, beneficiaries of land redistribution or restitution) to hold land as a juristic person. CPAs generally have defined membership based on various criteria, such as common dispossession or in the case of the ‡Khomani San, bushman-ness. CPA members elect an executive committee and other constituent bodies to govern the resources of the association.

12   I participated in wealth-ranking exercises with the extension workers of FARMAfrica. For some of the results see Bradstock (2006, 2007).

13   I have personally encountered a number of Xhosa-speaking people who had travelled from the Eastern Cape or Cape Town to visit Dawid Kruiper or one of his relatives. N/ooi (Dawid Kariseb) also receives many visitors from various regions of South Africa.

14   The 'rural poor' are probably as much a simulacrum as 'bushmen'. It is a matter of which simulacrum serves the people at any given time.

15   Dance dramas enacted from the holy texts reflecting the life of Lord Krishna, over 100 variations of these plays exist.

16   The 'problem of the native informant' is not a problem of the 'other'; rather it is an epistemic question and a representational issue. Simply put: Who speaks for the 'other'? Who is responsible for *giving* the world its *image* of the 'native' who is the recipient of assistance, of 'development'? Very often it is indigenous academics, intellectuals who speak to the 'West' about the subaltern, and these intellectuals are equally complicit in creating particular images of the other as impoverished, racialised, indigenised, etc. Hence, the problem of the native informant speaks back to Spivak's text 'Can the subaltern speak?' and its conclusions.

References

Adorno, T. 1964. *The jargon of authenticity*. USA: Routledge and Kegan Paul.
Adorno, T. 1987. *Minima moralia: reflections from damaged life*. London: Verso.
Adorno, T.W. 2003. *Can one live after Auschwitz? A philosophical reader*, ed. R. Tiedemann. Stanford: Stanford University Press.
Agamben, G. 2004. *The open: man and animal*. Stanford: Stanford University Press.
Barnabas, S.B. 2010. Picking at the paint: viewing contemporary Bushman art as art. *Visual Anthropology* 23(5): 427–442.
Barnard, A. 1990. 'Comment' on foragers, genuine or spurious? Situating the Kalahari San in history. *Current Anthropology* 31(2): 109–146.

Baudrillard, J. 1989. *America*. New York: Verso.

Baudrillard, J. and P. Petit. 1998. *Paroxysm: interviews with Philippe Petit*. New York: Verso.

Baugh, B. 1988. Authenticity revisited. *The Journal of Aesthetics and Art Criticism* 46(4): 477–487.

Benjamin, W. 1969. *Illuminations*. New York: Schocken Books.

Berman, M. 1970. *The politics of authenticity: radical individualism and the emergence of modern society*. Boston: Atheneum.

Biesele, M. and R.K. Hitchcock. 2008. Writing in the San/d: autoethnography among indigenous southern Africans – a review. *Collaborative Anthropologies* 1(1): 201–205.

Biesele, M. and R.K. Hitchcock. 2010. *The Ju/'hoan San of Nyae Nyae and Namibian independence: development, democracy and indigenous voices*. New York: Berghahn.

Boonzaier, E. and J. Sharp. 1993. Staging ethnicity. *Track Two* 10–13, February.

Boydell, T. 1948. *My luck's still in*. Cape Town: Stewart Printers.

Bredenkamp, H.C. 1991. Die Khoisan en vakterminologie na *The Oxford history of South Africa*: 'n Historiografiese dilemma. *South African Historical Journal* 25: 61–76.

Bruner, E. 1994. Abraham Lincoln as authentic reproduction: a critique of postmodernism. *American Anthropologist* 96(2): 397–415.

Bruner, E. 2001. The Masaai and the lion king: authenticity, nationalism and globalization in African tourism. *American Ethnologist* 28(4): 881–908.

Carrier, J. 2004. Ecotourism and authenticity. *Current Anthropology* 45(4): 483–498.

Carstens, P. 1966. *The social structure of a Cape coloured reserve*. London: Oxford University Press.

Chanock, M. 2000. 'Culture' and human rights: orientalising, occidentalizing and authenticity. In *Beyond rights talk and culture talk*, ed. M. Mamdani, 15–36. Cape Town: David Phillip.

Clifford, J. and G.E. Marcus, eds. 1986. *Writing culture: the poetics and politics of ethnography – experiments in contemporary anthropology*. Berkeley: University of California Press.

Coetzee, J.M. 1986. *Foe*. South Africa: Penguin.

Cohen, E. 1988. Authenticity and commoditization in tourism. *Annals of Tourism Research* 15(1): 371–386.

Comaroff, J. and J. Comaroff. 1999. Occult economies and the violence of abstraction. *American Ethnologist* 26(2): 279–303.

Comaroff, J. and J. Comaroff. 2009. *Ethnicity, Inc.* Chicago and London: University of Chicago Press.

Crawhall, N. n.d. Too good to leave behind: the N|u language and the ǂKhomani people of Gordonia district. Unpublished manuscript.

Den Hertog, T.N. 2013. Diversity behind constructed unity: the resettlement process of the !Xun and Khwe communities in South Africa. *Journal of Contemporary African Studies* 31(3): 345–360.

Derrida, J. 1972. *Limited, Inc.* Chicago: University of Chicago Press.

Dockney, J. 2011. Social power through self-imaging in participatory video. Unpublished Master's dissertation, Centre for Communication, Media and Society, University of KwaZulu-Natal.

Douglas, S. n.d. Do 'Bushmen' belong in reserves? Reflections on recent events at Schmidtsdrift and anthropological intervention. Unpublished seminar paper delivered in Social Anthropology Dept., University of Cape Town.

Douglas, S. 1995. The human isthmus: dangerous diluted sewerage poison; recuperating 'bushman' in the new South Africa. *Critical Arts* 9(2): 65–75.

Dyll, L. 2003. In the sun with Silikat. *Current Writing: Text and Reception in Southern Africa* 15(3): 135–150.

Dyll-Myklebust, L. 2013. Development narratives: the value of a multi-voiced epistemology in Kalahari research. http://www.inter-disciplinary.net/probing-the-boundaries/wp-content/uploads/2013/05/Dyll-Myklebust.pdf (accessed 14 March 2014).

Ellis, W. 2010. The ‡Khomani San land claim against the Kalahari Gemsbok National Park: requiring and acquiring authenticity. In *Land, memory reconstruction and justice*, ed. C. Walker, T. Kepe and A. Bohlin, 181–197. USA: Ohio University Press.

Erasmus, P.A. 1997. The harmless people: from Stone Age hunter to modern soldier. *South African Journal of Ethnology* 20(4): 165–169.

Feuser, W.F. 1988. Wole Soyinka: the problem of authenticity. *Black American Literature Forum* 22(3): 555–575.

Finlay, K. and S. Barnabas. 2012. Shifting representations of the Bushmen. In *Cultural tourism and identity: rethinking indigeneity*, ed. K.G. Tomaselli, 24–71. The Netherlands: Brill.

Geertz, C. 1971. *Islam observed: religious development in Morocco and Indonesia.* Chicago: University of Chicago Press.

Ghosh, A. 1992. *In an antique land: history in the guise of a traveller's tale.* New York: Vintage.

Gordon, R. 1995. Saving the last South African Bushman: a spectacular failing. *Critical Arts* 9(2): 28–48.

Gordon, R. 1999. Bain's Bushmen: scenes at the Empires Exhibition, 1936. In *Africans on stage*, ed. B. Lindfors, 266–289. Bloomington, Indiana: Indiana University Press.

Grant, J. 2011. Rural development in practice? The experience of the ‡Khomani Bushmen in the Northern Cape, South Africa. Unpublished doctoral dissertation, University of Edinburgh.

Guignon, C.B. 2004. *On being authentic.* London: Routledge.

Handler, R. and W. Saxton. 1988. Dyssimulation: reflexivity, narrative, and the quest for authenticity in 'living history'. *Cultural Anthropology* 3(3): 242–260.

Hart, T.B. 2011. Community radio: the beat that develops the soul of the people? A case study of XK FM as an SABC-owned community radio station and its role as a facilitator of community-based development. Unpublished Master's dissertation, Centre for Communication, Media and Society, University of KwaZulu-Natal.

Heidegger, M. 1927. *Being and time.* Germany: SCM Books.

Huhn, T., ed. 2004. *The Cambridge companion to Adorno.* Cambridge: Cambridge University Press.

Humphreys, A.B. 1985. A kaleidoscope of values: changing perspectives on San society. *Kronos* 10(1): 58–66.

Husain, M.E. and K.J. Ayotte. 2005. Securing Afghan women: neocolonialism, epistemic violence, and the rhetoric of the veil. *NWSA Journal* 17(3): 112–133.

Isaacson, R. 2001. *The healing land: a Kalahari journey*. London: Fourth Estate.

Isaacson, R. 2002. Last exit from the Kalahari: the slow genocide of the Bushmen/San. www. opendemocracy.net (accessed 25 January 2003).

Jay, M. 2006. Taking on the stigma of inauthenticity: Adorno's critique of genuineness. *New German Critique* 97: 15–30.

Jeursen, B. and K.G. Tomaselli. 2002. Romancing the Kalahari: personal journeys of methodological discovery. *Current Writing: Text and Reception in Southern Africa* 14(1): 29–58.

Kapoor, I. 2004. Hyper-reflexive development? Spivak on representing the Third-World 'Other'. *Third World Quarterly* 25(4): 627–647.

Kohn, E. 2007. How dogs dream: Amazonian natures and the politics of transpecies engagement. *American Ethnologist* 34(1): 3–24.

Lindfors, B., ed. 1999. *Africans on stage: studies in ethnological show business*. Bloomington, Indiana: Indiana University Press.

Lindholm, C. 2002. Authenticity, anthropology and the sacred. *Anthropological Quarterly* 75(2): 331–338.

Lyotard, J.F. 1991. *The inhuman: reflections on time*. Stanford: Stanford University Press.

Mahmood, M., ed. 2002. *Beyond rights talk and culture talk*. Cape Town: David Phillip.

Maingard, L.F. 1937. Introduction. In *Bushman of the southern Kalahari*, ed. J.D. Rheinallt Jones and C.M. Doke. Johannesburg: University of the Witwatersrand Press.

Marshall, L. 1976. *The !Kung of Nyae-Nyae*. Cambridge: Harvard University Press.

McCannel, D. 1973. Staged authenticity: arrangements of social space in tourist settings. *The American Journal of Sociology* 79(3): 589–603.

McLennan-Dodd, V. 2003. Hotel Kalahari: 'You can check out any time you like but you can never leave'. *Cultural Studies <–> Critical Methodologies* 3(4): 448–469.

McLennan-Dodd, V. 2004. 'The healing land': research methods in Kalahari communities. *Critical Arts* 18(2) (Literature and representation issue): 3–28.

Mhiripiri, N.A. 2012. A performative encounter with artist Silikat van Wyk in the Kalahari. *Critical Arts* 26(3): 375–400.

Mhlanga, B. 2006. Community radio as dialogic and participatory: a critical analysis of governance, control and community participation – a case study of XK FM radio. Unpublished Master's dissertation, Centre for Communication, Media and Society, University of KwaZulu-Natal.

Mufti, A.R. 2000. The aura of authenticity. *Social Text* 18(3): 86–103.

Paddison, M. 2004. Authenticity and failure in Adorno's aesthetics of music. In *The Cambridge companion to Adorno*, ed. T. Huhn, 198–221. Cambridge: Cambridge University Press.

Peters, R. 2013. Anthro-tourism, documentary film and method. *Journal of African Cinemas* 5(1): 19–31.

Prins, F.E. 2009. Secret San of the Drakensberg and their rock art legacy. *Critical Arts* 23(2): 190–208.

Rabinow, P. 1986. Representations are social facts: modernity and post-modernity in anthropology. In *Writing culture: the poetics and politics of ethnography*, ed. J. Clifford and G.E. Marcus, 234–261. Berkeley: University of California Press.

Ramos, A.R. 1992. The hyperreal Indian. *Série Antropologia* no. 135, Universidade de Brasília, Instituto de Ciências Humanas, Departamento de Antropologia.

Rassool, C. and P. Hayes. 2002. Science and the spectacle: |Khanako's South Africa, 1936–37. In *Deep histories*, ed. W. Woodward, G. Minkley and P. Hayes, 117–161. Amsterdam: Rodopi.

Rheinallt, J.J.D. and C.M. Doke, eds. 1937. *Bushmen of the southern Kalahari*. Johannesburg: University of the Witwatersrand Press.

Robbins, D. 2006. A San journey: the story of the !Xun and Khwe of Platfontein. Sol Plaatje Educational Trust.

Robins, S. 1997. Transgressing the borderlands of tradition and modernity: identity, cultural hybridity and land struggles in Namaqualand (1980–94). *Journal of Contemporary African Studies* 15(1): 23–43.

Robins, S. 2000. Land struggles and the politics and ethics of representing 'Bushman' history and identity. *Kronos* 2000: 56–75.

Robins, S. 2001. NGOs, 'Bushmen' and double vision: the ǂKhomani San land claim and the cultural politics of 'community' and 'development' in the Kalahari. *Journal of Southern African Studies* 27(4): 833–853.

Roy, A. 2002. *God of small things*. London: Penguin Books India.

Sharp, J. and S. Douglas. 1996. Prisoners of their reputation? The veterans of the 'Bushman Battalions' in South Africa. In *Miscast*, ed. P. Skotnes, 323–330. Cape Town: UCT Press.

Shiner, L. 1994. 'Primitive fakes', 'tourist art' and the ideology of authenticity. *Journal of Aesthetics and Art Criticism* 52(2): 225–234.

Simões, A. 2001. Issues of identity in relation to the Kalahari bushmen of southern Africa: a comparative analysis of two different bushmen groups during the late 1990s and into 2001. Unpublished Master's dissertation, Centre for Communication, Media and Society, University of KwaZulu-Natal.

Skotnes, P., ed. 1996. *Miscast: negotiating the presence of the Bushmen*. Cape Town: UCT Press.

Smith, A.B. 1990. On becoming herders: Khoi-Khoi and San ethnicity in southern Africa. *African Studies* 49(2): 51–73.

Solway, J.S., R.B. Lee, A. Barnard, M.G. Bicchieri, A.C. Campbell, J. Denbow and R. Gordon et al. 1990. Foragers, genuine or spurious? Situating the Kalahari San in history [and comments and reply]. *Current Anthropology* 31(2): 109–146.

Spivak, G.C. 1990. Theory in the margin: Coetzee's *Foe* reading Defoe's *Crusoe/Roxana*. *English in Africa* 17(2): 1–23.

Spivak, G.C. 1999. *A critique of postcolonial reason: toward a history of the vanishing present*. Cambridge, MA and London: Harvard University Press.

Steyn, H.P. 1984. Southern Kalahari subsistence ecology: a reconstruction. *The South African Archaeological Bulletin* 39: 117–124.

Suzman, J. 2001. *An introduction to the regional assessment of the status of the San in southern Africa*. Report no.1. Windhoek: Legal Assistance Centre.

Tobias, P.V. 1956. On the survival of the Bushmen. *Africa* 26(2): 174–186.

Tomaselli, K.G. 2001a. The semiotics of anthropological authenticity: the film apparatus and cultural accommodation. *Visual Anthropology* 14(2): 173–183.

Tomaselli, K.G. 2001b. Review essay: Rock art, the art of tracking and cybertracking: demystifying the 'Bushmen' in the age of information. *Visual Anthropology* 14: 77–82.

Tomaselli, K.G. 2003. 'Dit is die Here se asem': the wind, its messages, and issues of auto-ethnographic methodology in the Kalahari. *Cultural Studies <–>Critical Methodologies* 3(4): 397–428.

Tomaselli, K.G. 2005. *Where global contradictions are sharpest: research stories from the Kalahari*. Vrije Universiteit, Amsterdam: Rozenberg.

Tomaselli, K.G. 2012. *Cultural tourism and identity: rethinking indigeneity*. Amsterdam: Brill.

Tomaselli, K.G. 2013. Visualizing different kinds of writing: autoethnography, social science. *Visual Anthropology* 26(1): 165–180.

Tomaselli, K., L. Dyll-Myklebust and S. van Grootheest. 2013. Personal/political interventions via autoethnography: dualisms, knowledge, power and performativity in research relations. In *The handbook of autoethnography*, ed. S. Holman Jones, T.E. Adams and C. Ellis. California: Left Coast Books.

Trilling, L. and L. Trilling. 2009. *Sincerity and authenticity*. Cambridge, MA and London: Harvard University Press.

Voss, A.E. 1990. 'Die Bushie is dood: Long live the Bushie' – black South African writers on the San. *African Studies* 49(1): 59–69.

Walker, C., T. Kepe and A. Bohlin, eds. 2010. *Land, memory, reconstruction and justice*. USA: Ohio University Press.

Wang, C. 2001. Is pro-poor tourism viable? Cultural tourism as sustainable development in Zulu and Bushman communities. Unpublished Master's dissertation, University of Natal, Durban. http://ccms.ukzn.ac.za/images/MA_dissertations/caleb%20wang%20-%20ma%20dissertation.pdf (accessed 25 January 2014).

Wessels, M. 2010. *Bushman letters: interpreting /Xam narrative*. Johannesburg: Wits University Press.

Wilmsen, E.N. and J. Denbow. 1990. Paradigmatic history of San-speaking people and current attempts at revision. *Current Anthropology* 31(5): 489–524.

Woodward, W., G. Minkley and P. Hayes, eds. 2002. *Deep histories: gender and colonialism in southern Africa*. Amsterdam: Rodopi.

Žižek, S. 1991. Grimaces of the real, or when the phallus appears. *October* 58(1): 45–68.

Development narratives: the value of multiple voices and ontologies in Kalahari research

Lauren Dyll-Myklebust

Abstract

This article is based on findings from a PhD study that explored the development communication processes between partners in the establishment of !Xaus Lodge in the Kgalagadi Transfrontier Park, South Africa. Framed within the critical indigenous qualitative research approach, it reveals the importance of local narratives in the coproduction of knowledge that may guide development initiatives. The ‡Khomani and Mier, as community partners, are San and Khoe descendants with a rich storytelling tradition, and so many interviews turned into what I term 'development narratives'. The study also adopted participant observation as a data-collection method and was guided by constructivist grounded theory. In presenting quotations from the ‡Khomani and Mier's development experiences it illustrates the way in which researchers as 'collectors of quotations' can create a polysemic narrative that mobilises individual narratives and in so doing offers a space for local partner agency to be acknowledged. The 'development narratives' presented in the article foreground the fluidity of identity revealed in the integration of San, Khoe and Nama spirituality and Western Christianity, the connection to ancestral land, everyday life and power relation practices expressed via animalistic motifs, reconciliation, and, briefly, the value of participation as empowerment.

Introduction[1]

This article interrogates the methodological use of local oral narratives in either development or research projects. It is based on findings from my PhD study that explored the development communication processes between different partners in the establishment of !Xaus[2] Lodge in the Kgalagadi Transfrontier Park (KTP), South Africa. Framed within the critical indigenous qualitative research approach (Denzin, Lincoln and Smith 2008), both the study and this article reveal the value in foregrounding narratives in research by drawing on examples from the field.

Local people's ontology (ways of being) and epistemology (ways of knowing) cannot be ignored in making recommendations for development. Development practitioners cannot compartmentalise indigenous modes of thinking and views of development, but should take them into account in planning and implementing programmes. Listening to and recording the narratives of the local communities who are impacted by development result in a holistic understanding of the pros and cons of an initiative. This article offers a framework that foregrounds the importance of narrative in mobilising research participants' voices for the coproduction of knowledge on which meaningful development initiatives may be guided. The local community partners in the !Xaus Lodge partnership are the ǂKhomani and Mier communities. Both groups are San and Khoe descendants with a rich storytelling tradition and so many interviews turned into what I term 'development narratives'. Oral narratives – especially in an oral society which speaks in imagery – reflect the intangible, in this case the spiritual beliefs of the community, which are as real to them as food in their stomachs and roofs over their heads.

In presenting quotations from the ǂKhomani and Mier's development experiences and expectations, the article aims to illustrate the way in which theorist-as-storyteller (Arendt 1968; Benhabib 2000) fits within critical indigenous qualitative research. As 'collectors of quotations', researchers/theorists can create a polysemic narrative that mobilises individual narratives, and in so doing offer a space/an audience for research participants to be heard and their agency acknowledged.

Background and methodological framework

In 2007 a public–private–community partnership (PPCP) was formed in the establishment and operations of !Xaus Lodge (Dyll-Myklebust 2011 and 2012; Dyll-Myklebust and Finlay 2012). My PhD study explored the interface between community development via tourism and the field of development communication *vis-à-vis* a case study of !Xaus Lodge. It valorised the voices of *all* lodge stakeholders, analysing their expectations and how they negotiate the processes involved in establishing and operating the lodge. It is my interaction with the ǂKhomani and Mier partners that is the focus of this article.

Traditionally, the ‡Khomani's political economy was one based on a hunter-gatherer society, whereas the Mier's political economy is founded on farming. Both groups were previously dispossessed of their land under processes of colonialism and apartheid. In 1995 the ‡Khomani met human rights lawyer, Roger Chennels, who explained that the new land laws gave them the right to restitution for the losses they had experienced since 1913 (Crawhall 2001). That same year the ‡Khomani lodged a claim for the restitution of land in and around the then Kalahari Gemsbok Park, from which they had been removed against their will. In 1997 the Mier Local Council attended the ‡Khomani land claim negotiations in 'opposition to the claim' (SASI 2004: 2), as they wanted to protect their existing land use in Mier – especially their game camps which were located in the rural reserve within the park (Ellis 2010). This led to the Mier lodging their land claim in December 1998. In addition, South African National Parks (SANParks) opposed the land claim. What followed was a period of intense negotiations on the rights in/to the KTP and challenging community dynamics (see Kepe, Wynberg and Ellis 2005). Part of these negotiations was an 'interpretation and reinterpretation of San identity, whereby San authenticity was either required or acquired in the process' (Ellis 2010: 181). Finally, in 1999 the land claim was settled, resulting in the return of land to the ‡Khomani and Mier.

This enabled a 'return home' for many ‡Khomani and Mier, as the park is where many of their ancestors are buried and where some grew up as children. The land claim saw the restitution of land in and around the park and an agreement to transfer the title deeds of six Kalahari farms, approximately 37 000 hectares, to the ‡Khomani Communal Property Association (CPA). In addition, approximately 25 000 hectares within the park was awarded to the CPA, in conjunction with an adjacent 25 000 hectares being awarded to the neighbouring Mier community, to be managed as 'contract parks' (Grossman and Holden 2002). This is private land that has been made available for inclusion in a national park, subject to terms and conditions agreed to by the ‡Khomani and Mier land owners and SANParks as the conservation authority (De Villiers 2008). !Xaus Lodge was built in the centre of the two contract parks.

The South African Department of Environmental Affairs and Tourism (DEAT) and SANParks represent the public partner in the !Xaus Lodge partnership. The lodge's construction was undertaken by SANParks and DEAT-sponsored poverty relief funds, with the Minister of Environmental Affairs and Tourism being a signatory to the *!Ae!Hai Kalahari Heritage Park Agreement* (2002: 167). In this agreement SANParks, the Mier Local Municipality and the ‡Khomani CPA committed to jointly establish the lodge, which aimed to symbolise cooperation between the principal partners and establish a facility for eco-tourism – the lodge would generate an income for all parties, and contribute to poverty alleviation in the region (ibid: 194). The private operating partner is Transfrontier Parks Destinations (TFPD), a South African-registered company that signed the !Xaus Lodge contract with the lodge's existing Joint Management Board (JMB) on 24 January 2007. The appointment of TFPD witnessed a paradigm shift that placed the emphasis on dialogue, contextual sensitivity and social entrepreneurship (Yunus 2007). These are all characteristics of a culture-centred approach (Dutta 2011) to a development project, yet they are not always commonly found.

Historically, from an indigenous perspective, the domain of research and science was mobilised to suit the imperialist agenda. Linda Tuhiwai Smith (1999) calls for a decolonisation of research methodologies as part of a wider project of reclaiming control over indigenous ways of knowing and being. She urges researchers to disrupt the rules of the 'research game' by employing practices that are respectful, ethical and useful, rather than merely founded on ethnocentric assumptions. Similarly, Norman Denzin and Yvonna Lincoln (2008a) propose a critical indigenous qualitative research approach along with interpretive research practices that aim to be ethical, transformative, participatory, and committed to dialogue and community. In their view the researcher must consider how his/her research has 'use-value and promotes self-determination for research participants' (ibid: 2). Narrative inquiry and storytelling form part of such an interpretive practice. The aim is for the researcher to represent the texture of fieldwork, along with the complexity of indigenous ontology and epistemology, in the coproduction of knowledge through the inclusion of local voices. This article centres on the use of local 'development narratives' in the methodological approach to my PhD, through which I experienced and analysed the partner perceptions related to !Xaus Lodge.

As a longitudinal study from 2006 until 2011, my PhD focused on the processes involved in transforming a failed built tourism asset, aimed at poverty alleviation, into a successful commercial product with a range of benefits for the community partners (see Dyll-Myklebust 2011, 2012). The processes involved were studied and shaped via participatory action research (Reason and Bradbury 2001).[3] Based on the findings of the !Xaus Lodge case study, the thesis generated a generalised PPCP development communication model that is sensitive to multiple ontologies. The model suggests that success should not only be determined by a venture becoming operational and commercially viable, but also by its capacity to 1) stimulate socio-economic empowerment, and 2) build local social skills and capacity that equates with individual empowerment (Dyll-Myklebust 2011, 2012).

The use of semi-structured in-depth, face-to-face interviews and participant observation, guided by constructivist grounded theory (Charmaz 2009, 2000) facilitated my understandings of the complexity of the Northern Cape as a research area. The interview excerpts provided in this article are possibly similar to those collected by other researchers. However, the specificity of this article is that it highlights the methodological merit of including local voices in research towards a development project – a practice frequently ignored in such projects (Smith 1999).

Although it uses !Xaus Lodge as a case study, the article aims to highlight the value of this method in general, and is not simply a report on the success of !Xaus Lodge. I was not part of the !Xaus Lodge partnership; I was an observer in the chain of constant reproductions of meaning attached to the project and between partners. I analysed these dynamics in connection with (participatory) development communication theory and empirical evidence within a cultural studies framework. In addition, the approach to this study was not necessarily to use narratives *per se*. However, the interviews often turned into a type of narrative that revealed the centrality of local cosmology in understanding a development initiative. This cosmology signifies the fluidity of the Northern Cape people's identity in merging traditional San spirituality (which merges indigenous and Western[4] beliefs), Khoe and Nama beliefs, as well as structured Western religion. This article aims to demonstrate that it benefits a development partnership to acknowledge the agency of local discourse.

Theory and/or sense-making?

The study adopted a sense-making approach. Brenda Dervin (2003) outlines the treatment of information in Western thought via seven chronological perspectives, starting with the treatment of information as a natural description of natural reality. However, over time 'information's capacity to deal with reality (i.e. its ontological assumptions), have first been tempered and then directly contested' (Dervin 2003: 327), leading to a sense-making conception of information as a theoretic perspective and methodological approach, where 'information is a human tool designed by human beings to make sense of a reality both chaotic and orderly' (ibid: 328).

I view the information in both the narratives told to me by the ǂKhomani and Mier, and in the PPCP model, from this perspective as it considers several aspects of critical indigenous qualitative research. This approach 1) acknowledges the existence of cultural as well as personal relativity; 2) recognises that all attempts to formalise information are framed within discourses of power; 3) concedes that information is made and unmade in communication (by humans collectively and individually); 4) recognises that information is theoretically incomplete and always open to potential change; and 5) privileges the ordinary person as a theorist involved in developing ideas to guide an understanding of his/her personal/collective/historical and social worlds.

Sense-making could thus be considered one example of an interpretive research practice, as it urges researchers to reach out to the sense made by others, in order to understand what insights they may bring to their understanding of a phenomenon, as 'sense-making explicitly enters the research situation in the "in-between" spaces between order and chaos, structure and individual, self 1 and self 2' (ibid: 332).

The sense-making approach is valuable in its insistence that meaning-making happens in the pragmatic interaction with research participants, and it therefore stresses the interpretive nature of research in recognising that the local is grounded in the politics, circumstances and economies of a particular moment (Denzin and Lincoln 2008a). Theory, if preconceived prior to engagement with the research area, and without the flexibility to be modified when tested and challenged in the field, often becomes irrelevant and 'forced' in its attempts to make sense of a phenomenon (Denzin and Lincoln 2008a; Tomaselli 2005; Tomaselli, Dyll-Myklebust and Van Grootheest 2013). However, theory is instrumental in interpretive research, as data collection, analysis and subsequent theory stand in close relationship to one another – theory that is *inductively* drawn from data is likely to offer insight, enhance understanding and provide a meaningful guide to action (Strauss and Corbin 1998).

Shifting conceptions of development

Development is defined in varying ways according to differing fields of study and application. This research is located within the field of development communication as the study 'of the relationship between the practical application of communication processes and technologies in achieving positive and measurable development outcomes' (Servaes 2008: 15). Within this field, development is theorised and practised differently, depending on different development communication paradigms ranging from the dominant top-down approach to the dialogic approaches of participatory perspectives.

Participatory development approaches appear to be the preferred paradigms taught in universities, and included in international and governmental development policy. However, empirical examples reveal that top-down communication remains the preferred development strategy, and behaviourist theories remain the preferred option in attempting to explain what is seemingly unexplainable in development projects with indigenous communities – this often results in blame being apportioned to communities if a project fails (Bond 2004; Dyll 2009; Hirsch 2005). The dominant paradigm is premised on a (capitalist) economic model. While this has its place in dealing with the practicality of socio-economic development outputs, the process of development within this perspective is often insensitive to local culture, or views it as a barrier to 'progress'. Cultural identity and indigenous ontology are inextricably linked with land (Kincheloe and Steinberg 2008). Understanding the relationship indigenous people have with the land on which projects are implemented is vital, if local partners are to truly form part of a partnership where their development discourse and expectations are taken into consideration.

This article thus highlights the necessity of contextual knowledge and seeks to demonstrate the way in which local communities have agency: while the 'subjects of development' may be unfamiliar with learnt development discourse, they are deeply aware of their positions within the chain of relations, and are therefore valid and necessary voices in the coproduction of knowledge.

What I present below as 'development narratives' is aligned to Mohan Dutta's (2011) explanation of social change. In contemporary literature, 'development' is often replaced with 'social change' (Dutta 2011; Figueroa, Kincaid and Rani et al. 2002; Gumucio-Dagron and Tufte 2006; Servaes 2008). The term accounts more closely for the intangible processes and manifestations of change, as opposed to the connotations of infrastructure, economic growth and authoritarian, Western communication processes which are often automatically associated with the term 'development'. While 'development' is frequently used in this article (and arose in the interviews), the study is framed according to the goals of social change, as conceptualised in the context of those communicative process, strategies and tactics which are directed at changing hegemonic structures. It is also built on the foundations of subaltern studies (Guha 2001; Guha and Spivak 1981, 2001; Spivak 1988).

Recognising the role of indigenous ontology and epistemology

Avoiding the appearance of 'speaking for' research participants is tricky. How do researchers/development facilitators voice their concerns and expectations without assuming a paternalistic stance? One way is through the use of narrative inquiry. I draw on my research participants' own words following the call by critical indigenous qualitative research for discourses to produce a multi-voiced epistemology.

This study pursues ontology in relation to the ǂKhomani and Mier and development as 'the cosmologies, values, cultural beliefs and webs of relationship that exist within specific indigenous communities' (Denzin and Lincoln 2008b: xiv). Many of the research participants' expectations include (but also go beyond) their material needs, linking strongly to their relationship with the land and 'spirit'/spiritual connections. 'Many indigenous peoples have traditionally seen all life on the planet as so multidimensionally entwined that they have not been so quick to distinguish the living from the non-living' (Kincheloe and Steinberg 2008: 151). This sense of interrelatedness speaks to 'both an epistemological and ontological dynamic – a way of knowing and being that is *relational* … Such relating is undoubtedly a spiritual process' (ibid.). This is illustrated in the ǂKhomani's frequent reference to their spiritual connection to the land within their 'development narratives'. I refer to epistemology as the philosophy of knowledge that considers the nature of knowledge and intelligence (Aluli-Meyer 2008). By including in my writings the Mier and ǂKhomani's expectations and vision for !Xaus Lodge, I aim to reveal them as coproducers of knowledge. Critical indigenous qualitative research honours and builds on the experiences of indigenous persons in a step towards empowering them in the research process, thereby documenting how they name the world for themselves (Smith 2000).

Development narratives

The main expectation the ‡Khomani and Mier had of !Xaus Lodge, is that it was to be an economic driver in a poverty-stricken area. However, other expectations/'development narratives' inductively emerged from interviews and conversations with the local people. The discussion of those 'development narratives' can be contextualised with two similar studies.

The Taita people of Kenya interpret development thought and practice in line with their changing understanding of witchcraft (Smith 2008). They express their views on the consequences of development (for example, the unequal distribution of wealth) in terms of magic or the occult. James Howard Smith (2008) has chronicled a useful way of framing development not in terms of economic indicators, but as part of the Taita cosmology, hence providing an indigenous view of wider politics and instances of resistance to Western conceptions of development.[5] This article aims to provide a similar discourse in terms of the ‡Khomani and Mier's views of !Xaus Lodge as development 'phenomenon'. Their views of the lodge became a lens through which to gain an understanding of issues that could be helpful in facilitating dialogue between them and lodge management/other partners, and so could be relevant for the PPCP model. These issues range from the research participants' conceptions of identity, land, skills, development, ownership, tourism, politics in the area (historical and contemporary) and the nature of work and participation, which are often linked to the metaphysical world.

The second study which has a bearing here is Mary Lange's (2011) research on water stories by the Eiland Women[6] in the Upington Gariep area of the Northern Cape. Her research illustrates how San and Khoe worldviews continue to be reflected in present-day oral narratives by the local people. 'This continuation is not likely a simple lineal passing on but often rather the result of ... a significant reworking and reconfiguration' (Lange 2011: 74). Despite shifting identities, particularly amongst the Khoe and San, the Gariep River people's cosmology continues to include a belief in the Water Snake.

I present only three overlapping 'development narratives' that foreground 1) the fluidity of identity amongst the ‡Khomani and Mier, as revealed in their integration of San, Khoe and Nama spirituality and Western Christianity; 2) the connection to the land, everyday life and power relation practices expressed via animalistic motifs; and briefly 3) the role of reconciliation and the value of participation as empowerment.

Shifting identities, spirituality and religion

Belinda Kruiper grew up in Cape Town and married late ‡Khomani artist, Vetkat Kruiper, when she moved to the Kalahari. She affirms the need to rid oneself of Western scepticism when working with or engaging the ‡Khomani:

SAN REPRESENTATION

Before I came to the Kalahari, my rational self would have dismissed [a lot of] stories. But the desert teaches you to think differently, to be more open to what is less tangible, to the world of the spirit. Things happen here that have no logical explanation. In these desolate open spaces, where technology does not impose, a different energy holds…I can't explain how Oom Jan could call rain by watering the *vygies*[7] … My Dutch Reformed upbringing had conditioned me to believe that such manifestations were of the devil. However, little by little I came to understand them in the context of the Bushman world, and to accept that the spirit world is as much a part of God's design as the physical world is. (Bregin and Kruiper 2004: 18)

Being alert and respectful to these instances of 'spirit'/'connections' can help development practitioners understand the role of spirituality in development with local communities, and assist them in moving away from overly-deterministic explanations for development successes or failures.

Returning to the Kenyan context, Smith (2008: 38) chronicles the Taita's reactions to development as linking to their cosmology, which is centred on the occult and religion:

[L]ate colonial development was synonymous with the modern and the future; it implied the victory of reason over primitivism, superstition and magic (all of which defied governance). But for Africans, development was something withheld, something spectral, and so too were the objects and institutions that were synonymous with reason and secularism for Europeans … Rather than referring to a known telos synonymous with civility and modernity, development became synonymous with the impossible and the absolute, and was permeated by religion and religious imagery of redemption and salvation.

Similarly, San and Khoe cosmology reflects a worldview where the levels of daily life and the metaphysical world interact (Lange 2011). The continuation of a Khoe and San cosmology is evident in some of the ‡Khomani and Mier's 'development narratives'. ‡Khomani CPA committee member, Hans Padmaker's (interview, 30 January 2007) response to my question about the possible benefits of !Xaus Lodge, sheds light on how the process of development is signified in terms of spirituality:

I think there are a lot of advantages for the ‡Khomani. Although some people have been sceptical for some time, you know, because of the [lodge's] remoteness … But if it could be possible and trust not only in our abilities or the operator's ability, or ‡Khomani CPA, or Mier Municipality. But also depend on the Messiah, or as the Bushmen say Thukwa … you see trust in God the creator of you and I. And I believe that despite our faults and our sins and things like that we could get somewhere.

For Padmaker, !Xaus Lodge's success is not only dependent on the partners' abilities, but also on the forgiveness of Thukwa 'who dwells on high, and to whom they showed great respect, especially during great storms of thunder and lightning …

saying, if it thunders, the Great Chief is angry with us' (Schapera 1930: 381). The shifting identities and reconfiguration of traditional beliefs *with* Western Christianity is evident in Padmaker's merging of Thukwa (Tsui ||Goab), a Khoe 'supernatural being' (Schapera 1930), and 'the Messiah', revealing a fluidity of identity. Padmaker also referred to practical elements in terms of what the lodge (management) would need to do to be successful. Directly following his explanation of the role of the Messiah or Thukwa, he acknowledged the importance of marketing and the need for skills development – in particular, a skill that some development practitioners and tourism operators may take for granted. Padmaker's development narrative illustrates the interaction between the practicalities of daily life in making a success of a development initiative and the role of a deity in 'allowing' this process to happen.

Another San belief which is evident in one of the 'development narratives' shared with me, was that of the creator god |Kaggen, a figure who holds shamanistic associations and takes the form of different animals. 'It is said that Mantis could become any animal he wanted, but most of all he liked becoming an eland bull. The elands are still his favourites and only they know where he is' (Leeming 1937/2010: 75). The lodge's development has been interpreted by some ‡Khomani as |Kaggen/ Mantis giving his blessing to the venture. This is evident in the multi-layered narrative provided below. Belinda Kruiper (interview, 22 August 2006) remembers the time when TFPD CEO, Glynn O'Leary, first visited what was to become !Xaus Lodge:

> *It's either the myth, or the coincidence or the spiritual stuff, it's big! ...When we go to scout and recce the lodge, the animals acknowledge us. When Glynn and Vetkat were alone in the vehicle they saw the leopard. When we left and Hannes Steenkamp stayed behind as one of the Mier guys to look after the lodge for that week he came back straight to my house and said:* 'There's an eland bull walking about, but there are not tracks. The eland walks and when I go on its trail, there are no tracks. There are big things happening.' *So there's a spiritual eland that's moving and in the Bushman lore the eland is the most sacred animal and it's the bull. So it seems like in the ancestral body they are blessing all of this.*

Significant here is not only that the above quote is evidence of San cosmology influencing how the local people viewed the lodge's development once TFPD came on board as the operator, but that it was a Mier community member, Hannes Steenkamp, who perceived *something* of the presence of the eland at !Xaus Lodge. The ‡Khomani are typically associated with traditional beliefs and folklore, but here Hannes, from the Mier (often nicknamed *westerse mense*)[8] also felt the presence of an eland as important for the lodge. This again points to the fluidity of identity and ontology in the Northern Cape. In addition, it highlights the role of interpretation and multiple layers of meaning, as it was a deliberate choice made by Belinda, who married into the ‡Khomani community, to stress the spiritual importance of this change in the establishment of the lodge. It would have been interesting to know whether Hannes would have attached the same prominence to this in his retelling of the event, if I had been able to meet with him.

Reinstatement of tradition and freedom in a return to the land

Smith's (2008: 38) research reveals more similarities between the ‡Khomani I spoke to and the Taita's interpretation of development:

> [I]n recent years, the sign development has become unhinged, and freed, from its referents in two major senses. First … it has become *dislocated from the state*, as communities try to acquire control over the meaning of the concept, and the *objects of their desire* while in the process defining themselves as communities. (emphasis added)

The day after the JMB signed the !Xaus Lodge contract, I interviewed traditional healer, Oom Jan van der Westhuizen, who was with his nursing wife and four children at Andriesvale, in the Northern Cape. Sounds of a community singing in Afrikaans and a pastor preaching during a church service, filled the air. Related to the notion that the sign of development has become *dislocated from the state*, Oom Jan does not simply view !Xaus as a state-funded development project, but rather sees it as part of his desire to live on the land again and to embrace a traditional way of life:

> *The park means much more to me than this Western life. The park is the joy of my heart. Because I can do all I want to in that park. And in that park no-one is an enemy of another. You make enemies for yourself if you so wish. Because in the Western world, in the people, are other things … And it is the fear of our hearts. We are at a point today where we can't tell right from wrong … I am keen to work for a living, for a future, for my wife and the children. I have eight children with this wife and two from the world …. I would very much like to live free, free in nature … dance a little at night – and if the male lion charges us, we can chase him away from the women and the children so that the spirit and soul can become stronger again. The heart of nature is far more beautiful than the heart of people.* (Van der Westhuizen interview, 28 January 2007)

Being in the park symbolises freedom that will allow their 'spirit and soul to become stronger again'. Oom Jan's expected benefit for the community is that !Xaus also presents a means for local children to have a future. This vision of the future is based on a reinstatement of the past, in a return to ancestral land and a sharing of traditional knowledge:

> *The elders who have been around for about fifty years hold the large portion of knowledge. This knowledge should be returned to our children. We don't know what the future holds for them or how they view their futures. But as we know the state in which our country finds itself we wish to plan a new future for them in the wild where they will be and become something else in the far future. And that is why I think !Xaus will perhaps give us a good future and life and a bright future ahead. That which we do,*

we do not do for ourselves. We do it for these children because I think it is the children of this day that will take us into a new way of life. (Van der Westhuizen interview, 28 January 2007)

This explanation resonates in Smith's (2008: 38) discovery of the Taita's reaction to and interpretation of development in Kenya:

[t]he concept [of development] has become increasingly disconnected from the categories of tradition and modernity, each of which seems increasingly beyond the control of any person or community. Kenyan development efforts consist, then, in attempts to acquire control over the future by drawing on the past.

Isak Kruiper, another traditional healer who is also on the CPA, explains: '*Look it was our dream, right from the start, to come to an agreement where our people have the privilege to come into the park and see their own place*' (interview, 28 January 2007). His expectations support the typical spiritual connection to the Park in which !Xaus is located:

[The park] is our source of love. It is our place. We were born here and we grew up here...Because, you see, our spirit and our source is after all in the park. And today I can sit here and say I am very proud of this place. (ibid.)

Being a traditional healer, his expectation of the ownership of !Xaus Lodge within the park is that it will allow him to source the indigenous plants which are important to his healing practices:

And I often think that – if you look at our indigenous plants – that it will be a very good thing for me. Because we are very close to our indigenous plants there that we use. And also the knowledge is linked widely to that place. It is a special place. (ibid.)

Thus, a return to the land not only relates to the spiritual connection, but with local communities there is valuable knowledge of the environment that needs to be respected in a culture-centred development project (Dutta 2011; Dyll 2009; Tomaselli 2012).

Reconciliation and empowerment through participation

Although there were signs of 'blessings', as discussed above, there was also some scepticism surrounding the lodge development, due, in part, to the numerous failed development attempts of the past. Isak Kruiper (interview, 28 January 2007) acknowledges the difficult process of getting !Xaus Lodge established, and the turn-around/paradigm shift once TFPD became involved:

We had different players who came to identify the place and who said: 'All right maybe I can take this over. Maybe I can build it up.' But up to now most of them had failed. And then some came and started to build the place up to what it is today. And now at last we can move forward ... with !Xaus Lodge we could ... if we can stand together then we can expand and we might now move forward.

Thus, !Xaus Lodge appears to be symbol of 'correcting wrongs' and an opportunity to 'move forward'. John Festus, a young ‡Khomani man who was raised by master tracker Vetpiet Kleinman, but who felt ostracised from his family and community, left the Northern Cape in 1996 for Pretoria, where he was unemployed and homeless. He returned to the Northern Cape in 2006, a few months before the JMB contract signing. Festus views the chance to work at !Xaus Lodge as an opportunity to reconcile his past and *'get connected to the people'*:

Everything had stopped there. Now I can say it's the second time I heard about the lodge and see how things are going. They are more on a mission to get everything in place ... It did not start as a dream of mine. But I will go there now. It's important for me for things to come right, and good things to happen. (Festus interview, 28 January 2007)

The motif of !Xaus as a symbol of reconciliation between the two communities themselves, and between them and SANParks, is illustrated in Isak Kruiper's response: *'if we can stand together'*. Traditionally, the holder of power in the !Xaus Lodge partnership is SANParks. Concerns over past unequal power relations between the people and the park are expressed via the development narrative of the jackal and the lion, offered by Oom Jan van der Westhuizen (interview, 28 January 2007):

We have also had a tremendous struggle with the park. We call them the young male lion as he is a rich gentleman and we are the small jackals that just get a small bit of bread, or just wait for a small piece here and there of the bones, or to scratch open the stomach contents once the young male lion is finished. And we ask that they share those moments with us in a free spirit and just see the troubles and the struggle of the poor and with us fight against it and try to work it out and also give back to the people what was lost to them over all the centuries.

The theme of reconciliation is echoed in Belinda Kruiper's vision that the success of the lodge will depend on good communication and the ability to rise above past conflict:

I feel that this lodge, spiritually, is a peace symbol to actually realise we're all power, we all have power – one has this knowledge and one has a degree. And I'm hoping that there's this underlying relationship in how it is operated and the decision making ... there will be a knowing that this place is running as a symbol of peace. (Kuiper interview, 22 August 2006)

The significance of !Xaus Lodge for Oom Jan ties in with the expectation that the lodge will providing an opportunity for community participation in their own development, and hence a sense of empowerment *'to see if we can't do something about it ourselves, and that is why it is so important to us'* (Van der Westhuizen interview, 28 January 2007).

Conclusion

The ‡Khomani and Mier's envisioned expectations of !Xaus Lodge, as revealed in the wider PhD study were: 1) a return to their ancestral land as their source of strength; 2) income generation through job creation; 3) skills development and training; 4) participation in their own development venture; 5) the creation of improved relationships between the community partners and SANParks, and between the community partners themselves; 6) the development of a sustainable project from which their children will benefit; and 7) access to the medicinal plants needed to practise traditional healing.

The 'development narratives' discussed in this article exhibit a 'consciousness of precedence' (Masilela 2003) in returning to the past, symbolised in a return to ancestral land as their desired development outcome. The land was, and still is, a physical and spiritual resource for survival. Nhamo Mhiripiri (2009: 184) highlights the complexity of the situation:

> …it is not the past [the ‡Khomani] want to return to. What they have is the symbolic language for describing their present marginalized position and what suffering was like. Bushmanness is a metaphor for where they are today as a development of past history – it is a language with a double register, literal and symbolic.

The use of 'development narratives' is essential in foregrounding the kinds of complexities development practitioners and researchers should consider when partnering with local communities. Development narratives are able to agitate, complicate, induct and animate, and thus have the power to challenge received 'rational' authoritarian modes of development. It is imperative, however, that a received and rationalist development discourse is not 'demonised' *in opposition to* local development narratives. A mastery of this discourse, that is dominant in policies and pronouncements, will enable local communities to take control of development projects and processes, albeit as they continue to share a worldview rooted in their spirituality and experiences. Going back to ontology, Belinda Kruiper (interview, 22 August 2006) says *'we all have power'*. All partners in a development project bring with them their own form of knowledge and being. It is essential that these forms are not compartmentalised and set up in contradistinction to one another, but rather that synergies are found.

Notes

1 Pronunciation note on symbols

! Alveolar: Place the tip of the tongue behind the alveolar ridge and pull away sharply. (Sounds like a bottle being uncorked if the mouth is kept round.) For example: !o (brother) (Cwi and Jones 2014: ix).

| Dental: Place the tip of the tongue on the back of the front teeth and pull tongue back sharply (as in the European 'tut' or 'tisk' to utter disapproval). For example: |am (sun) (ibid: viii).

ǂ Palatal: Place the blade of the tongue in the hard palate and the tip of the tongue against the front teeth and pull tongue back sharply. For example: ǂoah (giraffe) (ibid: viii).

2 All lodge partners agreed that it would be called !Xaus Lodge. ǂKhomani community members, Oom Tietes Rooi and Elsie Rooi, explain that it means 'heart' in the Nama language (Kruiper email, 2006). Nigel Crawhall, a sociolinguist who has worked closely with the ǂKhomani and the N|u languages since the early 1990s, supports this translation but adds another dimension: 'As I know, the name of the pan was original Xausendi, which means 'diarrhoea', as the water is brackish there. Ouma |Una pointed out that the pan was shaped as a heart, but that was a later observation, and she meant like a romantic heart, not literally like a human heart' (Crawhall email, April 2009).

3 'A participatory, democratic process concerned with developing practical knowing in the pursuit of worthwhile human purposes ... It seeks to bring together action and reflection, theory and practice, in participation with others, in the pursuit of practical solutions to issues of pressing concern to people, and more generally the flourishing of individual persons and their communities' (Reason and Bradbury 2001: 1).

4 'Western' in this article refers to an Occidental inclination that is not geographically bound to countries originally labelled 'the West' (see Chapman 1997). Rather it refers to ideological leanings towards Western culture that has been heavily influenced by the traditions of the Renaissance, Protestant Reformation, Age of Enlightenment and colonialism.

5 See also Peter Geschiere (1997, 2010), for his fieldwork with the Maka of south-east Cameroon. He discovered that 'it is hardly possible to talk about power without referring to the *djembe* (sorcery/witchcraft)' (1997: 2). He explores how witchcraft is implicated in various power relations, and is used to explain aspects of modernity: 'witchcraft discourse seems to offer an obvious language, both for the rich and for the poor, for trying to make sense of the modern changes – and notably the shocking news forms of wealth and inequality' (2010: 235).

6 Lange refers to the Eiland Women, as their relationship started at the island resort in the middle of the Orange/Gariep River at Upington. They are not a homogenous cultural group, and their individual, shared and shifting identities form a significant part of their contribution to Lange's research. The women gave Lange permission to use their names in related research. I have used their nicknames but have included their surnames for cultural links (Lange 2011).

7 A small, succulent, brightly coloured flower or ground cover that grows in dry conditions.

8   This group includes farmers and pastoralists in the area, and they differentiate themselves from the ‡Khomani whose primary source of income is generated via cultural tourism.

References

!Ae!Hai Kalahari Heritage Park Agreement. 2002. Document whereby the land restitution claims of the ‡Khomani San Community and the Mier Community are finalised, 29 May.

Aluli-Meyer, M. 2008. Indigenous and authentic: Hawaiian epistemology and the triangulation of meaning. In *Handbook of critical and indigenous methodologies*, ed. N.K. Denzin et al., 217–232. London: Sage.

Arendt, H. 1968. Introduction: Walter Benjamin, 1892–1940. In *Illuminations*, ed. W. Benjamin, H. Arendt and H. Zohn, 1–58. New York: Harcourt, Brace & World.

Benhabib, S. 2000. *The reluctant modernism of Hannah Arendt*. USA: Rowman and Littlefield Publishers.

Bond, P. 2004. *Talk left, walk right: South Africa's frustrated global reforms*. South Africa: University of KwaZulu-Natal Press.

Bregin, E. and B. Kruiper. 2004. *Kalahari rainsong*. South Africa: University of KwaZulu-Natal Press.

Chapman, M. 1997. South Africa in the global neighbourhood: towards a method of cultural analysis. *Critical Arts* 11(1-2): 17–27.

Charmaz, K. 2000. Grounded theory: objectivist and constructivist methods. In *The handbook of qualitative research*, ed. N.K. Denzin and Y.S Lincoln, 509–535. London: Sage.

Charmaz, K. 2009. Shifting the grounds: constructivist grounded theory methods. In *Developing grounded theory: the second generation*, ed. J. Morse, 127–154. Walnut Creek: Left Coast Press.

Crawhall, N. 2001. *Written in the sand: auditing and managing cultural resources with displaced indigenous peoples*. Cape Town: SASI/UNESCO.

Cwi, T. Fannie and K. Jones. 2014. *Ju| 'hoan Da'abi!oa N‡omtciasi Kokxuisi ‡Xanua, Ju| 'hoan prentewoordeboek vir kinders, Ju| 'hoan children's picture dictionary*. Pietermaritzburg: University of KwaZulu-Natal Press.

De Villiers, B. 2008. *People and parks: sharing the benefits*. South Africa: Konrad-Adenauer-Stiftung.

Denzin, N., Y.S. Lincoln and L.T. Smith, eds. 2008. *Handbook of critical and indigenous methodologies*. London: Sage.

Denzin, N.K. and Y.S. Lincoln. 2008a. Introduction: critical methodologies and indigenous inquiry. In *Handbook of critical and indigenous methodologies*, ed. N.K. Denzin et al., 1–20. London: Sage.

Denzin, N.K. and Y.S. Lincoln. 2008b. Preface. In *Handbook of critical and indigenous methodologies*, ed. N.K Denzin et al., ix–xv. London: Sage.

Dervin, B. 2003. Chaos, order and sense-making: A proposed theory for information design. In *Sense-making methodology reader: Selected writings of Brenda Dervin*, ed. B. Dervin and L. Foreman-Wernet and E. Lauterbach, 325–340. Cresskill, N.J: Hampton Press.

Dutta, M.J. 2011. *Communicating social change: structure, culture and agency*. New York: Routledge.

Dyll, L. 2009. Community development strategies in the Kalahari – an expression of modernization's monologue? In *Tourism strategies and local responses in southern Africa*, ed. P. Hottola, 41–60. Wallingford: CAB International.

Dyll-Myklebust, L. 2011. 'Lodge-ical' thinking and development communication: !Xaus Lodge as a public-private-community partnership in tourism. PhD thesis, the Centre for Communication, Media and Society, University of KwaZulu-Natal, Durban, South Africa.

Dyll-Myklebust, L. 2012. Chapter 13. Public-private-community partnership model for participatory lodge (tourism) development. In *Cultural tourism and identity: rethinking indigeneity*, ed. K. Tomaselli, 179–214. Leiden: Brill.

Dyll-Myklebust, L. and K. Finlay. 2012. Chapter 9. Action (marketing) research and paradigms in partnerships: a critical analysis of !Xaus Lodge. In *Cultural tourism and identity: rethinking indigeneity*, ed. K. Tomaselli, 119–136. Leiden: Brill.

Ellis, W. 2010. The ǂKhomani San land claim against the Kalahari Gemsbok National Park: requiring and acquiring authenticity. In *Land, memory, reconstruction and justice*, ed. C. Walker et al., 181–214. USA: Ohio University Press.

Festus, J. 2007. Interview with Lauren Dyll and Keyan Tomaselli at Molopo Lodge, Northern Cape, 28 January.

Figueroa, M.E., L. Kincaid, M., Rani and G. Lewis. 2002. *Communication for social change: an integrated model for measuring the process and its outcomes*. The Communication for Social Change working paper series No. 1. New York: The Rockefeller Foundation and CFSC.

Grossman, D. and P. Holden. 2002. Kalahari land claims: far from settled... Ecologists who have assisted the ǂKhomani San. Unpublished paper.

Guha, R.G. 2001. Subaltern studies: projects for our time and their convergence. In *Latin American subaltern studies reader*, ed. I. Rodriguez, 35–46. Durham: Duke University Press.

Guha, R. and G. Spivak, eds. 1981. *Selected subaltern studies*. New Delhi: Oxford University Press.

Gumucio-Dagron, A. and T. Tufte, eds. 2006. *Communication for social change anthology: historical and contemporary readings*. South Orange, NJ: Communication for Social Change Consortium.

Hirsch, A. 2005. *Season of hope: economic reform under Mandela and Mbeki*. Durban, South Africa: University of KwaZulu-Natal Press.

Kepe, T., R. Wynberg and W. Ellis. 2005. Land reform and biodiversity conservation in South Africa: complementary or in conflict? *International Journal of Biodiversity Science and Management* 1: 3–16.

Kincheloe, J.L and S.R. Steinberg. 2008. Indigenous knowledges in education: complexities, dangers and profound benefits. In *Handbook of critical and indigenous methodologies*, ed. N.K. Denzin et al., 135–156. London: Sage.

Kruiper, B. 2006. Interview with Keyan Tomaselli, Lauren Dyll and Kamini Moodley in Welkom, Northern Cape, 22 August.

Kruiper, B. 2006. Email to the author, 17 October.

Kruiper, I. 2007. Interview with Lauren Dyll at Witdraai, Northern Cape, 28 January. Translated from Afrikaans by M. Lange and N. Oets.

Lange, M. 2011. *Water stories and rock engravings: Eiland Women at the Kalahari edge.* Amsterdam: SAVUSA Publications.

Leeming, D. 1937/2010. *Creation myths of the world: an encyclopaedia.* 2nd edition. California: ABC-CLIO, LLC.

Masilela, N. 2003. The new African movement and the beginnings of film culture in South Africa. In *To change reels: film and film culture in South Africa*, ed. I. Balseiro and N. Masilela, 5–30. Detroit: Wayne State University Press.

Mhiripiri, N. 2009. The tourist viewer, the Bushmen and the Zulu: imaging and (re)invention of identities through contemporary visual cultural productions. PhD thesis, the Centre for Communication, Media and Society, University of KwaZulu-Natal, Durban, South Africa.

Padmaker, H. 2007. Interview with Lauren Dyll at !Xaus Lodge, KTP, 30 January.

SASI. 2004. *The ‡Khomani San: from footnotes to footprints – the story of the land claim of the ‡Khomani San.* Upington: SASI.

Schapera, I. 1930. *The Khoisan peoples of South Africa.* London: George Routledge & Sons, Ltd.

Servaes, J., ed. 2008. *Communication for development and social change.* India: Sage.

Smith, J.H. 2008. *Bewitching development: witchcraft and the reinvention of development in neoliberal Kenya.* Chicago and London: University of Chicago Press.

Smith, L.T. 2000. Kaupapa Māori research. In *Reclaiming indigenous voice and vision*, ed. M. Battiste. Vancouver: UBC Press.

Smith, L.T. 1999. *Decolonizing methodologies: research and indigenous peoples.* Dunedin, New Zealand: University of Otago Press.

Spivak, G. 1988. Can the subaltern speak? In *Marxism and the interpretation of culture*, ed. C. Nelson and L. Grossberg. Chicago: University of Illinois Press.

Strauss, A.L. and J. Corbin. 1998. *Basics of qualitative research: techniques and procedures for developing grounded theory.* 2nd edition. Newbury Park: Sage.

Tomaselli, K.G. 2005. *Where global contradictions are sharpest: research stories from the Kalahari.* Vrije Universiteit, Amsterdam: Rozenberg Publishers.

Tomaselli, K.G., ed. 2012. *Cultural tourism and identity: rethinking indigeneity.* Leiden: Brill.

Tomaselli, K.G., L. Dyll-Myklebust and S. van Grootheest. 2013. Personal/political interventions via autoethnography: dualisms, knowledge, power and performativity in research relations. In *The handbook of autoethnography*, ed. S. Holman-Jones, T.E. Adams and C. Ellis, 576–594. California: Left Coast Books.

Van der Westhuizen, J. 2007. Interview with Lauren Dyll at Andriesvale, Northern Cape, 28 January. Translated from Afrikaans by M. Lange.

Yunus, M. 2007. *Creating a world without poverty: social business and the future of capitalism.* New York: Public Affairs.

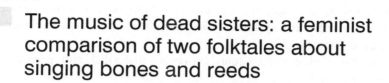

The music of dead sisters: a feminist comparison of two folktales about singing bones and reeds

Cheryl Stobie

Abstract

This article compares and contrasts two folktales. The first is the traditional ballad, 'The twa sisters', collected by Francis J. Child in the 19th century. The Canadian folksinger Loreena McKennitt compiled a variant of this, called 'The bonny swans'. Many of these ballads feature a musical instrument composed of the bones of the slain sister, which sings the name of her killer, who is her heartless sister. The second folktale is 'The singing reed', a story collected in Namibia by Sigrid Schmidt. This tale recounts the story of a girl who dies due to the cruelty of her peers. Some of her blood splashes onto a reed, which sings to her brothers. No claim is made for any direct connection between the two tales; however, transcultural traffic entailed the exchange of various stories, both in written and oral form. Using a feminist perspective, the effects created in both of the folktales are analysed, including the representations of family life, the use of oral features and music, the references to magic talismans and the yearning to transcend the boundaries of death. The consonances and pertinent differences between the two narratives, highlighting their significance socially, politically and spiritually, are explored.

Introduction

This article is about telling stories, via the spoken word, song and written form.[1] It is about tradition and change; language and culture; interpretation, mystery and hope. Long-lived folktales and ballads lose and accrue resonances, and evoke haunting, familiar yet deceptively simple mindscapes which tax the critic's ingenuity. These enduring stories are possessed of freshness, narrative force and immediacy, and the best lyrics of the ballads or chante-fables[2] embody depth and density. The most widely travelled stories have crossed continents and become transformed over centuries. They are living proof of transcultural conversations and transmutations that could be a model for 21st-century dialogue about Western and indigenous knowledge and belief systems, or in the context of this article, Anglo-American and African epistemologies.

For this dialogue to occur, however, historical and present inequities and asymmetries of power need to be acknowledged, instead of adopting falsely universalising assumptions. A particular example of unconscious patronisation can be seen in Bruce Chatwin's (1988: 280) meditations, from an outsider perspective, on nomadism, origins, Aboriginal Dreaming and myth-making:

> I have a vision of the Songlines stretching across the continents and ages; that wherever men have trodden they have left a trail of song (of which we may, now and then, catch an echo); and that these trails must reach back, in time and space, to an isolated pocket in the African savannah, where the First Man opening his mouth in defiance of the terrors that surrounded him, shouted the opening stanza of the World Song, 'I AM!'.

One way in which pervasive asymmetries of power are seen is connected to assumptions about gender, which are expressed unselfconsciously by Chatwin in the extract above. A recent article by Dean R. Snow (2013) uses research about differing finger ratios in men and women to analyse data from hand stencils on Upper Paleolithic cave sites of France and Spain. He concludes that the people who made hand stencils in European cave art were predominantly women, thus rebutting the traditional assumption that the stencils were made by male artists. Androcentric assumptions are clear in such widespread assumptions, as well as in English linguistic conventions, such as those employed by Chatwin, which have historically regarded men as prototypes of humanity. As Simone de Beauvoir (1988 [1949]: 16) notes, woman is frequently posited as the 'Other' of man: 'Thus humanity is male and man defines woman not in herself but as relative to him.'

In an African context, Chinua Achebe (1988) offers illuminating commentary on the value of language, literature, folktales and criticism in interpreting the past, the present and the future. He reminds us that 'we must not see the role of literature only in terms of providing latent support for things as they are, for it does also offer the kinetic energy necessary for social transition and change' (1988b: 115). However, despite his breadth of vision, he too falls prey to sexist language which unwittingly occludes the place and contribution of women in myth-making: 'Every people has a body of myths or sacred tales received from its antiquity. They are supernatural stories which man created to explain the problems and mysteries of life and death –

his attempt to make sense of the bewildering complexity of existence' (1988a: 92). This partial view, disseminated through gendered language usage by which women's role is forgotten, is one that I aim to widen by focusing on a female central protagonist in both folktales, women as creators of oral literature, and women as critics across cultural divides. Many versions of brothers exhibiting fraternal rivalry are well known, such as the biblical story of fratricide between Cain and Abel (which is particularly interesting because of the reference to a brother's blood crying out from the ground), and the narrative of the jealousy of Joseph's ten half-brothers because of their father's favouritism towards him. While I am aware of these accounts, aspects of the feminine will be my concern, in order to highlight women's position as self-defining subjects rather than othered objects; showing women as original creators, custodians of a living heritage, and agents of social change.

In analysing the two selected folktales I use the framework of comparative literature, which studies literature across linguistic and cultural boundaries, and I specifically adopt a feminist and postcolonialist perspective. Comparative literary study recognises that literary forms and practices cross cultural boundaries, and is interested in the ways this happens and the effects of the process. Historically, comparative literature focused on such matters as study of genres, historical periods, ways in which the *Zeitgeist* acted to produce a national literature, sources, influences, myths and themes. The influence of poststructuralism in the academy since the 1960s led to the criticism of comparative study as being a covert form of Eurocentric homogenisation. However, postcolonial theory reveals that while concepts of imperial binarism postulated a transfer of ideas from coloniser to colonised, the contact zone between different groups is in fact ambivalent and transcultural, with effects circulating between them in complex ways. In line with this insight, recent comparative literary studies refute the notion of national superiority, and focus on crossing borders of language, culture and nation, showing similarities as well as areas of incommensurability.

Mexican American poet and theorist, Gloria Anzaldúa, is an influential figure in transcultural literary studies. She uses the metaphors of the bridge, the borderlands and the *mestiza* (woman of mixed European and Native American ancestry) to explore issues of marginality, belonging, language, body and sexuality from feminist, postcolonialist and queer perspectives (2009). She appeals for alternatives to Western binarism, political activism and communication across borders. She recounts four near-death experiences she suffered, and develops a concept of spiritual immersion in an imaginary zone, with the effect of regeneration and personal improvement. Her later work explores the concept of spiritual activism – a combination of spiritual practice and politics designed to effect revolutionary change in society.

Feminist scholars such as Paula Gunn Allen (1992) explore the possibilities of sensitively applying ideas about gender to indigenous texts. Allen analyses a specific

Native American story from varying perspectives to show that both Eurocentric feminist and traditional tribal interpretations have clear limitations; by contrast, however, she proposes a combinational 'feminist tribal' (ibid: 223) reading that highlights the power of women in pre-colonial times in the culture under discussion. By drawing out the consonances between feminism and traditional epistemologies, Allen suggests a form of cultural relativism grounded in mutual dialogue, respect and understanding.

A useful theoretical text for my purposes is *Borderwork: feminist engagements with comparative literature*, edited by Margaret R. Higgonet (1994). In her introduction to the volume, Higgonet points out the challenge that feminist scholarship represents to comparative literature. She notes the importance of topics such as the construction of the female subject's identity, genre theory and the position of the critic (ibid: 5). She reveals the intersections between comparative and feminist approaches in investigating language usage, translation, texts dealing with female bodies and sexuality, and '[w]ho speaks for whom' (ibid: 11) in the act of criticism. Higgonet cautions critics who venture into this contact zone of the hazards:

> [T]he violation of the female body displaces some other, unspoken critical violation. How can one work at the border without absorbing, usurping, or silencing another? Understood in this way, ethnographic or cultural study is always implicitly ethnocentric, freighted with scopophilia, and prone to view the Other as a feminized and subordinate spectacle. (ibid: 13)

Despite this cogent reminder, however, the problem is not intractable. Without an attempt to transcend the limits of the individual ego, authors and critics alike would simply be bound within the silos of their own experiences. It is therefore incumbent on the critic to bear in mind the parameters of one's own frame of reference, and enter imaginatively into the world of the story-teller across the border, thereby attempting to bridge the divide between 'Us' and 'Them'.

The comparative, non-binarist approach I will follow in this article is informed by theories of postcolonialism, global literature and gender studies. I seek to highlight the similarities and differences between the two texts I have selected: 'The bonny swans', a composite version of strands of 'The twa sisters' devised by Canadian harper and singer Loreena McKennitt and recorded in 1994, and 'The singing reed', a story recounted in 1995 to Sigrid Schmidt by Helena Namases, who was then 75 years old, in Okombahe, Namibia (Schmidt 2001: 77–80). I have selected these particular versions as they were recorded within a year of each other, and they show that traditional ballads and folktales are still alive, popular, being adapted in particular contexts, and being transmitted and interpreted transculturally. These two texts are united by primal themes which are quotidian but numinous: family dynamics; struggles between good and evil, love and hate, altruism and selfishness;

and fear of mortality. Both texts have at their centre a sister descending into an unnatural death; her body parts being transformed into a magical musical instrument; her words, channelled through the musical instrument, revealing the crime; and an end exploring issues of social justice. Despite these similarities, one text is from the northern hemisphere, while the other is from the southern and each is very specific, requiring detailed analysis of significant differences. In addition, as Higgonet suggests, acknowledgement must be made of my own etic perspective arising from my socio-cultural positioning as a white South African, and my intellectual training, which could be construed as elitist.

The methodology I adopt is not formalist, functionalist, structuralist or reductively comparative, approaches to Bushmen studies which have been rightly criticised by Michael Wessels (2010: 47–48, 70–71, 105, 135–138). Although comparative study in its traditional guise is viewed with suspicion by Wessels, I hope to avoid the problems of ethnocentrism and false universalisation raised by him. Instead, I wish to build upon his own work of close literary analysis, in addition to the work of Roger Hewitt (1986, 2008), Duncan Brown (1995, 1998, 1999, 2006) and Anne Solomon (2009), amongst others. Each of these scholars promotes the need to investigate literary and other texts respectfully and within the frameworks of the cultures from which they emanate. In particular, Solomon (1992), Megan Biesele (1993) and Camilla Power and Ian Watts (1997) draw attention to negotiations based on physical and social differences between men and women in specific Khoekhoe groups, ethnography, rock art and stories. For me, working within the Humanities, and specifically English studies, allows for a comparison of stories and what they suggest about the values of cultures, communities and gender relations against the backdrop of global routes of connection.

'The twa sisters' was collected in four versions in Volume II of Francis J. Child's eight-volume collection, *English and Scottish ballads*, of 1861. He mentions that the first printed version known to him is 'The miller and the king's daughter' of 1658 (1861: 230). He observes:

> No ballad furnishes a closer link than this between the popular poetry of England [and Scotland and Ireland, it might be added] and that of the other nations of Northern Europe. The same story is found in Icelandic, Norse, Faroish, and Estnish ballads, as well as in the Swedish and Danish, and a nearly related one in many other ballads or tales, German, Polish, Lithuanian, etc., etc. (ibid: 231)

Child's expanded ten-volume work, *The English and Scottish popular ballads*, published between 1882 and 1898, contains 305 English and Scottish ballads and their American variants. In this magisterial work each ballad is ascribed a number; for number ten, 'The twa sisters', Child provides some 25 different versions of the basic story. Paul Brewster (1941: 187) gives his tally of British, Scandinavian and

American texts as 350, and tunes as 125. In addition he mentions similar verse and prose versions from countries including Greece, Hungary, Poland and Lithuania.

Brewster (1953) concludes that 'The twa sisters' originally ended with the resuscitation of the murdered sister. He believes the ballad moved from Scandinavia to England and Scotland, and speculates that the original source of the story may have been Slavic, probably Polish. Although it is impossible to excavate an Ur-text, it is clear that the ballad has existed in the form of song, folktale and chante-fable across a huge geographical distance, and for many centuries, and it is still in the process of reinvention. There are an impressive 486 recorded versions of 'The twa sisters', according to the Roud Folksong Index.

The names for this particular ballad include 'Minnorie', 'The cruel sister', 'The wind and rain' and 'The bonny swans'. The core story concerns two sisters. A young man falls in love with the younger, and the elder, in a frenzy of jealousy, pushes her sister into the water to drown. Some versions include the poignant line: 'Sometimes she sank, and sometimes she swam', which evokes the pre-Chaucerian alliterative tradition. Some variants then have a miller pulling her out of the mill-pond where she has fetched up, and he may or may not be considered jointly culpable of her demise. A passing musician chances upon her body, and he constructs an instrument, usually a harp or a violin, from elements such as her breastbone, hair and fingers, which then sings the story of the murder to the young woman's parents, who in some versions are a king and queen. Punishment of the guilty may occur, or may be implied by the denunciation of the song. In the folktale, the dead sister is sometimes resurrected, although this ending does not occur in the ballad forms.

'The twa sisters' ballad and folktale have certain consonances with 'The singing bone' fairy tale collected by the Brothers Grimm, tale number 28. This is classified as ATU (Aarne Thompson Uther) type 780. The tale concerns two brothers who decide to kill a boar which has caused widespread havoc. The younger brother kills the boar, and the elder then kills and buries him. The elder brother takes the dead boar to the king, and marries the king's daughter. A shepherd finds a bone of the younger brother, and makes a horn from it. The horn magically sings the tale of fratricide, and the king has the elder brother executed. It is noteworthy that Gustav Mahler made use of this story in his cantata, *Das klagende Lied*; in particular, the song 'Der Spielmann' (The Minstrel) depicts the bone flute singing the sorrowful tale. The Grimms note the connection between the Scottish ballad and the 'household tale', 'The singing bone'; further, they point out other similarities, such as Polish and 'Bechuana' versions (Grimm and Grimm 1884). This illustrates that the story existed in Africa in the 19th century, and the implication by the Grimms is that it travelled and was adapted in then-Bechuanaland (present-day Botswana), although this may be a Eurocentric assumption.

In verse or tale form, orally or in writing, 'The twa sisters' and variants based on it continue to be popular and to evolve further. A well-known example of this creatively reworked tradition is Loreena McKennitt's version, 'The bonny swans', from her fifth album which has sold millions of copies worldwide. In this economically conveyed rendition, the scene is set in 'the north country', with a farmer's three daughters walking next to a river, into which the eldest pushes the youngest. Dialogue between these two occurs, in which the youngest sister offers her sibling a house and land in return for saving her, appealing to her avarice, but the cruel eldest sister demands her younger sister's 'own true love'. This outlines the dynamic of jealousy and rivalry between two sisters, dating back to an age when the older sister was expected to marry first. Presumably the youngest sister refuses, as the next stanza has her alternately sinking and swimming, and ending up in the mill-dam, where the miller's daughter observes a swan which looks like a 'gentle woman', and father and daughter place her on the river's bank. The implication that the drowned woman has magically metamorphosed into a swan is emphasised by the burden of the song: 'With a hey ho bonny o' and 'The swans swim so bonny o', which is interspersed between the narrative lines. There are four types of burdens across the spectrum of 'Twa sister' ballads: those that reinforce the content, those that contrast with the content, those that repeat place-names, and nonsense syllables. In this case, strikingly, suggestions of all four types are collated. The first line of the burden is verbal padding close to nonsense, although the word 'bonny' in both lines implies a Scottish setting. For the bulk of the ballad the jolly burden seems to be at odds with a tragic story of sororicide; however, the tranquil image of gliding swans fittingly acts as a transitional signifier of the shape-shifting drowned sister, and presages the ethically satisfying exposé of the end of the text. The overall effect of the burden is to mediate the grim violence of the song, and to foreground the image of mute and traditionally faithful swans in their rightful element.

The harper enters the scene and fashions a mystical harp out of the drowned woman's fingers, golden hair and breastbone. This talismanic object, invested with metaphysical power from the body parts of the dead sister, immediately begins to play on its own, and the harper takes it to the hall of the sisters' father, where it expresses the soul-yearning for justice of the drowned woman. The final stanza is sung in the voice of the drowned sister, who recognises her father (whose status is now elevated from farmer to king), her mother the queen, her brother, and her beloved, 'William, sweet and true', then finally she exposes the crime of her 'false' sister, Anne. The use of specific names highlights the sense of intimate relationships, and the contrast between 'true' and 'false' aptly sets the scene for the tone of reproach and disbelief expressed in the line: 'Who drowned me for the sake of a man.'

This ballad recounts a dramatic story of human love, jealousy within families, and physical and psychological anguish. The water which flows throughout the story symbolises life, as it is used by the miller's daughter to bake bread; danger, as it is the medium used by the eldest sister to kill her youngest sister; and change and catharsis, as it is the means by which the harper receives the body which he disassembles and transforms in surreal fashion into a musical instrument which channels her voice and exposes the wrong done to her. It is noteworthy that all of the voices in McKennitt's version are female, indicating feminine agency, whether evil or good. The male personae are silent presences. The magical corpse is a powerful and allusive figure at the heart of this cautionary tale. The evocative drama charts the metamorphosis from the corporeality of the drowned sister, through her ambiguous appearance as a white swan, to her transformation by the craft of the harp-maker into an instrument by which music can spring forth, accompanied by words which memorialise loss and enchant the audience – both within the setting of the song, and for those listening to it. The ritualised repetition threaded through the narrative of the ballad entrenches memory, mourns the presence of evil and death, and offers the uncanny beauty of transformative art. In the world of the ballad, sisters are not depicted as automatically supportive of one another, but are pitted in competition for men's attention and love, and the social status of marriage. Female jealousy and rivalry can even lead to murder, a crime less usual and more socially condemned for women, given feminine stereotypes of loving-kindness and weakness. While men exist in the tale in the roles of father, brother and sweetheart, the primary drama entails the conflict between sisters as perpetrator and victim, respectively.

Widespread as Child acknowledges 'The twa sisters' to be, its geographical dissemination extends even further than he notes, and adaptations have been made according to local circumstances and cultural codes. Examples include a West Indian chante-fable, 'King Daniel' (Jekyll 1907: 14–15) and a Bengali variant, 'The story of two princesses' (Philipose 1990). A third pertinent example is an 'unusual' Polish text about a singing reed discovered in Springfield, Vermont. This folksong describes the murder of the younger sister during a raspberry-picking contest, and a flute made from reeds growing at her grave (Barry 1935: 2–5, 1936: 2–4). Unbeknownst to Barry, this is an offshoot of a well-established Polish folktale which is closely related to tales of 'The singing bone'. Nicole Marzac (1977: 401) summarises 17 Polish versions, with seven musical settings, and notes that Polish scholars have analysed versions of this tale since 1834. All versions feature a sibling murdered because of jealousy or hatred roused by her or his accomplishment at a task, usually picking berries; the truth of the murder is later conveyed by a magical pipe or fiddle made from the wood of a tree growing on the grave of the victim, and the murderer is punished. In one version, the victim is miraculously revived. This outline largely accords with the world archetype suggested by L. Mackensen (1923: 64; in Marzac 1977: 410–411), except that most versions from outside Poland include the resurrection of the murdered sibling. It is clear from the example of Polish versions of 'The singing bone' that a regionally specific type has developed, using references from the local context. In addition, Polish people have travelled across the globe, including to the United States of America and Namibia, taking this story with them on their transnational journeys.

In the southern African context, and particularly in Namibia, Sigrid Schmidt is known as a leading international folklorist who has spent decades collecting and commenting on oral literature. Prior to her research, only seven magic tales catalogued under ATU numbers 300–999 had been recorded from Nama, Damara and Hai‖om narrators (Schmidt 2001: 192). By 2001, Schmidt had expanded this tally to 89, many in several variants. She hypothesises that her success is related to the fact that previous collectors were men who may have focused on male informants, while in Namibia magic tales are related by women, who formed the bulk of Schmidt's informants (ibid: 192). While Schmidt notes that some Nama and Damara folktales followed transnational routes over centuries, she offers no specific evidence relating to the Namibian tale, 'The singing bone'. She points out that 'only orally transmitted tales keep to sung verses' (Schmidt 2007: 308). It may thus be inferred that 'The singing bone' followed an oral route of transmission, the precise details of which are unclear.

In the Nama and Damara oral tradition, there are two types of renditions of 'The singing bone' (ATU 780, and 984 in Schmidt's numbering in her catalogue of the Khoisan folktales of southern Africa). In the B type, which is less popular, a king promises two orphaned siblings that the one who finds a golden flower will be king. The girl finds it, and her brother kills her and becomes king. A servant finds a bone of the girl and makes it into a flute, which sings about the murder to the king, who has the bones of his sister collected and put in a calabash, and she returns to life (Schmidt 2007: 407). In the A type a group of playmates leaves a little girl in a well. Shepherds, an elephant or a giraffe swallow her. A drop of the girl's blood falls onto a reed, or the elephant regurgitates her onto the reeds, and she metamorphoses into a reed. Her brother creates a flute out of this reed, and the instrument sings the story of the murder of the girl. In different ways, according to the individual narratives, the girl is revivified. In some versions the tale ends with her secretly doing housework before her resurrection is discovered, and in others her betraying peers are punished by death (ibid: 405–406).

Schmidt itemises the tale elements of 16 different versions of 'The singing reed' known to her in Nama and Damara folktales. The first was recorded in 1934 by a German collector, and the second occurs in three publications written between 1938 and 1964 by a Polish author, R. Stopa. (Given Schmidt's comment that only seven magic tales were collected prior to her research, and given my previous comments about the long and deeply entrenched tradition of 'The singing reed' in Polish, one is tempted to imagine that a Polish scholar might be particularly interested in recording this Nama and Damara folktale in Polish and English.) The remaining 14 tales have been collected by Schmidt, and she has published five of them. Twelve of the tales include a sung component, and in one the narrator uses a singsong voice at stages to convey a similar effect (ibid: 406).

The particular story which occupies the centre of my focus is a version of 'The singing reed', which Damara narrator, Helena Namases, told to Schmidt (2001: 77–80) in Okombahe, Namibia, in 1995. This tale was recounted in Nama, and then Schmidt translated it into English (2013). The length of this story allows for more development and detail than that provided in McKennitt's condensed version of the ballad, 'The bonny swans'. There are three sections to the story. The first suggests the melding of transnational currents, as it begins: 'Once upon a time there were people. They lived in a little settlement' (Schmidt 2001: 77). The traditional Western folktale opening formula is combined with a statement implying community, unity and the values of the Khoekhoe, Nama and Damara people. However, very soon trouble looms, when the adults leave to search for food, and the children are left to play and swim in the river. Three of these children, a girl and her two younger brothers, belong to one family, and the group of other children obviously target and victimise the girl. They regularly demand that she climb into the well to scoop up water for them, and on this particular day they callously hatch plans to abandon her: 'When the girl climbs down today, we should not help her to get out! Let's leave her in the well! Let's go home without her!' (ibid: 77). Home and well are illustrated by the plotting children as contrasting places. The deep well functions as a liminal space, offering the life-sustaining gift of water but also imperilling one trapped in its depths, even though the children's intention might not have been to kill their companion by abandoning her. The well is a place of power and danger, and represents a portal to the spiritual realm of the underworld, particularly redolent in a range of Bushmen narratives. Anne Solomon (2000: 3) summarises the place of the San 'deity', !Khwa, who is associated with peril, death and the spirit realm: '!Khwa's home is the waterhole, which appears as an interface between this world and the domain of the spirits; [compared with |Kaggen, the trickster and creator] he appears as the lesser "deity", associated with death'. In 'The singing reed' the girl's little brothers weep and weep when their sister is deserted, but eventually they stop crying and join their playmates. They are presented as being ambivalent, torn between fraternal compassion and a desire to be accepted by the dominant group.

In the second section of the story elephants come to the well to drink, and an ancient elephant grandmother accidentally swallows the girl in the well. This improbability introduces some humour into the story, and continues to foreground its magical aspects. In addition, this account calls to mind the |Xam tale about |Kaggen's sister's child being swallowed by a she-elephant, whereupon |Kaggen creeps into the elephant's belly and kills her, saving the child (Bleek 1923: 41–44). Frequently, too, these swallowing tales result in a happy outcome. The swallowed person, usually a girl, exists in a state of limbo, occupying the threshold between life and death, reminiscent of seclusion rituals or initiations associated with menstruation. This interpretation is emphasised by the image of the girl protagonist in 'The singing reed' being engulfed by the massive force of traditional female animality embodied by the grandmother elephant. Later in the account, when the children return home, the boys' parents enquire about the whereabouts of their daughter, and her brothers confess that they did not assist her to climb out of the well; however, they assume that she will still be waiting there for rescue. Naturally the parents cannot find her at the well, despite a desperate search. They fruitlessly ask each other what they can do, but are powerless to act.

In the third section of the story, the children go out to play at usual; however, the two little boys are still grieving the loss of their sister. A flashback explains that when the elephant had finished drinking, she had coughed up a single drop of the blood of the girl she had swallowed, onto a reed. The reeds mysteriously swell, and the youngest brother cuts one to make a reed pipe. Of course it is the reed infused with the life-force of his sister, and it begins to play by itself:

Is this my mother's son who is playing me, playing me, playing me?

Is this my brother who is playing me, playing me, playing me?

The Beregan[3] children,

the chameleon-like children,

they have killed me! (Schmidt 2001: 78)

This refrain, like the final stanza of 'The bonny swans', is in the voice of the dead girl, and is sung by the narrator, Helena Namases, in the taped version, giving it the haunting force of combined music and words. In the written text the English refrain appears first, then a musical score appears with the original Nama refrain underneath the musical notation. Meaning is thus suggested by three different sets of signifiers, even though few readers will be able to decode all of them. The dramatic effect of the girl's song is amplified by the sequence of other direct speech voiced firstly by the plotting playmates, then the parents, the brothers and even the elephant, before the spectral song of the girl. Schmidt (2007: 265–266) points out that songs in Nama and Damara tales are usually voiced by women or girl protagonists, and that these songs may seek help, act as a bridge between two worlds, or expose secrets. She suggests that these songs may originally have functioned as incantations, very literal examples of en*chant*ment.

Here the dead sister seeks connection with her young brother, who shares her maternal heritage. In contrast to this ideal of family unity which is being evoked by the brother's intuitive act of creating an instrument to capture the breath and heartfelt sung words of his sister, the end of her song exposes the cold-heartedness and treachery of the other children, perceived in terms of chameleons which use their cryptic coloration as a means of concealment.

While the children have not killed her directly, they are exposed as being culpable, as their actions in deliberately abandoning her have resulted in her death. The story contains a number of triple repetitions, such as 'And they drank and they drank and they drank' (Schmidt 2001: 77), the coughing sound of the elephant: 'Kchchch! – Kchchch! – Kchchch!' (p. 78), 'the reeds swelled and swelled and swelled' (p. 78) and 'playing me, playing me, playing me' (p. 78–79) repeated in the refrain of the chante-fable. However, the repetition of the refrain breaks this threefold pattern. The pipe, which acts as a conduit for the message of the girl, only plays for her brothers, and the youngest brother plays the song four times. This alteration of the pattern makes the refrain particularly striking and memorable. On the fourth occasion the song is sung to the children's parents who, in this version, cover the blood-infused pipe with a blanket and place it in a locked room, giving strict instructions to the brothers not to enter. Again, this ritual evokes the seclusion of a girl during her menarche: she is kept covered with a blanket in a separate room, and only after a period of isolation may she be released and 'reborn'. In 'The singing reed', as usual, the parents leave to find food, and the boys go to play with their friends, who ask for the pipe. This time, however, the boys are able to reinforce their family unity, refusing to succumb to peer pressure to deliver the pipe. Almost as if the brothers' refusal contributes to the magical effects, the narrative continues: 'By that time the girl was already there, she had already crept out from under the blanket' (p. 80). When the parents return they discover that the pipe has been transmuted into the girl, and the penultimate sentence of the story is in their combined voice, again using triple repetition: 'Oh! […] here is our child, here is our child, here is our child!' The narrator concludes: 'And now the family was united again' (p. 80).

'The singing reed' represents a girl's ritual triple descent into otherness: into the otherworld of the well, the belly of the animal, and into the magical musical instrument. After this physically, psychologically and spiritually gruelling journey she rejoins her family and order is restored, reinforcing underlying Nama and Damara values in the same fashion as Megan Biesele (1993: 124–138) reveals patterns of gendered behaviour operating in Ju|'hoan creation tales.

Although I do not intend to dwell on the cataloguing systems used to separate different ballads and folktales, it is significant that the ATU number 780, 'The singing bone', is placed within a group headed 'The truth comes to light'. What unites these tales is not the didactic ending, found in some versions, of caution, punishment and vengeance, but a desire for justice, truth, family cohesion and support, within the framework of specific cultural contexts and values. In addition, these texts are united in having females as central protagonists, transmitters of the narrative, collectors and commentators.

Both 'The bonny swans' and 'The singing reed' are placed by folklore scholars into the framework of ATU 780. 'The bonny swans' in bare outline tells of a jealous older sister pushing her youngest sister into the river, and refusing her any help, as a result of which the younger girl dies, and is ambiguously transformed into a swan. Pieces of her body are made into a harp, which sings the story of the crime. A stratified society is evoked, as can be deduced by the uneasy shift from the father as a farmer to the parents as king and queen. Typically in the Child ballads there are many unnatural deaths, but generally the guilty are denounced. This pattern is followed in 'The bonny swans'. However, the ballad ends at the point of revelation of the crime, rather than offering the further supernatural twist of resuscitation of the corpse. From a feminist perspective, the ballad dramatises the threat to a woman from her alter-ego, who shares her heritage, under pressure from patriarchal customs. The family is an ambivalent site, where women are shown as being prone to negative emotions and violence, debunking stereotypes of femininity; however, the family is also the setting for the provision of justice. By extension, there is no sentimental universal sisterhood.

'The singing reed' clearly evokes a Namibian landscape, with a well and elephants, rather than a millpond and swan. The society is egalitarian, rather than hierarchical, and family unity and community amity are perceived as necessary virtues. The equivalents of the cruel sister of 'The bonny swans' are the vicious playmates of 'The singing reed'. The cautionary message that misdeeds will be discovered is emphasised in both texts by the magical female voice transmitted by the talismanic musical instrument. Both texts refuse the punishment offered by other versions of the ballad and Nama/Damara folktale respectively. 'The singing reed' gains a dimension not present in 'The bonny swans' by its representation of a completion of the cycle of death, metamorphosis and rebirth, which evokes a sense of redemption in the reader. In particular, this effect is enhanced by the use of imagery suggesting a loss of innocence in the young girl, who is trapped by her friends and has to face the brutality of humans which coexists with altruism and love. Most specifically, the archetypal pattern of initiation, descent, solitude, return, reconciliation and healing is given a local gendered resonance by the narrative's allusions to menarcheal seclusion rituals, thereby suggesting the hope associated with a nubile young woman's re-entering the wider society via the protection of her loving family.

The unnamed central character in 'The singing reed' is protean, functioning as both typical in her gendered rite of passage, and atypical as one who is special, the provider of symbolic water, yet picked out for suffering, which she manages to testify about and achieve transcendence over. The young girl illustrates an individual adolescent's survival of the frightening processes of physical change and social rites associated with the onset of menstruation. More than this, she demonstrates on a collective level women's hope for survival after violence and hardship, suggesting the possibility of social change for women through the combined efforts of the siblings and parents, implying intergenerational collaboration. As the young woman emerges from under the blanket at the end of the story, the effect on the reader or listener is heartening and inspiring, as one imagines the healed, reconstituted female body brought back into the fullness of life.

A comparison of my selected texts illustrates a common paradox and mystery portrayed in both, testament to the transformative power of cross-cultural traffic. Both 'The bonny swans' and 'The singing reed' display various similarities and differences, but enable a respectful insight into different cultures with particular value systems. Together, they offer hope for social justice for girls and young women whose bodies and lives are under threat. In particular, 'The singing reed' evokes the ideas of Gloria Anzaldúa in its presentation of issues of marginality, belonging, language and song, as well as by depicting a feminine body as a bridge between nature and culture, life and death, thereby refuting Western binarism and implying the possibility of spiritual regeneration and political change.

Notes

1   I am grateful for the gracious and helpful correspondence of Dr Sigrid Schmidt, and the assistance rendered by Samuel Mund of the Centre for World Music at the University of Hildesheim, who converted some of Dr Schmidt's tapes to digital format for me.

2   Stories with a sung component, such as a refrain.

3   I am at a loss to explain the reference to the Beregan children, despite making enquiries with Dr Schmidt and linguists. 'Beregan' is a variant of a surname of European origins, typically from Burgundy in France, but occasionally from the Netherlands or Norway. The word may be used here to indicate children who are behaving in a fashion which is alien to Damara cultural values. Also possible, however, is that a word-shift has occurred, in the same way that the refrain 'Juniper, gentian and rosemary' used in some examples of 'The twa sisters' and other ballads has been altered to such versions as 'Jennifer gentle and rosemary', 'Jinny flower jen, a rosemary', or 'Jennifer gentle, fair Rosie Marie'. In any event, not being able to pinpoint a rational explanation enhances the effect of mystery evoked by the tale.

References

Achebe, C. 1988a. Language and the destiny of man. In *Hopes and impediments: selected essays, 1965–1987*, 87–94. London: Heinemann.

Achebe, C. 1988b. What has literature got to do with it? In *Hopes and impediments: selected essays, 1965–1987*, 106–117. London: Heinemann.

Allen, P.G. 1992. *The sacred hoop: recovering the feminine in American Indian traditions*. Boston: Beacon.

Anzaldúa, G. 2009. *The Gloria Anzaldúa reader*, ed. A. Keating. Durham: Duke University Press.

Barry, P. 1935. Polish ballad. *Bulletin of the Folk-song Society of the Northeast* 10: 2–5.

Barry, P. 1936. Polish ballad. *Bulletin of the Folk-song Society of the Northeast* 11: 2–4.

Biesele, M. 1993. *Women like meat: the folklore and foraging ideology of the Kalahari Ju/'hoan*. Bloomington and Indianapolis: Indiana University Press; and Johannesburg: University of Witwatersrand Press.

Bleek, D. 1923. *The mantis and his friends: Bushman folklore*. Cape Town: Maskew Miller.

Brewster, P.G. 1941. Two Gaelic variants of 'The two sisters'. *Modern Language Notes* 56(3): 187–192.

Brewster, P.G. 1953. *The two sisters*. Helsinki: Academia Scientarum Fennica.

Brown, D. 1995. The society of the text: the oral literature of the |Xam Bushmen. *Critical Arts* 9(2): 76–108.

Brown, D. 1998. *Voicing the text: South African oral poetry and performance*. Cape Town: Oxford University Press.

Brown, D., ed. 1999. *Oral literature and performance in southern Africa*. Oxford: James Currey.

Brown, D. 2006. *To speak of this land: identity and belonging in South Africa and beyond*. Pietermaritzburg: University of KwaZulu-Natal Press.

Chatwin, B. 1988 [1987]. *The songlines*. London: Jonathan Cape.

Child, F.J., ed. 1861. *English and Scottish ballads*. London: Samson Low.

Child, F.J., ed. 1957[1882]. The twa sisters. *The English and Scottish popular ballads* I: 118–141. New York: Folklore Press/Pageant.

De Beauvoir, S. 1988[1949]. *The second sex*. London: Pan Books.

Grimm, J. and W. Grimm. 1884. *Household tales, with the authors' notes*. Trans. M. Hunt. The singing bone, *Sur La Lune Fairy Tales*. http://www.surlalunefairytales.com/authors/grimms/28singingbone.html (accessed 30 October 2013).

Hewitt, R.L. 1986. *Structure, meaning and ritual in the narratives of the Southern San*. Hamburg: Helmut Buske Verlag.

Hewitt, R.L. 2008. *Structure, meaning and ritual in the narratives of the Southern San*. Johannesburg: Wits University Press.

Higgonet, M.R. 1994. Introduction. In *Borderwork: feminist engagements with comparative literature*, 1–16. Ithaca and London: Cornell University Press.

Higgonet, M.R., ed. 1994. *Borderwork: feminist engagements with comparative literature*. Ithaca and London: Cornell University Press.

Jekyll, W., ed. 1907. King Daniel. *Jamaican song and story: Annancy stories, digging sings, ring tunes, and dancing tunes*. London: David Nutt.

Marzac, N. 1977. A Polish version of A.T. 780 in living oral tradition. *Ethnomusicology* 21(3): 397–413.

McKennitt, L. 1994. 'The bonny swans.' *The mask and mirror*. CD. Quinlan Road and Warner Bros.

Philipose, L. 1990. The twa sisters: a Santal folktale variant of the ballad. *Folklore* 101(2): 169–177.

Power, C. and I. Watts. 1997. The woman with the zebra's penis: gender, mutability and performance. *The Journal of the Royal Anthropological Institute* 3(3): 537–560.

Roud Folksong Index. 2013. English folk dance and song society website, for the Vaughan Williams memorial library. http://library.efdss.org/cgi-bin/query.cgi?cross=off&index_roud=on&query=8&field=20 (accessed 6 April 2013).

Schmidt, S. 2001. *Tricksters, monsters and clever girls: African folktales – texts and discussions*. Köln: Rüdiger Köppe Verlag.

Schmidt, S. 2013. Personal communication with the author, 3 April.

Snow, D.J. 2013. Sexual dimorphism in European Upper Paleolithic cave art. *American Antiquity* 78(4): 746–761.

Solomon, A.C. 1992. Gender, representation, and power in San ethnography and rock art. *Journal of Anthropological Archaeology* 11: 291–329.

Solomon, A.C. 2000. Issues and problems in the study of San *kukummi* (oral narratives). Unpublished paper presented at University of Natal English Studies postgraduate and staff seminar, 21 September.

Solomon, A.C. 2009. Broken strings: interdisciplinarity and |Xam oral literature. *Critical Arts* 23(1): 26–41.

Wessels, M. 2010. *Bushmen letter: interpreting |Xam narrative*. Johannesburg: Wits University Press.

The creation of the eland: a close reading of a Drakensberg San narrative

Michael Wessels

Abstract

For the most part, the narratives recounted by the San informant Qing to the magistrate, Joseph Orpen, who had employed him as a guide and scout in the Maloti mountains during the Langalibalele rebellion of 1873, have been discussed in terms of rock art. This is unsurprising since Qing's narratives were told, at least in part, in response to Orpen's questions about the rock art they saw on their journey through the Malotis. This focus has meant, though, that the discussion has generally been conducted with a careful consideration of only selected passages from Orpen's (1874) published version of Qing's narratives. Folklorists, linguists, archaeologists and historians are now turning to the whole text in ways that promise to produce more insight into both the text itself and the context in which it was produced. The aim of the present article is to contribute to the embryonic project of reading Qing's materials in new ways. In the course of offering a close reading of a single story it seeks to show that the stories possess a value as literature, quite apart from the information about rock art or ethnography that they also offer, and that the literary technique of close reading can bring an invaluable dimension to the study of the stories.

Introduction

In 1873, Joseph Orpen, a magistrate who formed part of the military force sent to intercept the rebellious Hlubi chieftain, Langalibalele, and his followers in the Maloti mountains in present-day Lesotho, was told a number of stories by his San guide,

Qing, which were published a year later in the *Cape Monthly Magazine* (1874(9): 1–13), with a commentary by the linguist and expert on the southern San |Xam language and literature, Wilhelm Bleek. Qing's stories have been celebrated as the only examples of traditional San narrative that were recorded from the Drakensberg area, and his comments on the rock art that he and Orpen saw on their journey have been central to the history of rock art interpretation in South Africa (see, e.g., the seminal study by David Lewis-Williams and Thomas Dowson [1989]). As Orpen's title intimates, Qing's stories offer a glimpse into a mysterious, hidden and vanished world, and tease the interpreter with their strangeness and elusiveness. With some exceptions, though, they have not been approached from the perspective of the literary technique of close reading.[1] This is largely true, too, of other bodies of San narrative, which have generally been read from a comparative, classificatory, structuralist or ethnographic angle, as in the invaluable work of Roger Hewitt (2008), Mathias Guenther (1989, 1999), David Lewis-Williams (1996, 1998), Sigrid Schmidt (1989, 2001) and Megan Biesele (1993). This article explores the possibilities that the approach of close reading offers in relation to the first of Qing's stories.

The story begins when Cagn's wife, Coti, ruins her husband's knife by using it to sharpen a digging stick. After Cagn scolds her and tells her that 'evil should come to her' (Orpen 1874: 3), she conceives and gives birth to the first eland. Cagn identifies the animal with the help of charms made from the powder of a plant, canna, which he sprinkles on it. This enables the eland to speak and affirm its identity. Cagn then takes the eland to a 'secluded kloof' and raises it (ibid: 4). When he is away visiting his nephew in order to obtain arrow poison so that he can make the eland 'fit for the use of men', a party of hunters led by his sons come across the eland. Gcwi, Cagn's younger son, stabs it when it is asleep and the men cut it up. Cagn is furious when he returns. He orders Gcwi to put some of the eland's blood in a pot and churn it so as to recreate the animal (as a species rather than as an individual animal), but Gcwi only manages to produce snakes and hartebeest. Cagn's wife then churns the blood, turning it into a bull eland which Cagn drives away. Eland spread across the earth. Cagn sends Gcwi to hunt an eland, but Gcwi is unable to kill one of the animals because 'Cagn was in their bones' (ibid: 5). Cagn kills three eland bulls himself before sending his sons out to hunt again. After this the men hunt game, including eland, but with difficulty because the game has been 'spoilt' and has become wild.

This extraordinarily concentrated narrative engages with social, gender and discursive power dynamics. It also evokes a landscape populated by plants, animals and people, and describes an ecology of intricate connections between them. The story's verve, pace, use of active verbs, ellipses, concentrated action and dramatic dialogue all point to Qing's proficiency as a storyteller, Orpen's assessment of the stories as 'fragmentary' and 'imperfect' notwithstanding (ibid.). This skill emerges despite the translation and the alien context of the storytelling event in which Qing acts more as an ethnographic informant than a performer, with an audience that shares a common cultural framework. He adapts his narrative technique to a new kind of audience – an aptitude that he no doubt cultivated over many years in the geographical, linguistic and cultural border zone he inhabited and had learnt to negotiate in different ways.

David Lewis-Williams (1996, 1998, 2010) provides detailed readings of both Qing's stories and the Bleek and Lloyd materials which interpret them as allegories for trance experience, readings he argues in relation to the |Xam stories which are invited by otherwise incomprehensible elements within the stories. In his discussion of what is considered the parallel |Xam story in which |Kaggen creates an eland from a shoe, Lewis-Williams (1998: 205) concludes that the story is a myth of the origin of |Xam shamanism: '[I]n making this mediatory, potent animal, the Mantis created the basis for |Xam shamanism.' A similar reading of Qing's story of Cagn and the eland, Lewis-Williams (2010: 13) intimates, is suggested by the correspondence between the waterhole in the |Xam story and the secluded kloof in Qing's narrative. Patricia Vinnicombe (2009: 155–172) situates the story within a widespread San eland complex in the region, linking it to ritual sacrifice, transgressive sexuality and the sympathetic and propitiatory relationship between hunter and hunted, which follows from the paradox that eland are both the San's most prized source of meat and a sacred animal that is intimately associated with Cagn. Their spiritual and economic role for the San parallels that of cattle among the pastoralists of the region. She points out, too, that humans and eland are symbolically conjoined, since they share a similar social structure in terms of gender dynamics and seasonal fluctuations in herd and band numbers.

Anne Solomon (1997, 2007) reads the story on a more literal level: the institution of hunting, necessitated by the going wild of the game, marks the end of the first times in which death did not exist and there was no clear distinction between the human and animal worlds. I, too, will look at the story on a less esoteric level. At the same time I will examine it in detail, treating all its elements as deserving of equal attention. As I argue elsewhere (Wessels 2010), stories are multivocal and their meanings unstable. This is in part a result of their intertextual relationship with other narratives and with different discursive formations (Foucault 1970, 1972; Kristeva 1986: 34, 111). To unravel the interpenetrating web of signification that would have been present for a San language speaker of the 19th century is, of course, impossible, although we do have a number of stories from Qing to work with, and tantalising echoes of the narrative in other traditions, San and otherwise. It must be conceded that interdiscursivity for a scholar of San literature inescapably includes a vast amount of other literature and cultural allusions from both inside and outside the broad field of study itself. My aim is not to recover an original or indigenous meaning in the story (if such a thing were possible) so much as to read it from the perspective of a reader situated in the 21st century who has some familiarity with the San oral literature of the region. While I welcome the work of folklorists, linguists and historians that makes more accurate readings possible, I am responding in this article to the text as we have it: a hybrid text in English from the contact zone in the colonial era – a text that has complex relationships with both San orality and folkloristics in the latter part of the 19th century and which has been accompanied by a range of writing, mostly academic, since its publication in 1874.

Central to Qing's narrative is the account of the creation of the eland, an animal that appears in several of his other narratives as well. The term 'eland' works, I would argue, not only to refer to an animal with potent symbolic associations, such as transformation, sexuality and economic plenitude, but also as a generator of discourse and narrative. The treatment of the eland in the story bears comparison with a large set of |Xam stories, including a number in which |Kaggen[2] creates an eland (Día!kwãin L V.-1. 3608–3683; ||Kabbo L II.-4. 489–493, 504–513, 515–519).[3] The commonalities between these narratives and Qing's story are clearly significant. In both, an eland is created through the agency of |Kaggen/Cagn, although the action is initiated by Coti in Qing's story, rather than by Cagn himself. Younger male relatives play a central role in both narratives, and in both they kill the eland. There are also significant differences between the stories from the two traditions, however. Cagn is granted greater powers than |Kaggen, wielding more authority over his wife and sons, for example. He does not have to resort to subterfuge, as |Kaggen does when he conceals his activities by pretending to be setting out to procure honey and then claiming that he has found none. He is not subject to the admonitions of his family members as |Kaggen is. Nor does he have to extricate himself from tight situations by magical means. There are indications, though, as we shall see when exploring the story, that his powers are less than his designation as creator of all beings might suggest.

The birth and creation of the eland

The action in Qing's story is initiated not by Cagn but by Coti, when she uses her husband's knife to sharpen a digging stick with which to dig roots. We are reminded of how women's determination to collect food more efficiently in the |Xam materials can have creative consequences. Their desire to be able to find ants' eggs more easily results, for example, in the propulsion of the sun into the sky (Bleek and Lloyd 1911: 44–55). The play of difference between the man and the woman that is set up from the beginning of the story gives birth here to both eland and discourse. This pattern is reproduced in other places in the corpus in which there is a creative disjunction between the sexes. An example would be in the movement between alienation and union in the story of a girl and the 'other chief, Qwanciqutshaa, the chief, [who] used to live alone' (Orpen 1874: 12).

Coti spoils Cagn's knife. The word 'spoilt' is Orpen's choice for a Baputhi rendering into Sesotho of a San concept that gathers together seemingly different ideas under the rubric of a single signifier. In the short space of Qing's narratives we encounter the term in what appears to be a number of unrelated contexts. We learn that '[M]en who had died and now lived in rivers ... were *spoilt at the same time as the elands* and by the dances of which you have seen paintings' (ibid: 4, emphasis in the original). This statement, Qing's answer to a question concerning paintings of men with rhebuck heads, has most generally been understood to refer to trance transformation. This reading forms one of the pillars of Lewis-Williams' theory of rock painting, and it is true that trance also seems to be the context later in the text when Qing refers to 'people spoilt by the dance, because their noses bleed' (ibid: 20).[4] The spoiling of the eland, though, to which the spoiling of 'the men who had died and now lived in rivers' is coupled, occurs in a narrative that is represented temporally as a formative period of becoming. Presumably trance sets up its own sort of temporality and this corresponds in some way with the process of formation of the first times. But even if we allow for this conjunction, there remains here a discursive split which invites, in part at least, a 'mythological' reading of the stories rather than a spiritual one, for the spoiling in the dances occurs at the same time as the spoiling of the eland. Interestingly, Orpen (or his editors) magnifies the focus on this disjunction by italicising the phrase: 'He said "They were men who had died and now lived in rivers, and were *spoilt at the same time as the elands* and by the dances of which you have seen paintings"'. Orpen (ibid: 4) then asks how the eland were spoiled: 'I asked when were the elands spoilt and how. He began to explain, and mentioned *Cagn*.' The story which forms the subject of this article is Qing's answer to this question.

The spoiling of the eland refers on a literal level to their going wild and the consequences this has for hunting them. Presumably had they not been spoilt they would have meekly allowed themselves to be slaughtered. The implicit contrast here seems to be with cattle. Later in the text Qing, speaking of Cagn, states that '[w]here he is, elands are in droves like cattle' (ibid: 5). Cattle had, of course, been present in southern Africa for many centuries before Qing tells his story. Mythology, it is useful to remember, is an articulation and representation of history, not some point of origin that is anterior to it. An imagined state of tractability of the game would have been suggested by the example of domestic animals, but this does not preclude other sources for the idea in economic, aesthetic and spiritual experience. The story represents, in any event, a fall, the inauguration of a disunity between culture and nature in some way, which also, though, establishes the space for prayer in which Cagn can be addressed for help in hunting (ibid: 4).

The narrative is prefaced by an assertion of Cagn's power and, as I have already observed, this seems both greater and more austere than |Kaggen's. The story, though, undercuts some of what is said of this power. Cagn is said to create all things, but his creation of the eland – a pivotal animal in both the symbolic and economic orders – is unintentional. The narrative points to the contingent and protean nature of the world rather than providing a stable, authoritative account of it. Cagn is part of the play of events rather than a figure who stands outside them in the fashion of the monotheisms' creator deities. While he undeniably possesses power and can harness it for different purposes, he is himself subject to its wilfulness.

As noted earlier, it is Coti rather than Cagn himself who initiates the action when she uses her husband's knife to sharpen a digging stick. She gives birth to the eland. It is also Coti who grinds the canna that enables the new animal to be identified as an eland and who later is able to successfully churn the blood – her sons fail in the attempt – and enable eland as a species to exist a second time after the first one is killed by her son. Whereas |Kaggen acts alone in creating the eland in the |Xam stories, the creation of the eland in Qing's account occurs in the domestic sphere, and results from the combined activity of the male and the female, albeit through a process of infraction, conflict and patriarchal command, rather than cooperation.

The eland is the creative consequence of conflict and difference. It is tempting to see in this an analogy with sexual intercourse. Both literally and figuratively, Coti takes the economic and/or sexual initiative that the male likes to think of as his prerogative. By using Cagn's knife to sharpen a digging stick she defies the categories that attend the gendered division of labour (and the codes of sexuality); she uses the male implement (organ) for the female pursuit of gathering rather than the male one of hunting. Her 'spoiling' of her husband's knife signifies, therefore, both physical damage to the knife and putting something to inappropriate use. Despite the fact that Coti procures food with the sharpened digging stick (or even because of it) Cagn is angry with her, scolds her and brings evil upon her. As a result, she falls pregnant and gives birth to an eland calf. What is the nature of Cagn's scolding here? His words have the power to inseminate? Could 'scolding' serve as a euphemism for rape? In the next story Cagn's daughter runs away after being scolded by her father, possibly a coded reference to rape and incest.[5] If the story concerns sexual relations, and Patricia Vinnicombe (2009: 169) infers that it does, we are left with a number of enigmatic narrative threads to reconcile. We know that in Ju|'hoansi culture there is a correlation between male sexuality and hunting, on the one hand, and between female sexuality and meat on the other (Biesele 1993), and that this correlation is also especially strong in relation to eland in the art of the western Cape (Parkington 1996: 282). In these cases, interestingly, the product of the woman's womb becomes the object of male hunting. But Cagn and Coti also have to work together to categorise the animal and ensure its survival. And then there is the question as to how hunting and sexuality pertain to the delineation of social roles and power relationships more generally. We also need to ask why Coti bears an animal and not a human child. She has, after all, already produced sons and daughters who appear as humans in the stories. Is giving birth to an animal instead of a human the evil that Cagn curses her with? Or does this evil reside in the fact that the animal she gives birth to will be central to the events that result in mankind's having to struggle to procure meat and so become a hunter? Why does the eland, the dominant image of the rock art and the antelope of supreme economic and symbolic import, originate in a context of evil, punishment and revenge? How does this relate to the ambivalence that attends hunting a sacred animal (Vinnicombe 2009: 168–170)?

Coti gives birth to an eland calf in the fields. The narrator retrospectively attributes the name 'eland' to the new-born animal, but its identity at the time of its birth is unknown to both its mother and to Cagn, who is in some way is its paternal progenitor, if not its father in the biological sense of the term. Presumably this follows a period of gestation[6] and must have been a tricky birth, to put it mildly, but in the story everything happens in the space of a single sentence. Coti goes out to the fields alone, here probably the place of the game and the wild plants that is situated away from the domicile, to give birth. She leaves the calf out in the wilderness before informing Cagn of the animal's birth and telling him that she does not know what sort of being the child is. Cagn himself is unable to identify the animal when he goes out to see it. He punishes Coti by making her fall pregnant but cannot predict the ultimate consequence of his scolding, the eland. He is a creator who can cause new forms of life to appear but who cannot always determine their nature; he is a conduit for other sorts of powers and the protagonist of a narrative, rather than an omnipotent author. He relies on divination in order to identify the animal, 'inquire what it was' (Orpen 1874: 6), and here, too, he requires the participation of the female. Coti prepares the canna, a plant, an item from the female realm of gathering, and sprinkles it on the animal before Cagn can enquire what it is. It is worth noting that the eland calf itself is born with the knowledge of its identity and also that Cagn, while unable to recognise an eland, is able, with the help of the canna, to include it in a list of possible animals: '"Are you this animal? Are you that animal?" but it remained silent till he asked it "Are you an eland (Tsha)?" when it said "Aaaa"' (ibid: 7). He possesses knowledge of a realm of potentiality and prototypes, but is unable initially in this story to match his knowledge of the idea of an eland with a real one.

The killing of the young eland

Once the animal's identity is revealed, Cagn takes it to a secluded kloof, a place between a lower and higher part of the mountains and, therefore, a liminal space of transformation (Lewis-Williams 2010: 13), just as Coti's womb was during the animal's earlier phase of formation. A kloof in the context of the Drakensberg and Maloti landscapes could indicate a number of different habitats, including exposed gullies in the high ranges of the basalt cliffs that lead to Lesotho. Here, the word 'secluded' suggests perhaps one of the numerous side valleys that run off the bigger river valleys of the Drakensberg foothills and the Malotis of Lesotho. These are protected and well-watered, with many overhangs and shelters in which a small animal could be hidden. In both the |Xam and Drakensberg stories, Cagn/|Kaggen assumes a female nurturing role with young eland; here we have an image of Cagn carrying the baby eland tenderly in a gourd, a womb-like receptacle, to a safe place in which it can grow.

It is notable that the world described in the story is already well-populated. There is a need to find a secluded place away from people and their pursuits. Later in the story, Cagn's sons set off to hunt in the company of a band of young men. A clearer separation between people and animals seems to already exist in the world of Qing's stories than in the |Xam narratives where the process of the separation of species is a major theme. Cagn's creative role consists partly, at least, of making the world easier for people to live in, aligning it with their needs. His nurturing and protection of the young eland are placed in a context in which he is 'making all animals and things, and making them fit for the use of men, and making snares and weapons' (ibid.).

Cagn nurtures in order to kill; this killing, though, occurs in an ecology of renewal. Even though Cagn makes the animals, he still has to perform certain actions to make them capable of being hunted. This is not accomplished without struggle. He sharpens three sticks – with the spoilt knife presumably; this is what Cagn's knife is for, not sharpening digging sticks! – and throws them at the young eland. Each time he misses and each time he calls the animal back. There is a considerable degree of pathos in this image – the beloved animal has to be made fit to be hunted. The animal tries to escape Cagn's spear, causing him to miss, but obediently returns to him when he calls it. Cagn, we are reminded once more, is not omnipotent; he has the power to summon the eland but not to hit it with his spear. He tries another strategy after he misses the eland a third time and sets out on a journey to procure arrow poison from a nephew, seeking outside help once more. While he is the central figure in the creation and re-creation of the world, he has, it seems, to act in concert with others if success is to be achieved. Here we also get an intimation of an extended family and a social world that is distributed across a wide area. The return journey takes three days. Cagn does not resort to magical means of self-transportation, as we might imagine |Kaggen doing. Insofar as this is a story of origin, of eland, of game going wild and of hunting, it is also a story of the origin of the use of arrow poison, or even of bows and arrows. The fact that the arrow poison already exists in the nephew's possession does not preclude this possibility, for in the elusive logic of these stories things pre-exist their origins. In the event, the poison is not used for the eland is already dead when Cagn returns, and later Cagn's sons hunt bull eland with spears.

Cagn's sons and their band of hunters find the young eland; no kloof, it would seem, is secluded enough to hide an animal away from hunters. They do not know what the animal is: 'it is a new animal'. Nor do they know that it belongs to Cagn. It is very difficult to kill even though they surround it. The punishment for the men's killing the eland at the conclusion of the story is that they will be fated to hunt the animals that elude them. But here the young eland is difficult to kill even though this punishment is yet to be instituted. Nor is the hunters' struggle caused by the 'wildness' of the animal; it does not flee after each attempt to spear it. The eland embodies a state at this point that is different from both the wildness of the game that follows its spoiling and the compliance that Cagn wishes to accomplish with his training; it instinctively eludes the spears and yet returns to its place and lies down. It is only when the antelope is asleep that Gcwi, Cagn's younger son, is able to kill it with a spear. As is the practice of San hunters across the region, the young men cut up the animal and take its meat and blood home. Too late, the men see Cagn's snares and traps and realise that the animal they have killed belongs to him. They are afraid; Cagn, after all, is a stern and punitive patriarch. Once again the story contrasts interestingly with its |Xam counterpart in which |Kaggen's family members intentionally kill one of his animals, without fear of his response.

The creation of eland

When Cagn returns after three days away – a recurring number in the story: he sharpens three sticks, goes away for three days, and Cogaz kills three bull eland – he finds blood on the ground in the place where he has hidden the eland. Gcwi is accused of being presumptuous and disobedient even though he could not have known that he was wrong to try to kill the eland. A degree of humour and performance enters the story at this point when Cagn impulsively punishes his son by pulling off his nose and throwing it in the fire. He quickly regrets his action, however, retrieves the nose and sticks it back on again. Cagn also comically articulates his own thoughts: 'No! I shall not do that' (ibid: 8). The tone shifts when he addresses his son directly, ordering him to undo his spoiling of the eland. Here 'spoiling' seems to refer chiefly to the killing of the eland. As in the |Xam story the eland can be resurrected with part of its body: with its gall or blood. These parts stand in a metonymic relationship with the animal, a structure which is replicated in the way in which the single eland represents eland in general – innumerable eland result from churning the blood, not just the original eland to which Coti gave birth. The eland, in turn, stand for game generally; their spoiling leads to the spoiling of all the game. But it might be incorrect to see this structure as simplistically metonymic; the eland, we suspect, is as much the sum as it is the part.

> 'Now begin to try to undo the mischief you have done, for you have spoilt the elands when I was making them fit for use,' so he told them to take of the eland's blood and put it in a pot and churn it with a little native churn-stick, which he made to spin in

the blood by rubbing the upright stick between the palm of his hands, and he scattered the blood and it turned into snakes, and they went abroad, and Cagn told them not to make frightful things, and he churned again and scattered the blood and it turned into hartebeests. (ibid.)

The passage is ambiguous. It is not entirely certain whether the pronoun 'he' refers to Cagn or Gcwi, and the switch between 'them' and 'he' is also confusing. Whoever spins the blood with the 'little native churn-stick' (a timely if somewhat rude reminder that we are in the midst of an ethnographic encounter) and scatters it, succeeds only in producing snakes (are these the first snakes, and are they also perhaps the snakes that appear in the next story [ibid: 9–10] – which are also men – and why are they frightful?) and then hartebeest. Whether or not Cagn spins and scatters blood himself, he holds Gcwi responsible for the production of the wrong animals. The creation of snakes and hartebeest also indicates the protean nature of the sign 'eland'; it is a sign that can slip out of control, that can easily turn into something else, either something other or something contiguous, something completely different or something not different enough. Snakes clearly have malign connotations but hartebeest represent something closer to eland. This is the only reference to hartebeest in the Qing materials, but the inescapable condition of intertexuality in which a San scholar is immersed reminds us that they have nearly the same status as the eland in the |Xam materials in which |Kaggen's heart is said to have been made from both eland and hartebeest (L.VIII.23: 8036). The hartebeest, in this instance, are born fully grown and already 'spoilt', for they immediately run away. Cagn is not impressed by them (as |Kaggen might have been): 'I am not satisfied; this is not yet what I want; you can't do anything. Throw the blood out!' (Orpen 1874: 8).

The process of restoring the eland begins anew with fresh blood and a clean pot. Cagn turns once more to his wife for help. At the beginning of the story he scolds her. Now he addresses her respectfully as 'my wife', a contrast with his dismissive treatment of his sons who 'can't do anything' (ibid.). While Cagn issues the orders, it is notable again that the creative act is a collaborative effort: Coti churns the blood, they (the sons?) add fat from the animal's heart and Cagn himself sprinkles the blood. This time, the third attempt, the drops produce eland. The creation of eland has proved to be uncertain, difficult and open-ended. Creation has a will and purpose of its own, if eland are anything to go by. It also has complex implications for different levels of experience and existence. The creation of eland involves the creation of much more than a species of large antelope, if we remember the multiple associations attached to the animal, such as sexuality and transformation.

The blood initially produces only bull elands, which butt the people. Their aggression, according to Cagn, can be blamed on the fact that the young men have spoilt the eland by killing the first one. The state of being spoilt manifests at this point in the story as hostility towards humans, rather than as intractable wildness. However, the going wild of the game will soon become integral to the new dispensation and what is chiefly meant by 'spoil'. It can be noted, too, that the elands' wildness results less from the young men's 'spoiling' them than from Cagn's chasing the bull eland away, both to protect his family and to punish the young men by making game difficult to kill. The bulls are soon joined by more eland, including cows, when the young eland's blood is churned again; this 'produced multitudes of elands, and the earth was covered with them' (ibid.). The young men's punishment is extended to all men, who from now on have to work to hunt game, not only eland. The compliance of the game that Cagn initially set out to achieve has been precluded by both the men's killing of the baby eland and Cagn's own response to this primal murder.

The rigours of hunting become men's burden. The eland stand in, as already noted, for all game, even the animals that Cagn had previously made 'fit for the use of men' (ibid: 7). Somewhat paradoxically, hunting itself is now new: spears, poison arrows and snares exist before the spoiling of the eland. What is new is the kind of difficulty that Gcwi experiences when Cagn orders him to go and hunt the eland – he comes back not only empty-handed but 'panting and footsore and worn out' (ibid: 9). He fails again on the second day. His lack of success is not chiefly attributable to his own lack of prowess, though, or even to the new intractability of the game, but to the fact that Cagn, in a fashion reminiscent of |Kaggen's role as protector of the game in the |Xam materials, 'was in the eland's bones' (ibid.). Gcwi's struggles. The original crime of killing the young eland is still responsible for Gcwi's struggles. Cagn then sends Cogaz to 'turn the eland towards him' (ibid.), which the young man accomplishes, although less through his own doing than Cagn's shouting at the eland. Cagn then kills three bull eland with assegais, and this opens the way for his sons to do the same. First Cogaz, sent to hunt with Cagn's blessing, kills two and then the rehabilitated Gcwi manages to kill one. The story closes with an aetiological declaration: 'That day game were given to men to eat, and this is the way they were spoilt and became wild. Cagn said he must punish them for trying to kill the thing he made which they did not know, and he must make them feel sore' (ibid.). People are simultaneously rewarded (given game to eat) and punished (fated to experience the rigours and challenges of hunting). This ambivalence pervades the story. It is present, as we have seen, in the relations between Coti and Cagn and between Cagn and his sons, and as Vinnicombe (2009: 155–173) points out, it is also present in the very activity of hunting eland, a sacred animal that is symbolically related to people.

Conclusions

The creativity exhibited by Cagn in the story is largely a product of speaking and the results of this speaking are unpredictable and unruly. Cagn's words have a generative capacity beyond his control. He scolds his wife for spoiling his knife, saying that evil will befall her. His words cause her to conceive and give birth to an unknown animal. Words, in the form of questions, are used to elicit an answer as to the animal's identity from the animal itself, but only after canna has been used to give it the power of speech (and comprehending speech?). The animal's negative responses are a reminder of Jacques Derrida's (1976) insight that signs always carry the traces of other signs. The animal is not this or that animal, but it might have been. Cagn's language frequently takes the form of an imperative. He commands first Gcwi and later Coti to churn the blood, with unpredictable and ambiguous results. He summons the eland and exerts power over their movements. He does not only command, though, he also confers a blessing on Cogaz, for example. But whether he commands or blesses his language is an active material force that shapes and creates in ways that are never predictable.

The eland are things of speech, Cagn's speech, as much as they are flesh and blood animals. They are brought into existence through a series of speech acts: speech initially causes the young eland to appear in Coti's womb, speech is necessary to bring it into the realm of the known and the named, and, finally, it is speech that sends the multitudes of eland out into the wild and across the earth. The young men's infraction lies, to a large extent, in their killing something which they did not know, something which they could not name, which had not yet been made available to them through language. Without this knowledge, they fail to identify the animal as belonging to Cagn.

Cagn embodies the ambiguities of language and of the world itself. He can both impede and facilitate hunting, an ambivalence, as noted earlier, that opens up the place of prayer (Orpen 1874: 4), for what would be the point of praying to a being that was either consistently helpful or unhelpful. He also slips between story and everyday reality. When he extends the punishment of the young men to all men at the end of the story of the creation of the eland, he demonstrates the permeability of this boundary.

Acknowledgements

Funds from this grant, along with funding from the School of Arts and College of Humanities of the University of KwaZulu-Natal, enabled me to hold the conference on San Representation at which an early version of this article was first delivered as a paper, along with most of the others in this special issue.

Notes

1   Close reading is fundamental to literary analysis, whatever the theoretical approach. It consists of the careful exposition of short texts or selected passages from longer ones. Attention is given to individual words and ideas rather than to generalities. Accordingly, the focus in this article is on the way that a single story generates meaning, rather than on comparisons with other structurally similar stories. It differs from a traditional close reading

in so far as the heavily mediated nature of the text makes a consideration of Qing's style, choice of diction or expression difficult, although such a study could potentially be conducted in relation to the rhetorical strategies that the translation and editing processes involve.

2   Cagn and |Kaggen are different spellings of the same name, used in Orpen's article and the Bleek and Lloyd collection of |Xam materials respectively. I retain the different spellings in this essay in order to distinguish between the Drakensberg and |Xam figures.

3   These references refer to Bleek and Lloyds unpublished notebooks.

4   Anne Solomon (2007, for example) has shown that other interpretations of these extracts are plausible.

5   I owe this insight to José de Prada, whose valuable annotated version of Orpen's text will hopefully be published in the near future.

6   Vinnicombe (2009: 169) points out that eland have 'a gestation period of similar duration to cattle and humans'.

References

Biesele, M. 1993. *Women like meat: the folklore and foraging ideology of the Kalahari Ju|'hoan*. Johannesburg: Wits University Press.

Bleek, W. 1874. Remarks by Dr. Bleek. In A glimpse into the mythology of the Maluti Bushmen. *The Cape Monthly Magazine* 9: 11–13.

Bleek. W.H.I. and L.C. Lloyd. 1911. *Specimens of Bushman folklore*. London: George Allen.

Derrida, J. 1976. *Of grammatology*. Trans. G.C. Spivak. Baltimore: Johns Hopkins University Press.

Foucault, M. 1970. *The order of things: an archaeology of the human sciences*. London: Tavistock.

Foucault, M. 1972. *The archaeology of knowledge*. New York: Tavistock.

Guenther, M.G. 1989. *Bushman folktales: oral traditions of the Nharo of Botswana and the |Xam of the Cape*. Wiesbaden: Franz Steiner Verlag.

Guenther, M.G. 1999. *Tricksters and trancers: Bushman religion and society*. Bloomington: Indiana University Press.

Hewitt, R.L. 2008. *Structure, meaning and ritual in the narratives of the southern San*. Johannesburg: Wits University Press.

Kristeva, J. 1986. *The Kristeva reader*, ed. T. Moi. Oxford: Blackwell.

Lewis-Williams, J.D. 1996. A visit to the lion's house: the structures, metaphors and socio-political significance of a nineteenth-century Bushman myth. In *Voices from the past: |Xam Bushmen and the Bleek and Lloyd Collection*, ed. J. Deacon and T. Dowson, 122–141. Johannesburg: Wits University Press.

Lewis-Williams, J.D. 1998. The mantis, the eland and the meerkats: conflict and mediation in a nineteenth-century San myth. *African Studies* 26: 195–216.

Lewis-Williams, J.D. 2010. The imagistic web of San myth, art and landscape. *Southern African Humanities* 22: 1–18.

Lewis-Williams, J.D. and T. Dowson. 1989. *Images of power: understanding Bushman rock art*. Johannesburg: Southern Books.

Orpen, J.M. 1874. A glimpse into the mythology of the Maluti Bushmen. *The Cape Monthly Magazine* 9: 1–13.

Parkington, J. 1996. 'What is an eland?' N!ao and the politics of age and sex in the paintings of the Western Cape. In *Miscast: negotiating the presence of the Bushmen*, ed. P. Skotnes, 281–289. Cape Town: UCT Press.

Schmidt, S. 1989. *Catalogue of the Khoisan folktales of southern Africa.* Hamburg: Helmut Buske Verlag.

Schmidt, S. 2001. *Tricksters, monsters and clever girls: African folktales, texts and discussions.* Köln: Rüdiger Köppe Verlag.

Solomon, A. 1997. The myth of ritual origins? Ethnography, mythology and interpretation of San rock art. *South African Archaeological Bulletin* 52: 3–13.

Solomon, A. 2007. Images, words and worlds: the |Xam testimonies and the rock arts of the southern San. In *Claim to the country: the archive of Wilhelm Bleek and Lucy Lloyd*, ed. P. Skotnes, 149–159. Johannesburg: Jacana.

Vinnicombe, P. 2009. *People of the eland: rock paintings of the Drakensberg Bushmen as a reflection of their life and thought.* Johannesburg: Wits University Press.

Wessels, M. 2010. *Bushman letters: interpreting |Xam narrative.* Johannesburg: Wits University Press.

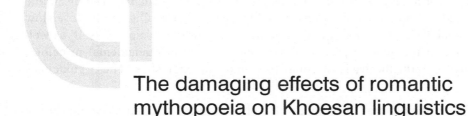

The damaging effects of romantic mythopoeia on Khoesan linguistics

Menán du Plessis

Abstract

The article outlines some basic guidelines that should inform studies in comparative linguistics, and notes a tendency in contemporary Khoesan linguistics for these to be neglected, while pre-theoretical assumptions of 'ancientness' and 'otherness' take their place. The article demonstrates the damaging effects of this romanticism through two brief case studies – one concerning the supposedly primordial stratum made up of the JU and !UI-TAA languages, and the other concerning a conjectured intermediate stratum made up of the KHOE (or 'Khoe-Kwadi') languages. It is concluded that the construction of these linguistic layers, so neatly in agreement with the layers proposed in certain models of southern African population history, has been enabled by a willingness to believe that perceptions of otherness have some absolute and meaningful value, and that they take precedence over fundamental principles.

Introduction: on guiding principles in linguistics

In its primary task of theoretical analysis and description, linguistics aspires to be a science. Yet, somewhat reluctantly, we have to acknowledge that there are many respects in which it cannot truly claim to be one. Linguists cannot speak with any great confidence about experiments and replicable results, just as they cannot write formulae that will invariably hold true, or invoke some constant value for a rate of change. Nevertheless, as the discipline has grown and developed over the past two centuries our basic knowledge has expanded considerably, so that we now have a better understanding, for example, of the great range of linguistic typologies that exist around the world, and the ways in which languages tend to change. The discipline has also had its share, like any other, of taking wrong turns. Out of all these slow processes, including lessons learned from the history of the discipline itself, as well as reference to the general philosophy of science, certain fundamental principles have come to form the basis of sound reasoning in linguistics. These guidelines include:

1. The principle that differences of a physiological or cultural nature do not preclude the possibility that the languages of the communities concerned might be related.

Neglect of this principle in the context of southern Africa accounts for the long time it took for linguists to recognise that the languages spoken by the Khoi-Khoi of the countries today known as South Africa and Namibia were, in fact, related to languages spoken by some of the 'Bushmen' or 'Masarwa' of modern Botswana. Although some of the typological and morphosyntactic affinities of the Khoe languages were already apparent by the early part of the 20th century,[1] it seems that arriving at the obvious conclusion was inhibited by an unshakeable belief that differences in physical appearance and economic culture were markers of some actually significant divide.

2. The converse principle that resemblances of a physiological or cultural nature do not constitute evidence that the languages of the communities concerned are related.

This principle was given formal expression by Joseph Greenberg (1963), following his dismantling of the 'Hamitic' hypothesis, as developed by Carl Meinhof (1912), amongst others. The Hamitic hypothesis proposed a set of far-flung connections between various languages from groupings that we would today identify as Niger-Congo, Nilo-Saharan, Afroasiatic, and Khoesan (or Khoisan) – and where the Khoesan candidate for membership was Nama.[2] The affiliations were suggested on the basis of a few elements of similar morphology, and various lexical items that bore a faint resemblance to one another. What made the 1912 version of the hypothesis particularly reprehensible (or ridiculous) was the appeal to biology for corroboration: *Die Sprachen der Hamiten* included a chapter by Felix von Luschan, in which he attempted to prove parallel affinities of the relevant speaker populations on the basis of measurements he had taken of people's noses.

3. The principle that it is advisable to have a reasonable comparative knowledge of other languages occurring in the neighbourhood of a language under study.

The dangers of a narrow focus were pointed out by William J. Samarin (1971: 230), in the context of comments by him on Gunther Tessmann's early study of the special languages used by young Gbaya-speaking men during their initiation into the West African secret societies of the Labi and To. Tessmann (1931), who was primarily an anthropologist, speculated that these languages might have preserved certain ancient or 'original' features. As Samarin noted, Tessmann was perhaps predisposed to imagine he was seeing evidence of ancientness because of his prior belief in the primitiveness of the society he was studying. In addition, Tessmann's ignorance of neighbouring languages meant that he failed to detect various borrowings: Samarin, for example, identified a Central Saharan base for Labi, and an Adamawa (Niger-Congo) base for To.

4. The general and overarching principle of parsimony, that the simpler explanatory hypothesis is to be preferred – at least in the first place – over one of greater complexity.

The good sense of applying this principle ('Occam's razor') in the context of linguistics has been pointed out on a number of occasions by the historical linguist and metatheoretician, Roger Lass (1997), in his discussion, for example, of situations where borrowing might be invoked as one of several explanatory scenarios; and also with regard to choosing between alternative candidates that might be projected as proto-segments in the context of linguistic reconstruction (Lass 1993).[3]

These four rationalist principles are among the fixed stars that should guide us in our modern practise of linguistics. As long as we keep them in sight, we have a fair chance of not losing our way, even when we enter a little-known linguistic territory, such as the field of Khoesan languages. As already noted, some of these guidelines were arrived at as a consequence of lessons learned from past errors. Since some of these historical false turns were made in the context of studies in African languages, it is dismaying that we occasionally find these hard-won principles flouted or ignored in current Khoesan linguistic studies – and in their place is an all-too-frequent reliance on beliefs concerning the 'ancientness' or 'otherness' of the Khoesan languages.

Romances concerning the 'ancientness' and 'otherness' of Khoesan (or Khoisan) languages

Belief in the 'ancientness' of the Khoesan languages, sometimes allied to a notion of their primacy, as well as conjectures about a former carpeting of Africa in a now almost entirely lost Khoesan linguistic substrate, are sometimes expressed even by the current generation of linguists. Only 13 years ago, for example, Bonny Sands (2001: 204), wrote:

> It is widely assumed that Khoesan languages were once spoken from southern Africa continuously to eastern Africa. Oral tradition speaks of 'Bushmen' or Twa in Zimbabwe and elsewhere, and the Twa (Kwadi) of south-western Angola became extinct only

recently. The presence of Sandawe-type words in the Cushitic language Dahalo of coastal Kenya is clear evidence Khoesan languages once had a greater distribution. But even within the 'Khoesan' area of southern Africa, we must not assume that the Khoesan groups were limited to their historically-attested distribution.

It is a mistake, of course, to think that use of the name 'Twa' implies some kind of specific 'Khoesan' identity, or that communities referred to in this way necessarily spoke a Khoesan language: the name is widely applied, and is typically a pejorative exonym. (The reconstructed Proto-Bantu, root *-tʊ̀à 'pygmy, bushman, servant' includes the variant *-tʊ́á, with the broad meaning 'member of neighbouring despised tribe' or 'bush dweller'.)

Beliefs of this kind on the part of linguists appear to arise, in part, from uncritical acceptance of the 'layer cake' model of southern African *population* history, where the first layer consists of an original population of hunter-gatherers. Since most speakers of the modern Ju and !Ui-Taa languages still preserved (until very recently) a hunter-gatherer mode of existence, it seems we thought it fair to conclude that they must be the direct and unique descendants of this earliest (or 'Stone Age') layer – and hence that their languages, too, must be ancient. In some cases there even appears to be an extreme version of this belief in play, namely that the Khoesan languages are not only ancient, but have failed to undergo any normal processes of change, so that they are imagined to be 'fossil languages' – or languages caught in amber – supposedly with the potential to provide insights into aspects of early human language as it was still evolving.

Conversely, since the archaeological record for southern Africa shows that domesticated animals and iron tools start appearing only in relatively recent strata, it has seemed reasonable to draw the neat conclusion that this layer must have been contributed by a much later group of 'Iron Age' immigrants, who – it is assumed – would have been speakers of various early Bantu[4] languages. While it may have been a popular argument at one time that various words associated with a distinctive 'Iron Age' culture could be reconstructed for Proto-Bantu, it has long since been demonstrated that almost all of these words are adaptations of older words with more basic meanings (De Maret and Nsuka 1977). For example, one of the words commonly used for 'iron' or 'metal' (such as Zulu *insimbi*) arises from a word meaning 'cowrie'. Words used for 'ore' are either older words for 'stone' or 'rock', or may be nominalisations (such as Nyanja *ntapo*) from a verb meaning 'take out honey or clay'. Likewise, words for 'smithing' seem to develop from words meaning 'beat', 'pound' or alternatively 'blow'; while further words for 'iron' are nominalisations from such verbs.

While some linguists (Schadeberg 2003) still allow that the earliest speakers of Bantu languages might have been making pottery and herding goats, we should note that the reconstructed word meaning 'heap up, mould' (*-bʊ́mb-) does not necessarily imply the making of pots, but may originally have had a general meaning more simply associated with the shaping of clay walls or fishing weirs. Lastly, we might note that words used in some southern Bantu languages for 'goat' were originally terms for species of antelope (such as *-bùdì 'kudu', or *-bàdì 'reedbuck'). Indeed, the *Khoekhoe* word for 'cow' (found in Nama as *goma*) appears to be another Bantu word for 'kudu' (found, e.g., in Nyanja as *mngoma*).

On the other hand, the reconstructed vocabulary of Proto-Bantu contains hundreds of words that are plainly associated with a primary culture of hunting, trapping, fishing and gathering, while individual Bantu languages typically have even richer repertoires of such terms which may include, for example, special names for the various methods of gathering winged ants (Van Warmelo 1989: 278), as well as terms for different types of arrows, including 'toy' arrows (or bird arrows), bird snares, small-game traps, pitfall traps and game-guiding fences (Scott and Hetherwick 1957: throughout). The very lore of hunting is embedded in the vocabularies of Bantu languages, as, for example, in Venda, where *tshiṭula-nama* was a traditional name for either a moth or a 'species of small bird that used to come in swarms, believed to augur meat' (Van Warmelo 1989: 426).

With all this in mind, it seems doubtful that early speakers of Bantu languages would have left any visibly distinct cultural signature in the material record, while the archaeological evidence for the first presence of domesticated animals and ironware in the southern region cannot be extrapolated to mean anything more than that these *things* (and perhaps the associated 'know-how') found their way by slow processes of diffusion (which might indeed have included some migration) to populations that were already here, and may well have been speakers of early Bantu varieties.

Sandwiched in-between these two layers, some have proposed that there might be a filling of somewhat earlier herders, speaking languages belonging to the Khoe family. This idea, which has a long history, has been given a contemporary reformulation by Güldemann (2008), who developed a theory of the staggered arrival of different linguistic communities in southern Africa, in a neat matching of the population model. The arguments will be discussed in more detail below.

In reality, none of the Khoesan language groupings shows the kind of extensive proliferation that would be commensurate with a great antiquity. Some contemporary linguists (Heine and König 2008) have lately conceded that the Khoekhoe languages in particular must be 'a fairly young genetic grouping', while it now seems, realistically, that the Khoe family as a whole cannot be older than perhaps two thousand years, considering the relatively limited extent of its branching and dialectal divergence. As for the Ju and !Ui-Taa groups,[5] these reflect no great diversity at all, and each on its own appears to be far younger than the Khoe family.[6] Of course the term 'old' is relative; and when it comes to the speed of language change, there are simply too many potential variables and intangible factors for us to propose a hard and fast rate.

But it seems at least unlikely that either Ju or !Ui-Taa could be very much more than a thousand years old, or perhaps two thousand years at the utmost.

Certainly we do not have a complete record for all of these groups, particularly for the !Ui languages. It is true that speakers of these varieties were among the victims of horrible 'extermination' campaigns carried out by Cape farmers called up on 'commando' at various times during the 18th century, and the official reports of that period – as later published by Donald Moodie (1838: Part III), for example – record with dreadful matter-of-factness exactly how many hundreds of people were killed. At the same time, the women and children were usually spared and taken to work on farms – which means their languages at least were not simultaneously wiped out. In some cases the women may have married Khoikhoi men working on these farms, and it is probably on account of an ensuing bilingualism that, by the time |Xam was recorded in the late 19th century, the speakers of this !Ui variety had numerous loanwords from Kora in their language. It is possible also that some of these small communities simply moved further away from the Cape, while others entered into new social formations. The Korana people indeed had an orally handed down historical tradition (Engelbrecht 1936: 67) that some of their clans had incorporated 'Bushmen' groups.

There are one or two fragmentary records of !Ui varieties that were made before Bleek and Lloyd started their major work on |Xam in the last part of the 19th century, including a brief wordlist written down by Lichtenstein (1815, Appendix 1), and another by Wuras (c. 1850). During the early and latter parts of the 20th century, scholars like Dorothea Bleek (2001), Meinhof (1928/29), Doke (1937) and Maingard (1937) collected more data from small communities of surviving speakers, while further material was later collected by Ziervogel (1955) and Lanham and Hallowes (1956), amongst others. Although these documentations are often sketchy, it is still reasonably clear, since lexical items shared across the dialects bear such a very close resemblance to one another, that the varieties of !Ui could not have been vastly divergent. (It is true that ||Xegwi seems to have been more of an 'outlier', but much of the data for this variety was obtained from just a single speaker, while at least some of the words appear to be either loans or innovations.)

Concerning the idea of Khoesan 'otherness', its sources are harder to pinpoint, because there is a sense in which the impression of difference is partly *created* by unusual linguistic analyses, while at the same time the very licence to engage in an exoticising type of linguistics seems to be granted by an assumption that the discovery of 'otherness' is a desirable possibility. In effect, the myth is self-confirming, while it undoubtedly derives further power from the adjunct belief in the 'ancientness' of Khoesan languages. Yet, as will be suggested below, supposedly rare or strange features in Khoesan often have a common occurrence in other languages, or else are amenable to simpler explanation.

The remainder of this article will focus on two of these proposed linguistic strata, and will attempt to show how their theoretical construction has been enabled, at least partly, by failure to adhere to the basic principles outlined above.

Construction of a 'first layer' supposedly contributed by speakers of the 'primordial' Ju and !Ui-Taa languages

The Ju and Taa groups both have a system of noun-classification based on a set of *multiple genders* very similar to those of the Bantu languages. While these genders are now largely covert, being expressed mainly through pronominal cross-reference, languages of the !Ui and Taa groups make some use of gender-indexical noun suffixes, while both Ju and !Ui-Taa groups have dialects where the nouns still carry *prefixes*. The existence of only a two-gender system in the !Ui language, |Xam, was recognised by Wilhelm Bleek, who nevertheless noted that this was 'probably the scanty remains of a former more extensive classification of nouns' (Bleek 1911: 147). The !Ui languages are considered (Güldemann 2004b) to form a unit with Taa, as implied by Dorothea Bleek's original (1927) classificatory entity, 'Southern Bushman'.

The best known and most extensively documented member of the !Ui family is |Xam. A preliminary contemporary analysis of the language is included in *The Khoesan languages* (Vossen 2013). In this account by Güldemann (2013a: 242) we read that '|Xam grams are to a considerable extent similar or identical between nominal and verbal expressions, in spite of the fact that there seems to exist a noun-verb distinction'.

Secondly, concerning adnominal modifiers in particular, we read (ibid: 245) that

> [s]ome lexical stems are used predominantly as modifying attributes of nouns; these all occur post-nominally. This functional and structural commonality aside, they reveal hardly any other characteristic in morphological design or grammatical behaviour which would justify subsuming them under the unitary lexical category 'adjective'. [...] In general, the data on lexical stems used for the semantic modification of nouns indicate that an incipient closed class of adjectives could exist; at the same time, almost all items concerned still betray the historical fact that they have been recruited from the two major lexical categories, viz. nouns and verbs.

With due respect, this characterisation invites us to regard the !Ui languages as not only still nascent, but also 'strange'. We could be forgiven for thinking, on reading them, that we are back in the 1930s, at the time of the great 'Empire Exhibition', when a linguist of that period (Maingard 1937: 239) wrote, concerning another member of the !Ui group, that the traditional nomenclature is not altogether discarded in these studies. It must, however, be pointed out that some of these terms are of doubtful application to ǂKhomani, where, for instance, 'verbs' (i.e. words expressing 'actions') have all sorts of functions which are represented in our European languages by other 'parts of speech'. Indeed the European conception of 'parts of speech' cannot strictly be said to be true of Bushmen.

In reality, the properties presented to us as so decidedly 'other' are perfectly familiar and normal in the context of other African languages – the Bantu languages in

Table 1: Relative stems in two Bantu languages, showing some that are interrogative and others that incorporate a deictic component

	Zulu (Doke 1950: 99–110)	Tswana (Cole 1975: 138–140; 173–174)
'True' adjectives	'c' = ǀ; 'q' = !	
Qualitative		
'short'	*-fuphi*	*-khutšhwabe*
'nice, good, beautiful'	*-hle*	*-ntlê*
'black'		*-ntšho*
'new, young, fresh'	*-sha*	*-ša, fša*
'very small'	*-nci*	*-nye, -ntʃe*
Quantifying		
'much, many'	*-ningi*	*-ntsi*
'other, some'	*-nye*	*-ngwe*
'two'	*-ɓili*	*-bêdi*
Interrogative		
'how many?'	*-ngaki?*	
'what colour?'		*-tsiang?, -tšang?, -tsabang?*
Relative stems		
Qualitative		
'black'	*-mnyama*	
'strong, hard, difficult'	*-qatha*	*-thata*
'pleasant'	*-mnandi*	*-monate* [denom]
'wet, damp'	*-manzi* [denom]	*-mêtse* [denom]
'sharp'	*-bukhali* [denom]	*-bogale* [denom]
'acid, salty'	*-munyu* [denom]	
Interrogative		
'how much, many?'	*-ngakanani?*	
'of what kind?'	*-njani?*	
'how much, how big?'		*-kaé?*
Deictic		
'like this'	*-nje*	
'like that'	*-njalo*	
'like yonder'	*-njeːyá*	
'so much/big as this'	*-ngaka*	*-kana*
'big as that'	*-ngako*	*-kalo*
'big as yonder'	*-ngakayá*	

particular. Since the latter typically each have only a few true adjectives (as reflected in descriptions, e.g., of Swahili [Ashton 1947: 46], Mwera [Harries 1950: 52], Mbukushu [Fisch 1998: 87], Venda [Poulos 1990: 126], Sotho [Doke and Mofokeng 1985: 118] or Zulu [Doke 1950: 99]),[7] we find extensive use of 'relative stems', plus denominatively derived descriptive stems. Just as in Taa and !Ui, stems used in relative constructions of this kind may include interrogative stems and others with a deictic (or demonstrative) component. Table 1 provides examples from two Bantu languages.

The !Ui languages have numerous other affinities with southern Bantu languages. These include:

- Use of an 'emphatic' (possibly topic-marking) particle *ke(n)*, which is used also in Venda and other Bantu languages, where it appears to be a construction incorporating the 'owner' root (< PB *(j)éné or possibly *(j)éní);
- Use of semi-homophonous yet semantically distinct morphemes (of the type *ha*) used for a past and a negative;
- Use of a venitive such as *saa* with future implication;
- Use of a possessive morpheme *ka*;
- Use of a morpheme *ka* in association with the adverbial phrase, much as in Tswana;
- Extensive use of multi-verb constructions comparable to (and sometimes even formally similar to) those of the Sotho-Tswana and Nguni languages. These constructions are used, just as they are in the case of the Bantu languages, to convey various micro-implications of tense, aspect and modality.

All things considered, there is no compelling evidence for the 'otherness' of the languages spoken by the imagined 'first layer' of people in southern Africa. Guidelines that seem to have been flouted in constructing such a layer include the principle that linguistic difference should not be pre-supposed on the basis of biological or anthropological considerations, and the principle that it is a good idea to know the linguistic neighbours of a language under study.

Construction of an intermediate layer, supposedly contributed by the arrival of Khoe (or 'Khoe-Kwadi') speakers

The Khoe languages are distinguished from the Ju and !Ui-Taa groups by their preference for a basic verb-final pattern. These languages also feature serial verb (or possibly multi-verb) constructions, and may manifest lexicalised compounds (or 'double verbs') that probably arise from the former. Nouns are sub-categorised as 'masculine', 'feminine' or 'common', where assignment is epistemically based in cases where natural gender applies, but otherwise arbitrary, although the masculine gender may carry connotations of greater height or length. Nouns may be reassigned to one or other of these genders, in which case the resulting implicational overlay may be augmentative, and is usually pejorative. The gender systems of languages in the Khoekhoe branch of Khoe are of an overt type, in that the genders of the nouns are explicitly indexed by post-placed affix morphemes.[8]

There is a long history to the theory that speakers of the Khoe languages were perhaps the earliest pastoralists to enter the region. In fact, two slightly different versions of the model have been put forward at various times. In the Hamitic scenario, the general connection proposed is between certain northern languages belonging to families that are today classified as Afroasiatic – and languages of the southern African Khoe family. The idea was first proposed by Bleek (1851), who suggested a connection between such languages as Coptic and Galla, and the Khoekhoe languages of South Africa, where the latter were at that time known to him only from some early fragments of 17th-century Cape Khoekhoe and a few missionary texts.

Bleek's hypothesis, based on resemblances involving aspects of nominal gender morphology, and a few other items such as a causative, must have seemed convincing at the time. After all, the likeness was somewhat intriguing, as the examples in Table 2 show.

A similar idea was put forward by Lepsius (1880), and was later expanded by Meinhof (1912), who developed it into the full-blown Hamitic hypothesis. In an extension of the Hamitic hypothesis, a link between Sandawe and Nama was proposed by Dempwolff (1916).

Robert Cust (1883: 435), on the other hand, while convinced that a northern group of people must have found their way to the southern part of Africa, expressed some doubt that these incoming people were necessarily related to speakers of Nubian or other 'Hamitic' languages. His alternative theory might be described as an early statement of the 'macro-Khoisan' scenario, and much the same belief was later expressed by Johnston (1919: 23–24):

Table 2: Suffixes of the third person

i. Suffixes of the 3rd person associated with the gender system of Nama (after Rust 1965)			
	Sg	Dual	Plural
Masculine	-b	-kha	-gu
Feminine	-s	-ra	-ti
Common	-i	-ra	-n
ii. Suffixes of the 3rd person associated with the gender system of Ancient Egyptian and later Coptic (after Loprieno 1995: 67)			
	Sg	Dual	Plural
Masculine	-f		-wj [vb suffix]
Feminine	-s		-tj [vb suffix]
Common		-snj	-sn (Early) -w (Late)

> We may imagine [...] some two thousand years ago, a South Africa beyond the Zambezi and Kunene rivers given up for a time to the dwarfish, steatopygous, yellow-skinned, click-using Bushman. The next disturbing element may have been the Hottentot; a hybrid between negro and negroid and some more northern Bushman race, which seems to have migrated from Equatorial East Africa south-westwards to the Central Zambezi and thence to the Atlantic coast near Walfish Bay, and on again southwards till the Hottentots entered (what is now) Cape Colony and displaced the Bushman.

In a recent reformulation of these ideas (Güldemann 2008), a group of supposed 'Khoe-Kwadi' speakers, who 'involve genetic profiles of both the Khoisan and Other-African type', are proposed to have entered the region a few centuries ahead of any Bantu-speaking communities, bringing with them the earliest domesticated livestock. It is suggested that these 'Khoe-Kwadi speakers', who may have come from somewhere in eastern Africa (ibid: 119), encountered on their arrival in the far south 'a different indigenous language group' (ibid: 111). It is added in this argument (ibid: 116) that these pre-existing speakers of the 'Non-Khoe' languages (Ju and !Ui-Taa) have a 'homogenous non-linguistic profile in that all relevant groups are foragers and show a strong genetic Khoisan profile' (ibid.). In short, the speakers of the Ju and !Ui-Taa languages are assumed to be the aboriginal or 'pristine' hunter-gatherer inhabitants of the region – where this belief is supported by an appeal to biology, insofar as these speakers are explicitly stated to be genetically (i.e., racially) different from other African communities. Two of the main components of this argument are considered next.

The Khoe-Kwadi hypothesis

The Kwadi language of southern Angola was briefly recorded by the anthropologist De Almeida in 1955, who reported that 'only four or five' senior men still spoke it, while 'their men, in particular, can speak Portuguese and also the language of the Kwanyoka' (De Almeida 1994: 240). Westphal (1963) reported that he went to Lisbon from December to January 1956/7 to work with De Almeida on his recordings of the Kwadi material. The notion that Kwadi might be very distantly related to the Khoe family was tentatively explored by Westphal, although he was inclined in the end (1971) to leave it classified as an isolate click language.

The feature of Kwadi that seems to have persuaded Westphal most strongly that the language was not Bantu was a pattern involving the infinitive verb, which he took to reflect an infixed particle –*la*. It appears, however, that what is essentially involved is a system of reduplication or partial reduplication (as noted by Güldemann 2013b: 263), with the occasional incorporation of a verbal extension or some other morpheme. Some of these verbs are plainly Bantu, as shown in Table 3. The other seemingly different and potentially Khoisan-like feature of Kwadi was a system of

Table 3: Examples of reduplicated or partically reduplicated verb stems in Kwadi

English	Other	Proto-Bantu	Kwadi
'read'	-tjanga 'write' [Herero]		taŋga-taŋga [HH-LL]
'drink'	-kalametsa [Tswana]		kala-ka [HH-L]
'cry'	-lela [Tswana]; -lila [Ndonga]	*-did-a	tyela-tyee [HH-L]
'put'	-pela 'give' [Kwanyama]	*-pá 'give'	pela-pɛ
'touch, feel'	-papatela 'hold' [Kwanyama]	*-pát-a 'hold'	pata-papata [HH-HHL]

Notes: Sources of data are listed at the end of the paper. The letters H or L indicate tones.

nominal suffixes. (Some Bantu languages of the same neighbourhood, such as Herero, regularly feature enclitic postnominal particles arising from a series of demonstrative morphemes with weak deictic force.) In the end, while Westphal identified a system of nominal genders indexed by the suffixes, and involving masculine and feminine sub-categorisations, and while he even believed he had found evidence of a dual, the suffixed morphology supposedly associated with the relevant agreement classes is not used with any great consistency, and bears only a slight resemblance to that of the Khoe languages. Examples of these suffixes, such as –di, –ndi and –i in the case of various singulars, can be seen in Table 4.

It appears from the limited material available that there were only a few dozen click words in Kwadi. The dental click was most commonly used, although one or two of the words are indicated with alternative pronunciations involving either a lateral click or the palato-alveolar. In short, the presence and distribution of clicks in this language does not seem to have been much greater than what is evident in Bantu languages of the Kwangari group, namely Mbukushu, Manyo (or Gciriku) and Kwangari. Certainly, a few words in Kwadi – including some click words – appear to be 'Khoe-like'. However, these few isolated words bear such a close resemblance to items of Khoe vocabulary, possibly from the Khwe language in particular, that the greatest likelihood is that they are direct loans, rather than evidence of any relationship.

In fact, by far the greatest part of the Kwadi vocabulary appears to be from a Bantu language – though *not* the Kwanyama-like language, Kwanyoka, that was predominantly used by the Kwadi and is occasionally reflected along with Portuguese in Westphal's transcriptions as one of the two languages used by De Almeida (1994) for purposes of communication and elicitation. Whereas Kwanyoka features the pre-prefix o- that is characteristic of certain noun classes in the western Bantu languages of Guthrie Zone R, such as Herero (R31) or Kwanyama (R21), the Bantu words in Kwadi are lacking in this element, so that they more closely resemble languages from groups of Zone K, such as the Lwena-Luvale group (K14) or the Kwangari group (K33) (see Table 4). To sum up: the evidence for a familial connection between the Khoe languages and Kwadi is slight; on the other hand, there is reasonable evidence

Table 4: Kwadi words of Bantu origin

English	Other	Proto-Bantu		Kwa-nyoka	Kwadi
'hunter'	*omu-koŋgo* [Kwanyama]	*-kong- 'hunt'			*mu-koŋgo-di* [H-HL-L]
'widower'	*omu-hepu-ndu* [Herero]	-			*mu-hepe-e* [H-LLL]
'hide, skin'	*omu-kova* [Herero]	*-kóbá			*mu-kotya*
'White man'	*osi-ndele* [Kwanyama]				*tçi-dele*
'day'	-	*-kòmbì 'sun'			*tçi-kume*
'root'	*omu-di* [Kwanyama]	*(3)-dì		*omwi-ɲi*	*tʃi-mu-θi-i*
'pig'	*ofi-ngulu* [Kwanyama]	*(9)-gòdó			*tʃuŋgulu-i* [LLL-L]
'tree'	*omu-ti* [Kwanyama]	*(3)-tí		*omu-ti*	*tʃi-di*
'ashes'	-	*(3)-tó		*e-to*	*tsu-ndi*
'egg'	*e-i* [Kwanyama]	*(5)-gí			*i-di*
'axe'	-	*(5)-gèmbè			*kx'eβe*
'pool, lake'	-	*(9)-jádé 'river'			*ɟade*
'rhino'	*omanda* [Kwanyama]	*(9)-panda			*phala-de* [HH-L]
'scorpion'	*on-dje* [Kwanyama]	*(9)-ge			*ge*
'bull'	*onuedi* 'bull' [Kwanyama]	*(9)-kudi 'bull'			*gwedi*
'goat'	*osi-kʰombo* [Kwanyama]	*(9)-kómbò			*kx'ɔ-(k)x'ɔbo-di* [H-HL-L] (*male*)
'snake'	*onyoha* [Umbundu]	*(9)-jókà			*kx'ɔ-ɲuwɜ-di* [H-HL-L] (*male*)
'chicken'	*sanji* [Kimbundu]	*-cangi			*k'ie-saŋgyi* [HL-LL] (*female*)

Note: Sources of data are listed at the end of the paper.

that Kwadi was most probably a Bantu language at heart, with a few unusual features, and a small complement of words borrowed from a range of sources.

It is worth adding, nevertheless, that the set of number names is particularly eclectic, and includes two terms borrowed from a Khoe source (for 'one' and 'two'), plus a pair for 'six' and 'seven' where the terms are reversed forms of typical Kwanyama number names, with Kwadi *li 'ɲau*, for example, substituting for Kwanyama *ñano na imue* 'six'. These inversions are so strongly suggestive of deliberate manipulation that it begins to seem a possibility that 'Kwadi' may have been some kind of 'inner language'. This likelihood is strengthened by De Almeida's (1994: 240) curious comment:

> The younger generation do not know it [Kwadi], either because they did not learn it, as it was a difficult language (a 'heavy one') or 'because they had grown up among the Whites', these being the words I have often heard from them.

A natural language is, of course, not normally learned in any formal sense, nor does it seem 'heavy' to its speakers. The fact that at the time of its documentation Kwadi was still used only by the men of a particular age grade, suggests that it may have been an old initiation language, of the kind that would have had to be specially learned and might well have seemed 'heavy' to young initiates. The use of such auxiliary codes, at least in earlier times, has been documented throughout Africa, and is discussed, for example, by Storch (2011).

The argument for a link between Khoe languages and the east African click language, Sandawe

Even if there is no ancestral 'Khoe-Kwadi', it remains open that speakers of the Khoe languages might have trekked down the continent perhaps two or three thousand years ago, bringing sheep or goats with them from somewhere in eastern Africa. After all, as noted above, the gender-associated morphology of the Khoe pronominal system certainly bears an uncanny resemblance to equivalent systems in Afroasiatic languages. Indeed, the affinities that Elderkin (1986) proposes as evidence for a Sandawe–Khoe connection could just as well be interpreted as evidence for a Sandawe–Afroasiatic connection. Yet, if it is a north-eastern connection involving some *Afroasiatic* affinity that is proposed for Khoe on structural grounds, then it is puzzling that nothing of this kind is reflected in the Khoe vocabulary. Alternatively, if we wish to discard the 'Hamitic' version of the theory and argue instead with Cust (1883) and Johnston (1919) that the north-east African link involves some

Table 5: Examples of words reconstructed for Proto-Khoe that appear to be Bantu

gloss	Proto-Khoe			Proto-Bantu		
'see'	*mũ [PKalK]	Nama:	*mũ*	*-bón-a [wide]	Herero: Kwany:	*-muna(u)* *-mona*
'tongue'	*dam [PKalK]	Khwe:	*dàm̀*	*-dámì [CD]		
'swallow' [vb]	*tom [PK:PKK]; *tóm̀ [PKalK]	Nama:	*tom*	*-tóm-a [CDELM] 'chew, drink'		
'night'	*thũ [PKalK]	Khwe:	*thùú*	*-túkò [wide]	Xhosa:	*ubu-suku*
'medicine, magic'	*tso [PK:PKalK]; *so [PKK]	Khwe:	*tcóò*	*-dòg- 'bewitch, curse' [wide]	Tswana:	*toô* 'witchcraft' < *-loa* 'cast spell'
sprout	*tsom [PKalK; PWK], *tsòm̀ [PEK]	Khwe:	*tcòm*	*-com- [AS] 'sprout'	Xhosa: Sotho: Venda:	*-hluma* *-hloma* *-ṭuma*
'lip'	*ts²om [PKalK]	Khwe:	*tc'óm̀*	*-dòmò [wide] 'lip, mouth,beak'	Venda:	*domo* (5) 'big mouth', [aug *mulomo*]
'breast'	*sam [PK]; *sam [PKalK, PEK]	Nama:	*sam-s*	*-jámu- 'suck' [EGKLMRS]	Karanga: Venda:	*zamu* *ḍamu*
'charcoal'	*gada [PKalK; PEK]	Shua:	*gada*	*-kádà [wide]	Tswana:	*ma-gala*
'navel'	*gobo [PKalK, PEK]	Khwe:	*gòvó*	*-kóbú [AGJKS] 'navel'	Tswana:	*khubu*
'year'	*kudi [PK]	Nama: Khwe:	*kuri-b* *kúri*	*-kútì [ADJ] 'cloud'	Karanga:	*gole* 'cloud, year'

Notes: Capital letters after a Proto-Bantu root refer to distribution of reflexes in terms of Guthrie Zones. 'Wide' means widespread. Abbreviations are explained at the end of the paper, along with sources of the data.

purely *Khoisan* ancestor, then we should probably try, as a precautionary measure, to eliminate from our supporting evidence any aspects of Sandawe that appear to be either Bantu or Cushitic. (Dempwolff [1916] identified a substantial proportion of words in the Sandawe lexicon that were Bantu, as well as a group of words that he clearly interpreted as borrowings from a Cushitic source.)

The difficulty here is to find words that truly reflect a unique 'Khoesan-ness', since, in reality, part of the vocabulary reconstructed for Proto-Khoe (Vossen 1997) appears to be Bantu. First, there are a number of 'non-click' words that fall into this category, as shown in Table 5. (There are several more examples not included here because they are less clear-cut, while in addition, the Khoe languages contain numerous words of Bantu origin not reconstructed for the ancestral language.)

It is nevertheless intriguing that one or two of the Bantu words in Table 5 seem to be characteristic of central Africa. For example, the Proto-Bantu reconstruction *-dàmì for 'tongue' has known reflexes only in Guthrie Zones C and D, which is to say in the central or interlacustrine regions of Africa.

Second, there are two classes of cross-Khoe comparative series where some of the cognates are words with clicks as initial segments, but others (typically from varieties of Eastern Kalahari Khoe) are not – and where the latter 'non-click' words are recognisably Bantu. Table 6 shows a few examples of these mixed series, from the class involving the palato-alveolar click [ǂ].

Despite such evidence for the great likelihood of *click emergence*,[9] the assumption has been made in formulating the reconstructions for Proto-Khoe that processes of click *loss* must have operated, and the relevant segments are accordingly projected as clicks. On one hand, it can be argued that this decision is in accordance with the historical linguist's rule of thumb known as 'Majority Rules'. However, the decision

Table 6: Examples of cross-Khoe comparative series where the palato-alveolar click alternates with a conventional segment - and where the 'clickless' form (bolded) is recognisably Bantu

gloss	Proto-Khoe	language		Proto-Bantu	language	
'black'	*ǂnu [PK]: *ǂu [PKK]; *ǂnu (*ǂu) [PKalK; PWK], **nju** [PEK	Nama: Naro: Shua: Tshua:	ǂnùù m̀ùú njú, yú ndú	*-jídò [wide] < *-jìd-a [FH] 'bec. dark'	Kgala: Tswana: Sotho: Venda:	-ntsʰo -tʃo -tsʰo -tsʷu
'food, foodstuffs'	*ǂʔũ 'food' [PK]; **ʔyũ** [PEK]	Nama: Naro: Shua:	ǂʔuũ [LH'] ǂʔõo ʔyũ	*(7)-diò [EGJLMNPS]	Tswana: Venda: Kwany:	di-yò nndyo e-lyo 'eating'
'egg'	*ǂʔubi [PKalK)]; *ǂʔúbí [PWK], **ʔyubi** [PEK	Naro: Shua:	ǂʔubi, gǂùi ʔyubi	*(5)-túmbí [EMNP] 'egg'	Xhosa	um-tʰubi 'yolk, colostrum'

violates the rule of thumb known as Lass's 'Oddity Constraint' – which is itself a version of Occam's Razor.

Overall, the picture remains somewhat complex, and while the possibility of some north-eastern or central African connection cannot be completely discounted, it is unclear what the nature of that regional affinity might have been, and what source languages are ultimately involved. At very least, though, it seems questionable that there is any intermediate linguistic stratum with a specifically 'Khoe-like' character. Rather, it begins to look as though we ought to be considering the possibility of a Bantu-like stratum.

The guidelines that have been ignored in formulating the notion of an intermediate layer include the principle that resemblances of a physiological or cultural nature do not constitute evidence that the languages of the communities concerned are related – in as far as it has evidently been assumed on the basis of physical appearance that some northern population group might be involved, and in as far as it has even been proposed to seek genetic corroboration for the theory. The decision to reconstruct words with clicks – when they appear to have unmistakeable Bantu antecedents – seems to have involved a flouting not only of the principle of parsimony, but also of the principle that it is generally wise to be mindful of neighbouring languages when working on a particular language group.

Conclusion

The brief studies above attempt to show how often and how far we have wandered off course in contemporary Khoesan linguistics, and it has been suggested that we have made these errors through failure to pay attention to the steady stars that should be our compass. This failure would seem to have come about because of our inability to shake off an overwhelming belief that perceptions of otherness have some absolute and meaningful value, and that they take precedence over fundamental principles.

Acknowledgements

A much earlier version of this article was originally intended as a contribution towards a book edited by the historian, Mike Besten, at the time of his premature death. I am grateful for the opportunity to present the chapter as a work in progress at a one-day symposium in the Department of Anthropology at the University of the Free State, in July 2010; and I am indebted to Chris Rapold for the useful comments he contributed on that occasion. This was while I was a postdoctoral research fellow at the University of Cape Town in 2010, and I am thankful for support received in the form of funding from the NRF and a departmental scholarship from the Linguistics Section at UCT. The current article reflects extensive revision and is effectively new work. This version has benefited from informal feedback received from colleagues who participated in the research seminar on Khoi and San Representation convened by Michael Wessels and held at the University of KwaZulu-Natal (Pietermaritzburg) in April 2013. In particular I am deeply grateful for ongoing correspondence with Anne Solomon, John Wright and Jill Weintroub. I also thank the two anonymous reviewers for their careful reading of this article and their constructive comments: I have tried to implement every one of their suggestions. Lastly, I thank the Department of Linguistics at Stellenbosch University for providing me with a supportive collegial environment and an academic home.

Appendix

Abbreviations

aug	Augmentative	denom	Denominative
Kgala	Kgalagadi	Kwany	Kwanyama
PB	Proto-Bantu	PEK	Proto-Eastern Kalahari Khoe
PK	Proto-Khoe	PKalK	Proto-Kalahari Khoe
PKK	Proto-Khoekhoe Khoe	PWK	Proto-Western Kalahari Khoe
sg	Singular	vb	Verb

Sources of data used in the tables

Note: The Bantu languages are grouped according to their Guthrie numbers, as updated by Jouni Maho (2009). These divisions are primarily geographic, although genealogical groupings may sometimes coincide with them.

Khoesan languages

Khoe

Proto-Khoe: Vossen (1997)
Khoe: Khoekhoe branch
Nambian Khoekhoe (Nama, Dama, Hai‖Om): Haacke and Eiseb (2002)
Khoe: Kalahari branch
Khwe: Kilian-Hatz (2003)
Naro: Visser (2001)
Eastern varieties (Shua, Tshua): Vossen (1997)

Kwadi

Westphal (1956/7)

Bantu languages

Proto-Bantu: Bastin and Schadeberg, eds. (2005)

S40: Nguni Group

S41: Xhosa: McLaren (1963); Fischer, Weiss, Mdala and Tshabe (2006)

S30: Sotho-Tswana Group

S31: Tswana: Brown (1982)
S33: S. Sotho: Mabille and Dieterlin, rev. Paroz (1988)
S311: Kgalagadi: Dickens (1986)

S20: Venda Group

S21: Venda: Van Warmelo (1989)

S10: Shona Group

S14: Karanga: Louw (1915)

K30: Luyana Group

K333: Mbukushu: Fisch (1998)

H20: Kimbundu Group

H21a: Kimbundu, Ngola: Pereira do Nascimento (1903)

R10: Umbundu Group

R11: Umbundu: Schadeberg (1990)

R20: Wambo Group

R21: Kwanyama: Tobias and Turvey (1954)
R22: Ndonga: Viljoen, Amakali and Namuandi (2004)

R30: Herero Group

R30: Herero: Viljoen and Kamupingene (1983)

Notes

1   Dorothea Bleek (1927) invoked a category of 'Central Bushman' for Kalahari varieties such as Naro and an eastern Kalahari variety described by Dornan (1917), which she perceived as being 'a link between the Northern Group and Hottentot' (p. 58). Beach (1938: 4) observed that Dorothea Bleek's *Comparative vocabularies of Bushman languages* (1929) made it seem "certain that there is a fairly close connection between Hottentot and Miss Bleek's "Central Bushman languages, particularly Naron", but added, almost as an afterthought, that it might be said 'that the language of the Naron [...] is really not Bushman at all, but simply a dialect of Hottentot"'. While this last point seems obvious today, it was some while before scholars like Maingard (1963) began to point out the systematic correspondences that clearly indicated the reality of this familial unity. An early set of reconstructions for the family was postulated by Baucom (1974), to be superseded by those offered by Vossen (1997).

2   Nama, a southern dialect of Namibian Khoekhoe, is also spoken in South Africa. Northern varieties include Dama and Hai‖om.

3   Linguistic 'reconstruction' involves the extrapolation of a hypothetical ancestral language that could plausibly have given rise to a range of actually observed offspring languages. The process begins with the assembly of arrays of comparative series consisting of cross-varietally distributed words that have similar meanings and display repeatedly similar phonetic alternations (but *not* necessarily identities). On the basis of known or universally likely sound shifts (such as *ki > /si/), a set of sounds is then postulated for the 'proto-language'. Known 'weak spots' in the process concern the quality and quantity of data used for the initial arrays, and assumptions about the directionality and naturalness of sound shifts.

4   As noted in the footnote to a previous work (Du Plessis 2014), the term 'Bantu' was invented by Wilhelm Bleek (1862: 3) as a label for a very large grouping of related languages within Benue-Congo, itself a subset of the Niger-Congo super-grouping of related language families. This abstract linguistic term was later misappropriated and abused by the apartheid regime in South Africa, being used in a generally contemptuous manner as a way of referring to black African people. As a consequence, South African linguists find it difficult even today to use this term in its original, neutral sense, and some have suggested alternative names for the family, such as Kintu or Sintu (see footnote 3, Herbert and Bailey [2002]). These have not taken hold, perhaps partly because the negative connotations are specific to the historical experience of people in South Africa, and partly because the country is home to only a few languages of this vast family, which has been variously estimated to consist of anything from 300 to 680 languages (Nurse and Philippson 2003: 2–3).

5   These language groups were named by Westphal (1971) after the basic word for 'person' in each. The revised spelling !Ui seems to date from Güldemann and Vossen (2000).

6   It is feasible that the Ju and !Ui-Taa groups might be related, and hence could share a common ancestor that would be much older. However, evidence from historical linguistics (Du Plessis 2013, in preparation) suggests that the two groupings are more likely to be cousins than sisters. The question of what the ancestral language, or related ancestral dialects, might have been is somewhat controversial, and really needs space of its own for the presentation of the detailed data and lengthy discussion required. Some of the evidence provided in the

present article nevertheless points, on a preliminary basis, to the possibility of associations of some kind (yet to be determined) involving regional varieties of Bantu languages.

7   The names of Bantu languages are given without their prefixes, in accordance with standard English usage.

8   The genders of Khoekhoe nouns are expressed by the suffixes *–b(i)* 'masculine' (plural *–ku* or *–ku(a)*) and *–s* 'feminine' (plural *–di* or *–ti*). A singular for the common (or neutral) gender is occasionally expressed by *–i* (with plural *–n*). In the case of Kalahari varieties other than Naro, genders are often expressed through agreement morphology alone, while the morpheme associated with the masculine singular is typically *–m(i)*. Identical morphemes function as dependent pronouns that may attach to other parts of speech for purposes of both discourse deixis and derivation.

9   At a subsequent conference at the University of the Witwatersrand (7–10 August 2013), the suggestion was made by Maddieson (2013) that clicks could, in principle, emerge from certain phonetic environments, such as those that occur naturally in languages of the Shona group (Guthrie Zone S) and Rundi-Rwanda (Guthrie Zone DJ60). At the same conference, Demolin and Chabiron (2013) independently demonstrated the actual emergence of clicks in just such environments in Rwanda.

References

Ashton, E.O. 1947. *Swahili grammar (including intonation)*. Harlow, Essex: Longman.

Bastin, Y. and T.C. Schadeberg, eds. 2005. Third Tervuren series of Bantu lexical reconstructions (BLR3). http://www.metafro.be/blr (accessed throughout 2012).

Baucom, K.L. 1974. Proto-Central Khoisan. In *Third Annual Conference on African Linguistics*, ed. E. Voeltz, 3–37. Bloomington: Indiana University Press.

Beach, D.M. 1938. *The phonetics of the Hottentot language*. Cambridge: Heffer.

Bleek, D. 1927. The distribution of Bushman languages in South Africa. In *Festschrift Meinhof*, 55–64. Hamburg: Augustin.

Bleek, D. 1929. *Comparative vocabularies of Bushman languages*. Cambridge: Cambridge University Press.

Bleek, D. 2000. The ǁD!ke or Bushmen of Griqualand West, *Khoisan Forum Working Paper* 15, ed. T. Güldemann. Cologne.

Bleek, W.H.I. 1851. *De nominum generibus linguarum Africa australis, Copticae, Semiticarum aliarumque sexualium*. Bonn: Adolph Marx.

Bleek, W.H.I. 1862. *A comparative grammar of South African languages. Part I*. London: Trübner & Co.

Bleek, W.H.I. 1911. The resurrection of the ostrich: part of the preceding tale parsed by Dr Bleek. In *Specimens of Bushman folklore*, ed. W.H.I. Bleek and L. Lloyd, 144–154. London: George Allen & Co., Ltd.

Brown, J.T. 1982. *Setswana dictionary: Setswana–English and English–Setswana*. Johannesburg: Pula Press.

Cole, D.T. 1975. *An introduction to Tswana grammar*. Cape Town: Longman.

Cust, R.N. 1883. *A sketch of the modern languages of Africa*. London: Trübner and Co.

De Almeida, A. 1994. *Os Bosquimanos de Angola*. Lisbon: Instituto de investigação cientifica tropica.

De Maret, P. and F.N. Nsuka 1977. History of Bantu metallurgy: some linguistic aspects. *History in Africa* 4: 43–65.

Demolin, D. and C. Chabiron. 2013. Clicks, stop bursts, vocoids and the timing of articulatory gestures in Rwanda. Paper presented at the Conference on Phonetics and Phonology of sub-Saharan Languages, 7–10 July, University of the Witwatersrand, Johannesburg.

Dempwolff, O. 1916. *Die Sandawe: Linguistiches und ethnographisches Material aus Deutsch-Ostafrika*. (Abhandlungen des Hamburgischen Kolonialinstituts: 34.B. Völkerkunde, Kulturgeschichte und Sprachen: 19.) Hamburg: L. Friederichsen.

Dickens, P. 1986. Qhalaxarzi phonology. Master's dissertation, University of the Witwatersrand, Johannesburg.

Doke, C.M. 1937. An outline of ‡Khomani Bushman phonetics. In *Bushmen of the southern Kalahari*, ed. J.D. Rheinallt Jones and C.M. Doke, 61–88. Johannesburg: Witwatersrand University Press.

Doke, C.M. 1950. *Textbook of Zulu grammar*. London: Longmans, Green and Co. Ltd.

Doke, C.M. and S.M. Mofokeng. 1985. *Textbook of southern Sotho grammar*. Cape Town: Maskew Miller Longman.

Dornan, S.S. 1917. The Tati Bushmen (Masarwas) and their language. *Journal of the Royal Anthropological Institute* 47(Jan–June): 37–112.

Du Plessis, M. 2013. New data on click genesis: further evidence that click-initial words shared by Khoesan and Bantu languages of southern Africa can be mapped as historically emergent from non-click forms reconstructed for Proto-Bantu. Paper presented at the Conference on Phonetics and Phonology of sub-Saharan Africa, held in honour of the late Tony Traill at the University of the Witwatersrand, 7–10 July.

Du Plessis, M. 2014. One hundred years of the specimens – a hundred years of linguistic neglect. In *The courage of ‖Kabbo: collected papers from the conference celebrating the 100th anniversary of specimens of Bushman folklore*, ed. J. Deacon and P. Skotnes, 275–302. Cape Town: University of Cape Town Press.

Du Plessis, M. In preparation. The systematic occurrence of Bantu-intrinsic click words in Khoesan languages, discovered by reference to reconstructions for Proto-Bantu.

Elderkin, E.D. 1986. Diachronic influences from basic sentence and noun structure in Central Khoisan and Sandawe. *Sprache und Geschichte in Afrika* 7(2): 131–156.

Engelbrecht, J. 1936. *The Korana*. Cape Town: Maskew Miller. [Previously published 1928, as Studies oor Korannataal, *Annale van die Universiteit van Stellenbosch* VI (2).]

Fisch, M. 1998[1977]. *Thimbukushu grammar*. Trans. S. Fitchat. Windhoek: Out of Africa Publishers.

Fischer, A., E. Weiss, E. Mdala and S. Tshabe. 2006. *English–Xhosa dictionary*. Cape Town: Oxford University Press, Southern Africa.

Greenberg, J.H. 1963. *The languages of Africa*. Bloomington: Indiana University Press.

Güldemann, T. 2004a. TUU – a new name for the Southern Khoisan family. In *Studies in Tuu (Southern Khoisan)*, T. Güldemann, 11–30. (*University of Leipzig Papers on Africa, Languages and Literatures* 23). Leipzig: Institut für Afrikanistik, Universität Leipzig.

Güldemann, T. 2004b. Reconstruction through 'deconstruction': the marking of person, gender and number in the Khoe family and Kwadi. *Diachronica* 21(2): 251–306.

Güldemann, T. 2008. A linguist's view: Khoe-Kwadi speakers as the earliest food-producers of southern Africa. *Southern African Humanities* 20: 93–132.

Güldemann, T. 2013a. Southern Khoesan (Tuu): morphology; syntax. In *The Khoesan languages*, ed. R. Vossen, 234–248; 408–430. London and New York: Routledge.

Güldemann, T. 2013b. Kwadi: morphology. In *The Khoesan languages*, ed. R. Vossen, 261–264. London and New York: Routledge.

Güldemann, T. and E.D. Elderkin. 2010. On external genealogical relationships of the Khoe family. In *Khoisan languages and linguistics: the 1ˢᵗ Riezlern symposium 2003. (Research in Khoisan Studies* 24), ed. M. Brenzinger and C. König, 15–52. Cologne: Rüdiger Köppe.

Güldemann, T. and R. Vossen. 2000. Khoisan. In *African languages: an introduction*, ed. B. Heine and D. Nurse, 99–122. Cambridge: Cambridge University Press.

Haacke, W.H.G. and E. Eiseb. 2002. *A Khoekhoegowab dictionary*. Windhoek: Gamsberg Macmillan.

Harries, L. 1950. *A grammar of Mwera*. Johannesburg: Witwatersrand University Press.

Heine, B. and C. König. 2008. What can linguistics tell us about early Khoekhoe history? *Southern African Humanities* 20: 235–248.

Herbert, R.K. and R. Bailey. 2002. The Bantu languages: sociohistorical perspectives. In *Language in South Africa*, ed. R. Mesthrie, 50–78. Cambridge: Cambridge University Press.

Johnston, H. 1919. *A comparative study of the Bantu and semi-Bantu languages*. Oxford: Clarendon Press.

Kilian-Hatz, C. 2003. *Khwe dictionary*. Cologne: Rüdiger Köppe.

Lanham, L.W. and D.P. Hallowes 1956. Linguistic relationships and contacts expressed in the vocabulary of Eastern Bushman. *African Studies* 15(1): 45–48. Repr. in *Foundations in southern African linguistics*, ed. R.K. Herbert, 253–256. Johannesburg: Witwatersrand University Press.

Lass, R. 1993. How real(ist) are reconstructions? In *Historical linguistics: problems and perspectives*, ed. C. Jones, 156–189. London: Longman.

Lass, R. 1997. Historical linguistics and language change. *Cambridge Studies in Linguistics* 81. Cambridge: Cambridge University Press.

Lepsius, R. 1880. *Nubische Grammatik, mit einer Einleitung über die Völker und Sprachen Afrika's*. Berlin: Wilhelm Hertz.

Lichtenstein, H.1815. *Travels in southern Africa in the years 1803, 1804, 1805 and 1806. Vol. II*. Transl. A. Plumptre. London: Henry Colburn.

Loprieno, A. 1995. *Ancient Egyptian: a linguistic introduction*. Cambridge: Cambridge University Press.

Louw, C.S. 1915. *A manual of the Chikaranga language*. Bulawayo: Philpott and Collins.

Mabille, A. and H. Dieterlen, reclassified, revised and enlarged by R.A. Paroz. 1988. *Southern-Sotho–English dictionary (South African orthography)*. Morija: Morija Sesuto Book Depot.

Maddieson, I. 2013. Clicks: primordial or derived? Keynote address, given at the Conference on Phonetics and Phonology of sub-Saharan Languages, 7–10 July 2013, University of the Witwatersrand, Johannesburg.

Maho, J. 2009. New updated Guthrie list.http://goto.glocalnet.net/mahopapers/nuglonline. pdf (accessed September 2012).

Maingard, L.F. 1937. The ǂKhomani dialect of Bushman: its morphology and other characteristics. In *Bushmen of the southern Kalahari*, ed. J.D. Rheinallt Jones and C.M. Doke, 237–275. Johannesburg: Witwatersrand University Press.

Maingard, L.F. 1963. A comparative study of Naron, Hietshware and Korana. *African Studies* 22(3): 97–108.

McLaren, J., revised W.G. Bennie and J.J.R. Jolobe. 1963. *A new concise Xhosa–English dictionary.* Cape Town: Longmans.

Meinhof, C. 1912. *Die Sprachen der Hamiten.* Hamburg: L. Friederichsen and Co.

Meinhof, C. 1928/1929. Versuch einer grammatischen Skizze einer Buschmannsprache. *Zeitschrift für Eingeborenen-Sprachen* 19: 161–88.

Moodie, D. 1838. *The record; or, a series of official papers relative to the condition and treatment of the native tribes of South Africa.* Cape Town: A.S. Robertson.

Nurse, D. and G. Philippson, eds. 2003. *The Bantu languages.* London: Routledge.

Pereira do Nascimento, J. 1903. *Diccionario Portuguez–Kimbundu.* Huilla: Typographia da Missão.

Samarin, W.J. 1971. Adamawa-Eastern. In *Current trends in linguistics 7: linguistics in sub-Saharan Africa*, ed. T.A. Sebeok, 213–244. The Hague: Mouton.

Sands, B. 2001. Borrowing and diffusion as a source of lexical similarities in Khoesan. In *Khoisan: syntax, phonetics, phonology, and contact*, ed. A. Bell and P. Washburn, 200–224. Cornell Working Papers in Linguistics 18. Ithaca, NY: Cornell University.

Schadeberg, T. 1990. *A sketch of Umbundu.* Cologne: Rüdiger Köppe.

Schadeberg, T. 2003. Historical linguistics. In *The Bantu languages*, ed. D. Nurse and G. Philippson, 143–163. London: Routledge.

Scott, D.C. and A. Hetherwick. 1957[1929]. *Dictionary of the Nyanja language (being the encyclopaedic dictionary of the Mang'anja language, edited and enlarged).* London: Lutterworth Press.

Storch, A. 2011. *Secret manipulations: language and context in Africa.* Oxford: Oxford University Press.

Tessmann, G. 1931. Die drei Sprachen des Bajastammes: To, Labi, Baja (Kamerun). *Mitteilungen des Seminars für Orientalische Sprachen* 34(3): 70–115.

Tobias, G.W.R. and B.H.C. Turvey. 1954. *English–Kwanyama dictionary.* Johannesburg: Witwatersrand University Press.

Van Warmelo, N.J. 1989. *Venda dictionary: Tshivenda–English.* Pretoria: J.L. van Schaik.

Viljoen, J.J., P. Amakali and N. Namuandi. 2004. *Oshindonga–English; English–Oshindonga dictionary.* Windhoek: Gamsberg Macmillan.

Viljoen, J.J. and T.K. Kamupingene. 1983. *Otjiherero woordeboek/dictionary/embo roMambo.* Windhoek: Gamsberg.

Visser, H. 2001. *Naro dictionary: Naro–English; English–Naro.* Gantsi: Naro Language Project.

Vossen, R. 1997. *Die Khoe-Sprachen: ein Beitrag zur Erforschung der Sprachgeschichte Afrikas. Research in Khoisan Studies* 12. Cologne: Rüdiger Köppe.

Vossen, R., ed. 2013. *The Khoesan languages.* Routledge Language Family Series. London and New York: Routledge.

Westphal, E.O.J. 1956/57. Manuscript Kwadi papers, amongst the Westphal papers in the University of Cape Town libraries' digital online collections.

Westphal, E.O.J. 1963. The linguistic prehistory of southern Africa: Bush, Kwadi, Hottentot and Bantu linguistic relationships. *Africa* 33: 237–265.

Westphal, E.O.J. 1971. The click languages of southern and eastern Africa. In *Current trends in linguistics 7: linguistics in sub-Saharan Africa*, ed. T.A. Sebeok, 367–420. The Hague and Paris: Mouton.

Wuras, C.F. 1919-1920 [c.1850]. An outline of the Bushman language. *Zeitschrift für Eingeborenen-Sprachen* 10 (ed. W. Bourquin): 81–87.

Ziervogel, D. 1955. Notes on the language of the eastern Transvaal Bushmen. In *The disappearing Bushmen of Lake Chrissie*, ed. E.F. Potgieter, 35–63. Pretoria: Van Schaik.

The boer and the jackal: satire and resistance in Khoi orature[1]

Hermann Wittenberg

Abstract

In the context of considerable scholarly and popular attention focused on Bushman narratives over the last 30 years, much of it centred on analyses and retellings of the Bleek and Lloyd archive,[2] there has been much less attention paid to Khoi story-telling and the comparative insights made possible by such a study. The monumental work on the |Xam carried out by Wilhelm Bleek and Lucy Lloyd in the 1870s and 1880s has overshadowed Bleek's own earlier studies of Khoi folklore. Soon after his arrival in Cape Town and his appointment as Lord Grey's librarian, Bleek had started to solicit Bushman and Khoi[3] folktales from missionaries stationed in the remoter areas of the colonies, and in 1864 a collection of 42 of these translated oral narratives was published in London as *Reynard the Fox in South Africa; or Hottentot fables and tales*. The book is South Africa's earliest publication of indigenous literature, and it remains one of the most important collections of Khoi orature. This article has two interrelated interests: first, drawing attention to the largely neglected area of Khoi orature, and second, developing an argument about the similarities and differences between Khoi story-telling and Bushman narratives. It is in this context that the contradistinctive idea of satire will be explored which is, in Khoi orature, associated with the transgressive trickster figure of the wily jackal. In Khoi stories the jackal is an attractive, roguish figure who is able to outwit the powerful – in particular, predators such as lions. In |Xam story-telling on the other hand, the jackal did not function as a trickster but was associated with negative connotations such as cunning, cowardice and selfishness, qualities that did not allow him to become a figure of identification. Such a bifurcation, this article will suggest, was not without political consequence in the often violent 19th-century Cape frontier.

I

Given a long and early history of European contact with Khoi people at the Cape, that even pre-dated the Dutch East India Company (VOC) settlement in 1652, it is surprising that not more Khoi stories have entered the colonial archive. Khoi self-representation in the form of a literary record is comparatively rare, despite the fact that they were South Africa's first indigenous people to come into contact with colonial literate cultures, a sustained and often intimate contact that stretched over 200 years from at least the late 16th century until the 1750s, when a coherent and distinctive Khoi culture disintegrated and became absorbed into the Cape underclass (Elphick 1985: xvii). Khoi languages persisted on the colonial fringes such as the eastern and northern Cape for another hundred years, but it is only in the remote Richtersveld and southern Namibia that one of the Khoi languages, namely Nama, is still spoken today. There is thus an almost inverse relationship between the long history of settler–native contact, and the volume of recorded narrative material, where we have the least number of records of Cape Khoi narratives, despite the extensive social history of pervasive and intimate interaction. The vast number of extant Khoi tales is drawn from more remote Nama and Koranna sources, as exemplified in Bleek's *Reynard* book, Leonhard Schultze's *Aus Namaland und Kalahari* (1907), L.F Maingaard's *Koranna folktales* (1962), and the much later assembled Sigrid Schmidt corpus from southern Namibia. Schmidt's comprehensive *Catalogue of Khoisan folktales of southern Africa* (1989) lists mostly Nama Khoi narratives. The small number of Cape Khoi sources cited in her bibliography is found in publications mostly devoted to other concerns (such as hunting, natural history and travel).

The paucity of Cape Khoi folklore and their incidental presence in the record may be ascribed to the late emergence of folklore as an object of scholarly study in the 19th century. Drawing on the philosophy of Herder and the philological work of the Grimm brothers, the emerging field of folklore studies in Europe sought to discover an authentic literary heritage that would reveal a people's essential and distinctive national character, uncontaminated by the homogenising forces of urban capitalist modernity (Bendix 1997). Such a paradigm of locating national and ethnic authenticity in a rural and primitive past could be readily transferred to the colonial arena, and this explains the interest of Bleek, Grey and other Cape intellectuals in collecting, studying and systematising indigenous literature. By the time folklore had emerged as a distinctive area of scholarly interest, Cape Khoi culture and language had already largely disappeared. Cape Khoi literature is thus very rare in the colonial record, and it is in this context that we need to consider the significance of the stories collected by the famous painter Thomas Baines. Born in England in 1820, Baines came to South Africa as a 21-year-old, embarking on a career as explorer artist. He travelled widely throughout the region, reaching as far north as the upper parts of the

Zambezi on an expedition led by David Livingstone. His prolific output of sketches and dramatic oil paintings remains the most valuable pictorial Africana of the 19th century. The Cape Khoi stories recorded by Baines were likely to have been picked up in the course of his many travels, possibly during his early four-year stay in the Eastern Cape in the 1840s (Carruthers and Arnold 1995).

The two Cape Khoi stories which Baines reproduced from his recollections were published in the little-known and short-lived *Folk-lore Journal*, published over 12 issues in 1879 and 1880. Issued by the South African Folklore Society, in which Lucy Lloyd was an influential member, the *Folk-lore Journal* must rank as the first scholarly journal published in the country, in any discipline. Under its epigraph 'Semper novi quid ex Africa' (Always something new out of Africa), it sought to make available 'a representative collection of traditional literature existing among South Africa's aboriginal races' which were 'rapidly passing away, under the influence of European ideas, and the spread of European civilisation' ('Preface' 1879: ii). The scientific ambitions of the journal were discernible in the language of the preface: it wanted to collect 'specimens of Native literature' drawn directly 'from the lips of the aborigines, written down in their own language and words, and accompanied by a translation into English' (ibid: ii–iii). The journal accordingly pioneered the columnar side-by-side printing of oral transcribed material and translations, well known in the subsequent publication of Lucy Lloyd's famous *Specimens of Bushman folklore* (1911). The journal also contains a number of significant contributions, among them |Han‡kass'o first *kumkummi* in print (the stories 'The Wind' and 'The Son of Wind'), as well as Wilhelm Bleek's posthumously published proposal to establish an anthropological institute in the region.

The *Folk-lore Journal*, together with more popular publications such as the *Cape Monthly Magazine*, must be understood as part of a short-lived Cape liberal enlightenment, a period between 1850 and the 1870s during which colonial intellectuals drew on universal knowledge and science to articulate more tolerant and open-minded attitudes towards indigenous people. As described by Saul Dubow in his study *A commonwealth of knowledge: science, sensibility and white South Africa* (2009), these enlightened attitudes in the Cape were inhibited after the discovery of diamonds in Kimberly in 1868 and self-government in 1872, when the demand for mining labour and the more assertive demands of settler agriculture militated against the liberal racial attitudes of an urban educated elite.

Baines's two Cape Khoi stories published in the *Folk-lore Journal*, 'The story of a dam' and 'The lion and the jackal, a Hottentot story' are both jackal trickster stories, of a type well known from other sources. The lion and the jackal story is found in similar form not only in the Bleek and Lloyd corpus (a story told by ‡Kasin 'The lion and the jackals' [Lewis Williams 2000: 165]), but also in the *Reynard* volume, as well as the Schultze collection. The story is briefly as follows: the lion and the jackal agree to hunt together and share the spoils, with the jackal volunteering to 'transport the game to their dens', taking 'care that Mrs Lion and her family should not want'. The hunt is exceedingly successful, but when Lion returns home, his family is 'on the point of death from sheer hunger, and in a mangy state'. The jackal, it appeared, had only given them a few 'entrails of the game'. Lion is in 'a terrible fury, vowing death to the jackal and his family', but the jackal has taken precautions, ensconcing himself and family on top of a steep 'krantz'. When the vengeful lion arrives, the jackal innocuously greets him with the words 'Good morning, uncle', to which the lion responds in fury: 'How dare you call me uncle? You impudent scoundrel!' The jackal pretends to be taken aback, and blames his wife. Taking a stick, he beats a hide loudly while instructing Mrs Jackal to scream. The jackal's wife utters such dismal howls that the lion begs him to be merciful. Having mollified the beast, the jackal then asks the lion to come up and eat meat, but on account of the steep cliff, he cannot. The jackal then offers to haul him up with a rope, and just as the lion nears the top, Jackal lets go the '*riem*', with the lion falling down. After a pretence of blaming and beating the wife, the operation is repeated, but the lion falls again 'with such force, that he was fairly stunned for some time'. After the lion recovers, the jackal suggests 'in a most sympathising tone' that he will drop down a 'nice fat piece of eland breast' into Lion's mouth. Instead of meat, however, the jackal takes a round stone, made red hot in the fire and wrapped in fat, and drops 'the hot shot right into the lion's capacious mouth, which ran through the poor beast, killing it on the spot' (Baines 1880: 54–57).

In the Baines version the story has been somewhat domesticated, as is evident in the Victorian language and metaphors (the hide is 'belaboured', the stone is equated with 'hot shot', etc.), making it clear that the story was not the outcome of a scholarly folkloristic collection effort (as in Bleek's *Reynard* volume) or ethnographic fieldwork (Schmidt 1989; Schultze 1907). Nevertheless, it presents us with one of the earliest and best elaborated jackal trickster narratives, showing clear linkages in oral tradition between the Cape Khoi and the more northern Nama cultures. If we compare the Baines story with the Nama jackal stories collected in Bleek's *Reynard* volume, we can see that both the Nama and Cape Khoi stories contain the same elements (unequal division of meat, an unreliable *riem*, an unclimbable cliff, a hot stone dropped into the lion's mouth).

Both Baines' and Bleek's narratives are, however, also illustrative of the 'processes of exclusion, occlusion and effacement that have occurred in the construction of the cultural history of this country' (Brown 1999: 4). As shown elsewhere (Wittenberg 2012), Bleek suppressed the disruptive, erotic and scatological elements of indigenous narration that he deemed not suitable for a Victorian reading public. As Bleek (1864: xxiii) put it in the preface, 'to make these Hottentot fables readable for the general public, a few slight omissions and alterations of what would otherwise have been too naked for the English eye were necessary'.

While Bleek may have been motivated by a Victorian reserve that could not entertain Rabelaisian material, we also need to see his editorial interventions in the light of progressive Cape liberal attempts to disassociate the stereotypical figure of the 'Hottentot' from the its well-established negative associations in colonial Cape discourse with disorderliness, idleness and licentiousness. Overall, though, Bleek's renditions of Khoi folklore need to be understood as limiting versions of indigenous orature.

II

The sanitisation inherent in 19th-century Khoi orature becomes particularly apparent when comparing the Bleek and Baines narratives with oral material collected by the German ethnographer, Leonhard Schultze, published in *Aus Namaland und Kalahari* (1907). Schultze's 67 tales were collected during extended field trips in the northern Cape and southern Namibia. While his scientific work became entangled with and tainted by his involvement in imperial Germany's notorious Herero and Nama wars of extermination (see Wittenberg 2012), his fluency in Nama, and his exacting fieldwork methodology of transcription produced a qualitatively different body of narratives:

> What I had listened to at night around the fire, I had repeated to me slowly the next day by the story teller, so that, after some practice, I was able to obtain a coherent dictation. In order to ascertain if the act of dictating had disturbed the sentence structure and sequence, I asked the Hottentot to repeat his story at normal speed and carefully noted down variations. (Schultze 1907: 752)

Schultze's corpus of tales was thus collected in more natural conditions than those that obtained in Bleek's research on prison convicts, and yielded stories that contained a fair share of risqué jokes, scatological references and politically disruptive material. Commenting on Bleek's stories, Schultze (ibid: 389) claimed that they 'do not reveal to me the Hottentot whom I have gotten to know. Since I was able to tap into the very source of their lore, I will disregard his versions completely.'

Schultze's Khoi stories, as will become immediately apparent, are told in a very different register than that of the Baines stories as well as Bleek's *Reynard* tales in which the 'naked' elements of indigenous storytelling had been censored. In Schultze's analogous story 'Der Löwe und der Schakal' (1907: 489–490), the narrative unfolds in much the same sequence, though elements are localised in order to adapt to different faunal and topographic conditions. For instance, instead of an eland, a giraffe is the object of the hunt, and the rocky *krantz* is replaced by a camelthorn acacia tree. The narrative outcome (the lion is killed by being duped to swallow a hot stone) is common to all the different versions, but in the Schultze narrative there is an additional small 'naked' or bawdy graphic detail: the hot stone tears apart the lion's anus as he tries to 'shit' it out. Hence, as explained to Schultze by his informant, lions will, to this day, always eat a piece of skin first, before wolfing down the meat, so as to plug up the hole.

In another lion and jackal tale in Schultze's corpus, similar 'naked' elements are even more visible. The following tale, 'The lions who pretended to be dead', is an exemplary instance of such transgressive humour:

> Two lions who were travelling were tired and they saw a jackal approaching. [Not wanting the trouble of a hunt] they lay down pretending to be dead, and the jackal came closer. He quietly crept up and softly touched the back hole [anus] of the one lion, and saw how it contracted. Then he knew that they only pretended to be dead and said: 'Thank you Lord, that you have given me this food!' Then he made a fire with some grass and said aloud: 'Let me first find some fire wood,' and he went off. And while he was breaking off wood, he gradually went further and further away, and once he had escaped he climbed on to a rock and called out: 'Luckily I touched your arseholes! You stupid, dirty, pus-encrusted dick heads! You could have almost killed me!' This is how he shouted, but the lions were very tired, and therefore they did not run after him. (Schultze 1907: 486)

Here the jackal evades being eaten through a neat bodily inversion when he approaches the lion from the wrong end: instead of being ingested by the lion's dangerous mouth, he cunningly approaches from the other side, exploiting the unguarded weakness of the master's delicately twitching anus. In Achille Mbembe's discussion of scatological humour as political strategy in the African postcolony, 'the significance of orifices' and of a body that drinks, eats, shits 'and is open' is fundamental to 'people's political humour' (Mbembe 2001: 107), a humour which in particular targets 'the president's anus' (ibid: 108). Both these Khoi tales may very well function in a similar subversive manner in their mockery of the 'king of the beasts' as they disallow faunal and political elites to eat easily at the cost of others, and skilfully deconstruct the lion's greed (figured by his ravenous, ever-hungry open mouth) by shifting attention to his vulnerable anus. As we have seen in Khoi orature, the wily jackal is an attractive and entertaining trickster figure who consistently manages to outwit the powerful and mighty by exploiting their vulnerabilities. In these narratives, the jackal is clearly a figure of identification for Khoi story-tellers and listeners, while the lion is the symbolically defeated and discredited enemy at whose misfortune one laughs. The cultural script implicit in the jackal trickster narratives allowed the weaker subject to outwit a dominant master, and I will argue that this was a template that seemed eminently adaptable in the face of historical change. With the entry of powerful colonial forces into the northern Cape frontier, the Khoi could deploy their jackal trickster narratives as a strategy of discursive resistance. But before we examine the political consequences of such story-telling modes as symbolic forms of resistance, we first need to examine the parallels in Bushman orature.

III

In Bushman cultures, the lion has a similarly negative connotation as in Khoi orature, so that we could speak of a considerable cultural overlap. As Mark McGranaghan (2012) has shown in a detailed study of |Xam society, identity and the idea of the human was not restricted to *homo sapiens* but was fluid and expansive enough to encompass other 'people' such as animals. Lions were, however, 'people who are different' since they 'eat other people' and display no restraint in their excessive consumption:

> Anti-social agents were for the |Xam fundamentally 'different', violent and angry 'beasts-of-prey' who went about by night to kill people (LL.II.3.421–422) and eat them (LL.II.16.1550) ... The most typical exemplars of persons who did not act in accordance with these norms and aims of |Xam society were to be found (unsurprisingly) in non-human communities such as those of lions (or 'beasts-of-prey' generally). (2012: 211, 204–205)

In |Xam culture, the lion was thus not only a dangerous marauder who posed a real and ever-present danger, but was also an exemplary figure for predatory anti-sociality, violating the accepted social norms of 'behaving nicely' (ibid: 183) and sharing food with others. People who displayed such qualities of greed or violence were regarded as 'different' (|xarra) and equated with lions (|xa), where the lexical similarity reinforced an overlap in meaning.

The similar negative treatment of lions in Khoi and |Xam orature points to a pan-Khoisan cultural world. Megan Biesele's (1993: 34) Kalahari-based work, for example, argues that 'Bushman folklore is itself practically indistinguishable from Khoisan tradition as a whole' and that it 'is very hard to tell the difference between a Bushman story and a Khoikhoi story'. Biesele's work points to the commonalities in pan-Southern African Khoisan culture, citing for example close similarities and linkages between |Xam and narratives collected among the Kalahari Ju|'hoansi during the 1970s. But assumptions of an undifferentiated commonality across diverse southern African Khoi and Bushman societies are also problematic, given pronounced divergences in economic mode, where Bushmen or San are generally associated with a hunter-gatherer lifestyle and the Khoi practised a pastoral subsistence. Earlier studies, such as Richard Elphick's (1977) influential materialist thesis, underplayed the role of intrinsic ethnic and cultural differences, arguing that many of the people whom the colonists called Bushmen and the Khoi called San were failed pastoralists who had fallen on hard times, lost their livestock and now had to rely on hunter-gathering; conversely that people who practised pastoralism where former hunter-gatherers whose economic fortunes had now improved. The difference between the Cape hunter-gathers and pastoralist Khoi was thus fluid, as people cycled between two different economic modes.

Elphick's study was important in destabilising essentialist notions of a pure and pristine hunter-gatherer Bushman culture, but more recent studies have revisited the cultural differences between hunter-gathering and pastoral societies – differences that are key to economic differentiation. Mark McGranaghan (2012: 339) argues that while hunter-gathering was not an absolute and exclusive mode for the |Xam (for example, Bleek's informant Dia!kwain possessed cattle), there remained 'meaningful distinctions between hunter-gatherers who have acquired livestock or started cultivating wild plants, and pastoralists or farmers who happen to hunt or who supplement their diet with wild plants'. John Parkington (2007) has proposed that hunter-gatherer and pastoralist world-views and ideologies were fundamentally divergent and incompatible, making a pragmatic cycling between two modes of economic subsistence highly unlikely. Bushman culture is inclusive and fundamentally shaped by an obligation of sharing, which not only solves the problem of waste in times of a sudden surplus of fresh food, but also permeates all other aspects of culture. The eland, whose successful hunt was productive of a huge supply of meat far in excess of the needs of the hunter and his family, is precisely so central in Bushman rock art and narrative because it represented an exemplary instance of this ideology of sharing, the basic social glue of a hunter-gatherer society. While Bushman culture is dispersive, distributive and egalitarian, Khoi pastoral culture, by contrast, is exclusive and accumulative, based on property ownership and fairly well-developed hierarchical political systems. As Parkington (2007: 86) puts it, 'herders or farmers who lost the ability to herd or grow crops may well have engaged in hunting and in the gathering of wild plant foods, but never lost the world-view of the accumulator'.

If we follow this argument, Khoi and Bushman cultures then shared commonalities shaped by distant ancestral links, by centuries of contact and by living in the same landscape, but they were also fundamentally divergent in ideological orientation or world-view. In the oral story-telling traditions, I will suggest, these differences articulated themselves in the way the jackal trickster figure could be utilised. So, while with respect to lions Khoi and |Xam beliefs coalesced, they were sharply differentiated around the jackal. Jackals, as we have seen, were sympathetic figures of identification for the Khoi, proxies for the human underdog in his dealings with powerful and oppressive masters. But in |Xam culture, jackals, like lions, were also primarily regarded as predators or 'different people'. As McGranaghan (2012: 183) has shown, the idea of a greedy person was 'applied to animals (e.g. jackals, LL.II.15.1477)[4] and people (LL.II.14.1319) noted for generally excessive consumption'. In a culture whose survival was premised on an ideology of distribution and sharing, such greediness was impermissible: 'people should work the excess food "nicely" instead of behaving like jackals by gorging themselves while food was plentiful (LL.VIII.16.7449')' (ibid: 254). In the Bleek and Lloyd archive, jackals thus function very differently from those in Khoi story-telling, associated generally with negative traits such as cowardice, cunning and selfish behaviour. According to |Hanǂkass'o, the places where jackals and hyenas urinate must be avoided (LL VIII.29.8584 rev.–8587 rev.), and they are also associated with dangerous black clouds ('jackal clouds') from which one should shelter (LL VIII-23. 8018–8029). He also warns that children should not eat its heart lest they imbibe his cowardly qualities (LL VIII-16.7457–7459).

If we accept that the |Xam held such sceptical and negative views of jackals, how do we then make sense of a |Xam trickster narrative which appears to violate this cultural logic and depicts the jackal as its hero? The story in question is ǂKasin's tale, 'The lion and the jackals', related to Lucy Lloyd in November 1873. In this story, a jackal shoots eland on two successive days, but always loses his game to a lion. A sorceress advises him to remain silent and stay at home; she then makes all the bushes and water disappear so that an eland comes right up to his house. The jackal shoots the eland, and the sorceress makes a mountain rise up with the dead eland upon it, together with all the other houses, water and 'also the people' (Lewis-Williams 2000: 165). The lion, smelling the feast above him, wants eland fat poured into his mouth and the jackal, with the help of other jackals, heats a stone and drops it into the mouth of the lion below. Lion's insides are burned up and he dies while running away. The story ends with all the jackals looking together at the dead lion, the first jackal saying: 'The man is dead' (ibid: 166).

At first glance the story is similar to the Khoi versions of Baines, Bleek and Schultze, but there are important differences, most significantly the added supernatural element of the sorceress. Overall, the resourceful, cunning trickster personality of the jackal is disabled in ǂKasin's story and he is strangely passive in the face of the lion's rapaciousness. Agency is less located in a wily animal than in the supernatural agency of the sorceress, through whose divine intervention social justice is eventually meted out. Although the story contains the basic plot structure and several narrative elements of the Khoi jackal trickster stories (dispossession of the game, refuge in a high place, a hot stone wrapped in fat), ǂKasin's version of the narrative destabilises its ostensive Khoi trickster structure and instead refashions the tale as a narrative permeated by the |Xam ideology of distribution and sharing, as is evident in the cooperative actions of the jackal community on the cliff:

He went and said to the other jackals, 'The lion is asking us for fat.' The other jackals told him to get a stone, and they all heated it. Another jackal took the stone, and they all heated it. The first jackal went and told the lion to wait. He went back and asked the other if the stone was heated. The others said yes. They took the stone out of the fire. The others told him to take fat from the pot which was on the fire and to fill up the dish. … Another jackal held the wet eland's skin. (ibid: 166)

The narrative clearly emphasises a multiplicity of actors engaged in communal action and cooperative behaviour, rather than individual heroic action, as in the conventional trickster tales. The hybrid nature of the tale and its anomalous relationship with other representations of jackals in the |Xam corpus is possibly explained by the genealogy of its narrator: ǂKasin was the son of a Koranna chief and a |Xam mother, and spoke both languages (Skotnes 2007: 220). ǂKasin went on to marry a |Xam wife and live with her community, and the hybrid nature of his story reflects a curious and revealing melding of two cultures. I am suggesting then that ǂKasin took a well-known fable from his own Khoi pastoralist cultural background and reshaped the narrative material to make it fit the ideological worldview of his adoptive |Xam community. The other jackal trickster fables in the Bleek and Lloyd archive, such as the stories 'The jackal deceives the hyena' and 'The jackal and the porcupine' are also drawn from Koranna sources and have undergone similar permutations.

The true trickster tales in |Xam orature are then not associated with the jackal but with the enigmatic |Kaggen or mantis figure, whose mischievous presence both destabilises and reinforces social conventions. A good example is ||Kabbo's famous opening story in *Specimens of Bushman folklore*, titled 'The mantis assumes the form of a hartebeest'. In this story the mantis disguises himself as a dead hartebeest, tricking the children to cut him up: 'The children jumped for joy (saying): "Our hartebeest! we shall eat great meat"' (Lloyd 1911: 23). But while they are busy dismembering the hartebeest, the pieces begin to move uncannily, eventually reconstituting themselves into the animal who chases the frightened children back home:

The children said: 'We thought that the hartebeest's horns were there, the hartebeest had hair. The hartebeest was one which had not an arrow's wound; while the hartebeest felt that the hartebeest would talk. Therefore, the hartebeest came and chased us, when we had put down the hartebeest's flesh. The hartebeest's flesh jumped together, while it springing gathered (itself) together, that it might mend, that it might mending hold together to the hartebeest's back. The hartebeest's back also joined on.

Therefore, the hartebeest ran forward, while his body was red, when he had no hair (that coat of hair in which he had been lying down), as he ran, swinging his arm like a man. (ibid: 26).

The extract here is an exemplary instance of the magical transformations of |Kaggen, the hybrid animal–human trickster. Like most of the Bleek and Lloyd material, the narrative is told in characteristic digressions, repetitions and reformulations, in which the narrative retains an open-ended allusive nature that is resistant to a linear reading and to neat closure. Unlike the jackal trickster in Khoi orature, the |Kaggen figure is much less reducible to a human subject, and the tale as a whole remains located in a mysterious and enigmatic mythical space. Matthias Guenther (1994: 259) writes that

> Bushman mythology is hauntingly asocial and pre-cultural, as well as liminal and surreal. This expressive domain is removed from, rather than informed by, social reality; indeed social and cultural reality is frequently inverted or disassembled. The beings hovering above and tampering with that reality are therianthropic creatures or precariously human men or women whose ontological state is fragile and slippery, ever ready to undergo transformation back into an alternate state of being.

In contrast to the mythic other-worldliness that makes the Bleek and Lloyd material so enigmatic, the Khoi tales, as we have seen, are more direct, earthy forms of story-telling in whose animal proxies we can easily recognise human characteristics. It is this groundedness and the social connection of the Khoi tales that allow them to adapt themselves more readily to changing historical circumstance, as is evident in the following discussion.

IV

By the time Bleek and Lloyd interviewed their informants in the late 19th century, |Xam society had already irrevocably disintegrated. After more than a hundred years of commando raids in which the |Xam had become the target for genocidal extermination and enslavement, their hunting-gathering lifestyle had been severely curtailed by encroaching faming settlement in their dry northern Cape heartlands. Driven by starvation to enter the service of farmers or risk arrest by engaging in stock theft, |Xam society was on the brink of dissolution (Bank 2006; Skotnes 2007). While the Cape Khoi society had earlier suffered a similar fate in the aftermath of a catastrophic smallpox epidemic in the early 18th century, and consequently became assimilated into a hybrid Cape underclass, autonomous Khoi societies persisted in the northern Cape regions of the colony. The Koranna waged successful wars against colonial encroachment in the mid-1860s (Penn 2005), forcing settlers to abandon the region, while the Nama retained a strong autonomous polity into the 20th century until eventually crushed by General von Trotha's infamous annihilation warfare, where they lost 50 per cent of their population (Adhikari 2005: 317).

The Khoi oral tradition, particularly in the case of the Nama, reflects a resisting engagement with colonial power, where the narrative template of the jackal trickster fable was adjusted to deal with the new realities on the northern frontier. This was achieved through a simple substitution of the figure of the lion with that of the boer or white settler. The lion, as we have seen earlier, was associated in both |Xam and Khoi culture with rapacious and dangerous predatoriness. This substitutive association had a long cultural history, as is evident in numerous colonial accounts, for example

Robert Gordon's travel diary from 1778 (in McGranaghan 2012: 205), where he records 'Sunei' Bushmen saying that 'they say we [colonists] are evil and come in the night like wolves [hyenas], and have hair like lions'. Boer commandos often attacked Bushman encampments at dawn, and the nocturnal habits of the enemy are further reinforced through the stereotypical figure of the bearded boer.

The connections between nocturnal, hairy predators (hyenas and lions) and powerful, hirsute settlers is a continuing cultural logic in the Khoi and Bushman imagination. In 2007, Jan van der Westhuizen (in Dyll-Myklebust 2011: 141), a member of the ‡Khomani group fighting SANParks for access to their ancestral hunting grounds in the Kalahari game reserve, used the motif of the jackal and the lion to illustrate the unequal power relations:

> We have also had a tremendous struggle with the Parks. We call them the young male lion as he is a rich gentleman and we are the small jackals that just get a small bit of bread, or just wait for a small piece here and there of the bones or to scratch open the stomach contents once the young male lion is finished. And we ask that they ... give back to the people what was lost to them over all the centuries.

This substitutive association of lion and boer is evident in several of the tales in the Schultze and Schmidt corpuses, showing clearly that Khoi orature was able to adapt dynamically to historical and social change in a manner that sought to critique and challenge colonial power relationships. In one of these stories, 'The jackal who sold a horse to the boers', the impish jackal outwits a greedy but dim-witted boer who eventually, once the penny has finally dropped, retaliates with characteristic and unrelenting violence:

> The jackal sold a horse to the Boers but beforehand he put some money into the horse's back hole. He then led the horse to them and said: 'Now I will first get some money from that horse!' And when the horse shat, he held his hand underneath, and they could see that the horse was shitting money.

> When the two Boers spoke about the price of the horse, the jackal said: 'I cannot put a price on this horse because I will not sell it. But any man would give me a wagon and its span of oxen for it.'

> The Boer gave him a wagon with a span of oxen. The jackal spanned in the oxen, climbed the wagon and said: 'Boer, wait for three days and the horse will shit money!' Thus spoke the jackal and he rode away.

> The two Boers however waited, and when the third day had passed, they waited until the fourth day. But the horse shat no money. Then they saddled their horses and gave chase. They came to a place next to the road and asked: 'Where is the wagon that came past here?' 'The day before he came past,' they were told.

They rode on and came to another place and asked: 'Where is the wagon that came past here?' And the people told them: 'Yesterday it came past here.'

They rode further and came to another place and asked: 'Where is the wagon that came past here?' And the people told them: 'This morning it came past here.'

So they rode further and when they came to the jackal's place they called: 'Uncle Fox, I will shoot you through your head!'

The jackal replied: 'What have I done wrong that you want to shoot me?'

The Boer said: 'You told me that the horse which does not shit money, shits money!'

But the jackal replied: 'No, do not speak to me so rudely! My older brother traded with you, not I.'

The Boers asked: 'Where is he?' And the jackal replied: 'There, further down that way is his place.' So the Boers went away to the other jackal who was innocent in order to shoot him dead. (Schultze 1907: 470–472)

In stories such as this, the antics of animal proxies, who are thinly disguised human subjects, are a window into the fraught colonial relationships between the settlers and the Khoi. Living on the fringes of a new colonial monetary economy that was beginning to replace the traded exchange of goods, the Khoi here mock the greedy acquisitiveness of the settler by conflating money with 'shit'. The narrative also imaginatively inverts the more common-place historical realities where indigenous people were routinely duped by colonial settlers in the form of unequal traded exchanges. In the early Dutch period, the Cape Khoi, for instance, bartered herds of oxen for a few nails, mirrors or other trinkets. In story-telling, a new inverted 'fictional reality' is manufactured through laughter and humorous consent which can rival or supplant their historical experience. The ending of the story is thus not necessarily readable as a retributive assertion of boer power, but it could also be understood as a narrative *mis-en-abyme*: that the next jackal will also in turn outwit the boer, and so on. Such 'discordant, unresolved endings of satiric texts can disrupt generic expectations' according to Connert and Combe (1995: 15). The open-ended conclusion and lack of closure are hall-marks of satiric narrative.

In the Schmidt corpus, such satire directed at settler authority proliferates and takes on even more extreme forms: in one tale, the jackal sells a boer a flute which is claimed to have the power to resurrect the dead. The duped boer kills his wife, but the flute proves useless. In another violent story the jackal sets the farmhouse on fire, becoming lord over the white children; in another fantastical cross-dressing narrative the jackal disguised himself as a woman and becomes a serving maid in a boer's household, using the opportunity to sleep with the boer's daughter. When she falls pregnant, the duped boer wants to kill the jackal, but he escapes (Schmidt 1989: 215). In such explicit, transgressive stories a counter-hegemonic resistance is clearly visible, but the substitutive logic established in Khoi culture (lion = boer) would also imply that seemingly naïve lion and jackal fables would be understood as if referring to contemporary lived reality, with the outwitted lion becoming a figure for the duped boer.

V

An overall evaluation of Khoi satire shows that Edward Rosenheim's famous definition of satire is particularly applicable. Rosenheim (in Ball 2003: 1) defines satire as 'an attack by means of manifest fiction upon discernable historic particulars'. The victims or dupes of satire must therefore never be entirely fictitious, but always be recognisable figures in actual lived reality, as in the case of the boers. The liberating comic potential of satire depends on such a referentiality in which the historic oppressor and the barely fictionalised target become merged. But satire is not simply reportage; it draws attention to its fantastical, absurd and at times grotesque aspects, an overt form of fictionalisation that shields its speakers from retribution. While satire seeks to associate the targeted figure of the dupe with 'discernable historic particulars' (ibid.), the genre as a whole therefore makes use of an extravagant and at times burlesque form of fictionality that draws attention to its non-referential literariness. Just like the jackal, who can take the moral high ground and reject the boer's accusation of 'speaking rudely', the Khoi story-teller can also shield himself behind the proxy figure of the crafty jackal and indulge in the fiction of simply telling innocent animal stories.

The deployment of the jackal in the Schultze and Schmidt corpuses suggests that Khoi orature was open to satirical and subversive discursive modes, but that on evidence of the Bleek and Lloyd records, the jackal trickster was absent from |Xam orature. The jackal trickster – an impish, subversive figure of identification in the Khoi imagination – could therefore become enlisted in a postcolonial strategy of resistance where the settler could be symbolically outwitted and defeated. Recalling Parkington's argument that Khoi society was already organised hierarchically long before the colonial intrusion into the Cape, we would expect that satiric modes of dissent could flourish in such a stratified social space and become transferrable to dealings with the colonial order. As Connert and Combe (1995: 15), in their discussion of the genre, put it, the primary function of satire is 'the process of unsettling hierarchies'. Conversely, the absence of satire as a discursive resource in |Xam culture would be keyed to a more egalitarian, classless social order in which such discursive strategies would have had no purpose. Roger Hewitt (1986: 32), in his early seminal study of the |Xam archive, notes the limited discursive engagement of the |Xam with the violent settler order which was imposing itself on their land: 'The dreadful conditions under which the |Xam lived at the time of the collection impinges only infrequently on the collected texts, and in only one narrative are the settlers even mentioned.'

Hewitt does not account for this ostensible gap in |Xam orature, and one may also speculate that Bleek's and Lloyd's ex-prisoner informants may have been reticent in sharing their candid views of the European invader. This article, though, suggests that deeper rooted differences in culture, visible in the oral tradition, need to be taken into account when considering how |Xam and Khoi societies engaged the colonial order.

In conclusion, then, the jackal stories show that the Khoi were able to deploy subversive humour – in particular, mocking satire – as a cultural strategy in dealing with the powerful, and to adapt them to the challenges of living with and under the colonial intruder, whereas in |Xam culture the option of this repertoire of discursive accommodation was evidently not available or took different forms that are not readily visible in the Bleek and Lloyd archive. Bushman and Khoi orature has a large overlap in terms of similar narrative material, but the way in which the building blocks of the story were narratively assembled, ordered and put to use, was different. This difference, I have suggested, may lie in the different social and cultural structures of Bushman and Khoi societies, where a hierarchically stratified pastoral society, as in the case of the Khoi, may be correlated to a culture in which mockery and satire flourished. These cultural modes were well suited to pull down the authority of the powerful and assert the agency of the weak, at least in an imaginary, fictional domain. In using animal proxies to mock the new boer masters who were imposing their violent order on the northern Cape region, the Khoi were thus able to reinvent an ancient but versatile figure in their folklore, the jackal trickster, and make him the imaginative vehicle for a symbolic reordering of colonial power relations in which they, and not the boer, could emerge triumphant.

Notes

1   The support of the National Research Foundation of South Africa (NRF) as well as the research fund of the University of the Western Cape is gratefully acknowledged. A much earlier, considerably different version of this article was published in the 2012 *South African Journal for Folklore Studies* 22(1): 1–13. This article draws on a conference presentation in Pietermaritzburg, in May 2013.

2   This famous archive of stories, personal testimony and paintings was assembled by the German philologist, Wilhelm Bleek, and his sister-in-law, Lucy Lloyd, in the 1870s. Their informants were |Xam prisoners who were serving sentences for stock-theft, murder and other offences in the Breakwater prison in Cape Town. What had originally been conceived of as a purely linguistic project to record a vanishing language, evolved into a massive and rich 12 000-page record of a culture, its mythology and vanishing way of life. For a good general introduction see Neil Bennun's *The broken string: the last words of an*

extinct people (2005), and Andrew Bank's careful historical contextualisation (2006). See also Pippa Skotnes' numerous publications, most recently *Claim to the country* (2010).

3   The use of racial terminology is complex and fraught in southern African studies. The term 'Bushman' instead of 'San' is now again widely in use, though guardedly. I have also referred to the |Xam when my comments have been limited to this group. Instead of Bleek's and Schultze's use of 'Hottentot', I have obviously used another less offensive term, choosing the generic, widely accepted word 'Khoi', or Nama and Koranna when referring specifically to these Khoi groupings. Where I have used the synthetic term 'Khoisan' to refer to both Khoi and Bushman societies collectively, this does not imply that these two groupings are conflated.

4   All direct references to the Bleek and Lloyd notebooks refer to the *Digital Lloyd and Bleek* resource (see Skotnes 2007). Most significant stories in the archive are published in Lloyd's *Specimens* (1911) and Lewis-Williams' anthology (2000).

References

Adhikari, M. 2008. 'Streams of blood and streams of money': new perspectives on the annihilation of the Herero and Nama peoples of Namibia, 1904–1908. *Kronos: Journal Of Cape History* 34(1): 303–320.

Baines, T. 1879. The story of a dam. *Folk-lore Journal* 1(July): 69–79.

Baines, T. 1880. The lion and the jackal. *Folk-lore Journal* 2(July): 54–57.

Ball, S. 2003. *Satire and the postcolonial novel*. London: Routledge.

Bank, A. 2006. *Bushmen in a Victorian world: the remarkable story of the Bleek–Lloyd collection of Bushman folklore*. Cape Town: Double Storey.

Bendix, R. 1997. *In search of authenticity: the formation of folklore studies*. Wisconsin: Wisconsin University Press.

Biesele, M. 1993. *Women like meat: the folklore and foraging ideology of the Kalahari Ju|'hoa*. Johannesburg: Wits University Press.

Bleek, W.H.I. 1864. *Reynard the Fox in South Africa, or Hottentot fables and tales*. London: Trübner.

Carruthers, J. and M. Arnold. 1995. *The life and work of Thomas Baines*. Cape Town: Fernwood Press.

Connert, B. and K. Combe, eds. 1995. *Theorising satire: essays in literary criticism*. New York: St Martin's.

Dubow, S. 2006. *A commonwealth of knowledge: science, sensibility and white South Africa*. New York: Oxford University Press.

Dyll-Myklebust, L. 2011. 'Lodge-ical' thinking and development communication: !Xaus lodge as a public-private-community partnership in tourism. Unpublished PhD thesis, University of KwaZulu-Natal.

Elphick, R. 1977. *Kraal and castle: Khoikhoi and the founding of white South Africa*. New Haven: Yale University Press.

Guenther, M. 1994. The relationship of Bushman art to ritual and folklore. In *Contested images: diversity in South African rock art research*, ed. T. Dowson and D. Lewis-Williams, 257–274. Johannesburg: Wits University Press.

Hewitt, R. 1986. *Structure, meaning and ritual in the narratives of the southern San.* Johannesburg: Wits University Press.

Lewis-Williams, D. 2000. *Stories that float from afar: ancestral folklore of the San of southern Africa.* College Station: Texas A&M University Press.

Lloyd, L., ed. 1911. *Specimens of Bushman folklore.* London: George Allen and Unwin.

Maingard, L.F. 1962. *Korana folktales.* Johannesburg: Wits University Press.

Mbembe, A. 2001. *On the postcolony.* Berkeley: University of California Press.

McGranaghan, M. 2012. Foragers on the frontiers: the |Xam Bushmen of the northern Cape, South Africa, in the nineteenth century. Unpublished PhD thesis, Oxford University.

Newton-King, S. 1999. *Masters and servants on the Cape eastern frontier, 1760–1803.* Cambridge: Cambridge University Press.

Parkington, J. 2007. ||Kabbo's sentence. In *Claim to the country: the archive of Wilhelm Bleek and Lucy Lloyd,* ed. P. Skotnes, 75–89. Cape Town: Jacana.

Penn, N. 2005. *The forgotten frontier: colonist and Khoisan on the Cape's northern frontier in the 18th century.* Cape Town: Double Storey.

Schmidt, S. 1989. *Catalogue of the Khoisan folktales of southern Africa.* Hamburg: Helmut Buske Verlag.

Schultze, L. 1907. *Aus Namaland und Kalahari: Bericht an die königlich Preussische Akademie der Wissenschaften zu Berlin über eine Forschungsreise im westlichen und zentralen Südafrika in den Jahren 1903–1905.* Jena: Gustav Fischer.

Skotnes, P. 2007. *Claim to the country: the archive of Wilhelm Bleek and Lucy Lloyd.* Cape Town: Jacana.

Skotnes, P., ed. 2007. The digital Bleek and Lloyd. Available as an optical computer disk in Skotnes (2007), as well as online: http://lloydbleekcollection.cs.uct.ac.za/index.html

Wessels, M. 2010. *Bushman letters: interpreting |Xam narrative.* Johannesburg: Wits University Press.

Wittenberg, H. 2012. Wilhelm Bleek and the Khoisan imagination: a study of censorship, genocide and colonial science. *Journal of Southern African Studies* 38(3): 667–679.

'Di-xɛrretən and the lioness'[1]: text and landscape of a |Xam narrative

José Manuel de Prada-Samper

Abstract

Focusing on the |Xam narrative 'Di-xɛrretən and the lioness', its recording history and possible connection with Springbokoog and its rock engravings, this article proposes a method for editing the |Xam *kukummi* (tales, accounts) collected by W. Bleek and L.C. Lloyd in the 19th century, making the case for the need to go beyond the received text of narratives and edit the English translations found in the manuscripts not only by modernising Lloyd's English, as other editors have done, but also by making informed changes on the text based on the |Xam original, which can be accessed by means of D.F. Bleek's *Bushman dictionary* (1956) and her grammatical sketches of the |Xam language. Using as a theoretical basis the work of Dell Hymes on the presence of 'measured verse' in Chinookan narratives, this article also proposes to lay out the texts in short lines.

Introduction

This article focuses on the |Xam narrative 'Di-xɛrretən and the Lioness', dictated by |Haŋǂkass'o to Lucy Lloyd on 21 January 1879. The recording history and formal features of the narrative will be discussed, along with its likely connection with Springbokoog, a major rock engraving site in the Northern Cape. A method is proposed for editing the English translations of the |Xam *kukummi* (plural of *kum*; a tale, piece of news or gossip) that form the bulk of the ethnographic and literary archive known as the Bleek and Lloyd Collection (hereafter, BLC). This method aims to improve the readability of the narratives and to better appreciate their aesthetic value as written records of oral performances. An edited and annotated edition of 'Di-xɛrretən and the lioness' is included as illustration.

Taking down and translating the text

|Haŋǂkass'o dictated this story to Lucy Lloyd on 21 January 1879, at the very beginning of his second and last year in Mowbray. The text occupies pages 8177–8197 of notebook L.VIII.25 or LL100.[2] Although other texts in this notebook were not translated until April 1897, when Lloyd was living in Germany, the translation of the story of Di-xɛrretən appears to have been made shortly after its dictation, on 26 January, when |Haŋǂkass'o drew a sketch to show the position of the different characters in the story. Both the text and the sketch were published in *Specimens of Bushman folklore* (Lloyd 1911: 163–169; hereafter *Specimens*).

'Di-xɛrretən and the lioness' is a good example of |Haŋǂkass'o's style: terse, patterned, showing a strong sense of overall structure. As is characteristic of his performances, the main event in the tale is repeated several times, in this case seven. 'Di-xɛrretən' belongs to a series of *kukummi* that he dictated in 1879, during his second year at Mowbray. Many of these were left untranslated. With one notable exception (the story of 'Biting-torn-apart and the lioness', Lloyd 1889: #37, De Prada-Samper 2009: 278–296), the *kukummi* dictated by |Haŋǂkass'o in 1879 tend to be short. This could be attributed to the fact that Lucy Lloyd was aware that |Haŋǂkass'o would not remain in Mowbray for long, as she had not been able to bring his small son to Cape Town. Also, in 1879 Lloyd was working at the Grey Collection, which reduced the amount of time she could devote to her research with |Haŋǂkass'o (on the circumstances surrounding Lloyd's work with |Haŋǂkass'o see Bank [2006: 277–301] and Bennun [2004: 308–319]). This explains not only why the narratives she collected that year from her |Xam teacher tend to be short, but also why many of them remained untranslated when he left Mowbray, which, in turn, explains why many of the left-hand pages of the notebook lack additional information about the plot and the characters that Lloyd normally elicited during the translation process.

That |Haŋǂkass'o complied with Lloyd's wishes to shorten the stories so as to record as many of them as possible, does not mean they are mere summaries or fragments, as some commentators have said (e.g., Biesele 1996: 145). There is reason to believe Lloyd's request for shorter versions suited |Haŋǂkass'o better, because an overall examination of the narratives and testimonies he dictated indicates that, as a storyteller, he preferred to give terser and more dramatically concentrated renderings of the narratives. In connection with this, it is interesting to note that 'Di-xɛrretən' was taken down in a single day, possibly during a single sitting. It is true that these stories often lack essential details, but we must bear in mind that all stories, even more traditional ones, possess a certain degree of assumed knowledge. In the light of this, |Haŋǂkass'o's 'fragmentary' narratives are complete in the sense that he told them to Lloyd as he would have to a |Xam audience, taking for granted a knowledge of the details that, of course, Lloyd seldom had. As Dell Hymes (1981: 322) says in relation to the telling of Clackamas tales:

> Narrative performances varied on another dimension as well – that of explicitness and length. An admired narrator could spin a story to any length desired by filling in detail, but could also convey the essence of a story in brief [...] Those who already knew the stories would have them brought to mind by the details that were given. The assumption that a part stands adequately for the whole remains alive, and people who credit one with knowledge of the stories sometimes act surprised that one has to ask about a detail that had not been given. [...] A story ends, as a story and an event, but the body of narrative and the world of stories is unending.

This is true, too, of those of |Haŋǂkass'o's *kukummi* that seem to be 'incomplete'. Being aware of this does not, however, help us to reconstruct the untold part of the narratives, and because of this the full sense of several of |Haŋǂkass'o's stories remains obscure. Having other |Xam variants of the same stories, or similar stories from related traditions could help fill in the gaps, but unfortunately in most cases we lack this complementary material. As in the case of 'Di-xeξrretən and the lioness', Lloyd often asked for additional information, but even in this story many things lack explanation (e.g., When did the lioness take away the children? What is the nature of her relationship with Di-xeξrretən?).[3]

Text and landscape

In her seminal article 'The power of a place in understanding southern San rock engravings' (1988), Janette Deacon established the importance that landscape and myth had in the belief system and rainmaking rituals of the |Xam, and suggested that '[i]f the power lay in the place and its legendary significance as well, then it would attract rock art and localize it' (1988: 138). Deacon focused on a *kum* told by |Haŋǂkass'o in which the mythical agama lizard becomes the Strandberg, three prominent hills south-east of Kenhardt. Deacon also mentions Springbokoog, a farm about 30km north of Vanwyksvlei in the Northern Cape, that has an unusual concentration of impressive rock engravings, as a place that 'attracted rainmakers/ artists over long periods' (ibid: 137). I argue that the *kum* discussed here is closely connected not only with this place, but also with the engravings themselves.

I noticed the possible connection of Springbokoog with this *kum* during my first visit to the farm in 2005. In 2010 I located among the Bleek and Lloyd materials kept at the Iziko-South African Museum in Cape Town a loose piece of paper with a note explaining some of the features in the sketch accompanying the story published in *Specimens*. The note – which Lloyd must have misplaced at some point – states that two of the ravines drawn in the sketch descend on the other side of the hill. This newly-found document reinforces the possibility that |Haŋǂkass'o was describing a specific place, a place with a wide hill cut by ravines, and with water and resources enough to allow several bands to camp not far from one another. As far as I know this type of landscape is found only in the vicinity of Springbokoog, not in the rest of the extensive area associated with the |Xam who collaborated with Bleek and Lloyd.

Although not included in it, the site is part of the general area covered by the map sketched by ||Kabbo and Bleek in 1871 (Deacon 1986). The map, however, includes Olifantvlei, whose |Xam name is !Nouraka !kwa. According to Deacon (ibid: 141), 'it is possible that Springbokoog once formed part of larger farm, Olifantvlei, an important landmark for the local |Xam'. There are indications that the area would have been familiar to Bleek and Lloyd's informants. ||Kabbo died on the farm of Charles St. Leger Devenish on 25 January 1876, and !Kwabba-aŋ, his wife, died on the same farm in January of the following year (Lloyd 1889: 5). The exact location of Devenish's farm remains unknown, but we can be certain it was not very far from the present town of Vanwyksvlei. Devenish was also instrumental in |Haŋǂkass'o's decision to travel to Mowbray with his wife and baby. The point of departure of his long and tragic journey, during which both his wife and baby perished, was Vanwyksvlei (Lloyd 1889: 5, Edith and Dorothea Bleek 1909: 41).

Although the territory that both ||Kabbo and |Haŋǂkass'o considered theirs is in the Flat Country, about 50km north-west of Vanwyksvlei, they moved with their families to the Vanwyksvlei area after their return to Bushmanland from Cape Town in the early 1870s, possibly because of Devenish's friendly disposition towards the |Xam. We know, too, that |Haŋǂkass'o's father 'was a mountain Bushman from |Khu: !humm' (LL 76: 6052). Although the mountain territory is normally associated with the Kareeberge (Bank 2006: 290) there are sound reasons to think the |Xam notion of this part of their homeland encompassed not only the Karee 'mountains', but also the generally quite hilly area north of them (that includes Springbokoog and neighbouring farms) which is quite visible in the distance as one travels westwards from Vanwyksvlei to Verneukpan. The location of |Khu: !humm is unknown, but it may have been near Vanwyksvlei. The presence of |Haŋǂkass'o and his parents-in-law in that area could then have resulted as much from Devenish's hospitality as from the former's connections in that part of the |Xam territory. This is relevant because there is evidence that at least part of |Haŋǂkass'o's repertory reflects the traditions of the 'mountain Bushmen'. 'Di-xɛrretən and the lioness' is one of the *kukummi* that appears to have originated there.

The *kum* describes a place with enough resources to allow a substantial number of bands to camp in the area. Given the favourable environment, Morris and Beaumon (1994: 26) suggest that 'it is possible to see Springbokoog site complex as an aggregation centre'. The main engraving site on the farm is located on 'a low hill to the north of a permanent spring' and has 'more than 150 engraved rocks including the older fine lines, pecked and recent scratched engravings' (Deacon 1988: 137). The hill in question has a flat top with a very extensive surface, which fits the description in the story closely; it is cut by ravines, in which the remains of several places of habitation can be seen at different points.

Figure 1: Google Earth aerial view of Springbokoog and environs.

The name(s) that the |Xam gave to this area are uncertain, but Springbokoog, 'the eye of the springbok', could very well be a literal translation of their name for the main water source, which in |Xam would have been *whai tsaxau*. We know of other |Xam toponyms with the element *tsaxau* ('eye') in them, including ||Gwattǝn-tsaξxau-!ka-!hu, 'the Cat's eye's waterhole', located 'on the other side of |Ku !khoξa: or "Sondak-Pan"' (LL 98: 8012'), that is, about 40km north of Springbokoog. It is unclear why, in the context of the |Xam worldview, certain waterholes were called 'eyes', although it seems clear that the name applied to permanent springs. In a semi-desert, where water sources are few and far apart and often seasonal, these permanent springs must have been considered by the |Xam as very special places. In all likelihood they were associated with the Otherworld and with supernatural potency, since they were the preferred dwelling of *!khwa-ka xoro*, the 'rain's bull'. In the |Xam language, 'eye' is sometimes used to convey the idea of intense heat. For example, the hottest moment of noon was called ||*koiŋ tsaxau*, 'the sun's eye' (*Specimens*, 399n, Bleek 1932: 338, 2004: 121), and live coals and sparks were called |*i tsaxau*, 'the eyes of fire' (*Dictionary*, p. 213). There is also the connection of eyes with stars, supernatural potency and springbok, beautifully stated in the well-known *kum* by |Haŋǂkass'o (*Specimens*, p. 80–83) in which he explains that in summer the stars 'cursed' (|*k"ao*) the eyes of the springbok (*wai tsaxaitən*). Another connection worth noting is that of eyes with water, resurrection and regeneration, as shown in the *kum* of !Gaunu-tsaxau, son of Mantis (|Kaggen) and the baboons, at the end of which Mantis puts the eye of his dead child in the waterhole and expresses the wish that he may become 'as he was before' (*Specimens*, p. 31). Interestingly, the name of the child, !Gaunu-tsxau, means 'the eye of !gaunu' – in all likelihood the star Vega, whose appearance in late February, together with Altair (‖*Xwhai* |*aiti*) and other stars of the neighbouring Aquila constellation, was associated with the end of the hot season and the coming (usually in March) of the late summer rains that renewed and sweetened the brackish pit water and other water sources, started the springbok migrations, and made bulbs and flowers grow again (*Specimens*, pp. 78–81, 230–231).

A landscape inhabited by stones

The presence of a permanent spring of the *tsaxau* or 'eye' type, in combination with other favourable traits in the area that has a richer vegetation than that of the Flat country, would have made Springbokoog a unique place. This explains, at least in part, the quality, quantity and originality of the rock engravings in the area, especially at its main site, which includes several 'spatially localized images sets' (Morris and Beaumont 1994: 27). Among these images is a group of felines, engraved on contiguous rocks – felines that resemble lionesses with their mouths wide open. One of them is situated next to a human figure. These visual images are very similar to the verbal one at the end of the *kum*, when the lioness opens her mouth wide to grab Di-xɛrretən's 'big head'.

It is not unlikely that this set of images is connected with the *kum*. Di-xɛrretən, a man whose 'head is a stone', could be the personification of one of the engraved boulders in the site, not necessarily one of the abovementioned group, although this is a strong possibility. That the |Xam thought engraved images could move is supported by ‖Kabbo's testimony on 'presentiments', which opens with the words:

The *!gwe:* of the |Xam people are in their bodies.

They talk,

they move,

they make their bodies [of the |Xam] move. (LL 34: 2531, *Specimens*, pp. 330–331)

As argued elsewhere (De Prada-Samper, in press), there are solid reasons to think that here the term *!gwe:* means 'images' rather than 'letters' (as Lloyd rendered it), and refers to the rock engravings.

Figure 2: Rock engraving of feline with mouth wide open, and human figure, Springbokoog, main site. Photo by the author.

The idea that these rocks could be animate will not surprise anyone who has visited the central and eastern parts of the former |Xam territory. Even when not engraved (and, of course, only a tiny fraction are), the brown boulders, randomly scattered for kilometres across hills and plains, with their impressive array of shapes, sizes and colours, are a presence in the landscape that conveys the feeling that the rocks actually inhabit it. The data strongly suggest that the |Xam saw the dolerite boulders – even those that were not engraved – as more than mere rocks.

In their landmark article 'Through the veil: San rock paintings and the rock face', Lewis-Williams and Dowson (1990: 5) argue that for the Bushman artists 'the rock was as meaningful a ritual element as the paint'. The same can be said of the rock engravings. In comparing the traditions of Aboriginal Australia and southern Africa, Paul Taçon and Sven Ouzman (2004: 40) call attention to widespread beliefs in 'worlds within stone' and in the idea of rock 'leading to another dimension of being'. Referring specifically to the artistic tradition of the southern African hunter-gatherers, the authors conclude that rock engravings 'inform us of a concern with the inner spirit world beyond the visible rock surface':

The very act of engraving – removing the dark outer rock cortex to expose the lighter, honey-coloured rock beneath – places the engraved image either directly within the spirit world or in a somewhat ambiguous space, part way into the inner spirit world but still visible and tangible from the outer ordinary world. (ibid: 52)

The representation, common in rock paintings, of figures that appear to emerge from the rock face or plunge into it, is found in the engraving tradition of the different areas of the |Xam home territory (see Figure 3), including boulders at Varskans (near Brandvlei, in the Grass Country), Franseville (south of Kenhardt, in the Flat Country) and in Springbokoog itself.

Figure 3: A pecked eland emerges from the rough part of the rockface. Franseville farm, Flat Country, Northern Cape, March 2001. Photo by the author.

In addition, the *kukummi* recorded by Bleek and Lloyd provide textual evidence that the |Xam saw the rocks in their home territory not only as potential doorways to a supernatural world, but also as being themselves endowed with life. In the *kum* about the Blue Crane and her friend the frog, told by |Haŋǂkass'o, the frog's husband, !kwoξmmaiŋ|ka ||kãu, runs away from his wife and 'goes in' what the narrator, in an explanatory gloss, said was 'a stone, a flat stone' (LL 107: 8820, 8820'; De Prada-Samper 2009: 323–233). In the continuation of the story, Blue Crane searches in vain for !kwoꞬmmaiŋ|ka ||kãu, and ends up being devoured by the evil lions Mat and Belt (LL 107: 8794–8811; De Prada-Samper 2009: 234–237). In the beginning of the tale Blue Crane recalls how, when pursuing her friend's husband, 'I snatching missed him, / as he entered in, / as he entered in here' (LL 107: 8795). Again, 'in here' refers to 'a stone (a flat stone)' (LL 107: 8795').

In another *kum* told by |Haŋǂkass'o (De Prada-Samper 2009: 250–256), also connected with Mat and Belt, the young Rhebok and her mother hide from the lions in the house of the ||*hoꞬru* (possibly a species of gecko). At one point in the story, the child, as instructed by its mother, is sitting behind the ||*hoꞬru* 'upon a bare place', about which the narrator explains that 'bushes were not there; for a rock it was' (LL 107: 8851, 8851'). When the lions try to get hold of the child, the stones 'came together', covering the young Rhebok, and causing the lions to break their teeth on the hard surface (LL 107: 8851–8852). Other examples could be offered, but those given here probably suffice to show that the |Xam believed in a world of living rocks – a world to which Di-xɛrretən belongs.[4]

The notion that a painted or engraved stone can be a supernatural being is known in other parts of the world. The Luiseño of southern California consider a painted rock in their territory to be woman of the early people (True and Griset 1988); Patricia Vinnicombe (2010: 243) found that for the Aboriginals of the Kimberley Mountains in Western Australia, 'the images, painted or engraved, are considered to be active and alive, and they are talked to as though they were real'. In the case of the |Xam there is evidence to conclude they had very similar beliefs regarding the rock engravings in their home territory. If so, the engravings were, for them, much more than simple representations; they would have considered them as living presences in the landscape, visible manifestations of the spirit world.

Editing Lucy Lloyd's translations

Returning to 'Di-xɛrretən', it can be argued that behind Lloyd's wish, expressed in the preface (see *Specimens*, vii), to make the book a learning tool for future students of the |Xam language, lies an awareness of the provisional nature of her translations – even the published ones,[5] which she probably saw less as a finished product than as an aid to access the |Xam original (see also Wessels 2012). She must have been quite aware of the fact that her own knowledge of the culture and world-view behind the texts was extremely limited, so that the full sense of many of the key metaphors and concepts conveyed by the stories and testimonies told by her informants, were beyond her grasp.

The issue of the translations of the |Xam texts in the BLC is a complex one, and I can only offer a bare outline here. As shown by entries in the preliminary pages of the notebooks, most of the texts were translated with the help of the teller soon after the testimony had been dictated. In other cases a different informant helped to translate a previously collected text. Other texts were translated by Lloyd when she was already living in Europe, years after they had been collected. Still others were translated by Dorothea Bleek, some while her aunt was still living and many others after her death in 1914. Although, generally speaking, Dorothea's style of translation follows her aunt's very closely, she departs from it in a number of points, using an English that is less Victorian and more steeped in the 20th century, and incorporates into her versions her more refined knowledge of certain aspects of |Xam grammar and vocabulary. Unfortunately, most of Dorothea's translations are undated, making it next to impossible to study the evolution of her style and criteria.

Referring to Bleek and Lloyd's style of translation of the unpublished texts, Guenther (1989: 25) writes that it 'impaired' their readability. He described this style as 'direct, word by word and passage by passage', resulting in a 'necessarily fragmented and irregular' syntax. He also mentions the 'antiquated and Victorian' diction and the use of biblical archaisms (ibid.). Lewis-Williams (2000: 38) suggests that the effort to keep the translation aligned with the |Xam original prevented the possibility of 'developing the longer, grammatically coherent sentences that are characteristic of English', adding that the 'loose punctuation' of the translations sometimes obscures the sense of the texts.

Regarding the arrangement of the narratives, Lewis-Williams (ibid.) observes that, when editing some of them himself, he 'resisted the very real temptation' to arrange them in verse, on the grounds that '[p]erhaps versification comes close to prettification, and the starkness of the narrator's dictated text, in its very proseness, better conveys the tragedy that permeates the whole collection'. This odd statement makes one suspect that the real problem with the 'verse' arrangement (an option already suggested by Brown [1998: 57–61]) was that it would occupy many more pages and would be an obstacle to the commercial viability of the book.

My own position is that the features mentioned by Guenther and Lewis-Williams (archaisms, odd syntax, etc.) do indeed compromise the appreciation of the texts as literature, and that any editor has to contemplate aspects like the standardisation of the syntax and the adoption of a less literal, and more literary, turn of phrase, while avoiding the temptation of 'domesticating' the narratives by submitting them to their own aesthetic conceptions. The grammatical and lexical tools available to us make it possible for the editor of |Xam literature to make *informed* modifications in the English text as we have it – modifications that can go beyond revising archaisms or syntax.

Regarding the page layout, the 'verse' arrangement that tempted Lewis-Williams is arguably the best option, although it can best be described as a short-line ethnopoetic arrangement. The theoretical framework for this is provided by Dell

Hymes (1981). The breakthrough that led Hymes to opt for this kind of arrangement was the identification, in several Chinookan languages, of linguistic markers that signalled the beginning and end of lines. Although it is possible that the |Xam language has similar markers, in the *kukummi* the basic unit of meaning and syntax is the clause. As D.F. Bleek (1929: 172) observes, |Xam speech 'is broken up into small clauses, joined either by connectives which precede the subject, by relatives, or by the meaning'.

It is important to stress that by arranging the |Xam texts in short lines I do not intend to transform them into poems, although the inherently poetic nature of the *kukummi*, both in content and in form, is beyond doubt. Wilhelm Bleek (1875: 15) was aware of this, and was even open to the possibility of considering some narratives as poetry, writing that 'it is not improbable that several of the larger mythological pieces are compositions, and ought perhaps properly to be placed under this head [poetry]. A further study of Bushman poetry and its peculiarities must decide this question.' I am convinced that if Bleek had been able to undertake such 'further study' and had decided that the *kukummi* in question were 'compositions', he would have opted for a short-line arrangement.

I am breaking with the typographical convention of printing as prose a type of verbal creation, oral narrative, that is much better served in this way (see also Tomaselli 1997). The much maligned 'repetitions' that abound in the *kukummi* become, for example, more 'palatable' to the reader once the text is presented in short lines. This arrangement also facilitates a greater concentration on the details and nuances of the narrative and, in so far as it also highlights the internal structure of each story, it contributes to a greater appreciation of its formal aspects and brings us closer to at least some of its oral-performative aspects that otherwise tend to remain hidden in the transcript of the narrative. As Robert Bringhurst (2008: 188) notes, learning to read this kind of transcript is akin to 'learning to read music'. This said, it is hoped that, as Wilhelm Bleek (1875: 15) wished, a proper study of |Xam 'poetry and its peculiarities' will eventually be undertaken so we can have a deeper knowledge of the prosody of |Xam verbal arts.

Di-xɛrretən and the lioness[6]

Editing criteria

My edition of 'Di-xɛrretən and the lioness' is based mainly on the original manuscript (LL 107: 8177–8197). However, as the text in *Specimens* (pp. 162–169) offers a more refined translation, I have taken it into consideration and added all the major corrections Lloyd made in the English version. My edited version is, in turn, based on a detailed 'diplomatic' transcription of the original which cannot be included here for reasons of space, although interested readers can compare my version with that in *Specimens*. In the edited text, Bleek's orthography has been converted to the system used by D.F. Bleek, that is, the International Phonetic Alphabet (IPA) as it existed in her time.

Following the principles expounded above the English has been modernised to convert Lloyd's 'word by word' literal translation into one in which the literary nature of the narrative can be better appreciated. To do this I revised the syntax and, in some cases, the use of verbal tenses. The more substantial 'informed modifications' are explained in the notes, but not the elision of the word *au*, that Lloyd always translated as 'while/when', but which is often redundant in English or can be rendered as 'and'. I have not noted the instances in which a noun is replaced by a pronoun, or vice versa.

The storyteller's explanations are included as footnotes, as are Lloyd's own notes, or the storyteller's clarifications. Following Lloyd's practice throughout *Specimens*, I replace the informant's European name, Jantje, with his |Xam name, |Haŋǂkass'o. The explanations in brackets are Lloyd's. Numbers in brackets and in bold type refer to the original manuscript pages.

The narrative is divided into six sections, each of which is given a short descriptive title, so as to highlight its formal structure, as normally this kind of division is not really necessary in |Xam narratives, except in some of the longer and more complex texts.

The edited text (8177)

Di-xɛrretən[7] and the lioness
|Haŋǂkass'o from ǂKaξmmi and also from |Xabbi-aŋ when he was older
Dictated 21 January, 1879
(LL 107: 8177–8197 = *Specimens* pp. 162–169)

i. The Lioness gathers in her camp the people's children
A long time ago,[8] Di-xɛrretən,[9]
when the Lioness was at the waterhole[10] dipping up water,[11]
had gone there to dip up water,
Di-xɛrretən, aware[12]
that the Lioness had gathered **(8178)** together the people's children...[13]
The Lioness knew
that her chest was ill;
that was the reason why[14]

157

she had gathered together the children of the people.
The[15] children could live with her,
the children **(8179)** *could work for her,*
because she was an ill
and couldn't do hard work...[16]
that being so,
Di-xɛrretən went to her camp[17]
when she was dipping up water.
For that reason
Di-xɛrretən went to her camp
when she was absent. **(8180)**

ii. Di-xɛrretən sends the children to their homes

Once there, Di-xɛrretən walked towards the children.
Di-xɛrretən went to the camp,
he reached the children.
Di-xɛrretən sat down.
And Di-xɛrretən said:
"Oh **(8181)** children sitting here! [18]
The fire of your people
is that at the top of the ravine[19]
which descends from the hilltop."[20]
And then
two children stood up,
they returned to their own people. **(8182)**
Di-xɛrretən said again:
"O children sitting here!
The fire of your people
is that below the top of the ravine
that descends on this side (of the hill)."
And three children[21] **(8183)** left,
they returned to their own people.
And he said again:
"O child sitting here!
The fire of your people
is that below the top of the ravine

that descends on this side (of the hill)."
And the **(8184)** child stood up,
he left,
the child returned to its own people.
He said again:
"O children sitting here!
The fire of your people
is that below the top of the ravine[22] **(8185)**
that descends on this side (of the hill)."
And two children stood up,
they went away,
they went away to their own people.[23]
And again he said:
"O children sitting here!
The fire **(8186)** of your people
is that at the top of the ravine
that descends from the hilltop."
And two children stood up,
they went away.
And again he said:
"O children **(8187)** sitting here!
The fire of your people
is that at the top of the ravine
that descends from the hilltop."
And three children stood up,
they went away,
they went away to their own people. **(8188)**
And again he said:
"O children sitting here![24]
The fire of your people
is that at the top of the ravine
which comes down from the hilltop."
And two children stood up,
they **(8189)** went away,
they went away to their own people,
while Di-xɛrretən sat and waited for the Lioness.

iv. The Lioness notices the absence of the children

And the Lioness came cantering from the water,

in this way she returned.

She **(8190)** came along looking (at the camp).

She did not spot the children.

And she exclaimed:

"Why do the children children children children (stammering with rage)

the children not do so to me?[25]

and the children do not play here,

as they **(8191)** usually to do?

It must be this man who sits at the camp,

his head looks like that of Di-xɛrretən,[26] yes."[27]

And she was angry, yes,

when she spotted Di-xɛrretən.[28]

She exclaimed: **(8192)**

"That one there is Di-xɛrretən!"

v. The Lioness confronts Di-xɛrretən

She arrived at the camp.

She exclaimed:

"Show me the children!"[29]

And Di-xɛrretən exclaimed:

"They are not our[30] children."

And the Lioness **(8193)** exclaimed:

"*Oeja!*[31]

Stop saying that!

Give me the children!"

Di-xɛrretən exclaimed:

"They are not our children!"

And the Lioness grabbed his head.

She exclaimed:

"*Xababu*"[32] (making a growling noise) **(8194)**

to the other one's head.

And she exclaimed:

"*Ouuu, |i! |i! |i! |i!*[33]

My teeth!

This must be why
this cursed[34] man's big head came to sit in front of my hut!"
And **(8195)** Di-xɛrretən said:
"I told you
that they were not our children."
The Lioness exclaimed:
"Curse![35] It really had to be yours,
the big head that came to sit (here). [36] **(8196)**
They were not our children."[37]

vi. Di-xɛrretən goes back
And he stood up,
he went away.
And the Lioness remained in her hut,
angry because Di-xɛrretən had come
and taken **(8197)** away from her
the children who had lived peacefully with her.
She knew
that she had taken good care of them,
she had lovingly
taken care of them.

Notes

1   My gratitude to Michael Wessels, whose support has been crucial in continuing the field and archival research on which this article is based. An earlier version was discussed in November 2010 during a workshop at the University of Cape Town's (UCT) Archive and Public Culture Research Initiative; my thanks especially to Professor Carolyn Hamilton, NRF Chair in Archive and Public Culture, for having invited me to join the group and for her valuable suggestions. Thanks also to Professor Pippa Skotnes, director of the UCT's Centre for Curating the Archive, for granting me (and extending several times) the postdoctoral fellowship that allowed me to pursue my research in South Africa, from September 2010 until April 2012. Thanks also to Janette Deacon, without whose pioneering and seminal work on the home territory of the |Xam my researches would not have been possible, and without whose generosity my first visit to Springbokoog, in May 2005, would never have occurred. Thanks go to Rina van Wyk for her hospitality and assistance during that and subsequent visits, and to Charles C. Kemp, the present owner of Springbokoog, and his son Karl. Last, I thank the anonymous reviewers of this article for their valuable suggestions.
2   L.VIII.25 means that the material is in notebook 25 of those *kukummi* collected by Lloyd (L) from |Haŋǂkass'o, whose code reference was the Roman numeral VIII. From now on, for convenience's sake, I use the number assigned to a given notebook on The

Digital Bleek and Lloyd: http://lloydbleekcollection.cs.uct.ac.za/index.html, followed by the page numbers. The notebooks derived from Lloyd's work are preceded by LL. The original manuscripts are kept in Special Collections section of the UCT libraries, where the collection is listed under the reference BC 151.

3 A potentially fruitful way of filling these gaps is turning to the knowledge of the contemporary descendants of the |Xam who still live in the area from which the Bleek–Lloyd informants came. Recent research has shown that, far from being mere acculturated 'residues' of the former hunter-gatherer bands, these descendants are in possession of a culture of their own that includes a rich oral literature – one that, in many ways, connects with that documented by Bleek and Lloyd in the 19th century (see De Prada-Samper and Winberg 2012, Swartz et al. in press).

4 One anonymous reviewer noted that 'the motif of people disappearing into rocks occurs in other tales from southern Africa' and mentioned Herero and Nama stories collected in the late 19th and early 20th century. Schmidt (2013, 2: 618) lists these and also cites Xhosa, Zulu and Venda parallels, as well as a few others from different parts of Africa. The folk motif present in those stories (D1552.2, 'Mountain opens to magic formula'), however, is not the one found in the |Xam stories, in which the characters penetrate the rock without needing a formula to do so (a form of motif D1552, 'Mountains or rocks open and close'), or the rocks act in a certain way as if of their own accord, or because a character orders them to do so (D2153, 'Magic control of rocks').

5 The published translations are not as 'raw' as the unpublished ones. A comparison of the translations published in *Specimens* with the notebook version and the printer's manuscript of the book shows how Lloyd refined her renderings of the stories, so as to make them more readable, even while retaining most of their strangeness.

6 Sigrid Schmidt has assigned this story number KH 886A1 in her *Catalogue of Khoisan folktales of southern Africa* (2013). For scans of the original manuscript, see http://lloydbleekcollection.cs.uct.ac.za/stories/837/index.html. – Ed.

7 **(8177')a**
His head was a stone.

8 In *Specimens*, 'formerly'. The |Xam has ||*kwaŋ haǯ oä* ||*nau*. As D.F. Bleek explains (in Bleek 1929: 166), *haǯ oä*, which in some instances, as here, can be preceded and followed by several verbal particles, is an opening formula for stories that tell about remote times, generally those connected with the Early People. – Ed.

9 **(8177')b**
He was a man of the early race.

10 In the manuscript and *Specimens* 'water', faithfully translating the |Xam original, although here 'water', as happens often in the |Xam corpus, stands for the place from which it is obtained. – Ed.

11 **(8177')c**
I think
that she probably dipped up water
with the stomach of a gemsbok,
because she killed gemsbok.

12 In the manuscript and *Specimens*, 'felt'. In the |Xam column *tatti e:*, literally 'felt which'. The verb 'to feel' (*tatti*) is used often in the |Xam corpus, but in many cases it clearly conveys the sense of 'being aware' or 'knowing'. In the lines that follow this one, the |Xam has *au ||khaǯŋ tatti e:*, translated in the manuscript and *Specimens* as 'because the lioness felt', although the function of this kind of construction appears to be that of stressing a condition or state. – Ed.

13 The |Xam, like other Bushman peoples of southern Africa, suffered greatly from the invading farmers' proclivity to kidnap their children and force them to work on their farms. This *kum* may perhaps be understood in the context of the devastating effect of this practice on the |Xam bands. – Ed.

14 In manuscript and *Specimens*, 'Therefore'. The formulistic phrase *he ti hing e:* (shortened sometimes as *he tikən e:*) means literally 'those things they are', and can also be rendered as 'therefore, then, that being so, this is why' (*Dictionary*, p. 59). Also as 'and it is so' (LL 18: 305) and 'then it was that' (LL 100: 8236). – Ed.

15 In manuscript and *Specimens*, 'that the children', but the 'that' is not in the |Xam column. Lloyd often added these connectives, perhaps to tone down the more 'telegraphic' nature of the |Xam narrative discourse. – Ed.

16 The lines I have put in italics and between dots somewhat interrupt the flow of the narrative, being the kind of information that usually goes in the verso page of the notebook. It is as if, having started the story, |Haŋǂkass'o realised he at least needed to explain to Lloyd why the lioness had gathered those children. – Ed.

17 In the manuscript and *Specimens*, always 'house', but the |Xam term is ||*neiŋ* which, according to the context, can be better rendered as 'camp' or 'hut' (*cf. Dictionary*, p. 619). – Ed.

18 Interestingly, the children sit in separate groups, according to the camp from which they come, and Di-xɛrretən knows them and the campsite in which they live. There are 2 + 3 + 1 + 2 + 2 + 3 + 2 children, that is, a total of 15.– Ed.

19 The |Xam term is *!kwirri*, which means 'river, riverbed' (*Dictionary*, p. 467) and usually refers to a type of dry riverbed, locally known as *liegte*, that is a common feature of the former |Xam territory in the Northern Cape. – Ed.

20 This sentence is repeated, with variations, seven times, yet it cannot be considered, as one of the anonymous reviewers suggests, 'a repeatedly sung (or chanted) refrain' like those widely found in African storytelling traditions. We can be sure we are dealing with something different here, because the |Xam also included this kind of refrain in their stories and |Haŋǂkass'o was a master of their use. – Ed.

21 **(8184')a**

Because the camp is in the ravine (i.e., not where the water flows, but among the bushes).

22 **(8184')b**

He also speaks of another ravine.

23 In the manuscript and *Specimens*, 'while [*au*] they went away', but for the reasons stated in the editing criteria, the *au* can be elided here. – Ed.

24 **(8188')**

No children of hers were there.

as those she had

were the children of the people.

25 Even in the original |Xam, this sentence does not make much sense, and it appears to reflect the state of confusion of the lioness. Another possible rendering would be 'Those children, where are they?' – Ed.

26 **(8191')a**

She knew him.

27 Here and in the following line the |Xam term *i:* is left untranslated by Lloyd, although in some cases she rendered it as 'on account of it'. On the basis of what D. Bleek (1929: 172) wrote, it is clear that when it is present at the end of sentence it can be best translated as 'yes' or 'indeed'. The very same word, apparently with almost the same pronunciation, is found in the Ju|'hoansi language (see Biesele 2009). – Ed.

28 **(8191')b**

As she realized

that she couldn't see the children.

29 **(8192')**

(|Haŋ‡kass'o's translation here appears to me somewhat doubtful.)

[In *Specimens* and the manuscript, 'Where are my children?'. In *Specimens*, p. 169, Lloyd's note appears as follows: 'The narrator's translation of |ne |auwaki !kaukən was "Where are my children?" but "Give me the children" or "Show me the children" may be verbally more accurate. – Ed.]

30 Here and in the following manuscript page Di-xɛrretən tells the lioness these are not *their* children, which indicates a relationship between them. – Ed.

31 Left blank in the manuscript. In *Specimens*, p. 169, 'Out on thee!' See following note. – Ed.

32 **(8193')**

Growling, she put the head inside [her mouth].

33 Left blank in the manuscript save for the initial 'Oh'. In *Specimens*, 'Oh! Oh dear! Oh dear! Oh dear! Oh dear!' – Ed.

34 In the manuscript and *Specimens*, 'cursed (?)'. The |Xam term is |nu, 'a word used signifying dead, departed, spirit, also used as a term of opprobrium' (*Dictionary*, p. 350). I am grateful to one of the anonymous reviewers of this article for pointing out to me the error in my initial reading of this sentence. – Ed.

35 The |Xam term is |a:, 'to fight, die, be killed' and, as a noun, 'fight, harm, curse' the emphatic form of which is |akən (*Dictionary*, p. 267). The term is remarkably similar, both in pronunciation and in meaning, to a !kung word mentioned by Lorna Marshall (1969: 351–352) |a, 'a fight', used frequently, says Marshall, 'for anything strong or dangerous'. Lewis-Williams (1983: 46–47, 1998: 207) says the word has a shamanistic use and is the |Xam equivalent of what modern !kung call n|um. – Ed.

36 Lloyd has in *Specimens*, p. 169, 'Thou hast been the one whose big head came to sit here'. – Ed.

37 **(8194')**

It was Di-xɛrretən who spoke thus.

References

Bank, A. 2006. *Bushmen in a Victorian world: the remarkable story of the Bleek–Lloyd collection of Bushmen folklore*. Cape Town: Double Storey.

Bennun, N. 1996. *The broken string: the last words of an extinct people*. London: Viking.

Biesele, M. 1996. He stealthily lightened at his brother-in-law (and thunder echoes in Bushman oral tradition a century later). In *Voices from the past: |Xam Bushmen*, ed. J. Deacon and T. Dowson, 142–160. Johannesburg: Witwatersrand University Press.

Biesele, M. 2009. *Ju|'hoan folktales: transcriptions and translations – a literacy primer by and for youth and adults of the Ju|'hoan community*. Victoria: Trafford Publishing,

Bleek, D.F. 1928. Bushman grammar: a grammatical sketch of the language of the |Xam-ka-!k'e". *Zeitschrift für Eingeborenen-Sprachen* 19: 81–98.

Bleek, D.F. 1929. Bushman grammar: a grammatical sketch of the language of the |Xam -ka-!k'e" (continuation). *Zeitschrift für Eingeborenen-Sprachen* 20: 161–174.

Bleek, D.F. 1932. Customs and beliefs of the |Xam Bushmen. Part IV: omens, wind-making, clouds. *Bantu Studies* 6(2): 323–342.

Bleek, D.F. 1956. *A Bushman dictionary*. New Haven: American Oriental Society.

Bleek, D.F. 2004. *Customs and beliefs of the |Xam Bushmen*, ed. J.C. Hollmann. Johannesburg: Wits University Press; Philadelphia: Ringing Rocks Press.

Bleek, E. and D.F. Bleek. 1909. Notes on the Bushmen. In *Bushman paintings copied by M. Helen Tonge*, 37–44. Oxford: Clarendon Press.

Bleek, W.H.I. 1875. *A brief account of Bushman folk-lore and other texts*. London: Trübner.

Bleek, W.H.I. and L.C. Lloyd. 1911. *Specimens of Bushman folklore*. London: George Allen.

Bringhurst, R. 2008. *The tree of meaning: language, mind and ecology*. Berkeley: Counterpoint.

Deacon, J. 1986. My place is the bitterpits: the home territory of Bleek and Lloyd's |Xam San informants. *African Studies* 45(2): 137–155.

Deacon J. 1988. The power of a place in understanding Southern San rock engravings. *World Archaeology* 20(2): 128–140.

Deacon, J. and T. Dowson. 1996. *Voices from the past: |Xam Bushmen and the Bleek and Lloyd collection*. Johannesburg: Witwatersrand University Press.

De Prada-Samper, J.M. 2009. Mitos y creencias de los bosquimanos |Xam: relatos orales acerca del león. Doctoral thesis, Universidad de Alcalá de Henares.

De Prada-Samper, J.M. 2010. Strokes in rock and flesh: presentiments, rock engravings and landscape in ||Kabbo's place. In *Rock art made in translation: framing images of and from the landscape*, ed. P. Skotnes, 75–79. Johannesburg and Cape Town: Jacana.

De Prada-Samper, J.M. [In press.] 'The pictures of the |Xam people are in their bodies': presentiments, landscape and rock art in ||Kabbo's country. In *The courage of ||Kabbo: conference proceedings*, ed. J. Deacon and P. Skotnes. Cape Town: University of Cape Town Press.

De Prada-Samper, J.M. and M. Winberg. 2012. 'The ouma and the lion': a contemporary |Xam tale of the upper Karoo. *Oráfrica: revista de africana* 8(2): 199–206.

Guenther, M. 1989. *Bushman folktales: oral traditions of the Nharo of Botswana and the |Xam of the Cape*. Stuttgart: Franz Steiner Verlag Wiesbaden.

Hymes, D. 1981. Discovering oral performance and measured verse in American Indian narrative. In *'In vain I tried to tell you': essays in Native American ethnopoetics*, 309–341. Philadelphia: University of Pennsylvania Press.

Lewis-Williams, J.D. 1981. *Believing and seeing: symbolic meanings in Southern San rock art*. London: Academic Press.

Lewis-Williams, J.D. 1983. *The rock art of southern Africa*. Cambridge: Cambridge University Press.

Lewis-Williams, J.D. 2000. *Stories that float from afar: ancestral folklore of the San of southern Africa*. Cape Town: David Philip.

Lewis-Williams, J.D. and T.A. Dowson. 1990. Through the veil: San rock paintings and the rock face. *South African Archaeological Bulletin* 45(1): 5–16.

Lloyd, L.C. 1889. *A short account of further Bushman material collected*. London: David Nutt.

Marshall, L.1969. The medicine dance of the !Kung Bushmen. *Africa* 39(2): 347–381.

Morris, D. and P.B. Beaumont. 1994. Portable engravings at Springbokoog and the archaeological contexts of rock art of the upper Karoo, South Africa. In *Contested images: diversity in southern African rock art research*, ed. T. Dowson and J.D. Lewis-Williams, 11–28. Johannesburg: Witwatersrand University Press.

Ouzman, S. and P. Taçon. 2004. Worlds within stone: the inner and outer rock-art landscapes of northern Australia and southern Africa. In *The figured landscapes of rock-art: looking at pictures in place*, ed. C. Chippindale and G. Nash, 39–68. Cambridge: Cambridge University Press.

Schmidt, S. 2013. *A catalog of Khoisan folktales of southern Africa*. Köln: Rüdiger Köppe Verlag.

Swartz, K., J.M. de Prada-Samper and M. Winberg. [In press]. The wolf and the man. In *The courage of ||Kabbo: conference proceedings*, ed. P. Skotnes and J. Deacon. Cape Town: University of Cape Town Press.

Tomaselli, K.G. 1997. Orality, rhythmography and visual representation. *Visual Anthropology* 9(1): 93–116.

True, D.L. and S. Griset. 1988. Exwanyawish: a Luiseno sacred rock. *Journal of California and Great Basin Anthropology* 10(3): 270–274.

Vinnicombe, P. 2010. Meaning cannot rest or stay the same. In *Seeing and knowing: understanding rock art with and without ethnograpy*, ed. G. Blundell, C. Chippindale and B. Smith, 241–249. Johannesburg: Witwatersrand University Press.

Wessels, M. 2012. The |Xam narratives of the Bleek and Lloyd collection: questions of period and genre. *Western Folklore* 71(1): 25–46.

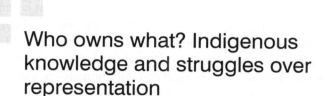

Who owns what? Indigenous knowledge and struggles over representation

Keyan G. Tomaselli

Abstract

Ownership of field research records involving informants and subject communities is discussed with regard to doing research amongst indigenous populations. Intellectual property rights (IPR) law often assumes, for example, that an age-old mythical story retold by a contemporary informant is owned by the legal entity that facilitated its being captured in writing. The implication is that if the story-teller now wants to tell the same story to someone else, written legal permission from the legal entity would be required. IPR contracts freeze the dynamism of knowledge, killing its 'lived' relation, and the process owned by others (our research partners/hosts/subjects) is transformed into commodities that the original storytellers no longer own or control. For our ǂKhomani Bushman hosts, this constitutes information theft. A third party, in our case the academy, claims ownership of ideas our subjects thought were theirs. This article examines ensuing issues of IPR and ethics in relation to doing research amongst indigenous communities.

Introduction

The relationship between ethical considerations, grant application and intellectual property takes us into the complicated realm of indigenous cultural considerations rarely acknowledged by legal regimes. Legal formulas, in contrast, are easy because they ignore complexity, eliminate contradiction and seek single, determining, interpretations. This suppression of complexity often results in academic myth-making, while the application of intellectual property rights (IPR) aims at ownership, rather than enabling our primary task of learning via doing research. Publicly-funded research is supposed to occur in the open creative commons that is being everywhere commercialised, copyrighted, patented and trademarked.[1] While the Berne Convention for the Protection of Literary and Artistic Works (1886) is necessary to prevent plagiarism and literary anarchy, the increasingly demanding IPR auditing regimes to which authors are now subject can only impede open commons research.

This article aims to engage academic researchers, legal representatives and indigenous communities in a discussion that brings to the fore the complexities of implementing indigenous IPR laws. Specific mention is made of the ǂKhomani San research informants of the Northern Cape, as this community is embedded in the Rethinking Indigeneity research track that is facilitated by the Centre for Communication, Media and Society (CCMS) at the University of KwaZulu-Natal (UKZN) (Finlay 2009).

Intellectual property (IP) refers to the intangible products of the mind, of which patents, trademarks, designs and copyright are the four forms. The first three are also known as *industrial property*. Patent law protects inventors of new products and processes from unauthorised manufacture, use or sale. Trademark law secures rights to distinctive words and symbols. *Copyright* confers upon creators of original forms of expression exclusive rights and protects authors from unauthorised usage (*Encyclopedia Britannica*). *Open access* and *creative commons* offer the right to access and to do so freely, sometimes with authorisation and/or payment for mass copying. Creative commons partially restricts use and commercial exploitation. Due citation is necessary to prevent plagiarisation. This issue is currently pertinent to academic researchers, authors and the like as the Department of Trade and Industry recently gazetted its draft national policy on IP. However, as the Authors' Non-Fiction Association South Africa (ANFASA) notes, there are omissions to the draft relating to IP in digital format, as well as a lack of provision made for materials created for the blind and visually impaired (ANFASA 2013). The draft Protection of Traditional Knowledge Bill was also gazetted in April 2013, which acknowledges the legitimacy of traditional knowledge as a *bona fide* category of IP. The Traditional Knowledge Bill, proposed by Wilmot James, allows for the IP rights to be held by 'community proxy', i.e., a member of a community is delegated to serve as a representative to the community as an entity. This takes into account the collaborative nature of traditional knowledge (see Anon. 2013; James 2013). These internationally pertinent issues are made sense of through specific encounters with indigenous groups in South Africa.

The task to be addressed here discusses a problem that the CCMS research teams encounter on every field trip when working with contemporary Kalahari communities:

how to deal with educational bureaucracy that sees the world only in terms of instrumentalist spread-sheets, quantifiable outputs and potential commercialisation. New forms of public accountability have lost sight of the lived, intangible practice of knowledge production in the field where remote rural communities live. It is exceptionally difficult to quantify and establish the origins of indigenous knowledge (IK). Due to the collective nature of knowledge production in cultures that rely on oral narrative as transmission, the boundaries and timeframes as to who composed collective narratives become blurred. In most cases IK emerges, adjusted and built upon in subsequent generations and in constantly occurring new contexts. As such, this fairly organic production of knowledge is incompatible with the rigours of copyright law. Copyright assigns protection to an original literary work for 50 years from the first date of publication. How does one ascertain the date of 'first publication' in a pre-literate society? Who determines when an oral narrative was first relegated to the public realm? Oral narratives are often used as a teaching device in indigenous communities; therefore they are subject to change and evolve with the current needs of the community. As the narratives are composed from within the community itself, it very often has close ties to a specific geographical location and to particular individuals in a community.

Predatory research versus knowledge production

The consequences of what is perceived as predatory research have resulted in some communities and many individuals within them resisting research, distrusting researchers and/or charging them for their cooperation and information/knowledge. They complain of maltreatment by researchers due to a lack of 'recognition' (Afrikaans: *erkenning*), theft of their 'knowledge' (*kennis*) and lack of due respect for them as individuals. DNA testing has resulted in more angry allegations of bio-piracy and bloodletting; now researchers are accused of stealing not only their '*kennis*' but also their bodily fluids. This perceived irresponsible behaviour by a minority of academic researchers undermines the indigenous communities' trust and rapport with all researchers. It is imperative that academic researchers behave in an ethically responsible manner when conducting fieldwork, so as not to break the tentative rapport established by other researchers. If both researchers and the researched do not implicitly agree to trust each other, then the research endeavour will result in an elaborate charade (see Metcalf 2002).

Academic institutions and IPR

It is not possible in anthropological and/or IK research to divide up holistic IK (*kennis*) and lived critical indigenous methodologies into separate parts, and to parcel each out for different ownership as the National Research Foundation (NRF) now demands.[2] This kind of Cartesian-derived IPR categorisation does not recognise the indigenous as the repositories of aspects/versions of that knowledge. Pre-capitalist Malawian oral traditions, for example, did contain notions of ownership, in relation to the individual, the community, and even the genre and form (see Kerr 2006). These 'notions' are excluded by IPR discourse as they are not written down, codified legally, and lodged in law. UKZN further wanted to claim *all* the IPR, to the exclusion of the rights of our other sponsors and collaborators, though the NRF stipulation would have required acknowledgement of these. Certain practices are imbued with spiritual significance and tied to folk history. Consequently, research informants are reluctant to share what they deem to be 'sacred' information with strangers (Brush and Stabinsky 1996). The intellectual commons that we have developed with our subjects over a 19-year-period could have been destroyed had I signed the UKZN contract, its 'Letter of Research', as it stands. One is precariously caught between having to honour the indigenous community's trust that is implicit when they impart their claimed *kennis* (IK) to the researcher on the one hand, and having to manoeuvre through institutional requirements on the other.

Like the Letter of Research, the UKZN Ethical Clearance Form, based on a bio-medical or clinical psychology model, leaves little space for culturally sensitive approaches stemming from ontological frameworks different from the Cartesian assumptions codified in IPR law. These contradict the practices of critical indigenous methodologies (see Denzin, Lincoln and Smith 2008; Mboti 2012; Watal 2001).

Critical indigenous methodologies use the ontologies and worldviews of the indigenous population with which they work as the entry point for their analysis, rather than imposing a Cartesian perspective on what is observed. While control and monitoring mechanisms are necessary, they should be sensitive to different contexts and needs. What is legally feasible does not necessarily equate with what has meaning in the ontologies of our research informants. These legal stipulations do not take into account the unpredictable and spontaneous context of conducting fieldwork. Cumbersome legal requirements (such as getting a-literate informants to sign informed consent forms) often hinder the research process, as legal documents are viewed with suspicion and contempt due to indigenous communities sometimes linking the signing of such documents with their experiences of land dispossession. Further, the research letter and ethics form disrespect our subject communities' rights to own their own information and to be treated in terms of the Kantian imperative. Finally, both documents need to address allegations by many subject communities and their representative organisations of 'theft of [IP] knowledge' perpetrated by researchers, their employers and their publishers, even if legitimised by IPR contracts.

In short, the question is: How do we practise Agnes Heller's reformulation of Immanuel Kant's injunction, 'Act in such a way that you will always treat humanity, whether in your own person or in the person of any other, never simply as a means, but always at the same time as an end'?[3]

For logistical reasons we had started a second phase of a cultural mapping project in July 2011 before the UKZN letter of research, the grant contract, previously unknown to us, had been received. On receipt via 3G transmission after our arrival at Witdraai in the Kalahari, we realised that the contract encoded a whole series of contradictions that needed resolution before we could accept the funding.

CCMS had responded to a call put out by the College of Humanities for strategic research funding that would involve students. Our proposal, 'Beyond Biesje Poort: extending participatory indigenous research',[4] was inserted into an ongoing 20-year project entitled Rethinking Indigeneity that had attracted financial support from a variety of international funders, including the NRF. Only one of the funders, M-Net, of a different sub-project with a different San community, had claimed copyright on any aspect of the overarching project (a television programme sponsored by the channel, made by a student).[5] UKZN, however, initially insisted on total ownership of the resulting 'intellectual property and information' generated by the research done in the specific Beyond Biesje Poort sub-project for which the College of Humanities funds were allocated.

Contracts and ethics forms assume that all parties are literate. Our informants/ co-researchers/subject community/hosts are largely a-literate. Conventional letters of consent and written permissions are often treated with suspicion by them. We thus largely work through their designated cultural, communal and development organisations which often require written research and/or media contracts. These list payment (i.e., a kind of facilitation tax) as being required.

The first phase of the Biesje Poort sub-project had secured multiple funding sources (National Heritage Council, McGregor Museum, the NRF and the Northern Cape provincial government). In the broader multi-institutional team, individual staff and students were separately sponsored by the Durban University of Technology (DUT), and the universities of Cape Town (UCT) and Pretoria (UP). UKZN, without consultation with CCMS, had declined the bulk of the costs – travel and accommodation – from the budget (for a project in the Northern Cape, a 3 400km round-trip from Durban). Nevertheless, the UKZN one-size-fits-all contract wanted total ownership of the IPR and information, no matter the multi-institutional intellectual composition of the team and its diverse financial sponsorship, of which the UKZN allocation was minuscule.

A-literate informants do not write or publish; however, academics and journalists do. Unless specified, copyright of someone else's idea thus resides with the author of the written document, not with the oral story-teller who relayed the narrative in the first place. This also applies to the taking of photographs, especially in public spaces; another irritation for our ‡Khomani hosts.

The issue here related to the university's confusion between patent, trademark and copyright laws, and the commodification of cultural research practice and outputs by tertiary institutions everywhere. What this contract did was to objectify the researcher–researched relationship, to commoditise it, thus turning it into a perishable good and putting a value on that which cannot be valued. Placing my argument into a legalistic perspective, Kundayi Masanzu, Director of ANFASA, responded:

> [The UKZN contract] is a typical 'run of the mill' contract from most institutions where they claim – and rightly so – ownership of the finished product because they either commission and/or fund it and it is also being done within the scope of the academic's employment. However, in scenarios where the foreseeable output is nothing more than a publication, some institutions will relax the rules and re-assign the copyright in the publication back to the academic/researcher in exchange for a non-exclusive licence.

Legal or not, by taking total ownership of both the research information and the final product, which were not defined in the letter of research, the potential consequences of the contract may have denied the research team the opportunity 1) to publish its findings, thereby ironically a) putting its staff in breach of university conditions of service and b) dissuading students from publishing from their theses, even though this is a requirement of their registration. Further, our informants might have accused us of 2) engaging in the theft of indigenous knowledge; and 3) in the event that publication did occur, the bizarre requirement was imposed that acknowledgement of the source of the funding (the College) was denied unless 'express permission' was obtained in writing; 4) the removal of the research ('release of information') from the public domain (through which it was to be funded), or acknowledgement of the grant, public or otherwise, without written permission, is incomprehensible in an academic environment which is supposed to be operating in the global intellectual commons. My making information about the source of this project's funding known to our co-sponsors without 'written permission' thus possibly implicated me in a legal transgression, should any gathering at which this analysis is presented be deemed by the university to constitute a 'public' event. And finally, 5) many of the instructions that emanated from the grant selection committee were ill-advised, insisting on all kinds of requirements that were financially and logistically impossible to meet. In the event, I insisted on the exclusion of the clause claiming for UKZN 'intellectual property rights and information' from the final contract which was acceded to. I was the only grant holder to raise these objections.

The implication is that if the indigenous story-teller wants to tell the same age-old story to someone else, 'express written legal permission' from UKZN will be required. The university's claim to ownership of local (indigenous) knowledge is exactly what the IKS paradigm questions. IPR freezes the dynamism of knowledge and the process owned by others (our research partners/hosts/subjects) into copyrighted and trademarked commodities that the original story-tellers no longer own or control. For our hosts, this is information theft, as the university has by this means now legally positioned itself to sell back to them (and anyone else) their own information and stories, whether original or inter-generationally transmitted. This, clearly, was *not* the university's intention. However, the contract nevertheless claimed ownership of ideas which our subjects claimed were theirs. Thus is knowledge thereby frozen, commodified and copyrighted by IPR.

In the letter of research, UKZN claimed ownership of *all* the IPR and *all* information gathered by its grantees. If the research generated is to become the 'property of UKZN', then *it is unlikely to be published even as a final product*, as most journal publishers require that copyright be assigned to them on publication. This consequence was not the university's aim, but the implication could be to prevent publication of the research by a third party. In the normal course of events, however, publishers are quite flexible in terms of specific considerations.

IK cannot be 'owned' by a corporation or a university, and, indeed, our subjects would not permit ownership of their stories by an external entity. We are dealing with intangible conceptual, spiritual and cultural knowledge here, not patents, procedures or inventions as might be the case in engineering, science or agriculture. What UKZN was doing, however, was to trademark (popular) information which it did not itself generate. This appropriation may be legal, but is it ethical?[6]

These issues are, to a good degree, addressed by Brill (Amsterdam) which has developed the following protocols in its 'Consent to Publish' agreement:

a. the right after publication to include the Contribution free of charge in a compilation of own works in print, such as a collection of own articles and/ or lectures, on condition that due acknowledgment is made of the original publication;

b. the right after publication to quote the Contribution and/or build on the content of the Contribution, on condition that due acknowledgment is made of the original publication;

c. the right to reproduce the Contribution in a limited number of copies for the sole purpose of private practice;

d. the right to include the Contribution in a collection by way of a support to lectures and presentations given by the Contributor, on condition that the normal exploitation of the Work by the Publisher is not harmed and that due acknowledgment is made to the original publication;

e. all the intellectual and industrial property rights or any similar rights with respect to (the protection of) methods, processes, designs and models described in the Contribution;

f. The right to post the post-print version of the Contribution on his/her own personal website free of charge. This means the Contribution may be shown exactly as it appears in print;

g. The right to allow the institute employing the Contributor to post the post-refereed, but pre-print version of the Contribution free of charge on its website. The post-refereed, pre-print version means the version which contains all adaptations made after peer reviewing. The Publisher's lay-out must not be used.

Within this framework, the IPRs are usually dealt with as follows in our own research: 1) our informants own the stories they tell us, but give us permission to publish them with acknowledgement; 2) we, the researchers, own the arguments and explanations that the stories illustrate; 3) the publisher might claim copyright of the article, book or chapter via which these stories are made known. In terms of this value chain, it is unclear what ownership the university was claiming. If the intention was to commercialise intangible humanities research, how is this is possible when we are simultaneously required to lodge our work with publishers who themselves often claim copyright? This clause would appear not to be of much use in the humanities, which, in contrast to science and engineering, *critique* processes, which have little or no commercial value.

Even where invention does occur, or where materials are processed into a commodity, with, for example, the *Hoodia* appetite suppressant, ownership is often contested. An IPR lawsuit against the Council for Scientific and Industrial Research (CSIR) by South African San Institute (SASI) resulted in the establishment of the Hoodia Trust to distribute a six per cent portion of proceeds earned by the patent to the San. However, other indigenous groups (and San in Namibia and Botswana) have also used the *Hoodia* plant and question the recognition of only some South African groups in claiming sole 'IK' of the plant's pharmacological properties.[7] In our case, we have secured from Unisa Press its agreement to cede full copyright to authors when republishing two independently produced works that have been largely authored by our informants (Kruiper and Kruiper 2011; Lange, De Wee and Van Rooi et al. 2007).

Ethical implications

Given that our projects are people-based, overall, the output or finished product will be the publication that comes out of this research and little more, unless action-based research is involved. The *South African Intellectual Property Laws Amendment Act* was referred by the president back to the National Assembly on 26 September 2012, partly because it had not been referred for comment to the National House of Traditional Leaders. The proposed act makes IK the commercial property of the community from which it emanates. But this poorly drafted law is unable to clearly define 'the community' that would own IK. In contrast, in the field of patents, benefit-sharing agreements are usually signed with the community involved in the research.

In the UKZN case, an unsuitable contract was applied to anthropology/archaeology/humanities/critical social science scholars, whose outputs should *not* be considered commercially equivalent. However, as a criminologist and lawyer who specialises in the protection of traditional knowledge in Africa, Andrew Mutsiwa notes that

> the UKZN letter of research does not draw distinctions between patents which have commercial and industrial implications, as is the case with engineering or industrial design, and the humanities which is much more fluid in terms of intellectual property ownership and commercial impact. Letters of research should be reviewed to ensure that it is relevant and appropriate to the discipline that it serves. (Personal communication, 24 April 2013)

He adds: 'The approach that has been here adopted by UKZN is tantamount to granting Indigenous Knowledge ideational dependence to the dominate culture of western knowledge regimes through integrating the former into the knowledge infrastructure of intellectual property' (Personal communication, 11 July 2013).

Institutions will try to secure ownership of IP in the form of patents and trademarks to leverage monetary value; the second reason cited by the president for referring the act back to Parliament was because certain provisions make it a 'Money Bill' – one that involves taxation or government spending, but whose provisions were not in accordance with the constitution. While these issues are under discussion, generally, *copyright* is excluded from these provisions, because it usually results in a publication which is governed by different criteria characteristic of the publishing industry. Issues surrounding IPRs are being negotiated on a global scale, as there are far-reaching cost implications for the publishing industry in both developed and developing countries (Maskus 2000).

I now return to the question of ethics with regard to the context in which my example has been framed. While statutory ethical procedures are intended to (and do) protect the researcher, the employer and the subjects, in the specific cases of the kind discussed here, the opposite would appear to be true in this particular instance. In such situations 1) ethics and legality are not necessarily co-incident; 2) ethical considerations can be overruled by commercial imperatives legitimised by IPR-led contracts; 3) the biomedical assumptions of the current ethical clearance form are often inappropriate for other kinds of social, cultural and historical research; and 4) IPR overrides the Kantian imperative.

What are the options facing researchers in light of these contradictions? Our researchers assess their location within the IP value chain and anticipate the likely consequences for their subject communities, which are also discussed in their theses and publications. Where subject communities might be disadvantaged by IP legislation, the following mechanisms might apply: 1) liaison with their representative organisations; 2) the making available of the research data generated to them; 3) ensuring that the published products are supplied to our hosts; 4) care is taken not to alienate the subjects from their intellectual labour or the researcher's labour from them, such work being potentially useful for the subjects' own purposes;[8] 5) never to commercialise academic research. Subject communities require that systems that work for them are to be incorporated, failing which researcher access to them may be compromised, and may be even denied; 6) facilitating organisations like SASI and the Working Group of Indigenous Minorities in Southern Africa (WIMSA) also enable such work, and due acknowledgement is given.

The non-governmental organisations (NGOs) which facilitate our research sometimes suggest that a 'payment' be made to the organisation (see WIMSA contract, p. 2).[9] This provision is difficult for academic researchers to comply with, as research funders like the NRF or universities do not normally approve this kind of expense as a legitimate line item. In any event, the sheer cost of doing field research – if the abovementioned reciprocity is adhered to – provides already funded research and data to representative NGOs, data which are statutorily lodged in the public domain, on open access where unpublished student thesis research is concerned.

It is not always clear with which organisations one is dealing when in the field or how to proceed when different agendas (and perhaps competing intermediaries) seem to be at work. For example, some of our ǂKhomani partners prefer to work directly with researchers and other professionals, irrespective of NGO contracts and policies claiming to represent and protect them. Organisations like the San Councils are WIMSA's representative bodies in Namibia, South Africa and Botswana. WIMSA is a regional advocacy San organisation; SASI, on the other hand, is a support organisation; while the Bushman Council seems to be a support-NGO in something of a competing space (see Francis and Francis 2010).

Where SASI and WIMSA act as enablers and sometimes seemingly as regulators, the San Council's agenda appears to include one of labour brokering for its own members, having twice insisted that CCMS employ one of its members on its short-term research projects. It was not clear what this person would be doing or why his/her employment was being requested. The San Council does not have statutory oversight as a gatekeeper between researchers and the researched, though WIMSA states that the councils, as political bodies, negotiate with governments and coordinate national issues regarding development programmes with their communities, donors and the industry. Except for Angola, each country has a San Council which is financially supported by WIMSA, the regional mother body and secretariat. The South African San Council (SASC) was mandated by the WIMSA annual general assembly (AGM) to negotiate with the CSIR, Phytofarm and, later on, Unilever, regarding royalties administered by the Hoodia Trust. About R500 000 was used by both the SASC and WIMSA to travel to and attend meetings, and also to communicate with the San communities. It was not meant to split the milestone payment amongst the countries and San communities.

In the Biesje Poort research project, contracts had already been signed with four ‡Khomani individuals with whom we have had a long-term relationship, whose employment had been approved and processed by UKZN and the McGregor Museum which administered the funds, and whose interpretations we wanted to elicit. We were scrupulous in applying labour law and in respecting the requests of our short-term employees who were wary of the San Council's claims to employment and representation. Members of councils may have no clear historical link to the IP they claim is part of their heritage (Prins, in Rønning et al. 2006: 12; Francis and Francis 2010).

Some organisations additionally insist that researchers pay 'taxes' to them, to enable them to facilitate the research, to 'protect' their constituents' interests, or to ensure access to such research subjects. We pointed out to the San Council gatekeeper that 1) an extra position (or tax) was not a line item in our or the funder's budget; 2) that we had already engaged four members of the community in terms of the research contract signed with the funder; 3) the local people to be employed had the cultural expertise needed for the project; 4) we were following labour law to the letter; and 5) we did not need his or his organisation's permission to do the research (though it would be helpful to have their blessing, as they could muddy the waters).

All over the country remote communities are held hostage, or supposedly represented, by kinds of 'cultural' and development gatekeepers who claim to exercise communal rights over individuals who are rarely consulted on the options available to them. The result is that such individuals are often eliminated from employment and opportunities by these gatekeepers who want to act as official labour brokers despite not being officially registered to conduct such business. They operate as a kind of rentier class who monopolise and manage access. This creates multiple layers of increasing dependency on the one hand, and resistance on the other, on the part of those being 'represented' – people who, on occasion, are eking out their survival despite these supposed development agents. That is one reason why they engage directly with researchers. Although these issues have been discussed largely in a southern African context, tussles over the ownership of IK have international resonance (see Brokensha, Dennis and Werner 1980).

Conclusion

Postmodern research methods, as we are developing them, respond constructively to the non-Cartesian ontology of our co-researchers/subjects (see, e.g., Mboti

2012). But these are now subject to claims of ownership placed in a positivist and objectified structurally violent commercialised IPR realm that is antithetical to the ways the indigenous make sense of the world as a set of interacting intangible (often unknowable) spiritual resources, elements of a landscape, linked to the ancestors, impacting them continuously. The final question in the logic here is: Who owns God or the ancestors – the copyright lawyers? The universities? Corporations?

Academic research is largely funded by taxpayers, yet ownership of this labour is conventionally ceded to publishers, many of whom then sell it back to the institutions within which it was produced. This is similar to the CSIR's appropriation of certain chemicals found in the *Hoodia* plant, without initially acknowledging centuries-old traditional knowledge. Scholarship in the Third World is similarly vulnerable: high-quality research is produced at a fraction of its actual cost (thanks to the public purse), which is then donated to international commercial publishers who package it and charge huge fees for it, with little direct material return to its authors or knowledge holders (Merrett 2006). In any event, just who gets the returns is always contested (Nwauche 2003), as has been the case with *Hoodia* royalties. What was previously a traditional commons has been translated into 'property' whose proceeds and recipients are now being questioned by those who still have access to the plant, but have been excluded from the monetised value chain once it had been processed as a product and marketed as a commodity. The stringent adherence to IP laws may, in effect, dispossess indigenous communities of even their indigenous oral history.

That the San Council, comprised of an educated group of town dwellers, has been receiving the (diminishing) *Hoodia* royalties is an indication of how copyright enclosures operate to create, or reinforce, class divisions. It is these very exploitative relations that perplex our traditional, rural, a-literate Bushman[10] informants, even as they may be unaware of the very complex and expensive international value chain that beneficiates their raw information into theory which itself frames the 'final product' as manufactured by academics and published in books, journals and films. It is these relations that the UKZN letter of research, ironically, sought to leverage in its favour.

Who owns what is no longer clear to our sources, who allege exploitation and knowledge-theft everywhere by everyone. By enacting what it saw as a protective mechanism, UKZN lost the plot of who owns what, how, and whether these ownerships can be identified and how due returns, if any, can be calculated and disbursed. What was once a non-rivalrous self-renewing free resource now becomes 'owned' by legal entities, and thereby a source of division, competition and contestation between representative bodies and between individuals and those bodies, purely because it has been monetised. IK cannot be privatised, which is in essence the aim of the university's research contract, as the university can only own the structure and analysis of the argument, as carried out by its employee. But the *content* should remain in the public realm, as it is communally produced. This is supported by Article 9(2) of the Trade Related Intellectual Property Aspects (TRIPS) agreement, which states that copyright protection extends to expressions but not to ideas, procedures or mathematical concepts.

If heritage is a bundle of relationships rather than a bundle of economic rights (see Puri 1997: 48), then forms of expression and what is innately known cannot be considered a commodity, a good or a property. One possible implication for critical indigenous research is the alienation of researchers, especially those in the field, from their subject communities, endistancing them from people and places that oral historians, anthropologists, cultural studies, and development and social work researchers, amongst others, take for granted.

Where official organisations appropriate ownership on the assumption of anonymity or unknown oral authorship, a category often elided with communal creativity, they marginalise the subjects of oral discourse, refuse individual human agency and confirm magical (timeless, uncopyrighted) sources of origin (see Kerr 2006: 146–147). The sense of extreme alienation from the collective has always been very strong amongst our traditionalist ǂKhomani sources, which may explain why the CCMS team seems to offer them ways of dealing with this sense of inclusion/ exclusion on the part of their own officialdom. They want to be recognised as individuals creating individually, acting individually and owning individually. Two of our autoethnographic anthologies have offered this almost in play script fashion (Tomaselli 2005, 2007), though attracting serious criticism from two key Kalahari scholars (Biesele and Hitchcock 2008; see also Tomaselli's reply 2013). IPR, the lawyers that write it, and academic bureaucrats often forget this human dimension. Too often, our hosts/subjects become objects of study and a means to someone else's ends. An appropriate balance needs to be found.

It is worth citing a UNESCO statement at some length:

> Knowledge itself, as an inexhaustible commons available to all human beings, is, if not a *global public good* (cf. Box 10.5), at least a '*common public good*'. For not only can knowledge not be regarded as a marketable good like others, but also knowledge only has value if it is shared by all. Such a mode of appropriation by way of sharing and making commonly available has long been formally regulated by law. Roman law thus made a distinction between *res communes* (what is owned in common and at the disposal of the public by virtue of a law), *res nullius* (what cannot be owned and is by nature at everyone's disposal) and *res publicae* (what is owned by a civil community as a public body). Unlike information which only has value if it is fresh and little known, knowledge is lasting by nature. It grows and intensifies with time, as it is propagated and shared. To paraphrase an African proverb, knowledge is like love, these being the only things that grow through sharing.

Knowledge-sharing is the cornerstone of the practices and values that should be at the heart of knowledge societies. It cannot be thought of in terms of a distribution – of something like the sharing of booty. Knowledge-sharing cannot be reduced to the apportionment of knowledge or to a parcelling out of skills, whereby each person is able to take possession of a field of specialisation or expertise (or separate ownership of fragments of content in published papers, as the NRF requires). The advance of knowledge requires the collaboration of all. Often the most novel ideas germinate out of older knowledge, when they are not born – as is frequently the case – from the refutation of knowledge previously held to be irrefutable (*UNESCO World Report* 2005: 170).

Network societies rely on collaboration, free modes of cooperative organisation, and a clear reversal of the shrinkage that currently typifies the public domain.

Notes

1   See, e.g., *Critical Arts* theme issue 20(1) 2006 on IPR regimes as they apply in Africa and for a discussion of the creative commons. http://www.tandfonline.com/toc/rcrc20/20/1#. U3CqToGSxCY

2   The National Research Foundation (NRF) Online Submission System from 2013 wants reports (current and previous) to disaggregate publication outputs as follows: 1) conceptualised idea for research; 2) responsible for data collection/analysis/design; 3) lead author; 4) writer of first draft, editorial input; 5) postgraduate supervisor; 6) owner/co-owner of intellectual property of research; 7) co-developed and executed research; 8) project leader/ budget owner. A distinction needs to be made between *economic rights*, which commercialise the academic work – claims ownership on the fact that research was conducted by the employee as part of his/her duties to the university – and *moral rights*, which give the authors the right to be identified as the creators of the work.

3   See Paton (1948: 91) and Heller (1987).

4   For reports on the first phase see *SUBtext*, Autumn 2011: http://ccms.ukzn.ac.za/ index.php?option=com_content&task=view&id=1064&Itemid=142

5   Tom Hart's *Voice of our forefathers* (2009); see also Dockney's (2011) reception analysis of the video.

6   In ensuing discussion with the College, it was agreed on presentation of a short response reflecting the above arguments, that Clause 11 could be deleted.

7   For more information from Lawyers Challenging Poverty on Hoodia and ownership see: http://www.protimos.org/what-we-do/iprs-and-biodiversity/san-ipr-project/background/ See also Maharaj (2011) and WIMSA (2004). WIMSA's Axel Thoma reports that

the South African San Council (SASC) were given a mandate by the Working Indigenous Minorities of Southern Africa (WIMSA) AGM to negotiate with CSIR, Phytofarm and later on Unilever. *Hoodia* royalties are administered by the Hoodia Trust. About 500 000 Rands were received as a milestone payment. This income was used by both the SA San Council and WIMSA to travel to and attend meetings and also to communicate with the San communities. The milestone payment also made it possible to have San representatives from Botswana and Namibia to attend meetings in South Africa. A great disappointment for the San was that farmers and companies who exported *Hoodia* did not pay their share for the San's intellectual property rights (benefit-sharing). The South African government did not disclose the export figures since the necessary legislation was not yet in place. (WIMSA, personal communication, 4 July 2012).

8   CCMS reciprocates as follows: 1) hard and video copies of all publications are lodged with SASI; 2) research is reported on annually at the Wildebees Kuil auditorium, to which Northern Cape provincial, museum and local NGO personnel are invited; 3) research is also reported on at the public Northern Cape provincial heritage meetings; 4) students (and sometimes) our hosts publish in *SUBtext*, a student-produced magazine where our work is popularised in accessible language. Theme issues on the Kalahari are sponsored by the Northern Cape government and circulated throughout the province; 5) CCMS and its affiliate NGOs organise exhibitions to showcase Kalahari artists; 6) where methods, budgets and contracts allow, CCMS will formally employ San individuals on a contract basis; 7) CCMS has facilitated the publication of a number of books authored by our Kalahari research partners, and so on.

9   The WIMSA Research and Media contract evolved because the Nyae Nyae Ju|'hoansi felt they had not benefited from films such as *The Gods Must be Crazy*. A French student, who researched and recorded San music, published San music on CDs without permission. All the San want is that the research is beneficial to their community, to receive copies of the findings, to be able to read what has been written about them (although they naturally often complain about the academic language) and to be able to offer corrections. The contract is not a money-making tool: it is a protection of San individuals and communities' intellectual property rights. As one leading San person observes: 'Many people from overseas and our countries have gained their academic qualifications with our information. I am still waiting for the San to get the chance to become academics as well' (Axel Thoma, email, 4 July 2012).

10   This is a term they use as a means of subverting top-down political namings forced upon them by authority. See Bregin and Kruiper (2004).

References

Authors' Non-Fiction Association of South Africa (ANFASA). 2013. Draft national policy on intellectual property, 2013, Academic and non-fiction association of South Africa (ANFASA) submission to the Department of Trade and Industry (DTI). http://www. anfasa.org.za/upload/files/ANFASA-Submission-DTI-IP-Policy-2013.pdf (accessed 3 December 2013).

Anon. 2013. Traditional knowledge: Will Wilmot's Bill make law? *Legal Briefs*, 30 April. http://www.polity.org.za/article/traditional-knowledge-will-wilmots-bill-make-law-2013-04-30 (accessed 3 December 2013).

Biesele, M. and R.K. Hitchcock. 2008. Review of Keyan G. Tomaselli, ed. 'Writing in the San/d: autoethnography among indigenous southern Africans'. *Collaborating Anthropologies* 1(1): 201–205.

Bregin, E. and B. Kruiper. 2004. *Kalahari rainsong.* South Africa: University of KwaZulu-Natal Press.

Brokensha, D.W., M.W. Dennis and O. Werner. 1980. *Indigenous knowledge systems and development.* USA: University Press of America.

Brush, S.B. and D. Stabinsky, eds. 1996. *Valuing local knowledge: indigenous people and intellectual property rights.* Washington, DC: Island Press.

Denzin, N.K., Y.S. Lincoln and L.T. Smith. 2008. *Handbook of critical and indigenous methodologies.* London: Sage.

Dockney, J. 2011. Social power through self-imaging in participatory video amongst the Khwe Bushmen community of Platfontein. Unpublished Master's dissertation, the Centre for Communication, Media and Society, University of Kwa-Zulu Natal. http://ccms.ukzn.ac.za/images/MA_theses/dockney_ma_binding_copy%5B1%5D.pdf (accessed 3 December 2013).

Finlay, K. 2009. The un/changing face of the ‡Khomani: representation through promotional material. Unpublished Master's dissertation, the Centre for Communication, Media and Society, University of KwaZulu-Natal. http://ccms.ukzn.ac.za/images/MA_dissertations/kate%20finlay%20dissertation.pdf (accessed 3 December 2013).

Francis, M. and S. Francis. 2010. Representation and misrepresentation: San regional advocacy and the global imagery. *Critical Arts* 24(2): 210–227.

Heller, A. 1987. *Beyond justice.* Oxford: Basil Blackwell.

James, W.G. 2013. Protection of Traditional Knowledge Bill: Republic of South Africa. http://www.rcips.uct.ac.za/usr/rcips/resources/wilmot.pdf (accessed 3 December 2013).

Kerr, D. 2006. 'Folklore', cultural property and modernisation in sub-Saharan Africa. *Critical Arts* 20(1): 144–157.

Kruiper B. and V.R. Kruiper. 2011. *Mooi loop, the sacred art of Vetkat Regopstaan Kruiper.* Durban: Centre for Communication, Media and Society.

Lange, M., J. de Wee, M. van Rooi, M. Malo, E. Sixaxa, M. Hlopezulu and N.P. Saaiman. 2007. *Water stories.* Durban: mel.

Maharaj, V. 2011. From plant to production: the *Hoodia* story. *Quest* 7: 24–27.

Maskus, K.E. 2000. *Intellectual property rights in the global economy.* Washington, DC: Peterson Institute.

Mboti, N. 2012. Research, method and position: What are we doing? In *Cultural tourism: rethinking indigeneity*, ed. K.G. Tomaselli, 53–70. Amsterdam: Brill.

Merrett, C. 2006. The expropriation of intellectual capital and the political economy of international academic publishing. *Critical Arts* 20(1): 96–111.

Metcalf, P. 2002. *They lie, we lie: getting on with anthropology.* Canada: Routledge.

Mutsiwa, A. 2013. Personal email communication to the author, 24 April 2013 and 11 July 2013.

Nwauche, E.S. 2003. Intellectual property rights, copyright and development policy in a developing country: options for sub-Saharan countries. Paper presented at the Copyright Workshop at Zimbabwe's International Book Fair, 30 July. www.kopinor.org/content/download/1777/13422/file/zibf.pdf.

Paton, H.J. 1948. *The moral law: Kant's groundwork of the metaphysic of morals.* London: Hutchinson.

Prins, F. 2006. Intellectual property rights and the political economy of culture. *Critical Arts* 20(1) (theme issue edited by H. Rønning, P. Thomas, K.G. Tomaselli and R.E. Teer-Tomaselli): 1–19.

Puri, K. 1977. The experience of the Pacific region. *UNESCO-WIPO, World Forum on the Protection of Folklore*: 41–59.

Tomaselli, K.G. 2005. *Where global contradictions are sharpest: research stories from the Kalahari*. Amsterdam: SAVUSA and Rozenberg.

Tomaselli, K.G., ed. 2007. *Writing in the San/d: autoethnography amongst indigenous southern Africans*. New York: Altamira Press.

Tomaselli, K.G. 2013. Visualizing different kinds of writing: auto-ethnography, social science. *Visual Anthropology* 26(2): 165–180.

United Nations Education, Scientific and Cultural Organisation (UNESCO). 2005. *Towards knowledge societies*. A UNESCO world report. Paris: UNESCO.

Watal, J. 2001. *Intellectual property rights in the WTO and developing countries*. The Hague: Kluwer Law International.

Working Group of Indigenous Minorities in Southern Africa (WIMSA). 2004. *Biopirates in the Kalahari?* Bonn: Church Development Service.

Wynberg, R., D. Schroeder and R. Chennells. 2009. *Indigenous peoples, consent and benefit sharing: lessons from the San-Hoodia case*. London: Springer.

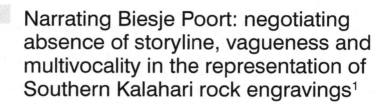

Narrating Biesje Poort: negotiating absence of storyline, vagueness and multivocality in the representation of Southern Kalahari rock engravings[1]

David Morris

Abstract

Rock engraving sites at Biesje Poort near Kakamas have been the focus of work by researchers and participants from the Kalahari. Narratives arising from this joint encounter with rock art and spatially associated artefacts, Later Stone Age and colonial in context, within this landscape and the contemporary socio-political setting, have highlighted issues of interpretive ambiguity and vagueness. There are marked gaps in the storyline, the different emerging accounts are often incommensurate, challenging efforts at constructing any single synthesis or representation. The material traces of the past in this landscape throw up the provocations of multivocality, but can be resources for engaging alternative narratives and the ways in which places, peoples and histories are constructed, inter alia by the heritage sector, in the present.

Introduction

Arguably, narrating Biesje Poort is a topic tangential to the seminar theme of 'Khoi and San Representation',[2] even if, on the face of it, the connections – including rock art and contemporary Kalahari community interaction with archaeological traces – seem obvious. The subject matter here echoes issues and content from debates on representation in the pages of this journal – notably the 1995 issue, *Recuperating the*

San (*Critical Arts* 9(2)) – and at the preceding year's 'People, Politics and Power' conference that was reviewed (Guenther 1995) in the same issue. Simultaneously, those debates, which continued in other venues (not least through and in relation to *Miscast*), highlighted the situated and contingent nature of any given representation. Widespread essentialism in heritage and tourism contexts (in particular) had been readily targeted and critiqued (and so had pre-revisionist academic writing, along with some features of more recent work). It is in light of those debates that the seemingly obvious connections of Biesje Poort, as site of rock art and Stone Age traces, with 'Khoi' and/or 'San' and their representation, need to be demonstrated rather than assumed. Least secure of all, some would argue, are these socio-cultural ascriptions – with a call being made at the April 2013 seminar, by John Wright, indeed for an end to 'bushman studies'. The fixing (and the unsettling) of 'Khoi' and 'San' as categories for this sort of discussion is not without a history (e.g., Wright 1996). But any sense of déjà vu at the 2013 meeting, at which a version of this article was presented as a paper (see also Morris 2013), needs to be tempered by the realisation that the landscape has become more complicated, not least with recognition of 'strategic essentialism' (Robins 2001, invoking Spivak) on the part of those represented. For the latter, connecting the dots (as happened at Biesje Poort) from rock art to stone artefacts and pottery, to colonial era objects, to histories of conquest and on to contemporary indigenous knowledge systems (IKS) and community rock art and landscape interpretation, comes rather more easily and coherently than it would for an archaeologist cautious about evidence and causality. Narrating Biesje Poort in the terms projected by some community voices becomes more squarely one of representing Khoi and San, somewhat untrammelled by the kinds of issues and subtleties that would worry academic commentators, and spurred on by current concerns over recognition and quests for land and language rights (e.g., Le Fleur and Jansen 2013).

The different perspectives on Biesje Poort to which this article refers have been brought into focus by a recent project involving joint fieldwork (and subsequent narration) by participants from the Kalahari, together with students and academic researchers (Lange, Müller-Jansen and Fisher et al. 2013). Biesje Poort, the place, is a landscape of hills that divide the Orange (Gariep) River Basin near Kakamas, in the Northern Cape, from the plains of the southern Kalahari fringe near Lutzputz (Figure 1). A number of rock engraving clusters occur on expansive rock exposures embedded in the hills (Figures 2 & 3). The fieldwork sought to enhance an existing record of the engravings (Lange 2011; see Morris 2013 for a summary of archaeological encounters with the Biesje Poort sites), with the points of departure of our trans-disciplinary group ranging from indigenous knowledge,[3] to archaeology, to landscape architecture (Figure 4). The emergent histories and understandings not only recognise the pertinence of much more than just the images on rock, but they also turn out often to be

Figure 1

Figure 2

Figure 3

Figure 4

discontinuous, ambiguous, or incommensurable – in the sense of being difficult to compare or synthesise within a single narrative. The tendency in practice – especially in heritage discourse, notes Lindsay Weiss (2012: 225) – is to gloss over such difficulties and to make the diverse histories, readings or versions 'available through a common set of assumptions'. She argues, instead, for engaging the sites and histories concerned on their own terms, as the dissonances and mismatches, where they emerge, provide important resources and opportunities for challenging the traditional narrative forms of heritage discourse.

Archaeological accounts, characterised by Mark Pluciennik (1999; *cf.* Hodder 1989; Tilley 1989), have tended to be single-voiced, usually androcentric, third-person sequential narratives, given often with a 'spurious sense of objective description' – advantaged by hindsight and a bird's-eye view. Echoing such narrative forms, in heritage or museum contexts, didactic 'presentations' are often unavoidably authoritative, hierarchical and closed to discourse, disagreement or challenge (*cf.* Tilley 1989). They 'tend to stop "conversation" before it starts', suggests Carol McDavid (2002: 305). But the material record, the stuff of archaeology, fragmentary in nature, yields no unambiguous sequence, no self-evident storyline: it surrounds us as a present-day palimpsest, an intermingling of remains; vestiges that have endured to varying extent, in processes of decay. Behind the perhaps overly stereotyped versions alluded to above, archaeology's interrogative methods and techniques, developed to interpret the traces, for picking apart and joining up strands of evidence, make for an impressive story in themselves. Hence, the foregrounding of 'method as message', advocated by Leone (1983) as one alternative narrative approach. There are, indeed, as Pluciennik suggests (echoing Tilley's earlier call), 'underexplored other ways of telling' – ways, for example, where *conversations*, contingent and historically situated, are opened up. McDavid illustrates how, in creating one such conversation on the Internet, the role of the archaeologist as *the* expert about the multiple pasts of a place or a community could be decentred so that it remained as an important voice, but one of many. The Biesje Poort project, as both praxis and narration (Lange et al. 2013), has sought to emulate this sort of interaction and conversation.

I have argued (Morris 2013) that an archaeology of rock art at Biesje Poort, deploying methods and epistemologies that define the discipline, should not shrink from acknowledging the gaps and limitations of its quest. Inherently there would be absences of storyline, degrees of ambiguity and vagueness, and uncertainties as to linkages between key perspectives arising through different 'voices' or ways of construing evidence. It would be important, I have suggested, to be sensitive to the contemporary, 21st-century imperatives that spur some of the alternative narratives. Notwithstanding archaeology's reputation for authoritative closure, it may, in a more open, socially engaged and reflexive mode, play a significant role in keeping the conversation going. As part of its ways of knowing it should surely admit a range of voices otherwise marginalised, and, relative both to the gaps and the range of insights reflected, acknowledge the provisional nature of its own conclusions.

Heritage discourse and the challenge of unresolved questions

Just as the heritage sector seeks to define its resources, and a spectrum of stakeholders (ranging from tourists and tour operators to communities) seeks to use or draw upon them for a range of purposes (recreational, commercial, academic, political), so the sites themselves (the places, the engravings, the artefacts occurring there, and the diverse interpretations that are possible) throw up challenges, defying the kinds of synthesis and closure that many stakeholder constituencies tend to assert. Advocated here, as elsewhere (Morris 2012a, 2013), is an archaeology and an approach to heritage sites that admits multivocality, a jostling of voices and perspectives; a public archaeology that envisages participation by visitors in the making of meaning rather than as mere consumers – who, as Tilley (1989: 280) puts it, discuss and interpret rather than merely being talked to and told.

At the April 2013 launch of the Palaeosciences Centre of Excellence at the University of the Witwatersrand, Francis Thackeray made an important point that is relevant. With reference to the fossil specimens found at Malapa, *Australopithecus sediba*, he cited the name given by a Johannesburg schoolgirl to the key individual amongst the fossils (the holotype), her competition-winning suggestion being 'Karabo' – a Setswana word meaning 'the answer' (Chauke 2010). The answer – a reassuring certainty – is what many constituencies seek in our heritage sites and objects as they are mustered or constructed as histories for sundry present-day uses: tourism, community identity quests, and so on (*cf.* Wright 2013). The point that Thackeray went on to make with regard to Karabo is that the fossils, far from presenting any definitive *answer*, in fact pose myriad questions. The rock art and its contexts at Biesje Poort should be no different.

One question that has ramifications across the full spectrum of concerns about the rock art here, is that which asks: Who were the engravers? As will be clear, this question about authorship would have much to say to contemporary issues around identity and aspirations for political recognition. It is indeed a primary question behind the 2013 seminar theme: Khoi and San representation.

Research perspectives on the matter of rock art authorship (just one of the many questions that are of interest) are as yet far from being resolved. Some of the earlier pronouncements based on associated archaeological artefacts, taken to denote a herder rather than a hunter-gatherer context (Beaumont, Smith and Vogel 1995), had implied a probability of the engravers having been Khoekhoe pastoralists rather than San or Bushmen. But this conclusion, based to some degree on stereotype, would need to be qualified in light of subsequent work which looks more closely at the variability both in rock art more generally (e.g., Morris 2012b) and specifically at Biesje Poort, in the artefact assemblages and evidence for subsistence (Parsons 2007). Isabelle Parsons' study based on Biesje Poort Later Stone Age (LSA) assemblages arrives at a more provisional and nuanced conclusion as to some of the linkages involved.

Beyond the level of academic debate, the heritage context at Biesje Poort is redolent of the tensions that arise in situations where answers are brought to bear, often before the questions have even been asked: Milan Kundera (2003: 18) notes how what he calls a spirit of complexity can be subverted by 'the din of easy, quick answers that come faster than the question and block it off'. In such a context the anticipated questions may not be the most pertinent. Many of the current heritage issues at Biesje Poort, for instance, prioritise the 'who?' question – presuming a narrow choice of options, or even that the matter is already settled – whereas the answer(s) may turn out to be rather complex, the associated histories somewhat dynamic.

One of the defining contexts in the present is that Biesje Poort lies within the axis referred to as a |Xam-‡Khomani Heartland (itself a prime example of a heritage construct eliding social and historical complexity: populations there today are testimony to diverse [often disruptive] interactions and convulsions in the region over the last few centuries). This 'Heartland' has been on South Africa's World Heritage Tentative List since 2004 (Department of Environmental Affairs and Tourism – Republic of South Africa 2004). Moreover, a National Khoe and San Heritage Route currently under consideration by the Department of Arts and Culture, in discussion with the National Khoisan Council (Francois Odendaal pers. comm.), includes Southern Kalahari and Karoo nodes in which Biesje Poort potentially could feature as a key site, already having been used as a venue for heritage tourism. One of the Kalahari participants from Witdraai had taken part in a promotional film featuring the engravings. A presumption that rock art, wherever it occurs, is self-evidently a resource for tourism, regardless of management status, explains the seemingly inevitable listings of sites in Northern Cape tourist literature generated over some decades. Recognising Biesje Poort's potential for tourism use, but also considering the major constraints of its geographical remoteness and the site's physical fragility (crumbling rock surfaces were noted by Gerhard and Dora Fock on their first visit in 1967, see Fock and Fock 1989), one of the aims of the fieldwork of 2011–13, besides enhancing the existing record of the site, was to draw the attention of heritage authorities to its significance and sensitivity, and to establish some of the parameters for a conservation management plan. It was a moot point whether or not Biesje Poort ought to be considered for public access at all (Barnabas 2013). Important questions about the challenges and sustainability of public rock art projects have been raised in recent evaluations (Duval and Smith 2012; Morris 2012a; Morris in press), and in purely economic terms it was not clear how self-representation by community-based tour guides, and community beneficiation, could be entertained even within the context of the |Xam-ǂKhomani Heartland proposal. Experience elsewhere in South Africa indicates that any commercial expectations by communities or individuals should be tempered by the finding that rock art has limited niche appeal within South Africa's tourism market (Morris, Ndebele and Wilson 2009).

Kalahari participants

A key aspect of this project has been the involvement of participants from the Kalahari, some of them artists and crafters, and all self-identifying as members of the ǂKhomani Bushman community. They joined the project as co-workers, principally through the Centre for Communication, Media and Society (CCMS) at the University of KwaZulu-Natal, in the processes of recording the engravings and in offering their insights into the meanings or significance of the art. Some of the students from CCMS made this participatory aspect of the project the focal point of their particular involvement (Magongo 2013). Training of our colleagues from the Kalahari in rock art and heritage resource recording and GPS plotting was one of the objectives; and follow-up work in 2011, not at Biesje Poort but at Witdraai (at the request of the Kalahari participants), was aimed at documenting local places and stories using skills acquired through participating in the rock art project further south. Their involvement in the Biesje Poort project arose out of their work with CCMS over a period of some 12 years, as part of its research programme Rethinking Indigeneity (Tomaselli 2013), through which various individuals developed an express interest in heritage. There was a prior link with Biesje Poort, as indicated, by way of tourism promotion here, and a strong affinity with the place and the engravings came to be expressed by the Kalahari participants in the course of our work. It was anticipated that aspects of an 'insider' perspective vis-à-vis the art might be gained as the Kalahari participants engaged with the engravings and the landscape.

Certain assumptions concerning affinities and insider understandings need to be unpacked. Pertinent is Ben Smith and Geoff Blundell's (2004) paper which challenges the possibility of discerning the landscape experience of past actors on the basis of phenomenological readings, grounded in intuitive or empathetic experience, or present-day 'immersion' in a landscape. Access to past understandings is possible only via ethnographically-derived worldviews, they argue. However, the somewhat Cartesian application of the alternative worldview approach may itself be subjected to critique (Morris 2012b: 165–167); and further difficulties pertaining to representation by worldview are discussed below.

Heritage and land

Beyond this particular project and the Kalahari participants' involvement, ǂKhomani elders have sought to reconnect with a past prior to colonialism and land loss which, for them, these kinds of sites represent. This is made explicit, for example, in the documentary *My Hunter's Heart* (Foster and Foster 2011). In the centenary year of the 1913 *Natives' Land Act* this matter was of no small importance, indeed having acquired somewhat greater significance following President Jacob Zuma's February 2013 State of the Nation Address. Zuma promised to reopen the lodgement of land claims to those who had not lodged claims by 31 December 1998; and specifically to create exceptions to the 19 June 1913 cut-off date to accommodate claims by the descendants of the Khoe and San, 'including claims on heritage sites, and historic landmarks' (Mxotwa 2013). A lively consultative meeting between government and Khoe and San representatives took place in Kimberley on 15 and 16 April 2013 (Kwon Hoo 2013), at which, in all probability, the full implications of these promises barely began to be realised. Hardly a segment of the South African landscape exists that is not, one way or another, embodied, as far as Khoe and San history goes, by 'heritage sites and historic landmarks'. Just as the ramifications of what are (in their detail) rash promises would soon, surely, become clear, so an opportunity will have been opened up for places such as Biesje Poort to feature more prominently in debates about access to, and ownership of, land.

The recent television screening of *My Hunter's Heart* highlighted the ǂKhomani land claim and their journey, as the blurb puts it, to 'recapture knowledge and save heritage'. It depicts community elders visiting rock art sites somewhat distant from their reclaimed Kalahari farms: sites such as Driekopseiland near Kimberley and, in the Karoo, Varskans and Springbokoog. It is by no means clear in historical terms whether the ǂKhomani, specifically, would have had any direct connections even with the rock art of Biesje Poort, let alone links with engravings further away. Yet the connections are being asserted. If a more generalised 'San' association is implied, then others in the landscape may have equally compelling claims, though the latter may lack the cultural attributes most strongly signalling indigeneity.

The political and legal entailments of indigenous identity and intellectual property rights encourage thinking in terms of an evolving matrix of classificatory traits, including language and cultural elements (Humphreys 1998), which may define who is or is not Khoekhoe or San or a representative of some more specific level of identity within the Khoisan constellation (see Morris 2008, 2012a). An asserted affinity with rock art in this connection – an obvious move, given its manifest age and accepted LSA context – adds advantage not only with regard to indigenous identity, but also as a link to land.

A role for rock art as the 'title deeds' of former Bushman occupation is a powerful idea raised as far back as the late 19th century by George Stow (Stow 1905: 397; Morris 2008), who referred to rock engravings at Driekopseiland near Kimberley in these terms. Often coupled with this idea, but having less empirical substance, is a persistent notion, also originating in Stow and propagated latterly through 20th-century school history texts (e.g., Van Jaarsveld 1969: 123–124), that had the Bushmen retreat into the desert from the south, as the reach of the colony swept inland. This version of history might provide a rationale for ‡Khomani elders (*cf.* Morris 2012a: 238–239 on !Xun and Khwe commentators' projection of this very formula at Wildebeest Kuil) to cast a proprietary eye over sites such as those in the Karoo. But the more likely scenario (although movement of people cannot be discounted completely) is that at least many of those |Xam people of the Karoo who survived disease and conquest were incorporated into colonial society locally as an underclass (Adhikari 2010; De Prada-Samper 2012; Penn 2005). Descendants today of the makers of Karoo rock art, it follows, would not be people allegedly once forced into the desert, but, predominantly, the Afrikaans-speaking so-called coloured people of the Karoo itself – 'culturally nearly extinct, though genetically very much alive' (Parkington, Morris and Rusch 2008: 122) – many of them still on farms, or living as peripatetic seasonal workers and often jobless *karretjie* people (De Jongh 2012).

The connections surely exist and even quite specific linkages may be echoed in the present-day proximity of some people to rock art in their particular landscapes. But these would be hard to demonstrate. Attempting to adjudicate between competing claims based on appeals to history (e.g., local but lacking cultural repertoire) or to culture (e.g., possession of a click language or other recognised traits, but from afar) would be to miss the point, however. It is argued that a focus, rather, on place and multivocality would open up opportunities for a more inclusive sense of custodianship acknowledging the historical overlays and nuances likely to exist in any given place.

Reading traces of the past in a landscape

I have referred to the somewhat bold earlier pronouncements on the archaeological associations of artefact assemblages at Biesje Poort, and the subsequent qualification of these views with more provisional assessments. The view that the occupants of the places were most likely not San/Bushman but Khoekhoe now gives way to an acknowledgement of greater complexity (just as complexity must be acknowledged in contemporary settings where some ‡Khomani, erstwhile N|uu-speakers, have since been speakers generally of Nama, and now predominantly of Afrikaans – and with some individuals tracing mixed ancestry which includes Damara forebears). The kind of pottery usually linked (perhaps stereotypically) with Khoekhoe pastoralists is found on the sites, but as yet there is little evidence of domesticates – although proxy evidence for sheep in the form of vitrified dung is found at a related site in the nearby Riemvasmaak (Parsons 2007). For now it is considered that the occupants of some of the Biesje Poort sites were perhaps hunters with sheep, with lifeways possibly divergent from those of the |Xam in the Karoo or the hunter gatherers of the Kalahari – but to what degree they diverged remains, as Parsons (2007) suggests, a matter for ongoing enquiry.

Quite how these artefact scatters then relate to the nearby rock art is also far from certain – any link remains, on present evidence, hypothetical – not least because there is still no reliable means to date the engravings and establish their contemporaneity with the artefacts.

During our fieldwork in 2011 we gained a profound sense of how the rock art of Biesje Poort is enfolded in a landscape replete with other traces of a long and dynamic intertwining of cultural and natural histories (Morris 2011, 2013). One site was a palimpsest with artefacts of varying age providing much fuel for discussion about the meanings and ambiguities of the variety of material culture remains that may occur in any given locale (Figure 5). What were the implications of these at this particular spot?

Figure 5

The place is a flat sandy area abutting the Biesje Poort hills, near 'T'jammiekloof' (Müller Jansen 2013). The artefacts strewn across its surface (Figures 6–10) are a disassembly of at least two or more histories, a succession of erasures, of over-printing: on the face of it, chaotic. A few flaked stone tools; several brass cartridge cases (darkly patinated); an upper grindstone; a

Figures 6–10

single postage-stamp-sized clay potshard; a glass marble (of the type from a circa 100-year-old mineral water bottle); and a variety of metal items, brown with age, including short bits of wire, steel loops (resembling either part of a broken padlock or cut chain links), nails (both flat and round – any wooden objects they once fastened long since having disintegrated), and a belt buckle with snake-motif clasp. Nearby are rock engravings of elephant, giraffe, antelope and strange complex designs. In an intermediate space, stone artefacts include flakes and a lower grindstone. It, too, is a palimpsest: alongside LSA traces, perhaps of the order of 500 years old, was a classic Middle Stone Age (MSA) triangular stone point, possibly some 125 000 years old. Widespread, if often diffuse, scatters of similar artefacts in the region suggest a pulse of MSA inhabitation during one of the warmer, wetter intervals within the generally cold, dry Pleistocene.

Lively discussion ensued as members of our group, from their different perspectives, sought to make sense of these traces and to construct storylines to 'read' what we were encountering.

Broadly, it was possible to distinguish objects of European and local derivation, separating out along a timeline from LSA to recent, with some potential for overlap between 'precolonial' and 'colonial'. Just as it was impossible to be certain which of the 'precolonial' artefacts were precisely contemporaneous on this flat erosion surface, and whether any could be linked with nearby engravings, so too it was hard to say whether or not all of the more recent artefacts could be read in terms of a single set of circumstances or events. The Kalahari participants were seemingly predisposed to explaining their separation from the kinds of 'precolonial' landscapes into which we had been dipping, in terms of conflagration: if not a massacre, then some kind of battle, they were convinced, had taken place here. Battle narratives concerning German colonial atrocities have been a feature of recent oral memory, given during the follow-up fieldwork at Witdraai in 2011, and featuring centrally and traumatically in Patricia Glyn's (2013) subsequent account of *What Dawid knew: a journey with the Kruipers*. A hypothetical scenario referencing a nearby 'Bushman grave', the cartridge cases, the military buckle clasp, the tunic button found upslope, the abandoned stone tools and grindstone, and the other items variously woven as components of a single dramatic episode at the edge of these hills, make for a remarkably coherent – and poignant – story. Liana Müller Jansen (2013) gives some sense of the evolving account, and the confusion over the nearby 'Army Kloof'/'T'jammiekloof'.

But the real story – or stories – one suspects, would be less spectacular and altogether more complex. The evidence is riddled with gaps. There are only fragments to go on, bits of potential storyline, each of them individually debatable.

What if the button, or the buckle, once parts of a military uniform, arrived on-site on the shoulders or around the waist of a farm-hand? Old bits of uniform or other clothing, beyond their prime, are known to be handed down to clothe labourers and may end their days (dropping into a future archaeological context) in quite unanticipated circumstances. Evidence for shooting may refer to such quotidian farm activities as predator control – or, as literature from Biesje Poort farm attests, shooting dassies (Müller Jansen 2013). Bits of wire and some of the other items may point to the site having been a temporary work area for the erection of farm fencing.

Micro-histories emerge from the interrogation of these and other left-over objects on-site – momentarily illuminated (from whichever perspective), as in Foucault's (2000: 161) 'lives destined to pass beneath any discourse', but caught for an instant, as by a beam of light, and thereby 'able to leave traces – brief, incisive, often enigmatic

…'. Indirectly they may point to macro processes and larger historical events, ultimately including those of conquest and the workings of sub-continental and world industrial and economic regimes (we spoke of manufacturing and commerce in relation to the two kinds of steel nails that were noticed, while the possibility that we had part of a broken padlock stimulated discussion on the history and local advent of concepts of private property relative to communal ownership). Contexts beyond the immediately local place were noted with respect to the raw materials on which precolonial stone tools were made: some we had seen were exotic to Biesje Poort, made from stone procured along the banks of the Gariep, a full day's walk away (or traded in via intermediate groups). The history of trauma hinted at near Witdraai, and more fully elaborated in Dawid Kruiper's unburdening of disturbing atrocities in the dunes further north (Glyn 2013), contextualises a predisposition to understand bullets and buttons in certain ways. Social, material and historical entanglements (Hodder 2012; Ingold 2011) across sweeps of time and space, were much in evidence.

The different possible readings arising from this one site highlight the ambiguity that is often inherent in artefacts – and places. The final circumstances under which an item ends up in any given setting may differ somewhat from its more usual connotations and the better interpretation may often be the less obvious one. While speculating, our debates made us particularly aware of the multivocality of things and of places, and the assumptions and preconceptions, even relations of power (Wolf 1999), that we bring to our acts of characterisation and narration.

From sites to zones of entanglement

Mapping site distributions and stratigraphic sequences is a basic modus operandi in archaeology for tracking change through horizontal (spatial) and vertical (temporal) dimensions. As a heuristic device, the Cartesian geometries involved – indeed, the Foucauldian 'grid of intelligibility' by which the 'order of things' is determined – can distort one's view. The conventional idea of 'site', itself, all too easily implies that the archaeological record is confined to small 'spot' occurrences separated by empty tracts – as they usually appear in maps (Chippendale and Nash 2004: 12). Because of past human behaviour patterns that tend to cluster spatially, or because of unequal preservation of the record, the traces may often indeed be localised. But the division of abundant spreads of, say, engravings into numbered localities, as in our Biesje Poort records, is often an entirely arbitrary enterprise in which misrepresentation may arise. Beyond the heuristic device, one comes to appreciate the engravings and 'sites' nested or enfolded in dynamic landscapes, and better conceived as being, as Tim Ingold (2000) suggests, part of the working out of the involved activity of their makers – and of those who afterwards 'used' these marks that endure; and indeed of those making sense of them today.

By contrast, cadastral logic in the modern setting (reaching an epitome in the context of heritage management practices) favours the neatly circumscribed site, static, fenced-off, legally segregated and defined in terms of 'use' and as 'protected' management unit (Byrne 2003). Such parceling out of small portions of landscape and segments of history, often along with their respective stakeholder communities, unwittingly reifies ethnicities while fragmenting the continuous patterns of past activity into the discontinuous pods of activity that constitute the heritage landscape (ibid.). Each such 'site' becomes what Ingold (2007a: 96, emphasis in the original) refers to as a kind of reconfigured place 'within which all life, growth and activity are *contained*'. Denis Byrne's (2003: 188) critique of the continued hegemony of the 'site' concept envisages a total cultural landscape that radiates outwards to and beyond the horizon, with 'off-site' scatters of artefacts or rock art spreading in variable densities over kilometres, rather than metres. !Kung hunter-gatherer *n!oresi*, the overlapping ranges of natural resources in the landscape exploited by neighbouring bands on a daily basis (Smith 1994), exemplify just this sort of scenario.

'Life will not be contained,' contends Ingold (2011: 83), 'but rather threads its way through the world along the myriad lines of its relations'. He opposes the idea of 'network' with a concept developed from Lefebvre, namely 'meshwork'. A 'network' presupposes the prior separation of elements, whereas 'things *are* their relations' (ibid: 70): they live along multiple pathways in the course of their involvement in the world, as entanglements with one another. Lefebvre's conception is defined as 'the reticular patterns left by animals, both wild and domestic, and by people (in and around the houses of ... a small town, as in the town's immediate environs')' (in Ingold 2007a: 80), where these various movements 'weave an environment that is more "archi-textural" than architectural'. It is in the entanglement of lines of life, not in the connecting of points, that the mesh is constituted. In this view, 'environment' falls away as a separate entity beyond or surrounding the lives of individual organisms (including persons) and instead becomes a 'domain of entanglement' (Ingold 2011: 70–71), with particular 'places' or 'sites' being formations that arise within the process of movement. They come into being in relation to the perpetual comings and goings of people, as a nexus of the activities in which people engage: they become, as Ingold (ibid: 168) puts it, 'a particular enfoldment of the lives of persons'. Conversely, he adds, places and journeys between them are implicated in the lives of individuals as 'every person would come into being as an enfoldment of the experience' (ibid.) that places and journeys afford.

The patterning of rock art and occupation/activity debris relative to resources, particularly water, at Biesje Poort evince this sense of 'comings and goings' in which the lives of persons and the formations of places were no doubt closely articulated. How personhood itself could be shaped and redefined in such relations is a theme explored through the rock engravings in another setting, at Driekopseiland where, it is suggested, the place and the rock art were intimately part of the coming-of-age rites of young women (Morris 2002). Similar processes may well have been enacted amongst the Biesje Poort hills.

There is, further, a political impulse in place-making, Ingold (2005)[4] argues, with people's activities revolving, to different degrees, on dwelling in relative peace and prosperity, securing protection or power against theft, sorcery, aggression, fire, storms, diseases and dangerous wild animals. Involved would be the workings of cosmologies and structural power (see Wolf 1999), and expressions of, for instance, territorial behaviour (see Humphreys 2009) – domains in which rock art possibly had a role. It appears that women's rituals (and with them, arguably, at a site such as Driekopseiland, rock engraving activity) were intensified and became more visible as the social environment, through increased interaction with outsiders, became more complex (Morris 2002). Might similarly politically significant actions lie behind some aspects of the marking of rocks at Biesje Poort, inscribing the hills in an enduring way?

Palimpsests

Ingold (2011: 96, 126) adds the insight that we inhabit weather worlds, which in the arid areas of the Northern Cape include eroding landforms that feed fields of wind-blown dunes, and sediments gravitating towards the Gariep. Because of weather, says Ingold (2007b: 533), the land is continually 'growing over' – which is why archaeologists have to dig to find traces of the past. When traces mount up or are swept away by erosion (the more predominant land-shaping process at Biesje Poort), what results are palimpsests that, as inherent features of the world we inhabit, constitute some of the gaps and fragments we contend with in our daily lives and, particularly, as scholars who would understand the past.

Geoff Bailey (2007) rejects the view that regards palimpsests negatively as the transformation of traces for which some correction is needed in order to read the past. They are 'not some degraded or distorted version of a message that needs to be restored to its original state before it can be interpreted. To a large extent,' he insists, 'they *are* the message.' In similar vein, Michael Shanks (2013) characterises the archaeological endeavour as, instead of discovery of the past, 'work on what remains'. Panels containing rock art are also palimpsests, featuring older and younger images, sometimes overlapping and sometimes in processes of destruction. Deterioration is very much in evidence at Biesje Poort, resulting from erosion, perhaps accelerated by locally increased seismicity (the area is geologically highly deformed by numerous fault lines, and has lately experienced an earthquake swarm [Council for Geoscience 2012]). The trampling of animals and people across crumbling gneiss exacerbates the situation.

Different forms of palimpsest occur (Bailey 2007: 203–208): true palimpsests in which successive layers of activity displace preceding ones, completely or nearly so; cumulative palimpsests (common in open sites of the Northern Cape) in which successive layers build up or are winnowed down, such that deposition episodes mingle and become 'mixed'; spatial palimpsests in which the traces of spatially discrete events are difficult to correlate chronologically, or where spatially clustered materials disaggregate through time; temporal palimpsests in which objects of differing age are deposited in a single event, as in a burial; and, finally, palimpsests of meaning revealed in the life histories or cultural biographies of objects or places which, as they endure, may be put to continuous or changing uses or acquire different meanings.

It is hard to think of any situation or place either in the archaeological past or in the contemporary world which is not, one way or another, a palimpsest. Any given object, moreover, might be characterised in terms of 'moments in time' – a stone artefact, for example, relative to the moment of raw material acquisition, of manufacture, use, trade and eventual discard; with yet further moments including those of recovery by an archaeologist, curation or display in a museum, of use in a publication, and the place it may come to occupy in scholarly discourse. Such moments extend, in the present, to the politics of identity and entitlement.

Representation

Part of an archaeological representation of Biesje Poort could take the form of a map, the rock engravings – along with distributions of artefact scatters and shelters and grinding grooves, relative to other features such as expanses of rock panels, watercourses, waterholes and seeps (after rains), graves, and so on – dotted across it, and a chart hazarding a hypothesis as to age for different engravings based on technique or degree of weathering or archaeological association (in the absence as yet of reliable dating methods). To this, archaeologists would seek to add insights on the meaning of the traces, often grounded in ethnographic analogy, with much progress having been made in the elaboration of interpretive frameworks in South Africa since the 1970s.

I have sought to indicate some of the gaps, uncertainties and ambiguities in the material record and in terms of absences of storyline – as much as the eruption of often incommensurate accounts arising from encounters with the site (or parts of it) from different perspectives or with diverse priorities in the present. From this has sprung a multi-stranded, often less-than-coherent narrative in which archaeology provides one thread. Against the background of unresolved questions, I have sought to illustrate something of the likely complexity of this zone of entanglement, as Ingold would put it, and of the palimpsests that, as Bailey says, are the message. Many voices come to us out of the Biesje Poort hills, which we weave, adding our own twists. The 'uppermost' layer in the Biesje Poort palimpsest consists of the arguments and interpretations of the present day.

At the level of representation, Rane Willerslev (2007: 156) has contributed an important critique of the concept of 'worldview', often deployed in the interpretation of archaeological materials and rock art. He regards 'worldviews' as an unhelpful, even fundamentally misleading, way of characterising the nature of cultural knowledge. It implies the existence of a universal, underlying substrate or code, a stable corpus of conceptual knowledge prefiguring individual belief and custom. His observations, consistent with Ingold's formulation, suggest instead that people generate representations of their beliefs, for instance, in the course of their everyday practical lives in local performative contexts. Our 'world versions', as Nelson Goodman (in Elgin 2000: 9) puts it, 'are made rather than found'. This is not to suggest that world-making does not start with worlds already on hand, again citing Goodman. But it is anthropologists, asserts Willerslev (2007: 156), and not the people studied, who have constructed the ideal cosmologies, cognitive templates and worldviews as a kind of cultural grammar somehow implanted in people's heads. History matters, suggests Silvia Tomášková (2013) in her analysis of the origins and use of one such anthropological construct, namely *shaman*. As a concept cobbled together from particular historical situations, it has come to be generalised as an ahistorical transcendental category, universally applicable (ibid: 196). Vince Miller (2006: 464) refers to qualities of vagueness and ambiguity which tend to get written out of our accounts in acts of representation. He adds that it is in the movement from vagueness to precision where power relations are enacted, and the open-endedness of social life gets to be constrained or closed down.

The fragmented, fragile traces at Biesje Poort, and the disparate narrative threads that have emerged, frustrate the construction of any definitive synthesis. But the inherent multivocality becomes, as Lindsay Weiss (2012) suggests for situations such as this, an opportunity for alternative narratives to be brought alongside one another.

Amongst these are the interpretations of the engravings given by the Kalahari participants. They would differ from the 'informed' views that rock art scholars tend to advance (noting that rock art scholars do not speak with one voice, despite aspiring to epistemological consistency; also often being explicitly sensitive and open to indigenous or local insights). The Kalahari experience is of a 21st-century context, with its own historical perspectives and contemporary priorities, and, however 'authentic' or linguistically immersed that experience may be, it would remain separated geographically and historically from the practice of rock art – a point made recently by David Lewis-Williams and Sam Challis (2011: 11–12). Nevertheless, the participants contributed rich readings of landscape and insights into social and cultural practices in the course of the fieldwork.

In the 1980s, Ed Wilmsen (1986) interviewed a group of Ju|'hoasi men to record their understandings of rock paintings through a selection of copies, and elicited from each quite idiosyncratic perspectives on the art. A century before that, as Andrew Bank (2006: 338–339) has shown, each of the |Xam informants had a distinct voice and, in their comments on copies of rock paintings, he suggests, 'their understanding of these pictures was often far from clear'. As Michael Wessels points out, citing Gayatri Spivak, and in light of Willerslev's remarks (above) on 'worldview', one should not expect the individual voice to be the 'authentic ethnic fully representative of his or her tradition' (Spivak 1999: 60 in Wessels 2010: 43) – whatever that might be. One should not presuppose either the cohesive, bonded and determining, collective consciousness, any more than the image of a bounded and stable individual subject who is completely defined by his/her cultural context.

The individual voices, as fragments of storyline, speak to histories that converge on or stretch out through landscapes like Biesje Poort. A tendency in heritage discourse often is to 'map' them in the flat, to generalise and iron out any ambiguities and discordances, reducing them through a common set of assumptions, as Weiss has noted. The authorised versions, 'feel good histories' (Wright 2013), would seldom admit questions or discrepancies. Advocated here is a kind of 'mapping' that does not reduce the multivocality in these ways. Instead, with Titlestad (2001: 31), 'we need to conceive of a map which announces the "creaking", the strain of representation, while celebrating fluidity and the divagations of meaning, force and signification'.

Narrating Biesje Poort has been about acknowledging the strain of representation, indeed announcing the 'creaking', the gaps, the vagueness, the not-always-coherent multi-strandedness of the available accounts. The conversations that ensue challenge our constructions of places, peoples and storylines in the present.

Notes

1   This article is based on a presentation given at the Seminar on Khoi and San Representation, 19–21 April 2013. A different version of it was reworked as a chapter in the book *Engraved landscape. Biesje Poort: many voices* (Lange et al. 2013).

2   These terms being problematic, different conventions and spellings have pertained. Khoisan is an anthropological term, coined by Schultze and popularised by Schapera (Barnard 1992), referring to speakers of click languages in southern Africa, historically known as 'Bushmen' (San) and 'Hottentots' (Khoi/Khoe/Khoekhoe). Where possible or appropriate, specific groups names such as ‡Khomani, !Xun or Khwe are used. Different current spellings include: 'National Khoe and San Heritage Route' and 'Khoisan Council.'

3   'History matters when considering categories' (Tomášková 2013: 197). For a considered understanding of IKS or indigenous knowledge, see Green (2008).

4   See also the preface to the 2011 edition of Ingold (2000). The author moves beyond an earlier focus on 'dwelling perspective' with its connotations of 'snug, well-wrapped localism', lacking in political dimension.

References

Adhikari, M. 2010. *The anatomy of a South African genocide: the extermination of the Cape San peoples*. Cape Town: UCT Press.

Bailey, G. 2007. Time perspectives, palimpsests and the archaeology of time. *Journal of Anthropological Archaeology* 26(1): 198–223.

Bank, A. 2006. *Bushmen in a Victorian World: the remarkable story of the Bleek–Lloyd collection of Bushman folklore*. Cape Town: Double Storey Books.

Barnabas, S. 2013. Biesje Poort as a rock art resource: conservation and tourism. In *Engraved landscape. Biesje Poort: many voices*, ed. M.E. Lange, L. Müller-Jansen, R. Fisher, K. Tomaselli and D. Morris, 103–109. Gordon's Bay: Tormentoso.

Barnard, A. 1992. *Hunters and herders of southern Africa: a comparative ethnography of the Khoisan peoples*. Cambridge: Cambridge University Press.

Beaumont, P.B., A.B. Smith and J.C. Vogel. 1995. Before the Einiqua: the archaeology of the frontier zone. In *Einiqualand*, ed. A.B. Smith, 236–264. Cape Town: UCT Press.

Byrne, D.R. 2003. Nervous landscapes: race and space in Australia. *Journal of Social Archaeology* 3(1): 169–193.

Chauke, P. 2010. New hominid skeleton named Karabo. *Mail & Guardian*, 1 June: 24. http://mg.co.za/article/2010-06-01-new-hominid-skeleton-named-karabo (accessed 7 August 2013).

Chippindale, C. and G. Nash. 2004. Pictures in place: approaches to the figured landscapes of rock art. In *Pictures in place: the figured landscapes of rock art*, ed. C. Chippendale and G. Nash, 1–36. Cambridge: Cambridge University Press.

Council for Geoscience. 2012. Seismicity in the Augrabies area. http://www.geoscience. org.za/index.php?option=com_content&view=article&id=1455:seismicity-in-the-augrabies-area&catid=288&Itemid=226 (accessed 29 April 2014).

De Jongh, M. 2012. *Roots and routes: Karretjie People of the Great Karoo – the marginalisation of a South African first people*. Pretoria: Unisa Press.

De Prada-Samper, J.M. 2012. The forgotten killing fields: 'San' genocide and Louis Anthing's mission to Bushmanland, 1862–1863. *Historia* 57(1): 172–187.

Duval, M. and B.W. Smith 2012. Rock art tourism in the uKhahlamba/Drakensberg World Heritage Site: obstacles to the development of sustainable tourism. *Journal of Sustainable Tourism* 21: 134–153.

Elgin, C.Z. 2000. Worldmaker: Nelson Goodman, 1906–1998. *Journal for General Philosophy of Science* 31(1): 1–18.

Fock, G.J. and D.M.L. Fock. 1989. *Felsbilder in Südafrika, Teil 3 (Vaal-Oranje-Becken)*. Köln: Böhlau Verlag.

Foster, C. and D. Foster. 2011. Documentary film *My Hunter's Heart*, dir. Craig Foster and Damon Foster. United International Pictures South Africa, 83 mins.

Foucault, M. 2000. The lives of infamous men. In *Essential works of Foucault, 1954–1984, vol. 3: Power*, ed. J.D. Faubion, 157–175. New York: The New Press.

Glyn, P. 2013. *What Dawid knew: a journey with the Kruipers*. Johannesburg: Picador Africa.

Green, L.J.F. 2008. 'Indigenous knowledge' and 'science': reframing the debate on knowledge diversity. *Archaeologies: Journal of the World Archaeological Congress* 4(2): 144–163.

Guenther, M. 1995. Contested images, contested texts: the politics of representing the Bushmen of southern Africa. *Critical Arts* 9(2): 110–118.

Hodder, I. 1989. Writing archaeology: site reports in context. *Antiquity* 63(3): 268–274.

Hodder, I. 2012. *Entangled: an archaeology of the relationships between humans and things.* Oxford: Wiley-Blackwell.

Humphreys, A.J.B. 1998. Populations, prehistory, pens and politics: some reflections from north of the Orange River. *Southern African Field Archaeology* 7: 20–25.

Humphreys, A.J.B. 2009. A Riet River retrospective. *Southern African Humanities* 21(2): 157–175.

Ingold, T. 2000. *The perception of the environment: essays in livelihood, dwelling and skill.* London: Routledge. Reprinted with new preface, 2011.

Ingold, T. 2005. Epilogue: towards a politics of dwelling. *Conservation and Society* 3(4): 501–508.

Ingold, T. 2007a. *Lines: a brief history.* London: Routledge.

Ingold, T. 2007b. Earth, sky, wind and weather. *Journal of the Royal Anthropological Institute (NS)*: S19–S38.

Ingold, T. 2011. *Being alive: essays in movement, knowledge and description.* London: Routledge.

Kundera, M. 2003. *The art of the novel.* New York: Harper Collins Perennial Classics.

Kwon Hoo, S. 2013. Government apologises to Khoisan people. *Diamonds Fields Advertiser*, 16 April: 4

Lange, M. 2011. *Water stories and rock engravings: Eiland women at the Kalahari edge.* Amsterdam: Rozenberg Publishers.

Lange, M.E., L. Müller-Jansen, R.C. Fisher, K.G. Tomaselli and D. Morris, eds. 2013. *Engraved landscape. Biesje Poort: many voices.* Gordon's Bay: Tormentoso.

Le Fleur, A. and L. Jansen. 2013. The Khoisan in contemporary South Africa. *Konrad Adenauer Stiftung Country Report*, August.

Leone, M.P. 1983. Method as message: interpreting the past with the public. *Museum News* 62(1): 34–41.

Lewis-Williams, J.D. and S. Challis. 2011. *Deciphering ancient minds: the mystery of San Bushman rock art.* London: Thames and Hudson.

Magongo, M. 2013. Participatory communication: a tool for social and heritage development. In *Engraved landscape. Biesje Poort: many voices*, ed. M.E. Lange, L. Müller-Jansen, R. Fisher, K.G. Tomaselli and D. Morris, 93–100. Gordon's Bay: Tormentoso.

McDavid, C. 2002. Archaeologies that hurt; descendants that matter: a pragmatic approach to collaboration in the public interpretation of African-American archaeology. *World Archaeology* 34: 303–314

Miller, V. 2006. The unmappable: vagueness and spatial experience. *Space and Culture* 9(3): 453–467.

Morris, D. 2008. Driekopseiland rock engraving site, South Africa: a precolonial landscape lost and re-membered. In *Landscapes of clearance: archaeological and anthropological perspectives*, ed. A. Gazin-Schwartz and A. Smith, 87–111. Walnut Creek: Left Coast Press.

Morris, D. 2011. Engaging the traces: archaeological meanings and ambiguities in the artefacts in and around Biesje Poort Site 10. *Subtext* (Autumn): 16–17, CCMS, University of KwaZulu-Natal.

Morris, D. 2012a. The importance of Wildebeest Kuil: 'a hill with a future, a hill with a past'. In *Working with rock art: recording, presenting and understanding rock art using indigenous knowledge*, ed. B. Smith, K. Helskog and D. Morris, 228–245. Johannesburg: Wits University Press.

Morris, D. 2012b. Rock art in the Northern Cape: the implications of variability in engravings and paintings relative to issues of social context and change in the precolonial past. Unpublished doctoral dissertation, Department of Anthropology and Sociology, University of the Western Cape.

Morris, D. 2013. Engaging absence of story-line, vagueness and ambiguity: towards an archaeology of rock art at Biesje Poort. In *Engraved landscape. Biesje Poort: many voices*, ed. M.E. Lange, L. Müller-Jansen, R. Fisher, K.G. Tomaselli and D. Morris, 47–55. Gordon's Bay: Tormentoso.

Morris, D. 2014, in press. Wildebeest Kuil Rock Art Centre, South Africa: controversy and renown, successes and shortcomings. *Public Archaeology* 13.

Morris, D., B. Ndebele and P. Wilson. 2009. Who is interested in the Wildebeest Kuil Rock Art Centre? Preliminary results from a visitor questionnaire. *The Digging Stick* 26(2): 17–18, 23.

Müller Jansen, L. 2013. Reading the Biesje Poort landscape. In *Engraved landscape. Biesje Poort: many voices*, ed. M.E. Lange, L. Müller-Jansen, R. Fisher, K.G. Tomaselli and D. Morris, 21–41. Gordon's Bay: Tormentoso.

Mxotwa, M. 2013. The Khoi and San people agree to work with government in restoring their land rights. Statement on behalf of Minister Gugile Nkwinti, 16 April. http://www.politicsweb.co.za/politicsweb/view/politicsweb/en/page71654?oid=370251&sn=Detail&pid=71654 (accessed 19 August 2013).

Parkington, J., D. Morris and N. Rusch. 2008. *Karoo rock engravings*. Clanwilliam: Krakadouw Trust.

Parsons, I. 2007. Hunter-gatherers or herders? Reconsidering the Swartkop and Doornfontein Industries, Northern Cape Province, South Africa. *Before Farming* 2007/4, article 3.

Penn, N. 2005. *The forgotten frontier: colonist and Khoisan on the Cape's Northern frontier in the 18th century*. Athens, Ohio and Cape Town: Ohio University Press and Double Storey Books.

Pluciennik, M. 1999. Archaeological narratives and other ways of telling. *Current Anthropology* 40: 653–678.

Robins, S. 2001. NGOs, 'Bushmen' and double vision: the ǂKhomani San land claim and the cultural politics of 'community' and 'development' in the Kalahari. *Journal of Southern African Studies* 27: 833–853.

Shanks, M. 2013. Archaeological manifesto. http://documents.stanford.edu/MichaelShanks/112 (accessed 29 April 2014).

Smith, A.B. 1994. Metaphors of space: rock art and territoriality in southern Africa. In *Contested images: diversity in southern African rock art research*, ed. T.A. Dowson and J.D. Lewis-Williams, 373–384. Johannesburg: Witwatersrand University Press.

Smith, B.W. and G. Blundell. 2004. Dangerous ground: a critique of landscape in rock-art studies. In *Pictures in place: the figured landscapes of rock art*, ed. C. Chippendale and G. Nash, 239–262. Cambridge: Cambridge University Press.

Stow, G.W. 1905. *The native races of South Africa*. London: Swan, Sonnenschein.

Tilley, C. 1989. Excavation as theatre. *Antiquity* 63(2): 275–280.

Titlestad, M. 2001. Contesting maps: musical improvisation and narrative. *Pretexts: Literary and Cultural Studies* 10(1): 21–36.

Tomaselli, K.G. 2013. Setting the scene: What's in a landscape? In *Engraved landscape. Biesje Poort: many voices*, ed. M.E. Lange, L. Müller-Jansen, R. Fisher, K.G. Tomaselli and D. Morris, xi–xvii. Gordon's Bay: Tormentoso.

Tomášková, S. 2013. *Wayward shamans: the prehistory of an idea*. Berkeley: University of California Press.

Van Jaarsveld, F.A. 1969. *New illustrated history, Standard VI*. Johannesburg: Voortrekkerpers.

Weiss, L.M. 2012. Rock art at present in the past. In *Working with rock art: recording, presenting and understanding rock art using indigenous knowledge*, ed. B. Smith, K. Helskog and D. Morris, 216–227. Johannesburg: Wits University Press.

Wessels, M. 2010. *Bushman letters: interpreting |Xam narrative*. Johannesburg: Wits University Press.

Willerslev, R. 2007. *Soul hunters: hunting, animism, and personhood among the Siberian Yukaghirs*. Berkeley: University of California Press.

Wilmsen, E.N. 1986. Of paintings and painters, in terms of Ju|'hoasi interpretations. In *Contemporary studies on Khoisan 2*, ed. R. Fossen and K. Keuthmann, 347–372. Hamburg: Helmut Buske Verlag.

Wolf, E.R. 1999. *Envisioning power: ideologies of dominance and crisis*. Berkeley: University of California Press.

Wright, J. 1996. Sonqua, Bosjesmans, Bushmen, abaThwa: comments and queries on pre-modern identifications. *South African Historical Journal* 35: 16–29.

Wright, J. 2013. Heritage as feel-good history. *The Digging Stick* 30(2): 1–3.

!Xun and Khwe elders. 2009. Wildebeest Kuil Story. Digital story (told in !Xun and in Khwedam, with English sub-titles) on YouTube. http://www.youtube.com/watch?v=CQVHs9yPFZs (accessed 28 September 2011).

Zuma, J.G. 2013. State of the Nation Address on the occasion of the Joint Sitting of Parliament, Cape Town, 14 February. http://www.thepresidency.gov.za/pebble.asp?relid=14960 (accessed 29 April 2014).

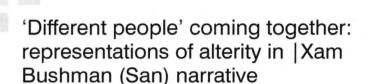

'Different people' coming together: representations of alterity in |Xam Bushman (San) narrative

Mark McGranaghan

Abstract

Colonial processes around the world had major impacts on the indigenous populations with whom colonists interacted – this is particularly true for small-scale populations that relied heavily on foraging subsistence practices. Historical sources that document these impacts are in the main highly skewed toward representations made by colonial populations themselves. The dominance of these representations forms a major challenge to attempts to reinterrogate colonial historical accounts of the processes of colonisation, and renders opaque the ways in which indigenous populations themselves understood and manipulated their historical interactions with 'Others'. The Bleek–Lloyd archive – focusing on the |Xam Bushmen of the arid interior Karoo of South Africa – offers the opportunity both to question colonial presentations of 'Bushman' identities, and to explore Bushman representations of their 19th-century situation. This article discusses one aspect of these representations, focusing on the way in which |Xam individuals constructed 'alien' identities, and how these were manipulated in social discourse.

The Bleek–Lloyd archive

Beginning in the late 1850s and continuing throughout the 1860s and 1870s, the German linguist Wilhelm Bleek interviewed several |Xam Bushman (San) informants, hunter-gatherers, herders, and farm labourers of the Northern Cape (Figure 1), and colonial convicts in the Breakwater prison. Hoping to produce a record of a language in imminent danger of extinction, Bleek was assisted by his sister-in-law, Lucy Lloyd, who came to play an increasingly central role in the project, continuing it and bringing it to fruition after his death in August 1875. The information they collected constitutes what is now known as the Bleek–Lloyd archive, a corpus of traditional narrative, personal histories and ethnographic information. It was recorded from records from six main informants: five men (|A!kunta, ||Kabbo, ǂKasin, Dia!kwain, |Hanǂkass'o) and one woman (!Kweitən-ta-||kəŋ).[1]

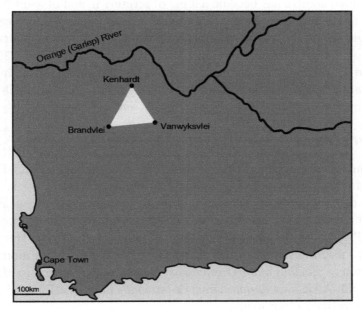

Figure 1: The 'Bushmanland triangle' approximating the homelands of the Bleek-Lloyd informants

In total, over 11 000 notebook pages, or approximately half a million (translated) words were recorded, around 85 per cent of them collected by Lloyd. First published in the late 19th century as summaries and short reports (Bleek 1874, 1875a and b; Lloyd 1880, 1889), *Specimens of Bushman folklore* (Bleek and Lloyd 1911) represented the first major dissemination of the material. Bleek's daughter, Dorothea, oversaw the publication of further notebook material in a short book (Bleek 1924) and in a series of *Bantu studies* papers (Bleek 1931, 1932a, b and c, 1933a and b, 1935, 1936a and b; reprinted with commentary in Hollmann 2004); she also undertook substantial research of her own on extant Bushman communities, culminating in the production of the *Bushman dictionary* (Bleek 1956) after her death.

There now exists an extensive body of literature exploring the Bleek–Lloyd archive and the narratives contained therein, from historical (Bank 2006; Deacon and Dowson 1996; Skotnes 2007), comparative anthropological (Barnard 1992; Guenther 1999), archaeological (Deacon 1988, 1996; Lewis-Williams 1981), folkloric (De Prada-Samper 2009, 2010; Hewitt 2008 [1986]; Schmidt 1996, 2013) and literary critical (Wessels 2010) perspectives, as well as several publications of artistic responses to the narratives it contains (e.g., James 2001; Krog 2004; Watson 1991); indeed, the study of the history of academic interest in and use of the Bleek–Lloyd archive has become a topic of scrutiny in and of itself (see Wessels 2010: 177–193). Although |Xam communities are no longer linguistically extant, anthropological and folkloric work amongst descendants of (among others) Northern Cape |Xam individuals (De Prada-Samper 2012; Hoff 1997, 1998, 2007, 2011, 2012), when placed in conjunction with the 19th-century records, hint at the continuance of certain narrative and ontological themes, providing new data with which to explore the transformation of |Xam identities into the 20th and 21st centuries.

!ke e: |xarra ||ke

Although the |Xam language is not included as one of the 11 official languages of South Africa it forms a key component in the iconography of the post-1994 democracy, used in the South African motto (*!ke e: |xarra ||ke*) alongside imagery derived from rock art panels produced by past southern Bushman communities (Barnard 2004; Smith, Lewis-Williams and Blundell et al. 2000). The motto was created as a loose translation of the phrase 'unity in diversity',[2] a motto recalling both the famous *e pluribus unum* (from many, one) as well as the motto of the former Union of South Africa, *ex unitate vires*, or 'strength in unity' (Barnard 2003a: 20, 28).[3] It is comprised of four words:

- *!ke* (more usually written *!k'e*), plural noun referring to people, men
- *e:* a relative or demonstrative particle, who, which, that, this
- *|xarra*, different, differently, separately
- *||ke*, to meet or be together, possible a variant of *||k''e:*, to be or talk together. (Bleek 1956: 36, 363, 419–420, 566, 604)

Barnard (2003a and b, 2004) has examined the grammatical structure of this sentence, discussed the implications of the various possible translations, and situated the motto within the broader context of the use of Khoisan-derived symbolism on the part of the post-apartheid South African state. Here, I am more concerned with the fact that the motto (whether or not it can be considered grammatically sound as a |Xam phrase) contains a concept that *is* an idiomatic expression found in the Bleek–Lloyd notebooks: *!k'e e: |xarra,* or in the singular *!kwi a |xarra,* 'a person who is different'. This discussion centres on how the |Xam conceived of 'difference' as a personal quality, and how this was deployed in their definitions of certain identities.

|Xam personhood

Recent digital scans of the Bleek–Lloyd texts, first published alongside Skotnes (2007) and now available online,[4] have raised the profile of the archive and vastly increased its accessibility. Although the material it contains can be readily seen as deriving from a specific colonial endeavour (Bank 2000; Moran 2001, 2009), the archive preserves substantial evidence of |Xam idioms – both at a grammatical level and in the deployment of recurrent representational 'themes'. These representations were not only made explicit to Bleek and Lloyd, but are also contained in the narratives the informants told to and about other |Xam individuals, presenting a glass that reflects 'darkly' the way in which |Xam agents represented themselves to one another. This dimension is evident both in the meta-narrative (i.e., the ways in which the tales were told, by whom, for whom, and with what emphases) as well as in the content of the stories themselves: the kinds of agent that the tales portray and the judgements made regarding these agents, both on the part of the narrators and by other characters in the stories.

This article relies on a wholesale transcription of the (translated component of the) archive generated from the digitised resource. This process transformed the scanned images into a fully-searchable archive, allowing for the extraction of key themes: every instance of the use of particular words and phrases can be located and examined for its associations. Bleek and Lloyd recorded parallel English and |Xam texts, and thus the archive allows us to revisit the |Xam terminologies that exist behind the English phrasing provided by Bleek and Lloyd's translations. Although issues concerning the extraction of |Xam (or any 'subaltern') 'voices' from the colonial archive are manifold,[5] by exploring repeated, connected associations of ideas and by constructing patterns and deviations from these patterns, we can hope to outline something approaching '|Xam belief' and attitudes (as much of a reification as these may turn out to be). The discussion that follows explores some of the connections the informants made between physical descriptions and personal traits, looking at the ways in which these were linked to positive and negative assessments of personhood. In outlining these connections I do not purport to define the entirety of '|Xam thought' on these matters (if such a thing were even possible), but instead draw attention to some of the likely components, as supported by specific textual references (see Wessels [2010: 217–240] for discussions on the 'multi-vocal' nature of |Xam narrative).

The identification of a 'foraging mode of thought' (Barnard 2002) has become a major preoccupation of later 20th-century anthropological hunter-gatherer scholarship, emerging from a reconceptualisation of 19th-century definitions of ideological and ontological components of hunter-gatherer cultures (De Castro 1998; Descola 1992, 1996; Tylor 1871, 377–453; for a review, see Bird-David 1999). A key element in this reconsideration has revolved around exploring elements involved in the definition of personhood. Ingold (2000) suggests that 'animic' ontologies have as their most basic emic premise the idea that the quality of 'being animated' is a principle shared amongst human and non-human communities. Drawing on ethnographies of indigenous American societies, Ingold (ibid: 113–114) suggests that notions of circulation and reciprocity in exchanges of 'vital force' are salient in these ontological understandings. Agents share ontologically-equivalent vitality but live in a manner consistent with their form, relying for their continued existence on sharing their vitality though interactions with a range of different forms. Although these understandings have typically been derived from (and usually applied to) foraging populations, it is important to note that Ingold does not attempt to construct an ahistorical essential 'hunter-gatherer' form of personhood, but instead draws upon ethnographic data to create heuristic models that can then be reapplied to new case studies. It is with this in mind that I now turn to the narratives of the Bleek–Lloyd archive.

Beastly difference

These 'new animisms', then, suggest that many communities commonly assign 'personhood' status to a range of non-human groups. Evaluations of appropriate and inappropriate forms of behaviour thus incorporate interactions not only with other (human) people, but also shape encounters with non-human species. The most typical exemplars of persons who did *not* act in accordance with the norms and aims of |Xam society were to be found (unsurprisingly) in non-human communities. In the animic model, certain species (or individual members of species) are marked out by unusual modes of interacting with people, which emphasise their agency: where these might be polar bears in the circumpolar north (Saladin d'Anglure 1994) or jaguars in South America (Reichel-Dolmatoff 1975), for the |Xam such species were best exemplified by the ||ke||ke or 'beasts-of-prey' (Bleek 1956: 571). Though the term describes carnivores in general (including smaller species such as bat-eared foxes, *Otocyon megalotis*), the lion (*Panthera leo*) and hyena (most commonly, the brown hyena, *Hyena brunnea*) best typified the category. Beasts-of-prey displayed a series of physical traits, most notably hairiness (LL.II.2.333; LL.II.30.2693–2694; LL.V.3.4127–4128; see figures 2 and 3) and a |kai:nja colour (yellow, green, or 'shining', Bleek 1956: 297; LL.II.18.1657), especially about the eyes (LL.II.18.1653'– 1654; see figure 2); more specific traits such as hair that covered the feet and 'closed

Figure 2: Lion at night, displaying distinctive physical traits of ‖ke‖ke (shining eyes and hairiness) © Kristoffen and Leah Everatt, used with permission.

Figure 3: Characteristic 'hairy' coat of brown hyena (*Hyena brunnea*). © Bernard du Pont 2011 (CC BY-NC-SA 2.0; http://www.flickr.com/photos/berniedup/6472939035/sizes/o/in/photostream/)

in' claws (LL.II.18.1655–1656) and a 'great' stomach (LL.II.18.1670) were linked with superlative 'bestial' identities.

This distinctive physicality was matched by an equally characteristic morally-dubious personality that governed their interactions with people and with one another. They were 'different' creatures (LL.II.9.914) that came at night (LL.II.9.914–915; LL.II.18.1660), 'greedy' animals (LL. II.20.1844–1846) that 'swallowed down' food in an immoderate fashion (LL.II.20.1862; LL.II.30.2695; LL.VIII.29.8554'), and angry folk (LL.II.30.2731; LL.II.30.2767) that wanted to chase and bite people (LL.V.3.4128).[6] They therefore did not act 'nicely' (‡hannũwa, Bleek 1956: 650) or do 'good' (a:kən, Bleek 1956: 7) in their relationships with people, by eating the game that the latter had killed (LL.II.23.2121) or, in perhaps the most apposite demonstration of their status, attempting to kill and eat people (LL. II.26.2339'–2340). In these references, the concept of |xarra (difference) is strongly associated with an antisocial personal identity, and with actions that attack |Xam individuals directly or undermine their attempts to behave properly in negotiating relationships.

Anger and greed

The angry, violent tendencies of 'beasts-of-prey' were made most obvious in personal attacks, which (although often recounted in stereotyped forms of narrative)[7] were a real danger in everyday life: genealogical information and several personal history narratives indicate that trauma or mortality from big cat encounters was not uncommon. This included individuals killed by lions in camp (LL.III.1.485') and people killed when out on the hunting-ground (LL.III.1.488'). ‡Kasin himself recounted his own violent encounter with a leopard (LL.IV.1.3461–3464), which left him seriously injured and unable to hunt for a time; hyenas as well as these big cats were considered 'angry' animals that would chase the hunter (LL.IV.2.3539–3542). Beasts-of-prey, then, formed a very real concern for |Xam groups, and correct methods of dealing with them are prominent themes in many narratives (e.g., where to walk safely in a Karoo environment, LL.II.18.1682–1683).

Anger was not the only locus of negative evaluation in the behaviours of these 'beasts-of-prey': of equal importance was the manner in which they dealt with comestible resources. Jackals (*koro*, black-backed jackal, *Canis mesomelas*, Bleek 1956: 101) were beasts-of-prey characterised as ugly, greedy lovers of fat, who would (like lions) eat people if the opportunity presented itself (LL.II.2.351; LL.II.3.418–419), although they were foolish or timid scavengers (LL.VIII.14.7229'– 7230'; LL.VIII.16.7459) rather than angry predators. In addition to their greedy consumption of the choicest portions, they also dealt poorly in their distribution of meat, burying it to finish it later rather than sharing it (LL.VIII.16.7449'–7450'). In this last point, they displayed their connection with the inappropriately-consuming 'beast-of-prey' *par excellence*, the hyena. Like jackals, hyenas were considered ugly, nocturnal, man-eating 'beasts-of-prey' (LL.II.3.420).[8] They behaved 'cunningly' (LL. II.21.1915) and were often in conflict even with other carnivores, both in stereotyped narratives (as when attempting to kill the lion with boiling soup, LL.II.2.362–366; LL.II.20.1774–1776) and in contemporary experience: despite their close connection with jackals, hyenas were so lacking in basic sociality that they could not even work with these creatures, driving them away from meat (LL.II.20.1764–1766).

The key attributes of hyenas (greediness) and lions (wrathfulness) were both deployed in recursive descriptions relating to specific human identities. On the one hand, lions were 'angry men' (LL.II.17.1598) and on the other, the impatient and 'passionate'[9] Tsatsi (|Han‡kass'o's maternal grandfather) was a man who 'talked to the lion' (LL.VIII.28.8464'–8465). !nuin |kuitən, an angry man (who *was* a !*gi:xa*)[10] was feared as a person who went about at night (as a lion), potentially to kill people (LL.V.5084–5085). In the case of hyenas, their improper attitudes toward distribution led to the imposition of the epithet !*k"wakkən*-||*kun* ('decayed-arms'; LL.II.21.1915), a term more commonly applied to people (see below). Conversely, human hunters who ate up springbok without sharing (LL.II.20.1793') were described as 'hyenas', a powerful statement of the inappropriate nature of their actions.

|*Xam-ka-!k'e-e:-*|*xarra* ('Different Bushmen')

Concerns regarding unregulated violence and excessive consumption as personal attributes were relevant across species boundaries, with animal communities providing striking referents in the construction of the negative consequences of disregarding |Xam norms. The *!k"wakkən-*||*kũŋ*; 'decayed-arms' was a term used to describe people who did not properly share or allow access to resources. Sometimes translated by Bleek and Lloyd as the quality of being 'stingy', it was connected with a wide range of forms of resource control. A man who ate meat with fat while only giving 'lean' food to others was acting in a 'stingy' manner (LL.VIII.25.8216–8217), but the term might equally apply to *!gi:tən*, who were considered to be able to influence resource availability in a more esoteric fashion (*cf.* Lewis-Williams and Pearce 2004: 185–204): an old man who would not 'dip out' food despite the fact that he 'owned' locusts was, for example, behaving as a *!k"wakkən-*||*kũŋ* (LL. VIII.7.6638–6640).

Non-human persons might themselves act inappropriately by transgressing the norms of their interactions with humans: |Hanǂkass'o (LL.VIII.16.7376'–7377') described a porcupine that dug its way out of the burrow to escape the hunters as *!k"wakkən-*||*kũŋ* (i.e., failing an obligation to distribute), implying that in behaving correctly toward the porcupine during the hunting process, the hunters required it to 'give' itself to them. The failure of the porcupine to do so marked a transgression somewhere in the relationship; in this instance, |Hanǂkass'o chastised the women at home for allowing children to break porcupine bones, on the principle that some incorrect (human) behaviour may have entitled the porcupine to an escape attempt.

Here we see the deployment of specific negative evaluations of behaviours and relationships in attempts to coerce or persuade people to act in particular ways. This was not limited to the concept of *!k"wakkən-*||*kũŋ*: the 'beast-of-prey' address was mobilised when attempting to cajole people into undertaking tasks within the context of specific relationships. Women used it when asking their husbands to fetch wood (LL.II.30.2699'), and men addressed their wives as ||*ke*||*ke* when asking them to 'work nicely' the houses, covering them with bushes (LL.VIII.23.8017'–8018'); people also called *!gi:tən* 'beasts of prey' when asking them to alleviate uncomfortable conditions (LL.VIII.7.6639'–6640'; LL.VIII.26.8305'). Such associations may have mobilised the generally 'irresponsible' stereotype of these bestial characters, reminding people that acting in a manner reminiscent of a 'beast-of-prey' was not appropriate in their relationships with their 'fellows'.

The 'man-who-was-different' character was also subject to an explicit moral evaluation, being otherwise described as a *!kõ!koiŋ*, or 'bad man' (Bleek 1956: 446). Elaborated in a narrative given by ||Kabbo concerning the maintenance of correct relationships with wives and children, a female protagonist described the 'different man' as one who would beat her children, as they were not his own (LL. II.14.1317), and who would eat up the desirable food (especially fat), bringing only hard, ugly flesh to the house (LL.II.14.1319–1322); Dia!kwain also commented on this element of 'different' identity, pointing out that such people would not feed orphans (LL.V.6.4410). The man 'who was different' was portrayed as one who did not maintain amiable social relations, being an angry, ugly and selfish person (LL.II.14.1317–1320), akin to the lions. The emphasis placed on beating – a violent action – was obviously congruent with this, as violence was equally valorised as a 'different' practice: 'strangers' were those who would shoot at people (LL.II.22.1981), while less tangible manifestations of antipathy sent by malevolent !*gi:tǝn* or spirits of the dead were also described as being sent from or by 'different' places or things (LL.V.19.5512; LL.V.22.5833).

Portrayals of 'difference' were not, however, limited to evaluations of the behaviours of specific individuals, but were also deployed in a more general sense to the practices of groups as markers of identity. |Han‡kass'o noted that 'Flat Bushman' (a geographical-bounded and dialectially-marked group of which he himself was part, see Deacon [1996: 251–253]) men were supposed to bring porcupine meat back to camp before eating, in a 'gendered' performance (LL.VIII.6.6590'–6594'): men brought it to camp, women cooked it, men divided it, and each gender consumed it differently (women eating the flesh, men 'gnawing' the backbone). |Han‡kass'o contrasted this with the behaviour of 'Grass Bushmen' (living to the west of his homelands; see Deacon [1996: 265–267]) who 'ate up' porcupines on the veld: the negative connotations of unrestrained consumption implied by 'eating up', alluded to above, make it clear he considered Flat Bushman behaviour more 'proper' in this regard. Part of the distinction – the 'Other-ness' – of the Grass Bushmen was therefore displayed in their attitudes towards consumption, just as 'beasts-of-prey' displayed their alien nature in more dramatic fashion in the ways they devoured food.

Korana violence

The Bleek–Lloyd narratives thus provide evidence of a clear |Xam terminology suited for discussing appropriate and inappropriate behaviours, which could be applied equally well to friends and relatives as it could to non-human species. These descriptive epithets were applied just as easily to non-|Xam human individuals and groups: indeed, it is in the characterisation of these 'Others' that this terminology might be said to have been most fully explored, discussing communities that were outwardly human but who often behaved in strikingly 'non-|Xam' ways.

Paramount among these 'Other' people were the Korana, overwhelmingly associated with the inappropriately directed or unregulated violence that was prototypically antithetical to |Xam notions of propriety. Korana populations represented the dominant indigenous 19th-century pastoralist groups of the middle

Orange River, and are by far the most frequently mentioned indigenous pastoralists in the archive. It is likely that 19th-century Korana groups incorporated immigrant Cape Khoekhoen, as well as populations occupying the middle Orange River prior to historical documentation (Penn 1995; Strauss 1979). Historically-recorded Korana (and other trans-colonial Khoekhoe populations) were rapidly reconfiguring their societies to deal with the new opportunities presented by the colonial scenario, and attempting to deal with the limitations of a colonial culture that sought to alienate them from their traditional subsistence strategies (Ross 1975; Strauss 1979). Small-scale stock raiding of colonial farmers was incorporated into Korana strategies from the early 19th century, taking livestock from farmers who took their animals to graze beyond the colonial boundary in territories claimed by the Korana, and coming increasingly to rely on colonial material culture in the form of horses and firearms (Ouzman 2005).

A common |Xam epithet for Korana populations was *xuaken-!ku* or 'bloody-browridges' (LL.II.32.2960'), referencing a homicidal stereotype and recalling the phrase 'overhanging cliffs' that was applied to baboons, a violent, non-human population (LL.V.24.5931'; Barnard 2010: 13). The latter component of the Korana's alternative name *!giri[11]-||kein* (Bleek 1956: 382) connoted stabbing or piercing, with the use of spears in conflict being a notable 'Korana' trait as far as the |Xam were concerned (LL.VIII.21.7968'). This formed part of a suite of 'violent' material culture that included particular kinds of knife (LL.VIII.18.7606), firearms that they acquired from Europeans through cattle trading (LL.VIII.18.7606'), and ornaments that were bound on for 'war' (LL.VIII.25.8261). Even practices that the |Xam informants found intelligible, and cognate to their own behaviour, were structured by this general violent schema: where the |Xam incised their hands to improve their skills in shooting springbok, the Korana incised their hands to help their aim when shooting at their fellows and to render deadly their blows in fist-fighting (LL. II.36.3244')

The virtually ubiquitous role of the Korana in more formalised narratives was adversarial, whether in the Early-Race times (LL.VIII.28.8494) or in 'legends' such as |Karran's escape from the Korana commando (LL.VIII.26.8269). Korana 'commandoes' (*k"a:o*) were a danger to Early-Race people (LL.VIII.18.7593; LL.VIII.25.8251) just as much as they were to 19th-century |Xam groups, for whom being 'killed by Koranas' was a real danger, of a piece with lion attacks, starvation, and disease as a component of the causes of death collected in the genealogical information (LL.III.1.497). The Korana, then, by seemingly embracing cultural attitudes based on similar principles to those that governed the behaviours of hyenas and (especially) lions, were demonstrating their 'difference' from the ideals of |Xam society.

However, it is important to note here that this presentation of adversarial Korana – in Early-Race and personal history narratives – did not translate into neat, bounded and isolated 'ethnic' identities only occasionally interacting with one another. The actual historical contingencies of the mid-19th-century Northern Cape region were, of course, rather more 'messy' than the |Xam presentations of Korana alterity might suggest. The circumstances of the arrests of |Xam individuals make it clear that they were (at least in the minds of the colonial authorities) closely involved in Korana raiding practices (LL.II.1.243). The genealogies recorded by Bleek and Lloyd (e.g. WB.XXIV.2337–2338, 2351) point to shared histories of intermarriage between |Xam and Korana: ‡Kasin himself had a Korana father (Bank 2006: 205).

Writing on the fluidity of group membership and the construction of identities among Khoe and Bushman populations, Barnard (2008: 67) suggests that while *individuals* (and even groups) might shift between subsistence modes and cultural practices, '[t]his does not mean that San and Khoekhoe are the same, but on the contrary, that they are opposites – poles to which individuals and groups gravitate, and about whose existence they are acutely aware'.

Fully enmeshed in their historical circumstances, the |Xam individuals represented in the narratives of the Bleek–Lloyd archive shifted between multiple identities – Bushman, raider, convict, family member, and so on – or perhaps more accurately, enacted multiple identities simultaneously. The construction of an (idealised) anti-social Korana identity among the Bleek–Lloyd informants thus emerges as a highly political act, attempting to govern individuals who might be inclined to 'act Korana' themselves: ‡Kasin spoke of his father's subjection to the norms of a positive |Xam identity when noting that his father's heart was made 'uncomfortable' because of his relative lack of skill in acquiring food while ‡Kasin himself was lying injured (LL. IV.1.3463').

Colonial 'Others'

Although relatively few narratives in the archive focus on interactions between Bushmen and white farmers, many allusions to colonial presence are to be found, especially in the supra-narrative framework of *reverso* notes and work-in-progress translations. Even Bleek and Lloyd's vocabulary and grammatical work can elucidate relationships with colonial populations: a note contrasting the 'stout' (!*kui:ja*, big, great, abundant, see Bleek [1956: 450]) Dutchman with the 'small' (‡*erri*, small, thin, see Bleek [1956: 643]) Bushman (WB.I.40), establishes particular physical attributes as distinguishing markers of European identities. Incorporating phenotypic variation, these distinctive features were situated in a wider cultural schema, as 'smallness' and 'greatness' were traits associated with concepts evocative of the wider relationship between |Xam and European colonists.

Thinness was linked with starvation, ugliness and hardship (LL.II.14.1321–1322), describing the Moon as it decayed (LL.II.6.658) or the kaross that would not keep one warm (LL.II.14.1341), connoting inadequacy or privation and according well with |Xam characterisations of their standing with Europeans as reminiscent of the 'orphan state' (LL.VIII.12.7108'). However, 'smallness' was also sometimes portrayed as a positive trait: the smallness of the Caracal's head was a constituent of her handsomeness (LL.II.15.1450–1451), the small pot was one made 'handsomely' (LL.VIII.23.8059), and the 'small-eater' was one who controlled his appetite rather than 'eating-up' in a unrestrained, bestial fashion (LL.V.3.4349'). These all placed notions of 'smallness' within the realm of the construction of appropriate |Xam sociality, and may be contrasted with the negative aspects of 'greatness'. The immoderately-consuming ||khwai-hem monster was not a 'small man' (LL. VIII.20.7812) and the lion with a 'great' body swallowed down even bones to fill his stomach (LL.II.18.1670): leonine characteristics emblematic of censurable social behaviour were thus mobilised in depictions of European characteristics.

Colonel Gordon, travelling in the Northern Cape in the late 18th century, recorded from the 'Sunei' Bushmen their opinions on the colonists, whom they said 'are evil and come in the night like wolves [i.e., hyenas], and have hair like lions' (Raper and Boucher 1988: 194). Although this forms a rather obscure aside in Gordon's account, by placing it in the context of the Bleek–Lloyd archive the cultural logic underpinning this statement becomes apparent. Based partly on observed behaviours of colonists – violent commando raids would, for example, often occur in the darkness of the early morning, as noted by |Xam informants (LL.V.16.5199) – and partly on their physical characteristics, this description situates an alien population that behaved in decidedly unfamiliar ways within the wide context of 'Other' communities.

|Xam relationships with 'Bastaard' (kwobbo)[12] communities were more or less contiguous with their encounters with Europeans: the extent to which these creolised groups should be characterised as indigenous responses to (rather than agents of) colonial expansion is contentious (Besten 2006; Waldman 2007), and it is an obvious distortion to imagine that the two were necessarily distinct. When describing their relationships with Bastaards, the |Xam employed identical terminology to that used for Europeans, with women referred to as 'mistresses' (LL.II.6.650) and men as 'masters'. This term (|hu) was also translated as 'white man', European or Boer (Bleek 1956: 289), and phrases talking about Bastaard 'masters' are therefore, in |Xam, linguistically indistinguishable from references to Europeans. This similarity is also present in the content of interactions, with the |Xam acting as herders and providing other kinds of labour (e.g., tanning sheep and goat hides, LL.II.6.650) for Bastaards (LL.VIII.8.6721') just as they did for Europeans.

If Northern Cape farmers constituted a relatively impoverished subset of European colonists expanding into unfamiliar ecosystems and depending upon incorporation of indigenous systems of knowledge (*cf.* Newton-King 1999: 18–36), then Bastaards arguably represented the extremes of this frontier. Certainly, they participated in the violent dimensions of interaction: the men who killed Dia!kwain's cousin were described as 'half whites (and half *kwobbo*'s)' (LL.V.21.5702'). Bastaards were the proximate agents of much of the disruption that engulfed the interior Karoo in the 19th century: the renaming of the|Xam landscape with Afrikaans alternatives, for example, occurred largely through their agency (LL.VIII.14.7215; Burchell 1822: 286), and ||Kabbo noted that Bastaards (Albert Meintjes and Oud Gert)[13] now occupied the places he once owned (WB.XII.1182'). His presentation of this 'ownership' stressed that his own inhabitation of the pits was part of a proper social order: he described his desire to 'work nicely' and to 'put in order' the water-pits that he possessed (LL. II.32.2894–2896). Further, transfers of this ownership along consanguineal family lines transmitted occupation 'properly' (LL.II.13.1300): while he lived there, his (adult, married) children came to live with him, allowing his grandchildren to grow up 'understandingly' (LL.II.32.2897–2898). This state of affairs was contrasted with the current occupation of his water-pits by 'different people'. Bastaards were in this instance 'different' – pursuing lifeways that were opposed to the proper, correct '|Xam' ways-of-doing.

However, Bastaards were also among the most 'creolised' of the northern Cape colonial populations, with numerous ties to both European and indigenous communities, including those forged by marriage (primarily |Xam women marrying Bastaard men). Unfortunately, Bleek and Lloyd collected little information from female informants, but the archive does demonstrate that some |Xam men attempted (on occasion at least) to use these marriages with Bastaard men as a means to access farmer resources: |Han‡kass'o went to live at a Bastaard named Jacob Kotze's place, because he was married to a |Xam woman named 'Silla' who supplied |Han‡kass'o with food (LL.VIII.8.6724). This access was situated within his characterisation of Bastaard identity more generally, as he contrasted the appropriate |Xam practice of 'liberally giving' food (lit. *!kou-a:kən*, to give well or nicely, Bleek 1956: 7, 444; LL.VIII.8.6723–6724) with the Bastaards' reputation for 'stinginess' with food – that is, their propensity for acting as *!k"wakkən-||kũŋ*. Though wed to social practices alien to Bushman morality, Bastaards could become subject to |Xam evaluations of appropriate sociality through their relationships with |Xam individuals, and as |Han‡kass'o's account suggests, subject to sufficient coercive pressure as to conform (at least to some degree) to expectations derived from |Xam norms.

Social significance of 'difference'

Bleek and Lloyd did not intend in their interviews with |Xam informants to explore the ways in which southern Bushman populations defined and understood 'personhood'; the narratives therefore contain little explicit commentary on this topic. Rather, |Xam ideas regarding personhood are revealed piecemeal through narratives (both anecdotal and 'mythological') that describe the interactions of a wide range of persons. As was evident above, these informants consistently assigned importance to particular attributes that were used in describing a wide variety of persons – human or otherwise.

These attributes included physical markers (hair, eyes, size) as well as behavioural traits or moral orientations (sharing, greed, anger) that demonstrate 'ways-of-being (or doing)' considered significant by the informants. The narratives make clear statements that there are appropriate '|Xam' ways of behaving, and inappropriate, anti-social non-|Xam attitudes (even if particular |Xam individuals may not have always adhered to these standards in practice). This presentation of personhood may thus be characterised as a 'political' domain, with various agents attempting to enforce certain interpretations of propriety (and the behaviours derived from these). The narratives display a particular concern for the regulation of the realm of comestible resources, and demonstrate the use of these evaluative practices as part of a suite of tools used in attempts to enforce particular norms in a society that largely lacked overt means of coercion.

Further, these characteristics of personhood were deployed as a way of understanding the behaviour of non-|Xam groups. In part, these constructions allowed the |Xam a 'way into' the difficult-to-understand behaviours of some of the non-|Xam groups that shared their 19th-century Karoo landscape. In other instances, these evaluations were employed in attempts to enforce |Xam norms even across different identities (as with the Bastaards) – although these may not always have been successful, the fact that |Hanǂkass'o was able to access resources from these colonising groups suggests that such definitions of (in)appropriate relationships had the potential to be able to act cross-culturally and that |Xam representations of 'personhood' formed a key component in their attempts to negotiate and manipulate the resources of their 19th-century Karoo landscape.

Acknowledgements

The doctoral research that produced the searchable transcription of the Bleek–Lloyd archive was undertaken with funding from the School of Archaeology, University of Oxford, which is gratefully acknowledged. This article developed from a presentation given at the Khoisan research seminar hosted by Michael Wessels and Keyan Tomaselli at the University of KwaZulu-Natal; my thanks go to the organisers, and to the participants for their useful discussions and commentary, and to the two anonymous referees who provided valuable comments on the original draft.

Notes

1   The symbols |, !, ǂ, and || refer to dental, palatal, alveolar, and lateral 'clicks' respectively

2   http://www.info.gov.za/aboutgovt/symbols/coa/

3   see Barnard 2003a

4   http://lloydbleekcollection.cs.uct.ac.za. Citations to Bleek's (WB) notebooks use a roman numeral (notebook number) followed by a page number; Lloyd's (LL) notebooks use the roman numeral to refer to the informant, followed by a notebook number, and then the page. Reverso page are indicated with ' (e.g., LL.II.12.1200')

5   Exploration of the voluminous literature devoted to these issues is beyond the scope of this article, but see Clifford and Marcus (1986), and particularly Spivak (1988) for an introduction. With respect to the Bleek–Lloyd archive specifically, Wessels (2010: 25–46, 2011) has discussed these issues in depth.

6   These tropes were repeated in more stereotyped 'mythological' narratives, where 'monstrous' figures (such as the 'all-devouring' ||khwai-hem, LL.II.33.3083–3084) were also notably greedy, angry and 'different'.

7   The jackal and hyena were, for example, described as 'angry folk' for poisoning the caracal (LL.II.18.1678–1679) in a 'mythological' narrative.

8   Hyenas and jackals were linked in a particularly close fashion, both possessing a distinctive, 'different' odour that smelt 'badly' (LL.II.15.1442).

9   !kwã:-'a, the word translated as passionate here, was more commonly rendered as wrath (Bleek 1956: 457).

10   !gi:tən, 'sorcerers' (Bleek 1956: 328); now commonly rendered as 'shaman' (see Lewis-Williams 1992: 58).

11   The meaning of this first component is obscure. It may represent a version of !gerri, the Gariep or Orange River (Bleek 1956: 381), which formed the heartland of Korana territories.

12   Translated by Bleek (1956: 115) as 'coloured person' and 'black man'. In the narratives it usually denoted creolised colonial populations rather than Bantu-speakers (LL. II.6.645'; LL.V.21.5702').

13   Although Bank (2006: 151) associates this figure with Gert van Wyk (a white farmer), the reverso note at WB.XII.1182' explicitly states that these two men were Bastaards.

References

Bank, A. 2000. Evolution and racial theory: the hidden side of Wilhelm Bleek. *South African Historical Journal* 43(1): 163–178.

Bank, A. 2006. *Bushmen in a Victorian world: the remarkable story of the Bleek-Lloyd collection of Bushman folklore*. Cape Town: Double Storey.

Barnard, A. 1992. *Hunters and herders of southern Africa: a comparative ethnography of the Khoisan peoples*. Cambridge: Cambridge University Press.

Barnard, A. 2002. The foraging mode of thought. In *Self- and other-images of hunter gatherers: papers presented at the Eighth International Conference on Hunting and*

Gathering Societies (CHAGS 8) (SENRI Ethnological Studies 60), ed. H. Stewart, A. Barnard and K. Omura, 5–24. Osaka: National Museum of Ethnology.

Barnard, A. 2003a. *Diverse people unite: two lectures on Khoisan imagery and the state (Occasional Papers No. 94)*. Edinburgh: Centre of African Studies, University of Edinburgh.

Barnard, A. 2003b. Comment !ke e: |xarra ke – multiple origins and multiple meanings of the motto. *African Studies* 62(2): 243–250.

Barnard, A. 2004. Coat of arms and the body politic: Khoisan imagery and South African national identity. *Ethnos: Journal of Anthropology* 69(1): 5–22.

Barnard, A. 2008. Ethnographic analogy and the reconstruction of early Khoekhoe society. *Southern African Humanities* 20(1): 61–75.

Barnard, A. 2010. Mythology and the evolution of language. In *The evolution of language: proceedings of the 8th International Conference (EVOLANG8)*, ed. A.D.M. Smith, M. Schouwstra, B. de Boer and K. Smith, 11–18. Singapore: World Scientific Publishing Co.

Besten, M.P. 2006. Transformation and reconstitution of Khoe-San identities: A.A.S. le Fleur 1, Griqua identities and post-apartheid Khoe-San revivalism (1894–2004). PhD diss., Universiteit Leiden.

Bird-David, N. 1999. Animism revisited: personhood, environment, and relational epistemology. *Current Anthropology* 40 (Supplement): S67–S91.

Bleek, D.F. 1931. Customs and beliefs of the |Xam Bushmen, 1: baboons. *Bantu Studies* 5: 167–179.

Bleek, D.F. 1932a. Customs and beliefs of the |Xam Bushmen, 2: the lion. *Bantu Studies* 6: 47–63.

Bleek, D.F. 1932b. Customs and beliefs of the |Xam Bushmen, 3: game animals. *Bantu Studies* 6: 233–249.

Bleek, D.F. 1932c. Customs and beliefs of the |Xam Bushmen, 4: omens, wind-making, clouds. *Bantu Studies* 6(1): 323–342.

Bleek, D.F. 1933a. Customs and beliefs of the |Xam Bushmen, 5: the rain. *Bantu Studies* 7(1): 297–312.

Bleek, D.F. 1933b. Beliefs and customs of the |Xam Bushmen, 6: rain-making. *Bantu Studies* 7(1): 375–392.

Bleek, D.F. 1935. Customs and beliefs of the |Xam Bushmen, 7: sorcerors. *Bantu Studies* 9(1): 1–47.

Bleek, D.F. 1936a. Customs and beliefs of the |Xam Bushmen, 8: more about sorcerors and charms. *Bantu Studies* 10: 131–162.

Bleek, D.F. 1936b. Special speech of animals and moon used by the |Xam Bushmen. *Bantu Studies* 10(1): 163–199.

Bleek, D.F. 1956. *A Bushman dictionary* (American Oriental Series 41). New Haven: American Oriental Society.

Bleek, W.H.I. 1874. On resemblances in Bushman and Australian mythology, with preliminary remarks. *Cape Monthly Magazine* 8: 98–102.

Bleek, W.H.I. 1875a. Bushman researches. *Cape Monthly Magazine* 11: 104–115, 150–155.

Bleek, W.H.I. 1875b. *A brief account of Bushman folk-lore and other texts. Second Report concerning Bushman researches presented to both Houses of Parliament of the Cape of Good Hope.* Cape Town: Juta.

Bleek, W.H.I. and L.C. Lloyd. 1911. *Specimens of Bushman folklore.* London: George Allen & Company.

Burchell, W.J. 1822. *Travels in the interior of southern Africa,* vol. 1. London: Longman, Hurst, Rees, Orme and Brown.

Clifford, J. and G.E. Marcus, eds. 1986. *Writing culture: the poetics and politics of ethnography.* Berkeley and Los Angeles: University of California Press.

De Castro, E.V. 1998. Cosmological deixis and Amerindian perspectivism. *Journal of the Royal Anthropological Institute* 4(3): 469–488.

De Prada-Samper, J.M. 2009. Mitos y creencias de los bosquimanos |Xam: relatos orales acerca del león. PhD diss., Universidad de Alcalá de Henares.

De Prada-Samper, J.M. 2010. Strokes in rock and flesh: presentiments, rock engravings and landscape in ||Kabbo's place. In *Rock art made in translation: framing images of and from the* landscape, ed. P. Skotnes, 75–79. Johannesburg and Cape Town: Jacana.

De Prada-Samper, J.M. 2012. 'The ouma and the lion': a contemporary |Xam tale of the Upper Karoo. *Oráfrica* 8(1): 199–216.

Deacon, J. 1988. The power of a place in understanding Southern San rock engravings. *World Archaeology* 20(1): 129–140.

Deacon, J. 1996. Archaeology of the flat and grass Bushmen. In *Voices from the past: |Xam Bushmen and the Bleek and Lloyd collection,* ed. J. Deacon and T.A. Dowson, 245–270. Johannesburg: Witwatersrand University Press.

Deacon, J. and T.A. Dowson, eds. 1996. *Voices from the past: |Xam Bushmen and the Bleek and Lloyd collection.* Johannesburg: Witwatersrand University Press.

Descola, P. 1992. Societies of nature and the nature of society. In *Conceptualizing society,* ed. A. Kuper, 107–126. London: Routledge.

Descola, P. 1996. Constructing natures: symbolic ecology and social practice. In *Nature and society: anthropological perspectives,* ed. P. Descola and G. Pálsson, 82–102. London: Routledge.

Guenther, M.G. 1999. *Tricksters and trancers: Bushman religion and society.* Bloomington: Indiana University Press.

Hewitt, R. 2008[1986]. *Structure, meaning, and ritual in the narratives of the Southern San,* 2nd edition. Johannesburg: Wits University Press.

Hoff, A. 1997. The water snake of the Khoekhoen and |Xam. *South African Archaeological Bulletin* 52(1): 21–37.

Hoff, A. 1998. The water bull of the |Xam. *South African Archaeological Bulletin* 53(1): 109–124.

Hoff, A. 2007. *Medicine experts of the |Xam San: the !kwa-ka !gi:tən who controlled the rain and water.* Köln: Rüdiger Köppe Verlag.

Hoff, A. 2011. *The |Xam and the rain: views by a group of Southern San.* Köln: Rüdiger Köppe Verlag.

Hoff, A. 2012. Guardians of nature among the |Xam San: an exploratory study. *South African Archaeological Bulletin* 66(1): 41–50.

Hollmann, J.C., ed. 2004. *Customs and beliefs of the |Xam Bushmen.* Johannesburg: Wits University Press.

Ingold, T. 2000. *The perception of the environment: essays on livelihood, dwelling and skill.* London: Routledge.

James, A. 2001. *The first Bushman's path: stories, songs and testimonies of the |Xam of the Northern Cape.* Pietermaritzburg: University of KwaZulu-Natal Press.

Krog, A. 2004. *The stars say 'Tsau':|Xam poetry of Dia!kwain, Kweiten-ta-||ken, |A!kunta, |Han‡kass'o, and ||Kabbo.* Roggebaai: Kwela Books.

Lewis-Williams, D. 1981. *Believing and seeing: symbolic meanings in Southern San rock painting.* London: Academic Press.

Lewis-Williams, D. 1992. Ethnographic evidence relating to 'trance' and 'shamans' among Northern and Southern Bushmen. *South African Archaeological Bulletin* 47(15): 56–60.

Lewis-Williams, D. and D. Pearce. 2004. *San spirituality: roots, expressions and social consequences.* Cape Town: Double Storey.

Lloyd, L.C. 1880. Bushman folklore. *Folklore Journal* II(III): 39–43.

Lloyd, L.C. 1889. *A short account of further Bushman material collected. Third report concerning Bushman researches, present to both House of the Parliament of the Cape of Good Hope, by command of His Excellency the Governor.* London: David Nutt.

Moran, S. 2001. Specimens of 'Bushman' studies. *Wasafiri* 16(34): 46–51.

Moran, S. 2009. *Representing Bushmen: South Africa and the origin of language.* Rochester: University of Rochester Press.

Newton-King, S. 1999. *Masters and servants of the Cape Eastern frontier, 1760–1803.* Cambridge: Cambridge University Press.

Ouzman, S. 2005. The magical arts of a raider nation: central South Africa's Korana rock art. *South African Archaeological Society Goodwin Series* 9(1): 101–113.

Penn, N. 1995. The Orange River frontier zone, c. 1700–1805. In *Einiqualand: studies of the Orange River frontier*, ed. A.B. Smith, 21–109. Cape Town: University of Cape Town Press.

Raper, P.E. and M. Boucher, eds. 1988. *Robert Jacob Gordon: Cape travels, 1777 to 1786.* Houghton: Brenthurst Press.

Reichel-Dolmatoff, G. 1975. *The shaman and the jaguar: a study of narcotic drugs among the Indians of Columbia.* Philadelphia: Temple University Press.

Ross, R. 1975. The !kora wars on the Orange River, 1830–1880. *Journal of African History* 16(1): 561–576.

Saladin D'Anglure, B. 1994. Nanook, super-male: the polar bear in the imaginary space and social time of the Inuit of the Canadian Arctic. In *Signifying animals: human meaning in the natural world*, ed. R. Willis, 178–195. London: Routledge.

Schmidt, S. 1996. The relevance of the Bleek/Lloyd folktales to the general Khoisan traditions. In *Voices from the past: |Xam Bushmen and the Bleek and Lloyd collection*, ed. J. Deacon and T.A. Dowson, 100–121. Johannesburg: Wits University Press.

Schmidt, S. 2013. *A catalog of Khoisan folktales of southern Africa* (2 vols.) Köln: Rüdiger Köppe Verlag.

Skotnes, P., ed. 2007. *Claim to the country: the archive of Wilhelm Bleek and Lucy Lloyd.* Johannesburg: Jacana.

Smith, B., D. Lewis-Williams, G. Blundell and C. Chippendale. 2000. Archaeology and symbolism in the new South African coat of arms. *Antiquity* 74(1): 467–468.

Spivak, G. 1988. Can the subaltern speak? In *Marxism and the interpretation of culture*, ed. C. Nelson and L. Grossberg, 271–316. London: Macmillan.

Strauss, T. 1979. *War along the Orange: the Korana and the northern border wars of 1868–9 and 1878–9* (Centre for African Studies, Communication 1). Cape Town: University of Cape Town Press.

Tylor, E.B. 1871. *Primitive culture: researches into the development of mythology, philosophy, religion, art, and custom*, vol. 1. London: John Murray.

Waldman, L. 2007. *The Griqua conundrum: political and socio-cultural complexity in the Northern Cape, South Africa.* Bern: Peter Lang AG.

Watson, S. 1991. *Song of the broken string: after the |Xam Bushmen – poems from a lost oral tradition.* Riverdale-on-Hudson: Sheep Meadow Press.

Wessels, M. 2010. *Bushman letters: interpreting |Xam narrative.* Johannesburg: Witwatersrand University Press.

Wessels, M. 2011. The story of !Khwe//na ssho !kui who brought home a young lion to use as a dog: character, identity and knowledge in a |Xam narrative. *Folklore* 122(2): 177–196.

Icons and archives:
the Orpen lithograph in the context
of 19th-century depictions of rock
paintings

Justine Wintjes

Abstract

Joseph Orpen's 1874 journal article, including a testimony by Qing, one of the last Bushmen in the region, has become a foundational 19th-century source for rock art research in southern Africa, and its illustrations have achieved iconic status. Against the backdrop of Orpen's images, I examine the pictorial qualities of four other 19th-century depictions of rock paintings, namely those by John Barrow (1801), James Edward Alexander (1837), Thomas Baines (1849) and Otto Mäder (1908). This comparative visual analysis entails an exploration of the archive in an extended archaeological sense – one that seeks to make connections between pictures, documents and sites in the landscape. Each of these depictions reflects different pictorial attributes of the originals, while also embodying different attitudes towards the art, but do not carry the textual 'authenticity' of Orpen's copies.

The icon

The point of departure for this article is a lithograph published by Joseph Orpen in 1874 (Figure 1). The plate consists of four clusters of figures, each copied from a different rock art site in the Maloti-Drakensberg range of Lesotho and South Africa. Orpen's article is one of two 19th-century sources that, alongside more recent ethnographic research, underpin San (or Bushman) rock art research in southern Africa. His

Figure 1

article carries this significance because it contains explanations gathered from Qing, one of the last Bushmen in the region. Qing's testimony is a string of story fragments, portions of which can be related to the illustrations. One of the groups is a rainmaking scene from a rock shelter that Orpen called Mangolong. Now known as Sehonghong, it is one of the most-researched archaeological sites in the Lesotho highlands, with Middle Stone Age deposits dating back 57 000 years (Jacobs, Roberts and Galbraith et al. 2008), and the focus of ongoing archaeological and historical interest (e.g., Mitchell 2010; Wright and De Prada-Samper 2013). The best-known feature of the site's archaeology is undoubtedly the rainmaking group, first published by Orpen, which has since been reproduced an astonishing number of times. I argue elsewhere that it has become iconic (Wintjes 2011).

Dictionary definitions for 'icon' put forward the notion of an image or sign most often bearing a likeness or visual resemblance to, or sharing the properties of, an original referent, while some hint at a more symbolic or metonymical function. An emerging definition more attuned to popular contemporary usage is a 'person or thing regarded as a representative symbol, especially of a culture or movement; a person, institution, etc., considered worthy of admiration or respect' (*Oxford English dictionary* 2014). Looking at a somewhat darker side of the icon, Martin Kemp (2012: 3) defines an iconic image as

> one that has achieved wholly exceptional levels of widespread recognisability and has come to carry a rich series of varied associations for very large numbers of people across time and cultures, such that it has to a greater or lesser degree transgressed the parameters of its initial making, function, context and meaning.

Kemp illustrates his emphasis on the transgressive with examples from popular culture. Here I examine an image that is widespread across a specialist field of academic enquiry, but common to both contexts is the idea that the iconic image is transgressive because it circulates at a problematic distance from the referent. Indeed, the icon–referent relationship can be more remote than alike, more strongly symbolic than visually representational; the further the icon moves from its referent, without becoming completely untethered, the more powerful the icon. Thus, icons develop lives of their own while carrying a claim of saying a great deal about the originals from which they derive. Often, however, their relationships to the originals are obscure.

Consistent with this definition of an icon, Orpen's copy of the Sehonghong rainmaking group retains a certain visual likeness to the original rock painting, but it has acquired a symbolic status that is far more significant. It is one tiny cluster of figures standing in for a whole rock shelter, and arguably for an entire corpus of art across the south-eastern mountain region of southern Africa. Moreover, it stands in for a historic moment that has been of central significance in the development of rock art research. This is particularly true for the last four decades, and for a particular kind of interpretative strategy that involves the application of ethnographic texts to archaeological materials. Challis, Hollmann and McGranaghan (2013: 2) summarise:

> The paintings at Sehonghong rock-shelter have attained particular prominence in southern African rock art research because certain images there were explained by Qing ... the only San person ever asked by Europeans to give interpretations of rock art while actually in a painted site. ... [Qing's] words, translated by Sotho interpreters and recorded by Orpen (1874), have proven a cornerstone in the ethnographically informed decipherment of San rock art ... They illustrate how the 'general character' of Maloti San mythology ... was coherent with that obtained from other San communities separated in time and space from the nineteenth-century Maloti context and underpin the use of these more extensive ethnographies in interpreting southern African San rock art.

This passage reflects the way in which Qing's story fragments have moved through several degrees of translation as they were woven into an interpretive framework for San rock art. By a closely related process, the Sehonghong group has been selected out, translated and recopied to crystallise into a graphic 'cornerstone' of the ethnographic approach, providing diagrammatic illustrations for aspects of Qing's stories, as well as the decipherment of the art more broadly. This transformation has come, however, at the expense of the copies' relationship to the original rock paintings.

The archive

To understand the influence of iconic images within visual representation, I find it useful to 'excavate' them, to explore the 'archive' that lies beneath. Theories of the archive have generated substantial scholarship in recent decades across different disciplines, revealing the complexity and ambiguity of the archive in terms of where it is located, what it consists of, what it is used for and what it means (e.g., Manhoff

2004). Here I do not distinguish between documents, pictures or sites, for, although these items are generally preserved separately in different kinds of storage facilities – or, in the case of the latter, remain out on the land – they cannot be disentangled in terms of their archival relationships. The archive behind a published copy of a rock painting would comprise the original field sketches and any intermediate versions between these and published illustrations, field notes or other texts, as well as the rock formation in the landscape. I therefore use 'archive' in an extended archaeological sense, where the site in the landscape is itself a kind of archive, and the documentary record an extension of that archive.

While archival materials associated with archaeological sites all carry some sort of link to those sites, they are also generated with particular kinds of selectivity, determined most notably by the interests and artistic skill of the recorder, and possibilities allowed by the recording medium. Indeed, while the Orpen image circulates at a particularly wide distance from the rock painting from which it derives, all copies, modern or ancient, ignorant or well informed, are selective in their own particular ways. Over the last few decades, for example, rock art researchers have developed a copying technique that involves a labour-intensive process of tracing and redrawing. It is a technique that turns the paintings into monochrome projections, emphasising a kind of accuracy that I call 'figural iconographic' (Wintjes 2012: 16–22; *cf.* Skotnes 1996). Although new techniques of digital photographic enhancement and 'art-in-context' visualisation seem poised to disturb the status quo, for example Kevin Crause's capture, process, enhance, display (CPED) method (e.g., Hollmann and Crause 2011; Challis et al. 2013), the tracing/redrawing technique is still the most common means of recording and reproduction. While this technique is considered to serve ethnographic interpretations of the art well, it is based on a narrow definition of what an image is made of, where the meaningful visual content is defined by a fluency of line, and, in particular, the contours of discrete motifs (animal, human, shape, line and so on). Alongside this figural interest, aspects such as colour, texture, liminality, natural rock features and wider landscape setting tend to be downplayed or ignored.

The interpretation of all images is vastly challenging, whether the rock art itself or the copies. The Orpen image has become iconic because it opened up the way for an explanation, in words, of a seemingly intractable corpus of art, but the centrality of textual explanation to the interpretation of San rock art has shifted attention away from pictorial aspects of the imagery. Extending the writing of San history to include 'pictoriographic' exploration – an unpacking of its 'imaging' – is an important project, for images do not constitute transparent windows onto the world. Despite their appearance of naturalness, immediacy and transparency, they conceal an 'opaque, distorting, arbitrary mechanism of representation, a process of ideological mystification' (Mitchell 1984: 504). There is no clear separation between the empirical implications of a mode of reproduction and its epistemological inferences. One moves quickly into the realm of attributing meaning because copying is never a purely material or intuitive exercise; it is always related to discursive practice. The distortion inherent in images justifies a questioning of dominant kinds of representation and an exploration of archives and alternatives.

Exploring the archive behind the icon

Elsewhere I examine the various iterations of the Orpen image and their archival relationships (Wintjes 2011). I summarise those findings here to establish the terms of the present analysis. Thereafter, I examine four other 19th-century depictions of rock paintings as comparative examples, focusing on their pictorial qualities and the kinds of accuracy they embody. These accuracies are multiple, not least because the rock paintings themselves are unstable physically, perceptually and epistemologically. They are affected by weathering, which causes colours to change over time, and certain pigments to disappear while others remain. Further, perception of the paintings fluctuates with individual visual acuity and changing light, in daily as well as seasonal cycles. Many of the paintings surely now look very different from when they were first created, but, in any case, the Western notion of an 'original' artwork – complete, presentable, unique and permanent – is quite at odds with what we understand of hunter-gatherer creativity, where process and transition are as significant as product. But for all their instability and impermanence, the paintings as we see them today nonetheless constitute 'originals', and a productive dialogue can take place between them and the copies they have inspired.

I provide a comparative pictorial survey of a selection of lesser-known 19th-century copies, because engagement with historic copies has typically been superficial or performed through the figural iconographic lens (e.g., Flett and Letley 2007; Lewis-Williams, Dowson and Deacon 1993). Closer visual assessments do exist of some 19th-century materials, including that of George Stow's copies (Skotnes 2008), and consequently I do not deal with Stow here. Embedded within the story of early copies is a history of economics, politics and technologies of printing, but rather than examining in any great depth these wider circumstances, I focus on the intimate pictorial relationship between these illustrations and the rock art that inspired them. The history of 19th-century science, and of the intellectual milieu in which Orpen and other copyists lived, also has a bearing on our understanding of how their illustrations came to exist in the form that they did, but this too is worthy of a separate study.

An important finding in my study of the Orpen rainmaking group was that the four supposed 'field copies' from which the 1874 plate was created, are more likely preparatory sketches drawn by the lithographer – they are not Orpen's field sketches. The four pieces of paper once formed one larger sheet that corresponds in scale and layout to the published plate, and would have been the result of the lithographer redrawing field copies supplied by Orpen into a publishable format, refracting them into separate layers, one for each colour.

The original field copies are missing, just like the original field notes. They must have been messier, because the clean, flattened character of the published motifs is, partially if not primarily, a consequence of the reproduction technique, for which it would have been necessary to reduce colour, flatten gradients and smooth texture. As a general rule, because fewer translations separate them from the original imagery, field copies often contain contextual information, notes or sketches describing other features of the site or surrounding landscape that never make it into print. Even between the lithographer's preparatory sketch and the final plate – two tightly related versions – we see an important omission: faint dashes are visible in-between the figures in the sketches, but are not present in the published illustration, possibly for technical reasons. A number of authors have flagged this absence as problematic, because the dashes are thought to denote water (e.g., Frobenius 1931: 23; Lewis-Williams 1980: 469; Smits 1973: 33; Vinnicombe 1976: 336). In Orpen's transcription of Qing's words, they are described as 'things growing under water' (1874: 10). Scholars have interpreted this to mean the scene depicts rainmaking, and the animal is a mythical, rain-related creature (Bleek 1874: 12; Lewis-Williams 1981: 34; Vinnicombe 1976: 336–337). Apart from this one significant 'error', however, the 1874 plate has been considered essentially correct in terms of its figural iconographic content.

While Orpen's drawings were originally published in colour, albeit limited to three flat hues, they have been reproduced much more frequently in a redrawn monochrome form. Almost 100 years after Orpen's expedition into the Maluti Mountains as part of a team of researchers, Patricia Vinnicombe rediscovered the site and made a tracing of the rainmaking group. The field tracing reflects the 'messy' recording process, with annotations and different colours of paint, and Vinnicombe cut the top edge of her polythene-plastic tracing-sheet to follow a natural break in the rock. None of these aspects were retained when she prepared a tidy monochrome redrawing for publication (Smits 1973: 32). Like Orpen's copy, this version lifts the painted scene from its context.

Both monochrome versions are 'diagrammatic' because they present the simplified shapes and features of the original, rather than depicting its actual appearance. A comparison of the Orpen and Vinnicombe images reveals that the figural iconographic content is essentially the same, but the latter is more accurate in terms of its graphic configuration. We also observe greater dynamism in Vinnicombe's version, a kind of gliding, eddy-like movement, whereas the Orpen version stiffens the figures and arranges them into two parallel horizontal registers. This difference is suggestive. Challis et al. (2013: 8) believe Orpen copied the upper and lower portions of the scene on separate pages of a small notebook, as this might explain the similarity in size between the two rain-animals in his copy (whereas on the rock the lower rain-animal is much bigger). Orpen was surely influenced by the rectangular page format, but the height and proportions of the human figures have also been standardised, showing that he performed a more generalised kind of reordering of this unfamiliar imagery. Not only is the entire scene warped to fit a rectangle, but each individual figure is confined to a vertical allotment that does not overlap much with the others, almost as if adjusted to fit into an invisible orthogonal grid like a typeset text character (*cf.* Wintjes 2011: 29). As a result, the Orpen translation turns the highly dynamic, supple and expressive leaping and lunging postures of the original figures into more restrained 'skipping' or 'jogging' actions. Perhaps Orpen lacked artistic training, but the stiffness and lifelessness of his copy may also convey something of the unease felt by members of colonial society towards African dance, considered a primordial physical expression associated with animality and loss of control, and opposed to the higher, aesthetic, dance traditions of 'civilised' societies (Castaldi 2006: 37–42).

Because Vinnicombe's versions are derived from a tracing, they capture these extreme postures more accurately. She was a talented copyist concerned with the accurate recording of colour, and she also prepared a painted version: subtle, yet striking and very colourful (Vinnicombe 1976: 337 in black and white; subsequently published in colour in Mitchell 2010: 161; Mitchell and Challis 2008: 435; Vinnicombe 2009: 329; Wintjes 2011: 21). The painterly qualities and dynamism are even more evident in her tracing than in this painted version, but it is when we compare all of these colour versions to a photograph of the panel (e.g., Mitchell and Challis 2008: 434; Wintjes 2011: 21, 33, 35) that the greatest visual gap still needs to be bridged, because the rainmaking group is almost unrecognisable. Yet it is the photograph that has the most indexical relationship to the original, i.e., it reflects more of what the rock paintings actually look like. Photographs of the panel (e.g., Mitchell 2010: 161; Mitchell and Challis 2008: 434; Wintjes 2011: 33, 35, 36, 37) show some of the natural rock features surrounding the group (absent from all versions mentioned so far, except, indirectly, in the way Vinnicombe's cut her tracing sheet), as well as numerous other painted figures in its vicinity. Although not reflected in the published texts, the position of the group as an excerpt from a wider pictorial context is captured in the archive, where the rainmaking group is clearly visible as a tiny cluster among a vast number of painted figures all along the back wall of a rock-shelter about 90 m long and 20 m deep.[1] Many have noted how difficult it is to locate in the shelter, so it is fascinating to ponder why Orpen and/or Qing singled out this particular group.

Rock paintings from another site provide us with a clue that this kind of scene might have had special significance for Qing. Challis et al. (2013) suggest a connection between the rainmaking scene at Sehonghong, where Qing enigmatically identified one of the four-legged rain animals as a 'snake' (Orpen 1874: 10), and another painted group centred around a giant coiled snake at Rain Snake Shelter on the other side of the Sehonghong River. They suggest that 'Qing's description of the capture of the Sehonghong "snake" is equally apposite' for the imagery at this other shelter (ibid: 12, 18). Because of the intimate connection in San cosmology between snakes, water and rain, and narratives involving the ritual capture of animals associated with water in order to control aquatic resources, Qing's use of the term 'snake' may refer to the category of rain-animals more generally. Challis et al. (2013: 13) push the connection further, observing that the 'running and dragging postures of [the rain-animal's] captors [at Rain Snake Shelter] are so similar in style to those at Sehonghong that one wonders if the same hand was at work'. Furthermore, certain iconographic elements such as bladder headdresses (ibid: 13–14) suggest a 19th-century date. At both sites certain colours remain bright, but the paintings are nonetheless highly degraded, consistent with the fragile constitution of 19th-century rock paintings observed elsewhere (e.g., Vinnicombe 1966, 1976: 141; Ward and Maggs 1994). It is therefore tempting to suggest that Qing had some sort of privileged, living connection to these paintings. He may even have watched these paintings being created as part of the community the artist came from, or involved in some activity that took place around them. This possibility would explain the selection of the rainmaking scene out of all the panels at Sehonghong: Qing may well have taken Orpen directly to a scene with which he was intimately familiar.

Qing's interpretation of the Sehonghong rainmaking scene in terms of elements of other rock paintings points to the interconnectedness of the sites, with imagery overlaid onto the landscape in a recursive pattern that is also varied and site-specific, forming a kind of cosmological map or 'imagistic web' (Lewis-Williams 2010). Yet despite this web of connections, the Sehonghong group dominates in the literature to the virtual exclusion of all else. Considering the greater knowledge we now have of the actual appearance and (inter-)site context of the group, we should reflect on why the Orpen copy has persisted in its authority. Most likely, this image exerts a particular power because of the accompanying text that promises 'insider' insights, rather than for its visual likeness to the original rock painting. The copy's power is further accentuated by a textual bias within Western scholarship. As I noted earlier, the manner in which the painted figures are lifted from their canvas, turned into smooth projected shadows and ordered into rows is well adapted to their treatment as something more akin to text than picture. In a way, the Orpen diagram stands as something quite contrary to the maxim, 'a picture is worth a thousand words', for here we have a picture that is validated by the words with which it is associated, rather than being a rich source of pictorial information in the first instance. Instead, the Orpen image functions more convincingly as a symbol, an icon, of the ethnographic approach than of the actual rock paintings. And yet Orpen's illustrated text stands as a benchmark for 'authenticity' in 19th-century recording practices, while other early copyists, considered ignorant of the ethnography, are readily sidelined. To explore some of these alternative positions, I revisit four depictions of rock paintings produced during the 19th century, focusing especially on their pictorial qualities.

John Barrow's unicorn

John Barrow (1764–1848) forged the first of his voyages into the eastern interior beyond the boundaries of the Cape Colony from 1797 to 1798. His personal account of these travels provides a glimpse into his first experience of rock paintings in the Sneeuwberg in 1797 (Barrow 1801: 239–240). David Lewis-Williams (1983: 7, 10) notes that Barrow 'was not the first white traveller to see Bushman rock art, but he was one of the first to appreciate both its extraordinary aesthetic worth and its significance for a more realistic assessment of the much maligned Bushmen'. Barrow certainly observed the 'brutal conduct' of Dutch farmers towards the 'Bosjesmans' (1801: 236) and seems to write about them with a mixture of fear and compassion. Others have recognised that Barrow was, for his time, outspoken in their defence (Penn 1993) and perhaps not as derogatory as some of his writing sounds to our 21st-century ears (Knox-Shaw 1997: 20). Elsewhere Barrow (e.g., 1801: 237, 283, 288) expressed more conventional opinions of them as filthy and gluttonous savages, with voices scarcely human, speaking an inarticulate language and living an uncivilised, marauding and ruthless way of life. But this hatred seems expressed with somewhat of a remove, perhaps reflecting the positions of others, rather than his own. In that he was impressed by the 'spirit', 'force' and correctness of the paintings (ibid: 239), his position seems progressive for his time because the artistry he saw in the paintings did not conform to the perceived savageness of the people.

Although Barrow's book is largely without illustrations, his writing is descriptive in a visual way, suggesting that he was a sensitive observer of the landscape. At one painted rock shelter he observed animals depicted naturalistically enough for him to identify at least eight species, including a striking painting of a zebra. He described the presence of two distinct painting styles, one naturalistic and another more caricatural, and observed an 'effect of light and shadow', possibly referring to bichrome (or shaded) painting techniques, while his row of

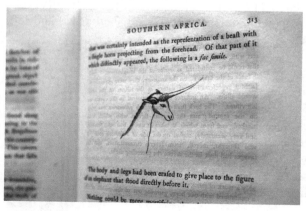

Figure 2

'crosses, circles, points and lines' suggests the presence of a more abstract, geometric tradition (ibid: 239–240).

As Barrow neared the end of his journey he had seen countless figures painted on rocks. Thus, when a member of the party claimed to have encountered a drawing of a unicorn some years before, Barrow set his heart on this particular subject and the party commenced a thorough search in the Zuureberg (ibid: 302). Eventually they found in 'a very high and concealed kloof' part of a figure 'that was certainly intended as the representation of a beast with a single horn projecting from the forehead' (ibid: 312–313) (see Figure 2).

Whether Barrow truly 'saw' an image of an animal with one horn (which might, for example, have been a partially preserved antelope with only one horn clearly visible), it is obvious from his words that he interpreted this subject matter from a depiction that was not very clear (or incomplete). By contrast, the line drawing in his book is quite unequivocally a unicorn in a highly conventionalised European form. We do not know what artistic skills Barrow had, what the original field copy looked like or what processes of translation it underwent before appearing in print, if indeed Barrow ever made a copy. The publishers probably used the services of an artist who was not even on the expedition. But, however inaccurate, it is sometimes credited as the 'first copy of African rock art to be published' (Bahn 1998: 25).

Michell's 'faithful copies'

British officer and writer-explorer, James Edward Alexander (1803–1885), reported on paintings observed in the districts of Uitenhage and George in his narrative of a 'campaign in Kaffirland' in 1835 (Alexander 1837: 314–317). In this publication he included three colour engravings derived from 'faithful copies' produced by his father-in-law, Charles Collier Michell (1793–1851), who was the first surveyor-general and civil engineer of the Cape Colony and an accomplished artist, and left

behind a rich archive of notebooks, watercolours and sketches (Richings 2006). Reflecting a sense of the fragility of historical traces, Alexander (1837: 315) records that Michell's field copies of the rock art 'executed by the former occupiers of the country' were 'faithful copies of all these drawings, such as still remain uninjured by time and the weather, by which great numbers have been almost entirely effaced'. The

Figure 3

monochrome figures depicted in these plates come from three sites, one of which is a rock shelter known currently as Ezeljagdspoort, located in a narrow gorge of the Brak River in the vicinity of Oudtshoorn (see Figure 3).

The copy from this site comprises a circular area delineated by a wavy line encompassing human figures with wing- or fin-like limbs that appear to be gliding (Alexander 1837: pl. III; Hollmann 2005: fig. 3; Lewis-Williams 1990: 8, 45). About this depiction Alexander (1837: 317) wrote: 'We are unable to assist the reader, even by a conjecture, in elucidating the meaning of that which he here sees represented: but it may, perhaps, have allusion to the amphibious nature attributed to the whites by the natives in the olden day.'

The group has been examined by numerous subsequent visitors to the site, such that its 'successive interpretations illustrate the ways in which our knowledge of San rock art has developed over the years' (Lewis-Williams 1990: 8). This history of interpretation also illustrates the multiplicity of possible, but never entirely certain, construals and the malleability of subject matter, as well as the cross-cultural nature of therianthropic characters and other aspects of myth. Amphibious interpretations have persisted, and not so long ago the figures were still described as 'fish-like up to the waist and human above, reminiscent of mer-people of European folklore' (Willcox 1963: pl. 11). This type of hybrid figure, also recorded at other shelters, is still familiarly referred to as a mermaid (e.g., Hollmann 2005: 25). In the more recent, ethnographically informed strain of interpretations, fins are read alternatively as wings and the figures' movement as flying rather than floating, denoting shamans who can embody or be embodied by swallows – animals that are symbolically related to rain and rainmaking (Lewis-Williams 1990: 8, 44–47). In an alternative analysis that combines natural modelling with ethnographic interpretation, Hollmann (2005) identifies these figures as swift-people, a unique class of spiritual being understood in terms of a correspondence between bird behaviour and aspects of San ritual. Others have associated a different kind of indigenous interpretation with this motif, suggesting that they represent spirit beings of the water known as *watermeide* in Afrikaans, linked to a Bushman version of a 'waterwoman' legend first recorded in the 1870s (Leeuwenberg 1970) and more recently (e.g., Prins 2001; Rust 2008).

In 1988, Thomas Dowson created another copy of the Ezeljagdspoort group by tracing the cluster of figures and redrawing it in black ink (Lewis-Williams et al. 1993: fig. 3). For Lewis-Williams (1990: 44), Michell's version is less accurate than Dowson's because he missed certain features (or did not record them in detail) that are significant for current ethnographically informed interpretations of the imagery. The omitted features include three dots on the lower right side of the group and several lines, including a wavy one, which Lewis-Williams argues are entoptics derived from optical responses of the nervous system in an altered state of consciousness. The identification of these spots and lines as entoptics seems tenuous, however, considering their formal simplicity, and because natural stains and older painting across the rock surface introduce a certain amount of ambiguity into the iconographic content of this particular example.

I rather agree with Richings' (2006: 50) assessment of the 'essential accuracy' of Michell's copy for the purposes of modern-day interpretations. The published plate also presents the figures like shadows projected onto a smooth plane, and, although it was not derived from tracing, comprises many of the same figural iconographic elements in a relatively accurate configuration. Moreover, Michell did capture one of the wavy lines, and despite the absence of the other lines and dots, his copy still fits reasonably well with modern interpretations. Interestingly, an earlier (1835) copy (Richings 2006: fig. 11), which may be the original field copy, includes extra lines, including a wavy one, in the right margins of this composition that were omitted in its translation to a lithographic engraving. Further, the figures of this group merge with the patterns and colorations of the natural rock surface, and it seems just as plausible that the lines and dots might depict something physical, for example, marking some kind of boundary or connection. Michell drew on the compositional significance of the lines, seeing the upper wavy line as part of an arc forming a frame encircling the group. This predilection for a 'framed' alignment might also have been at work in Orpen's isolation of the Sehonghong group, contained along the upper edge by a wavy line, rendered more horizontal in the copy to define the upper edge of an imposed rectangular layout. Michell's copy does not show an older layer of faded yellow figures beneath the rusty reddish ones, and this is also consistent with Orpen's treatment of the rock surface and that of many other copyists who lift off the clearest, uppermost layer for the purposes of discussion. However, Michell's copy retains a greater sense of the swirling movement within the original than the Orpen illustration does.

Not only can it compete with the accuracy of modern redrawn versions serving figural iconographic analyses, it also embodies a particular concern for colour and the 'rust of iron' from which the pigments were thought to be derived, as Alexander (1837: 315) claimed the rusty reddish colours in the reproduction replicated the colours of the rock drawings exactly. In its concern for colour, it is more accurate than the modern redrawing. In an otherwise relatively colourless sandstone setting, the painters' repeated return to this red-tinted patch points to the site-embeddedness and continual nature of their practice, and to the significance of the colour red. Colour seems to me absolutely fundamental to the visual and symbolic significance of the art, and would be worth pursuing in San rock art research in the future. On several counts, therefore, Michell's copy demonstrates an openness and interpretative restraint in relation to unfamiliar imagery, unusual in the times in which he lived.

Figure 4

Baines's haunted rocks

John Thomas Baines (1820–1875) was a traveller and skilled artist whose naïve yet shrewd and perceptive illustrations reflect various aspects of life in southern Africa in the mid-1800s. He produced thousands of sketches, watercolours and oil paintings of landscapes, people and events (Carruthers and Arnold 1995). Of his oeuvre, less than a dozen images and diary entries relate to southern Africa's San; several refer to rock art (Ouzman 2010: 11). Baines' diary from 1842 to 1853 (Baines 1961, 1964) alludes to sketches produced at four separate sites, one of which is the subject of the 1849 oil painting titled *Bushman's Krantz, Baviaans River, Animals painted on the rock by the Bushman. Much visited by the Poet Pringle*. It is located in the Bedford district of the Eastern Cape (Ouzman 2010) (see Figure 4).

Baines portrays, high up on the rock above the Bushman paintings, the inscription 'T Pringle 1825', a 'graffiti' signature which is an actual feature of the site, inscribed there by the poet Thomas Pringle (1789–1834). In the oil painting (and not at the actual site), Baines placed his own signature onto a 'cartouche' provided by a conveniently located rock projecting into the lower right corner of the picture. Baines' portrayal of this site, located on the Pringle family's farm, Eildon, depicts an irregular rock wall painted with a variety of figures (animal and human) and more abstract shapes including stars and dots. In the left foreground, Baines has autobiographically inserted himself in a sketching pose beside a napping companion.

Ouzman (2002: 7) points out that the interest in matching up historical copies with physical sites is not 'just for the thrill of (re)discovery', but that the process also provides us with a glimpse into colonial attitudes towards the Bushmen and rock art, and indeed outsider attitudes to the land more generally. Baines was 'a product of expansionist colonial times' (Ouzman 2010: 11), unimpressed by Bushman art which he considered 'debased' due to what he judged a poor technique and ugly, non-naturalistic style:

> The works of the aboriginal artists, which covered the face of the cliff to an average height of five feet above the ground, comprised rude but recognisable delineations of the rhinoceros, hartebeest, giraffe, eland, koodoo, the domestic ox and other animals, with grotesque representations of men engaged in chase or war, as well as many in which it was impossible to trace a resemblance to any living creature whatever. The pigments appeared to consist of red, yellow and white earths and charcoal, mixed as an old Hottentot informed me, with fat, which indurated by the scorching sun, rendered them indelible; and laid on without the slightest attempt at shadow, blending, or perspective, with feathers of different sizes. (Baines 1961: 116)

While Baines (1961: 115) did not seem to appreciate the role the imagery played in making this one of the 'spots hallowed' by his poetry, Pringle may have been paying 'homage to the spirit of the painters previous' in inscribing his name above these figures (Ouzman 2010: 13). Perhaps the rock painting merely played a supporting role for what really interested Baines at Baviaans Krantz, namely the signature of his literary hero. Indeed, in its details, the painting is not an accurate portrayal of this particular place, yet Baines successfully created an evocative impression: a flat patch of ground with grass next to an uneven vertical rock wall across which the Bushman images occur across natural subdivisions of the rock face. While the painted figures are anecdotal, caricatured and cartoonish, and not the main pictorial subject of the painting, their size and clarity are exaggerated, suggesting that they are depicted as something more than an incidental part of the background.

Baines' signature at the lower right corner of the canvas features a later date of 12 March 1849, indicating that the painting was completed a month-and-a-half after the visit, recorded in his diary under 25 January, suggesting it may have been created from memory. Demonstrating his gift for 'capturing the essential elements of a place' (Ouzman 2002: 6), Baines portrayed the rock art as an integral part of the setting, situating it in relation to other inscriptions on the land and acknowledging the layeredness of human traces, and in the process captured something specific enough about this place for it to be locatable over a century-and-a-half later.

Figure 5

Figure 6

Mäder's multiple vision

The final contribution I consider serves as a transitional example from the 19th to the 20th century, and to the era of photography. Otto Mäder was a German-born painter, also known as Brother Otto and Otto Trapp (1863–1937), who served the Mariannhill Missions as a draughtsman at various stations in South Africa. Adrian Flett and Penny Letley (2007) examine his work as a copyist and go some way to correct earlier views that he had 'quaint and fanciful' ideas about the art, instead positioning him as a skilled and faithful recorder who developed several important ideas about rock painting techniques and the meanings behind the art.

Mäder's better-known later work depicts the rock paintings of the Kei River Valley, where he was commissioned by Father Albert Schweiger to copy paintings in 1913–14, while based at Keilands Mission (on the Great Kei River, Eastern Cape province, South Africa). His recording procedure involved taking measurements and making sketches and notes *in situ*. From this first generation of working documents he produced more presentable composite illustrations, many dating from 1932 when he was stationed at Mariannhill, so a distinction can be made in Mäder's work between 'field watercolours' and paintings 'for exhibition purposes' (Flett and Letley 2007).

But his interest began in the mid-1890s in the southern Natal Drakensberg when he was stationed at the Reichenau Mission, near the village of Underberg.

From the Reichenau period, Mäder (1908) published three photographs and six hand-drawn copies from Sangwana Shelter (Flett and Letley 2007: 106). The three photographs are among the earliest documenting rock art in the region (dating to 1894–1895). The six copies were published in small format, grouped together onto a single journal page. The location of the original field copies is unknown, but in these drawings prepared for publication, Mäder's formal style appears stiff and caricatural (see Figure 5).

Several of the renderings show an incipient interest in copying the rock surface along with the painted figures, influenced by his practice as an architect, technical draughtsman and photographer.

In Germany, Mäder had been trained as a painter specialising in the restoration and reproduction of medieval works, and one of his primary responsibilities to the Mariannhill Missions was to convert architectural plans into working drawings (ibid: 103–104). A combination of this technical drawing skill, painterly technique and photographic vision is visible in his later composite depictions of rock painting sites, where he developed a method of representing different views on one sheet of paper: for example, a close-up, flattened view of the painted figures, a view of the natural configuration of rock around the figures, and a frontal perspective of the site (Figure 6), sometimes including wider views of the landscape.

Mäder intended his copies to be comprehensive:

> The pictures were copied completely and systematically, so that they form a record without selection or omission ... This method of wholesale copy is of great importance, because isolated elements were not taken and robbed thereby of their context; the pictures were carefully reproduced in water colours; great pains were taken in studying the technique whereby the originals were executed ... Notes were made concerning the technical execution of the originals at the time of copying and were written on the copies during the period of research. (Huss and Mäder 1925: 497)

Flett and Letley (2007) include a numerical assessment to gauge the accuracy of his copies in view of current figural iconographic requirements, establishing a narrow margin of discrepancy. Although he tended to avoid depicting facial features (possibly for religious reasons) he could 'very seldom be accused of subjective alteration; even in the few instances where points were deducted for alteration, there was no gross distortion of images' (ibid: 113). He also consciously sought to avoid allowing preconceived ideas to influence what he saw, seeming to have been able to 'separate the art from his religious beliefs and to examine it in a more methodical and dispassionate way' (ibid: 111, 118).

When Raymond Dart (1925) argued in a controversial article for external influences on the indigenous cultures of South Africa, claiming that foreigners were depicted in the art, he used information and pictures supplied by Schweiger and Mäder, thereby linking them to his dubious theories. Because of this association, Mäder has not received the credit due to him. Yet he recorded the paintings more holistically than many other copyists of his time (and indeed many since), discouraging people from viewing them 'as isolated images to be separated from their general context and analysed through Western eyes' (Flett and Letley 2007: 116). His presentation of the paintings is innovative because his drawings seem to encourage the viewer to locate and experience it first-hand in the landscape, rather than to rely on a copy.

Motifs embedded in the landscape

The first written references to rock paintings appeared in the 18th century. Similarly, early archival images also exist, such as those produced by Robert Jacob Gordon and/or his assistant Johannes Schumacher between 1777 and 1778, and which are apparently the earliest extant graphic copies (Bahn 1998: 27; Wilson 2005: 10), not only from southern Africa but the African continent (Davis 1990: 271). During the 19th century, depictions of rock paintings began to enter the literate realm and the examples discussed in this article form a significant sample (other examples include Bent 1892: 292–293, 303; Farini 1886: 124; Fritsch 1872: Tafel L; Holub 1881: facing 438; King 1855: 207).

At the eve of the 19th century, Barrow's unicorn is clearly erroneous and demonstrates the powerful impact of overlays of European mythology onto indigenous African imagery, or simply the desire of publishers to break and lighten the text with pictures. Yet Barrow's descriptions of rock art sites point to a sensitive, almost geographic observation of the landscape. In Michell's copy, published in 1837, the paintings are viewed through a cautious yet open-minded interpretative lens. From a graphic perspective this is a more accurate rendition than Orpen's image, which appeared in print almost four decades later. Furthermore, it expresses a novel interest in the importance of colour. From the middle of the century, Baines' oil painting also captures something of the physical configuration of the rock art site, and the notion of the rock paintings as one layer among many human markings placed onto the land over time. From around 1894 onwards, influenced by the new image-making technology of photography, Mäder began to produce depictions of rock paintings that capture something of the landscape context, ultimately producing in the early years of the 20th century a recording method which includes the art's geological and landscape setting, collating different views into one image.

The single most influential 19th-century depiction is, however, Orpen's four-group compilation, particularly the rainmaking scene, whose legacy can be tracked through a lineage of reproductions (Wintjes 2011). Authenticated by Qing's testimony and peeled off the rocks, this configuration of motifs 'floats' as an icon over the landscape. Its textual context sparked an entire field of contemporary rock art research. It also set the precedent for a diagrammatic mode of reproduction, which treats the painted imagery as if it were made up of discrete iconographic motifs, that can be lifted from the rock surface and transposed onto a reproducible rectangular medium without affecting what the paintings might mean or represent, or simply what the paintings might 'be', as 'self-sufficient wholes' (Davis 1990: 271).

This treatment echoes iconographic concerns of the scientific project of early art-historical and archaeological research, yet other 19th-century copyists working largely in isolation illustrate a number of alternative approaches, showing graphic experimentation and diversity in copying techniques – what Pippa Skotnes (1994: 319) calls 'creative exploration'. Although not authenticated by Qing's testimony, these are often more than simply quaint, uninformed, fanciful documents. They represent different positions, and at times experimental research processes, from which we can still learn today. People from different backgrounds trying to grapple with enigmatic pictures on the rocks, using a variety of strategies, present us with diverse ways of seeing, prior to an understanding of the semantics of their symbolic constituents in the ethnographic sense, but with a certain appreciation of their visual, even spiritual, significance. Considered against the backdrop of the Orpen icon, other 19th-century copies do not carry the same kind of 'authenticity'. As pictorial copies, however, they are not necessarily any worse or less instructive. On the contrary, they represent in various ways the imagery as a fragment of a wider, intractable whole, and demonstrate that other recording strategies can enrich and complicate our understanding of colonial positions in relation to the art, and ultimately the visual significance of the art itself.

Acknowledgements

Thanks go to Anitra Nettleton, Gavin Whitelaw and two anonymous reviewers, who commented on earlier drafts. Diana Wall, image curator at Museum Africa, provided me with access to the Baines painting. This article draws on my doctoral thesis, which was funded by Mellon Foundation, National Research Foundation, National Arts Council, University of the Witwatersrand and Maria Stein-Lessing bursaries. The inspiration to examine the Orpen materials through the icon-archive framework came from working with members of the Qing and Orpen Project, initiated by John Wright and José de Prada-Samper.

Note

1   The ARAL (Analysis of Rock Art in Lesotho) report on Sehonghong (ARAL 658) compiled by Taole Tesele in 1985, includes a site plan and schematic sketches of each of the

painted panels lettered A to Z and A1 to Z1. Vinnicombe's records from Sehonghong also reflect more than just this group.

References

Alexander, J.E. 1837. *Narrative of a voyage of observation among the colonies of western Africa, in the flag-ship Thalia; and of a campaign in Kaffir-land on the staff of the Commander-in-chief in 1835*. London: Henry Colburn.

Bahn, P.G. 1998. *The Cambridge illustrated history of prehistoric art*. Cambridge: Cambridge University Press.

Baines, T. 1961. *Journal of residence in Africa 1842–1853 by Thomas Baines: volume one, 1842–1849*, ed. R.J. Kennedy. Cape Town: Van Riebeeck Society.

Baines, T. 1964. *Journal of residence in Africa 1842–1853 by Thomas Baines: volume two, 1850–1853*, ed. R.J. Kennedy. Cape Town: Van Riebeeck Society.

Barrow, J. 1801. *An account of travels into the interior of southern Africa in the years 1797 and 1798: including cursory observations on the geology and geography of the southern part of that continent; the natural history of such objects as occurred in the animal, vegetable, and mineral kingdoms; and sketches of the physical and moral characters of the various tribes of inhabitants surrounding the settlement of the Cape of Good Hope*. London: A. Strahan.

Bent, J.T. 1892. *The ruined cities of Mashonaland being a record of excavation and exploration in 1891*. London: Longmans, Green and Co.

Bleek, W.H.I. 1874. Remarks by Dr. Bleek. *Cape Monthly Magazine* 9(49): 10–13.

Carruthers, J. and M. Arnold. 1995. *The life and work of Thomas Baines*. Vlaeberg: Fernwood Press.

Castaldi, F. 2006. *Choreographies of African identities: négritude, dance, and the National Ballet of Senegal*. Urbana and Chicago: University of Illinois Press.

Challis, S.W.R., J. Hollmann and M. McGranaghan. 2013. 'Rain snakes' from the Senqu River: new light on Qing's commentary on San rock art from Sehonghong, Lesotho. *Azania: Archaeological Research in Africa*. http://dx.doi.org/10.1080/006727 0X.2013.797135 (accessed 4 August 2013).

Dart, R.A. 1925. The historical succession of cultural impacts upon South Africa. *Nature* 115(2890): 425–429.

Davis, W. 1990. The study of rock art in Africa. In *A history of African archaeology*, ed. R. Robertshaw, 271–295. London: J. Currey.

Farini, G.A. 1886. *Through the Kalahari Desert: a narrative of a journey with a gun, camera, and note-book to Lake N'Gami and back*. London: Sampson Low, Marston, Searle & Rivington.

Flett, A. and P. Letley. 2007. Brother Otto Mäeder: an examination and evaluation of his work as a rock art recorder in South Africa. *Southern African Humanities* 19: 103–121.

Fritsch, G. 1872. *Die Eingeborenen Süd-Afrika's*. Breslau: Ferdinand Hirt.

Frobenius, L. 1931. *Madsimu Dsangara. Südafrikanische Felsbilderchronik*. Berlin and Zurich: Atlantis Verlag.

Hollmann, J.C. 2005. 'Swift-people': therianthropes and bird symbolism in hunter-gatherer rock paintings, western and eastern Cape provinces, South Africa. *South African Archaeological Society Goodwin Series* 9: 21–33.

Hollmann, J.C. and K. Crause. 2011. Digital imaging and the revelation of 'hidden' rock art: Vaalekop Shelter, KwaZulu-Natal. *Southern African Humanities* 23: 55–76.

Holub, E.M. 1881. *Seven years in South Africa: travel, researches, and hunting adventures, between the diamond-fields and the Zambesi (1872–1879)*, vol. two. London: Sampson Low, Marston, Searle & Rivington.

Huss, B. and Mäder, O. [Br. Otto, O.C.R.] 1925. The origin of the Bushmen paintings at the Kei River. *South African Journal of Science* 22: 496–503.

Jacobs, Z., R.G. Roberts, R.F. Galbraith, M. Barré, H.J. Deacon, A. Mackay, P.J. Mitchell, R. Vogelsang and L. Wadley. 2008. Ages for Middle Stone Age innovations in southern Africa: implications for modern human behavior and dispersal. *Science* 322: 733–735.

Kemp, M. 2012. *Christ to Coke: how image becomes icon.* Oxford: Oxford University Press.

King, W.R. 1855. *Campaigning in Kaffirland or scenes and adventures in the Kaffir War of 1851–2.* Second edition. London: Saunders and Otley.

Knox-Shaw, P. 1997. Unicorns on rocks: the expressionism of Olive Schreiner. *English Studies in Africa* 40(2): 13–32.

Leeuwenberg, J. 1970. A Bushman legend from the George district. *The South African Archaeological Bulletin* 25(99/100): 145–146.

Lewis-Williams, J.D. 1980. Ethnography and iconography: aspects of Southern San thought and art. *Man* 15(3): 467–482.

Lewis-Williams, J.D. 1981. *Believing and seeing: symbolic meanings in Southern San rock paintings.* London: Academic Press.

Lewis-Williams, J.D. 1983. *The rock art of southern Africa.* Cambridge: Cambridge University Press.

Lewis-Williams, J.D. 1990. *Discovering southern African rock art.* Cape Town: David Philip.

Lewis-Williams, J.D. 2010. The imagistic web of San myth, art and landscape. *Southern African Humanities* 22: 1–18.

Lewis-Williams, J.D., T.A. Dowson and J. Deacon. 1993. Rock art and changing perceptions of southern Africa's past: Ezeljagdspoort reviewed. *Antiquity* 67: 273–291.

Mäder, O. [Br. Otto, O.C.R.] 1908. Buschmann-Malereien aus Natal. *Anthropos* 3: 1047–1049.

Manhoff, M. 2004. Theories of the archive from across the disciplines. *Libraries and the Academy* 4(1): 9–25.

Mitchell, P.J. 2010. Making history at Sehonghong: Soai and the last Bushman occupants of his shelter. *Southern African Humanities* 22: 149–170.

Mitchell, P.J. and S. Challis. 2008. A 'first' glimpse into the Maloti Mountains: the diary of James Murray Grant's expedition of 1873–74. *Southern African Humanities* 20: 399–461.

Mitchell, W.J.T. 1984. What is an image? *New Literary History* 15(3): 503–537.

Orpen, J.M. 1874. A glimpse into the mythology of the Maluti Bushmen. *Cape Monthly Magazine* 9(49): 1–10.

Ouzman, S. 2002. Thomas Baines' 'lost' rock art site. *The Digging Stick* 19(1): 6–7.

Ouzman, S. 2010. Graffiti as art(e)fact: a contemporary archaeology. Paper presented at the Sociology, Anthropology and Development Studies Seminar, University of Johannesburg, 10 March 2010 (quoted with the author's permission). http://www.uj.ac.za/EN/Faculties/humanities/departments/sociology/seminar/Documents/Seminar%20papers/Ouzman%202010%20Graffiti.pdf

Oxford English dictionary. 2014. Oxford: Oxford University Press. www.oed.com

Penn, N. 1993. Mapping the Cape: John Barrow and the first British occupation of the Colony, 1795–1803. *Pretexts* 4(2): 20–43.

Prins, F. 2001. Call of the water spirits. In *Rock paintings of South Africa: revealing a legacy*, ed. S. Townley Bassett, 65–69. Cape Town: David Philip.

Richings, G. 2006. *The life and work of Charles Michell.* Simon's Town: Fernwood Press.

Rust, C. 2008. Meta-tourism, sense of place and the rock art of the Little Karoo. PhD thesis, Geography and Environmental Studies, Stellenbosch University.

Skotnes, P. 1994. The visual as a site of meaning. In *Contested images: diversity in southern African rock art research*, ed. T.A. Dowson, and [J.]D. Lewis-Williams, 315–330. Johannesburg: Witwatersrand University Press.

Skotnes, P. 1996. The thin black line: diversity and transformation in the Bleek and Lloyd collection and the paintings of the Southern San. In *Voices from the past: |Xam Bushmen and the Bleek and Lloyd collection*, ed. J. Deacon and T.A. Dowson, 234–244. Johannesburg: Witwatersrand University Press.

Skotnes, P. 2008. *Unconquerable spirit: George Stow's history paintings of the San.* Johannesburg and Athens, Ohio: Jacana and Ohio University Press.

Smits, L.G.A. 1973. Rock painting sites in the upper Senqu Valley, Lesotho. *The South African Archaeological Bulletin* 28: 32–38.

Vinnicombe, P. 1966. The early recording and preservation of rock paintings in South Africa. *Studies in Speleology* 1(4): 153–62.

Vinnicombe, P. 1976. *People of the eland: rock paintings of the Drakensberg Bushmen as a reflection of their life and thought.* Pietermaritzburg: University of Natal Press.

Vinnicombe, P. 2009[1976]. *People of the eland: rock paintings of the Drakensberg Bushmen as a reflection of their life and thought*, second edition. Johannesburg: Wits University Press.

Ward, V. and T. Maggs. 1994. Changing appearances: a comparison between early copies and the present state of rock paintings from the Natal Drakensberg as an indication of rock art deterioration. *Natal Museum Journal of Humanities* 6: 153–78.

Willcox, A.R. 1963. *The rock art of South Africa.* Johannesburg: Thomas Nelson.

Wilson, M. 2005. Early records of South African rock art. *The Digging Stick* 22(1): 9–10.

Wintjes, J. 2011. A pictorial genealogy: the rainmaking group from Sehonghong Shelter. *Southern African Humanities* 23: 17–54.

Wintjes, J. 2012. Archaeology and visuality, imaging as recording: a pictorial genealogy of rock painting research in the Maloti-Drakensberg through two case studies. PhD thesis in Art History, University of the Witwatersrand, Johannesburg.

Wright, J. and J. de Prada-Samper. 2013. Introducing the Qing and Orpen Project. *The Digging Stick* 30(1): 5.

Truths, representationalism and disciplinarity in Khoesan researches

Anne Solomon

Abstract

Khoesan studies today are the province of researchers in diverse disciplines, with markedly different epistemologies and priorities. In this article I consider Khoesan representations in relation to disciplinarity, and work designed to move beyond it, for instance, through creative curation. From a phenomenological perspective, an under-appreciated problem is that of 'representationalism' or a divide between 'the world and its meanings'. From this perspective, new practices and ways of working are required in order to discover new forms that are appropriate to the subjects of study, namely Khoesan peoples.

Introduction

The theme of Khoesan representations encompasses various issues and questions, centring on the ways in which Khoe and San peoples have been understood and portrayed in popular opinion, and in cultural and academic arenas. Other dimensions include the historical disenfranchisement and voicelessness of Khoesan peoples. In this article I raise questions about the theoretical underpinnings of the theme of 'representations', relative to alternative approaches to understanding Khoesan cultural materials; this in turn raises key issues of disciplinarity. Discourse and fact, material and ideal, art and science, worlds and meanings and qualititative versus quantitative, are some of the poles that organise different enquiries, from archaeological research through literary studies and museum curation. These

246

distinctions are themselves historically situated, and to recognise this is relevant to examining the problem of Khoesan representations and issues of the possibilities of authentic knowledge.

Self-representation?

George Stow, founder of rock art research, may have been the first to be aware of the problems of Khoesan representations. His stated aim of producing a history of San peoples 'as depicted by themselves' (Jones 1870) has been cited in support of the view that rock art provides a cultural insider's view (Lewis-Williams 2000), more authentic and less 'contaminated' by the perceptions of the researcher. For reasons that must remain unknown, ten years later, in the completed volume of his *The native races of South Africa*, Stow (1905: ix) had changed this to 'as illustrated by themselves'. The context of the quotation (which deals with San interviewees' lack of interest in, or even suspicion of, his historical project) suggests that he had become more aware of the difference between 'his' history (of tribal migrations) and that of the peoples who were the subject matter of his work. It seems that he thought that this problem could be mitigated, or perhaps minimised, by juxtaposing them. This strategy of acknowledging and contrasting different discourses is still with us, in new forms and contexts (see below), as is the divide itself, which turns on the very possibility of knowledge of past cultures. Are rock arts and the |Xam testimonies voices from the past? Or does our own historically situated consciousness render that proposition entirely untenable?

Positivism or scepticism?

Self-reflexive, critical awareness of the ways in which Khoesan peoples are represented is now a central concern, especially in arts and humanities disciplines. In archaeology, which has played a key role in Khoesan research, an allegiance to an ideal of value-free, 'objective' science was prominent throughout much of the 20th century, from the time of the professionalisation of the discipline in the 1920s, through to the 1980s and beyond. The dominant frame for archaeology of the 1970s, 'processual' archaeology, acknowledged that the discipline was not a hard science, but was concerned with increasing scientific rigour (e.g., via statistical analyses) and a quest for the 'laws' of cultural behaviour. In the 1980s this paradigm was challenged by 'postprocessual archaeology', exemplified by Shanks and Tilley's *Reconstructing archaeology* (1987). In a nutshell, the authors argued that archaeologists do not reconstruct the past, in a process akin to restoring a shattered pot to its former wholeness, but actively construct and recreate it in narratives and representations.

Postprocessualism was unenthusiastically received by traditionalists, who feared that it opened the door to epistemological anarchy, unfettered relativism, untestable interpretations and the injection of political agendas into scientific research. Today, few archaeologists would deny the importance of examining the representations of Khoesan peoples implicit in their work. However, there has also been a contrary effect. In practice, much archaeology seems to have retreated further into scientism, ostensibly for reasons of funding, with departments located in science faculties, and departments of environmental studies and geography. Proponents of a more 'discursive turn' such as myself have, to some extent, found more common cause with art history, cultural studies, and other arts and humanities disciplines that, in the words of Pauketat (2001), are open to more 'proximate' explanations. Ironically, research since the postprocessual debate seems actually to have become significantly further polarised along distinct disciplinary lines. It has fallen to people such as the artist Pippa Skotnes (see below), outside archaeology, to challenge this polarisation. Much archaeology remains largely wedded to a search for objective facts, while arts and humanities research has a strong focus on a critical examination of academic discourses about (Khoesan) cultural materials.

These are not, and should not be, mutually exclusive, but diverse attitudes to issues of authenticity and truth divide them. For most archaeologists, these are to be found in the factuality and materiality of the past, and there is no place for the hyperreal. Arts and humanities researchers rightly point out that trawling cultural materials for historical facts ignores the epistemological problems of the positivist project. Such approaches, according to Skotnes (1994), have traditionally subordinated the 'aesthetic and expressive' to the 'verifiable and verbalisable'. In my view, the most interesting and productive domain is intermediate, where perspectives meet, perhaps to be synthesised.

The postprocessualists 30 years ago in fact insisted on such a middle-ground position, where 'facts' constrain the narratives that we can tell about the past. Today, 'facts' appear more problematic than the early postprocessualists perhaps acknowledged. Then again, archaeology's facts and truths may indeed be contingent, but contingent facts are not the same as fictions. Empirical data remain important, and new evidence (finds, dates, excavation information) can still recast existing knowledge in a new light.[1] The other end of the spectrum from that which focuses on supposedly 'objective' scientific measuring and counting (i.e., the project that appears to have greater factuality), is that of prioritising discourse. But the problem here is that academic work itself – how 'we' write about, or otherwise re-present or speak for 'them' – can become the centre and subject of enquiry. It seems sometimes that attention to the mediations of the materials eclipses the materials themselves, with the experiences of Khoesan peoples almost secondary. To give an equivalent example, an historiography of writings about Khoesan peoples is not itself a Khoesan history.

Writing about writing has an important place in Khoesan studies, but is at a certain remove, and is not without its own ironies. Discourse analyses and work on representations are founded on scepticism about authenticity. Yet the appeal of rock paintings and texts such as the |Xam testimonies in the Bleek and Lloyd archive, for literary and cultural analysts, rests on notions of their authenticity and their status as under-mediated materials. A belief in authenticity more obviously grounds claims that the material remains of the past, and rock art in particular, indeed offer a more authentic view of the past, as is implied by Stow's initiative to produce a volume about San peoples 'illustrated by themselves', and the idea that rock paintings are a superior reflection of the culture of their makers.

Of course this is unsustainable, since rock paintings and other materials are only accessible to us through our own interpretations and contemporary consciousness. A belief in authenticity coexists uncomfortably with scepticism about the possibilities of knowledge in some postmodern thinking and arts/humanities scholarship, and frequently remains under-examined in scientific work. For example, rock art research might appear to be the flourishing 'cultural wing' of archaeology, but it was long the poor relation because strictly archaeological methods are inappropriate to investigate it. It was not Lewis-Williams' innovative semiotic approach to rock art (e.g., Lewis-Williams 1981) that brought rock art into the mainstream, but the approach that claimed to ground interpretations scientifically, by locating image forms in relation to neurological functioning (e.g., Lewis-Williams and Dowson 1988).

The effect of interpreting rock art as the reproduction of the contents of visions is a denial of the creative agency of the artists. Scepticism about the possibility of knowledge has its own problems. San rock art and narratives are often treated as deeply esoteric and complex; respect for cultural difference and an appreciation of the complexities of language segue into a pessimism about establishing meaning and a retreat from evaluating interpretations. Theories of authorship have highlighted the real complexities of identifying authorial intent, and also the problem of conflating authorial intent with meaning. But, in respect of the |Xam testimonies, the texts may not be transparent, but they are not entirely opaque either. Most of the narrators were perfectly articulate in many of their communications. Treating the testimonies as esoterica sails close to treating them as the utterances of the Other, when (inter alia, as 19th century products) they are no further removed, and perhaps less so than, for example, the texts of the ancient Greeks.

Some examples of questions that are more, rather than less, amenable to evaluation in terms of correct or incorrect readings, are required. From my own field of research (Solomon 1997, 2008, 2011, 2013a): Did the |Xam describe a healing dance? Do the accounts of people who walk by night in animal form describe shamans or spirits? Is the 'broken string' mentioned by Dia!kwain a severed bond with a spirit or the relation to the land severed by colonial incursion, as proposed by Watson (1991)?

However unamenable to ultimate proof, there *are* better and worse readings, and these questions are not beyond some kind of firm resolution.

In relation to the |Xam testimonies, on the one hand their language is ambiguous, but language also circumscribes the possibilities of meaning. Evaluating the limits of interpretation also sometimes seems to recede in work that focuses on the very real difficulties and ambiguities of the texts. In relation to rock art research, the art-historical critique has aptly pointed out that much work (archaeological and anthropological) has been in establishing an iconography of (more or less) verifiable 'facts', at the expense of formal and aesthetic considerations. But a 'correct' iconography remains important, since it is impossible to appreciate forms without an appreciation of 'content' (or, to be precise, of form:content relations and their possible configurations). These concerns have been allocated along disciplinary lines, relating to epistemological positions (formal considerations – art history, humanities; real world referents – archaeology, 'science'), but the divide is false, and also requires analysis, in discursive/historical terms, as a product of time and place.

Non-representational theory (NRT)

Alternatives have been proposed. What are the axes of divergence in Khoesan studies? Writing about 'the ontogenesis of sense', Anderson and Harrison (2010: 6) argue that a key problem in such research is a divide between 'the world and its meanings': 'On the one side, over there, the really real, "all things coarse and subtle", and on the other, in here, the really made-up, the representations and signs that give meaning and value. It's a classic Cartesian divide.'

Disciplinarity in Khoesan research – preoccupation with either the material and factual (the really real) or the discursive (the really made up) – replicates that Cartesian divide, as did the paradigm shift that took place in San research since the 1980s: from ecology to 'mind', away from viewing past San peoples as hunter-gatherers living perceptually in and of the landscape, towards examining systems of thought (a move that paralleled the shift from processualism to postprocessualism). Ecological approaches seemed to incorporate deterministic assumptions about the power of the environment to shape human behaviour. The replacement paradigm, emphasising worlds actively constructed in thought, may be disembodied in the way the advocates of non-representational theory (NRT) describe, and is not simply 'progress'.

The problem is, in part, the idea of 'representation' itself. NRT is inspired by phenomenology, and by the work of writers such as Deleuze and Latour. It can be summed up as an attempt to resist the 'conversion of life, matter and practice into text, sign and image' (Wylie 2007: 171). NRT is so named for its critique of 'representational*ism*' (Lorimer 2005; emphasis added), though it is not actually a theory, nor is it anti-representation; Dewsbury, Harrison and Rose et al. (2002, 438;

parentheses added) insist that it 'takes representation seriously [but] not as a code to be broken or as an illusion to be dispelled'.

An allied body of ideas is exemplified by Ingold's phenomenology, via Heidegger, on what he calls a 'dwelling perspective'. Like the NRT theorists, he develops Bourdieu's (1977) ideas on practice and habitus to consider embodied or corporeal knowledge, or knowledge produced 'without contemplation', rather than the idea that 'human beings inhabit discursive worlds of culturally constructed significance' (Ingold 2002: 172). It involves exploring 'the nexus of materiality, corporeality and perception' (Wylie 2007: 178), with the insistence that forms and 'meanings' arise in practice as fundamental. In rock art research this has been highlighted by Skotnes (1994) in her exemplary analysis of the relation of artistic praxis, figure and ground in a south-western Cape painted site. From a different angle, in my own work I have argued for attention to the practice of thoughtful 'making' of rock art, arising in particular circumstances (art as situated, instrumental action), rather than seeking the neurological origins of image forms (Solomon 2008).

Ingold's work also offers an interesting take on the issues of truth claims that are a key divide between disciplines. His work on landscape (e.g., Ingold 1993) and accompanying critique of representationalism emphasises the indivisibility of body/landscape, comparable to that of figure/ground – 'each implies the other' (ibid: 156). This is not the body marking the landscape: 'If we recognize a man's gait in the pattern of his footprints, it is not because the gait preceded the footprints and was "inscribed" in them, but because both the gait and the prints arose within the movement of the man's walking' (ibid: 162). He proposes that the archaeologist and the native dweller, attending to the cues of the landscape in the practice of being in and of it, are both engaged in much the same task, though the stories they tell will differ. In other words, comparable practices, both characterised by an 'education of attention' (Ingold 2003: 153), will (or can) produce isomorphic narratives, with some degree of authentic resemblance.[2]

There are other compelling reasons for returning at least some attention to these questions, even if historical meanings cannot simply be retrieved. In his critique of representationalism, Ingold considered anthropological studies of the Australian Pintupi, one of the last Australian aboriginal peoples to be forced to abandon their traditional lifeways. As indigenous dwellers they derive meaning from the landscape; but in anthropological readings 'we find a complete inversion, such that meanings that the people claim to discover *in* the landscape are attributed to the minds of people themselves and are said to be mapped *onto* the landscape' – this 'flatly contradicts the Pintupi ontology' (Ingold 2000: 54). Running parallel is the issue of the relation of the San artists' and |Xam storytellers' imaginative and creative works to the materiality and mundane factuality of everyday life. The flights and whimsicality of the former can only be properly appreciated against the backdrop of the latter (though to speak of a 'backdrop' belies the constitutive role of material culture in identity and sociality, and implies a separation that NRT theorists would reject).

It is not that replication of indigenous ontologies in our own work is necessarily either desirable or possible, but awareness of such contradictions is. For reasons why impositions matter we need look no further than the local example provided by Prins (2009: 204). He describes how, in his work with San descendants, he was initially told that making rock art related to acts of renewal, but that ten years later he was being told about trance metaphors and other things derived from a shamanistic interpretation. The mobilisation of academic readings that contradict indigenous ontologies and knowledge (or are plain wrong) can be an act of deculturation, however unintentional.

Though interpretations cannot be proven, and the San past exists in and through our narratives, I nevertheless contend that it is indeed possible to approach (if not flatly specify) what I have previously unwisely referred to as 'original meanings' (Solomon 2013b). I would now rather speak of 'historical meanings'. The iconography, meanings and worlds of rock art and stories may not be patent, but knowledge is not impossible. At the very least we know what (some of) it is (probably) not. Rock art was not interior décor, for example. We can securely identify various motifs (such as rain animals). It is not impossible to establish, with some confidence, whether narrators were describing x or y, though not in every instance. Many more motifs and their connotations may be amenable to understanding, with careful attention in a spirit of faithfulness to the narrators/artists and their experiences.

As mentioned above, acceptance of the intentional fallacy effects a transfer of authority from the writer (e.g., the |Xam narrators) to the reader/researcher. The representations of the |Xam themselves – *sensu* their efforts to convey their own experience, culture and reality – recede, with the balance tipped towards the analyst's role in the creation of 'meaning'. But it is not an either/or scenario. A quest for historical meanings is antithetical to the analysis of texts (or visual images) in terms of how they work for readers or viewers now, since the latter exercise is already infused and saturated with ideas about those historical meanings. They are simply inseparable. Yet these two tasks remain distributed disciplinarily, along the lines of the 'really real' or 'really made up' that NRT theorists identify.

Interdisciplinarity

No one has done more to address the problem of disciplinarity in Khoesan studies than Skotnes, with the 1996 'Miscast' exhibition a landmark event. Intriguingly, Skotnes wrote then that the exhibition was 'not, strictly speaking, about Bushmen', but an exploration of the term 'Bushman' (Skotnes 1996: 18). If so, then it might exemplify an academic displacement of the San as research subjects, but I suggest that a strength of the exhibition was that its attention to disciplinarity meant it did, in fact, locate 'Bushmen' as the centre around which so much scholarship has revolved, foregrounding the materiality of their lives at the same time as critically examining representations of San peoples. The involvement of scholars across disciplines around a common interest was effective. The accompanying publication, with its parallel texts, highlighted both the issue of disciplines running alongside each other and questions of representation.

Twenty years on, questions are still arising concerning multidisciplinary versus interdisciplinary research. While some researchers, including Skotnes, work across disciplines to a greater or lesser degree, multidisciplinarity remains more the norm. The work of artist Mark Dion, and the *wunderkammer* or cabinet of curiosities, provides an example from the arena of creative curation. (A key work is his 'Bureau of the Centre for Surrealism and its Legacy'.) According to Endt (2007: 3, citing Bourriaud 2002: 35), 'Mark Dion appropriates discourses and professional protocols of natural science and archaeology in order to mimic the "relational world" that these disciplines suppose, and to activate slippages between aesthetic and utilitarian functions'. His work deals with the 'alleged clash between science and art, between meticulous research and free imagination [that] lay at the very core of surrealism'. These juxtapositions, in the anarchic 'cabinet of curiosities', are said to 'offer a form of resistance to the totalising ambitions of reason, a place where the human mind can play instead of working' (Mason 2000: 28, in Endt 2007: 12).

I began this article with Stow's juxtapositioning of his history with copies of rock art, conceived of as the cultural insider's view, suggesting that this indicates a nascent understanding of discursive differences – though he probably regarded his parallel texts as mutually supportive. The strategy now is designed to be critical and productive. A problem, however, in this exhibition strategy and in multidisciplinary projects alike, is that this productivity remains mysterious. Somehow, in the interstices, something unspecified, even quasi-magical, is believed or expected to happen. But does it necessarily work like that? It is said that 'Dion proposes a form of interdisciplinarity that, instead of promoting the emergence of blinkered 'jacks of all trades, masters of none', combines thorough expert knowledge with productive collaboration and exchange between faculties, departments and disciplines' (Endt 2007: 11). The impulse is exciting, but it is questionable whether the strategy always goes far enough. Does it not equally risk reproducing and perpetuating separations, when the task now is to transcend them *before the fact*?

According to Nowotny (2003: 48) what is really required is transdisciplinarity – 'a joint problem solving that it is more than juxtaposition; more than laying one discipline alongside another'. This means research that is

carried out in the context of application, that is, problems are formulated from the very beginning within a dialogue among a large number of different actors and their perspectives. The context is set by a process of communication between various stakeholders. That requires great patience. But the problem is not formulated outside of that group and until that group comes to an agreement about what the problem is and how it will be carried out, no resources flow and no research activity can begin. (ibid: 48–49)

In other words, (new) forms (or representations) arise in (new) practices (*cf.* the phenomenological critiques of representationalism mentioned above).

Plainly, Khoesan research has not quite reached this point, where creative collaboration is undertaken in order to establish what problems require attention and what truly new questions can be asked. A problem highlighted by the 'Khoesan Representations' seminar was that of conferences predicated on ahistorical ethnic categories – 'the end of Bushman studies', in the words of John Wright. But this is ultimately another tussle of the disciplines – between history, by definition focused on the diachronic, and anthropology, concerned primarily with the synchronic. Rock art and stories, as cultural products, surely have to be considered primarily in cultural terms, but from a perspective strongly attuned to history. The task is to pose questions that are themselves not so deeply disciplinarily rooted to start with. Whereas notions of culture conceived of in terms of ethnicity tend to be short on history, to embrace the inverse is unsatisfactory. The historicist error is the assumption that historical context sufficiently explains cultural materials. For example, Mazel (2009), based on the hypothesis that shaded polychromes in the Ukhahlamba Drakensberg emerged c. 2000 b.p., explains the style in terms of incoming agriculturalists and social stress (i.e., ritual intensification = more painting). However, even if this were so, it is not an adequate explanation of the style itself, and its particular features. Context cannot account for the internal dynamics of the phenomenon of visual art (Solomon 2014). In a similar vein, the '500-Year Initiative' embraces multidisciplinarity at the same time as its core concept prioritises and even reifies history.

In Khoesan studies, inter- or trans-disciplinarity is not important for its own sake, or in terms of innovation in the organisation of knowledge, but because a more holistic picture can better 'represent' the subjects of enquiry and the many facets of their identities and experiences. Disciplinarity is specialisation, and specialisation is the direction in which knowledge production has long travelled, especially in the sciences. Research within all disciplines is further split among diverse specialists. The productivity of scientific reductionism is clearly apparent, but there comes a time when subfields of enquiry require reassembly to do justice to the subject(s). The individual polymath, now rare (and who might even be regarded these days as a dabbler), is differently equipped for that task (as opposed to a team), but is also well placed, or even better able, to achieve it. However, the opportunities in Khoesan research to broaden perspectives through interactions with practitioners in other disciplines are regrettably rather few and far between. An online platform that familiarises Khoesan researchers across disciplines with different perspectives and promotes discussion and, perhaps synthesis, would be a welcome development.

I will conclude by looking back to the history of Khoesan research, to the classic ethnographies and ethnographers and Khoesan researchers. Pre-eminent among them is the work of Lucy Lloyd. The value of her work owes much to the fact that she was not specialised in linguistic and philological enquiries, like Wilhelm Bleek. Contrary to the critique that she was a 'suburban' researcher who lacked a framework within which to formulate questions (Lewis-Williams and Pearce 2012), her strength lay in the fact that she took her cues primarily from the narrators (Solomon 2013a), attending to their voices instead of foregrounding her own. Another giant among ethnographers, Lorna Marshall, studied English literature before embarking on her ground-breaking Kalahari work (e.g., Marshall 1976, 1999), and initially had no anthropological training. Her work, too, benefits from being under-disciplined, and from its failure to conform to any particular tradition of anthropological thought (*cf.* Barnard 2007: 55). Next, there are the Harvard-Peabody Kalahari expeditions of the 1960s and 1970s, where teams of specialists from diverse disciplines travelled to the Kalahari, uniquely engaging with the Ju|'hoansi and their environments, and with their fellow scholars. This is not a matter of nostalgia, and of course there can be no return to 'naïve' ethnographies (so-called). But perhaps there is a study to be done that explores the quality (and qualities) of the work that emerged from these research engagements, in relation to questions of embodiment, disciplinarity and epistemologies, in order to embrace approaches of the kind that Lorimer (2005: passim) describes as being 'more than representational'.

Notes

1   However, as Mitchell (2005) noted, primary research into the Later Stone Age (which would include Khoesan materials) has in fact declined, except for work on rock art.

2   This does not have to pertain only to the experience of the physical landscape, but might also apply to the reader immersed in the world of the |Xam narratives.

References

Anderson, B and P. Harrison. 2010. The promise of non-representational theories. In *Taking place: non-representational theories and geography*, ed. B. Anderson and P. Harrison, 1–36. Farnham: Ashgate Publishing.

Barnard, A. 2007. *Anthropology and the Bushmen.* Oxford: Berg.

Bourdieu, P. 1977. *Outline of a theory of practice.* Cambridge: Cambridge University Press.

Bourriaud, N. 2002. *Relational aesthetics.* Dijon: Presses du Réel.

Dewsbury, J.D., P. Harrison, M. Rose and J. Wylie. 2002. Enacting geographies. *Geoforum* 32: 437–441.

Endt, M. 2007. Beyond institutional critique: Mark Dion's surrealist *wunderkammer* at the Manchester Museum. *Museum and Society* 5(1): 1–15.

Ingold, T. 1993. The temporality of the landscape. *World Archaeology* 25(2): 152–174.

Ingold, T. 2000. *The perception of the environment: essays on livelihood, dwelling and skill*. London and New York: Routledge.

Jones, T.R. 1870. Cave paintings by Bushmen. Letter to the editor. *Nature* 3: 107.

Lewis-Williams, J.D. 1981. *Believing and seeing: symbolic meanings in Southern San rock paintings*. London: Academic Press.

Lewis-Williams, J.D. 2000. *Stories that float from afar*. Cape Town: David Philip.

Lewis-Williams, J.D. and T. Dowson. 1988. The signs of all times: entoptic phenomena and Upper Palaeolithic art. *Current Anthropology* 29(2): 201–245.

Lewis-Williams, J.D. and D. Pearce. 2012. The Southern San and the trance dance: a pivotal debate in the interpretation of San rock paintings. *Antiquity* 86: 696–706.

Lorimer, H. 2005. Cultural geography: the busyness of being 'more than representational'. *Progress in Human Geography* 29: 83–94.

Marshall, L. 1976. *The !Kung of Nyae Nyae*. Cambridge, MA: Harvard University Press.

Marshall, L. 1999. *Nyae Nyae !Kung beliefs and rites*. Cambridge, MA: Peabody Museum of Anthropology and Ethnology.

Mason, P. 2000. The song of the sloth. In *re-verberations: tactics of resistance, forms of agency in trans/cultural practices*, ed. J. Fisher, 20–31. Maastricht: Jan van Eyck Editions.

Mazel, A. 2009. Unsettled times: shaded polychrome paintings and hunter-gatherer history in the southeastern mountains of southern Africa. *Southern African Humanities* 21: 85–115.

Mitchell, P. 2005. Why hunter-gatherer archaeology matters: a personal perspective on renaissance and renewal in southern African Later Stone Age Research. *South African Archaeological Bulletin* 60(182): 64–71.

Nowotny, H. 2003. The potential of transdisciplinarity. www.interdisciplines.org/medias/ confs/archives/archive_3.pdf, pp. 48–53 (accessed 2011).

Pauketat, T. 2001. Practice and history in archaeology: an emerging paradigm. *Anthropological Theory* 1: 73.

Prins, F. 2009. Secret San of the Drakensberg and their rock art legacy. *Critical Arts* 23(2): 190–208.

Shanks, M. and C. Tilley. 1987. *Reconstructing archaeology*. Cambridge: Cambridge University Press.

Skotnes, P. 1994. The visual as a site of meaning: San parietal painting and the experience of modern art. In *Contested images: diversity in southern African rock art research*, ed. T.A. Dowson and J.D. Lewis-Williams, 315–329. Johannesburg: Witwatersrand University Press.

Skotnes, P., ed. 1996. *Miscast: negotiating the presence of the Bushmen*. Cape Town: UCT Press.

Solomon, A. 2008. Myths, making and consciousness: differences and dynamics in San rock arts. *Current Anthropology* 49(1): 59–86.

Solomon, A. 2009. Broken strings: interdisciplinarity and |Xam oral literature. *Critical Arts* 23(1): 26–41.

Solomon, A. 2013a. The death of trance: recent perspectives on San ethnographies and rock arts. *Antiquity* 87: 1208–1213.

Solomon, A. 2013b. 'People who are different': alterity and the |Xam. In *The courage of ||Khabbo*, ed. J. Deacon and P. Skotnes. Cape Town: UCT Press.

Solomon, A. 2014. Central problems in southern African rock art research. Paper presented at the 'African Rock Arts colloquium', Sorbonne/Musée du Quai Branly, January.

Stow, G.W. 1905. *The native races of South Africa.* London: Swan Sonnenschein.

Wylie, J. 2007. *Landscape.* Oxford and New York: Routledge.

Researching the San, San/ding the research

Keyan G. Tomaselli

Abstract

Bureaucratic mechanisms adopted in universities which favour high publication output at the expense of inter-disciplinary collaboration translate into myopic vision within disciplines. Competition for limited resources often leads to academics clearly demarcating and jealously guarding their respective fields in order to justify their line of inquiry and, in the current economic climate, to emphasise the necessity of funding. This article argues for trans-disciplinary collaboration, using the field of 'Bushman studies' as a focal point. Trans-disciplinary researches around a single topic should be viewed as different components of an interlocking system. Myopic disciplinary vision should be cast aside in favour of more holistic approaches that incorporate multiple (and sometimes contradictory) viewpoints, to arrive at a more nuanced and realistic estimation of a particular field of inquiry.

Introduction

The postmodern (and post-apartheid) era with its emphasis on issues of identity has generated 'blackness studies', 'whiteness studies', 'ethnic studies', and studies of 'indigenous knowledge systems', all responding to postcolonial conceptual, class and political imperatives. Where does the certainty stem from, as expressed by John Wright, that the 'end of bushmen studies' has come? Is this the despair that is so characteristic of the postcolonial moment? Or, is it a new beginning? As one delegate responded: 'For my part, I think that, far from being pessimistic, John Wright's closing suggestion that we may have reached the "end of bushman studies" offers real hope, since it opens up the possibility of new and more rational approaches, some of which might even show us a way out of the muddy neo-colonial rut we seem to be stuck in right now' (Du Plessis, personal communication, 25 August 2013). Is the 'authentic Other' no longer findable as it once was? The Other is now within the academy, as is so bluntly and noisily depicted in the self-reflexive video, *I am, You Are?*[1] (Sætre 2002, 2003).

Rock art specialists, observes William Ellis, decipher an epitaph on a gravestone. Archaeologists exhume the poisoned and murdered corpse of the victim of genocide, colonial violence and the like. Linguists and folklorists decode the language and transcribe the holy book, a text that includes stylised nudity and scatological humour in addition to Victorian edits. The contrast and disgust of some delegates was evoked when presented with Marit Sætre's metaphorically pornographic video of rural poverty, disease, and the mess and confusion that typify lived researcher–researched interactions – all very raw. The veneer of culture, language, purity and whatever other aura of Bushmen, were stripped away by the video and some of the papers presented on studies of contemporary relations. What remains are naked, hungry, snot-nosed and dirty people from somewhere in the middle of nowhere.[2] Are these really our subjects in the postcolonial era?

Reconstructing the simulacrum holistically

The disciplines represented at the conference included history, archaeology, linguistics, rock art studies, literature, cultural and media studies, sociology, art and other disciplines. The often stark discontiguities that emerged in discussion led me to think of each of the disciplines as separately framed windows, each located in a circle (a point also made by other commentators). Their different disciplinary practitioners are standing on the outside of each window looking inwards into a common circular space. Within this circle is/are the object(s) of study: rock art, stories, languages, lived relations and individuals, development projects, the archaeological tracings of a particular people, both in history and contemporarily.

The perspective of each of the disciplines represented at the conference was framed by the small window through which it was observing its specific object of study. The practitioners of each discipline are aware of the other windows and of the other spectators looking into the circle. They are also keenly aware that their conceptual language – though English – is not common across all the disciplines looking into the common space. Each window uses a different kind of theoretical discourse to make sense of but a single fragment of the deep, complex and often bewildering multilayered world that is encapsulated under the combined gaze of the different disciplinary windows. Each window suggests its own way of looking, its own way of apprehending, its own ways of making sense. To a greater or lesser extent each window refuses, engages or reinterprets the methods brought to bear by other windows. This is a tolerant, if contested, relationship, as we all struggle to make sense of the other – in our case, our academic others (i.e., scholars located in disciplines and paradigms different to our own). It is a difficult relationship, especially when some ways of looking reveal disquieting situations which may cause anxiety, as was clear when Sætre's video was screened.

Each window is epistemologically limiting, each sees only a fragment, what its disciplinary assumptions allow it to see. But the window is beguilingly transparent – we see through it, but its opacity limits our understanding – in terms of both depth and breadth. Sometimes we are aware of the process of limitation; but more often we are not. Through each window can be heard different explanations, different constructions and competing interpretations of the same objects of study. Each knows that the academic other is out there, looking in, differently. Sometimes the dissimilar interpretations result in vigorous debates, anger or even horror at the other discipline's methods, explanations and outcomes.

While the differences are noted, they are not always fully understood, sometimes they are not engaged, and often they are simply rejected/ignored and may even be demonised. We are all looking into the same space, but we are suspicious of each other's windows, we are defensive of our own particular perspectives, and sometimes hostile to revelations from which our own frames of reference work to shield us. Few of us think about the people who actually inhabit the imagined circle – what do they think, feel and do? (See the poem by Deon Arends below.) They are perhaps Othered by us even as we seek to evade this positioning.

This is the situation that characterised the seminar. Let us now examine what those 'Bushmen' – our objects/subjects of study – on the *inside* looking *out* might have seen:

At the theoretical level (as William Ellis observes):

The conference (and this volume) drew on a small diversely specialist group; the dialogue was often productively interdisciplinary, but often at cross-purposes. Within the mix of disciplines common ground was hard to find. The tensions, and lest we forget and focus on difficulties only, the congruencies coalesce around issues of varied practice, theory, engagement and action spaces. The main tension was one of attempts to recover a rich past of a people versus very real presence in the here-and-now of a culturally mute and cosmologically autistic poor people.

A second related set of tensions circulated through, oscillate between, orbit around, bushman-ness as a fantasy acted out by academics-as-researchers, people (self-referential actors and volunteer bushmen), poets, bricoleurs, artists, musicians, by interlocutors and everybody who has something/anything to say versus the poverty of a people whose culture may have been incidentally bushman.[3]

Tensions of connection occurred between earlier and present, of a freely available past read from archives and archaeological record to the readings of the messy and disorientating present. (Ellis, personal communication, 27 August 2013)

From the *outside* the seminar provided an effective collegial working forum, a nuts-n-bolts environment to which graduate students significantly contributed. Some delegates queried student participation, but our students are the replacements of the 'elders', they must be apprenticed into the job, and the interdisciplinary environment – despite being separated by different windows – is a good place to explore disciplinary polygamy.

Disciplinary interstices enabled the identification of some of the hot, unresolved issues. These kinds of contestations opened up very productive inter-paradigmatic fissures, seeming contradictions, contestations and the need to address uncertainties through which we can manoeuvre in identifying new questions, new methods and new approaches. We started in a small way to replace the separate windows with their separate disciplinary frames and class assumptions with a large, single sheet of plate glass (which suggest a more integrated understanding). This plate, if slid open, will allow us to walk from the autistic outside, located as we are in each of our disciplinary imaginations, into the circular inner interconnected space, where those different imaginations can be fruitfully integrated, negotiated, and dialectically synthesised into more holistic frameworks.

At the level of method some taken-for-granteds were unsettled, some concepts troubled and some methods questioned. A new template may have begun to develop from these unsettling responses to certain presentations and videos. What the studies focusing on contemporary Bushmen generated was discussion of methods, reflexivity, ethics and the lived relations of doing action research – changing outcomes as we go. This approach attracted some criticism, as working in the contemporary realm was shown to be often chaotic, with researchers trying to make sense on the spot in relation to developing methods of interaction, writing and representation in which informants/subjects/hosts can recognise themselves and to which they can relate, and feel included rather than excluded (as objects of study, scientific language) from the final product. Nevertheless, as one delegate observed:

Certainly we are all 'different disciplinary practitioners', and certainly we each seem to stand 'on the outside of [our own] window looking inward'. But it is not clear that we are all contemplating the same thing, merely refracted differently by the different lenses we use. That we may be looking at very different things was suggested by one of the short films, which documented a journey on the part of postgraduate students and their academic mentors to discover some essential quality of 'San-ness', for a range of personal reasons that wavered chaotically in and out of the frame. The illusory nature of this quest was made dramatically plain when the camera collided with the stark truth of economic and social marginalisation, as the people invested with the burden of 'specialness' were filmed in a degrading scramble for handouts. I walked out of the room at this point because I was revolted – *not* by the graphic depiction of poverty, dismaying though it was, but by the project itself. (Du Plessis, personal communication, 25 August 2013)

The living are acutely aware that they are in the circle and being gazed at, and they do understand that their sale of the anthro-script requires some appreciation of the different windows through which the academic and journalist gazers make sense of them. Responses to the video vary starkly, depending on how viewers encounter it in relation to their own windows. Kalahari audiences recognise themselves and sometimes actively use the camera as their agent in negotiating their conditions and image with wider audiences. They do not necessarily see themselves as victims.

At the book launch, MA student Varona Sathiyah drew attention to a point of discomfort. She did what the academics did not do: Sathiyah argued for the diversification of ethnicities and subjectivities in the constitution of research teams. This is a *sine qua non* in the current postapartheid conjuncture. Diversity also changes the nature of the researcher–researched encounter, the quality of information offered, and how researchers are interacted with by living hosts/informants/co-researchers. This was done by the Biesje Poort rock engraving research team which employed and worked with four ‡Khomani informants/participants whose interpretations were requested (see Lange, Jansen and Fisher et al. 2013; Morris, this volume).

While Bushmen were in our narratives, regrettably, the conference resources could not stretch to include them at the conference venue. Remarking on this absence, Nhamo Mhiripiri observed:

In many ways the presentations made each and every one of us obliquely or directly counterpoise her or his own identity with that of the imagined San. This was not always reassuring since there were no San or Bushmen scholars to speak for themselves, or even to speak about us 'outsider' researchers who depend on their cultural capital for own academic careers. Indeed, at least one paper raised the issue of mentoring San graduate and postgraduate researchers who are a necessarily intellectual alter-ego to all those who attended the conference. This is a practical redressing of a glaring absence, where each one of us spoke on behalf of the San, notwithstanding our varied hesitations induced by that reflexive tendency that requires exposure of how we come to know about the San, why we want to know and for whose benefit. (Mhiripiri, personal communication, 25 August 2013)

My reciting of Deon Arends's contemporary poem/lament/curse (reproduced below with his permission) published on the iHoengeyqua Peoples Council of the Kat Rivier Facebook page, aimed to partly redress this lack. His poem encapsulates, in its own poignantly raw way, the subtext of much of our discussion over the three days. Arends, who was not present, uncannily speaks directly – as it were – to how we conducted ourselves at the conference. He offers a challenge to which academics should respond constructively.

Deon Sydney Arends
9:27pm Jan 8 2013

The Khoi inside of me....
As the morning sun rises and waves of the sea persist
So me and my people cannot be wish away
You have turned on the heat and you blocked your ears
But me cries and the drumbeat of my elders keep you awake
You have told the world that my people have died
Now our ghost will see you run
I shared our fight to destroy those who took my soil
Now I see that I should have killed him and you
You have tricked my kinsmen to your room
Now their stains will spoil your bed

Today I am dirt, return my land I insist
Your talks with them has made my people pay
I will rise and show your hidden fears
I am forced just for my children's sake
God's patience is running out, I sighed
With Him I need no spear or gun
You stood on me to make you tall
I am still coloured and you call it true
Simply that can bring your doom
You don't want to see a Hoena mad

On the Katberg Mountain the eagle cries
While the Eland grazes with inner fright
As the river crawls to the stormy sea
And the sweet aloes turns to bitter ale
So the patience of the Hoena shrink

My smile is fade and my laughter dies

My looks become a bitter sight

My pain has changed me to another me

You expected breeze now you will have a gale

Because you thought I could not think

'DJ Plaasnaar' Mackommershoek Kat Rivier

Perhaps it is within this kind of perceptual space created by Arends that Michael Wessels intended the conference to be located. While the indigenous were not present here as they were in 2012 Cape Town meeting during 'Miscast' (see Douglas and Law 1997; Jackson and Robins 1999) and during Thomas Dowson's 'People, Politics and Power' conference (Johannesburg 1994), the structure of this seminar opened up different kinds of dialogue, one of which was magnificently theorised by William Ellis, applied by Lauren Dyll-Myklebust in her analysis of lodge–community partnerships, and made contemporary by, for example, Matthias Brenzinger, Menán du Plessis, David Morris and others. Our living San sources want such acknowledgement; they crave recognition of their place in the academic sun, but they often feel like victims of intellectual property theft, they feel disempowered, even as they themselves may control many of the research interactions.

In postapartheid South Africa the indigenous are no longer considered indigenous and the new indigenous (i.e., those in power) now control what indigenous means. The idealist call made by Ntongela Masilela (1987) is that the study of original culture offers a route which is different to brutal contending black and white nationalisms. For him, 'Bushman studies' thus remains relevant in the face of new erasures of whole sections of minority ethnic histories. Redressing this erasure in the here and now, with all the mess and confusion that is depicted in Sætre's video, is why different groups of Bushmen collaborate with down-to-earth journalists like Rupert Isaacson (2001) and Patricia Glynn (2013), who interact with them on their own terms. Simultaneously, they very effectively leverage these relationships and the stories they tell and retell ad nauseum for the anthro-scripts that they sell and resell to visitors – the Jungian-derived myths spun of them by the Van der Postian kinds of writers.

There is, as another example, a vigorous Facebook discussion amongst the iHoengeyqua Peoples Council of the Kat Rivier on the way their ethnicity has been again imposed by state policy. This is compounded in the refusal by the state to acknowledge Afrikaans as an indigenous language. Overlaid on these issues is the way the Khoisan are allochronically imaged as being 'of the past', dislocated from the present and deprived of their futures (Fabian 1983; Tomaselli 1992).

Deon Arends's poem is very evocative and speaks on many levels (as did Piet Draghoender's curse/lament recited for my camera at Kat River in 1984; see Sienaert 1988; Tomaselli 1997). Where Draghoender poetically and powerfully agonised over betrayal by whites, Arends agonises over betrayal by blacks. The layers encoded by his raw, angry and threatening poem 1) identify the state's insensitive apartheid-derived classification of an original people still labelled as 'coloured' as during apartheid; 2) draws attention to the state's refusal to grant Afrikaans indigenous language status; 3) the poem addresses the 'stereographic metaphor', where government officials (and, dare I say it, some academics and many journalists) continue to allochronically image Kalahari and Khoi people essentially as living in the 'past', while some academics seem to be studying them from the vantage point of the present (see also Nichols 2008); 5) the poem indicates loss of citizenship. The KhoiSan are 'invisible', they do not exist in official categories, but are sandwiched between them. The retention of 'Bushman studies' may be one way of contesting this exclusion; 6) Arends's poem encapsulates a sense of fracture, a dualist subjectivity, a) the Khoi within; and b) the 'coloured' without. One's subjectivity is made officially indeterminate, neither here nor there, not connected to anything: neither origins, nor land, religion, ethnicity, psychology or language. This is the loss of citizenship, so to speak, of citizenship on their own terms. Finally, official state categories locate Khoisan as not knowing who they are. How can this be, given that we are all derived from this single genus?

Masilela sees the indigenous as having generated original culture at the dawn of Man – one that needs to be understood in relation to the contemporary struggles, anxieties and frustrations that have been so effectively communicated in both the Arends and Draghoender poems/curses. Original culture, argues Masilela, offers us a bridge between the past and the future, by helping us to avoid both white and black nationalisms, as these are destructive and squeeze minorities in their wake. For me, the time of the Bushman is now at hand. Bushman studies needs to start addressing contemporary issues in order to respond productively to the issues raised by both Masilela and Arends. Such studies will remain rooted on the ground, rather than pursuing the metaphorical Jungian and Van der Postian trajectories of the cultural isolate, postulated by Paul Myburgh in his film, *People of the Great Sandface* (1985) that he revisits in his recent book, *The Bushman winter has come* (2013). The claim to a 'true story' in Myburgh's title is an advance defence against critique of this kind of essentialist position that dismisses the type of mystical experience articulated by Myburgh (see, e.g., Gordon 1990), which is offered quite without any reference to competing interpretations of concepts of modernity and development (see Mikalsen 2008). These kinds of existential accounts are appealing because they affirm the

Western myth of Eden before the Fall, even after the Fall. Myburgh here locates himself at the centre of 'garden'.

In conclusion, Mhiripiri remarks:

> The credibility or 'authenticity' of the researched San or Bushmen informants is also not always uncontestable. The San/Bushmen sources are also part of the intricate process of representation, which process is further developed by different scholars and ends up as conference presentations, theses and publications. Perhaps no one holds the last word. The lingering question – is it necessary to conduct San or Bushmen conferences in future or was what we were experiencing one of the last of its kind? If practical ways to develop scholarship that train the autochthonous San graduate and postgraduate into researchers and writers of similar, if not better and much more erudite standards than our current crop of San scholars, then we might still have to see a reinvigorated San conferencing with 'new' voices and fresh insights.

Notes

1   *I am, You Are?* was constructed/represented in 1) documenting the nature (semiotics) of the researcher–researched encounter; 2) establishing the video maker/researcher position within the broader research team, and 3) to derive an in situ aesthetics that emerges from the research site itself. The fire dance catalysed by one of the research team unexpectedly enabled a Jean Rouch (1988)-like cinetrance, a surreality and rhythmography to emerge from the pro-filmic event unfolding in front of the two cameras. This enabled us to negotiate and reimagine Self–Other relations, operating at different levels; thereby enabling what film (and linguistic) scholars call parole (accent: texture, the experiential, the contradictory, the uncertainties, self-exposure of naivety). How to depict parole in relation to langue (genre, form, theory, finished video) in disaggregating and making visible/audible the constructedness of the representation/explanation offered, is the task of self-reflexive film-making. That is, how are we constructing our explanation? What sense do our audiences (as shown in the video) make of our imaginings and how do our research participants relate to the video? The student director's mini-dissertation explains her production approach to documentary film theory and principles of visual anthropology (Sætre 2003). Other writings on the video explain the context, particularly the fire dance and exchange sequences. The latter, where clothes are exchanged for camping rights, audiences appear to find amongst the most uncomfortable. Suffice to say that this exchange was requested by the community itself, which also negotiated in discussion with the research team the distribution mechanism depicted in the video. These proposals resolved the community's previously unhappy experiences where donated, rather than exchanged, goods were allegedly unfairly appropriated by a powerful official 'gatekeeper' within the community. The nature of the exchange – no matter its seemingly chaotic character – is indicative of 1) the Ngwatle community's self-agency and 2) its resistance to an emergent, corporately enabled village elite, where the gatekeeper (the shebeen owner/safari representative) allegedly hoarded resources donated to the community as a whole. In defying of the company's camping charge that was to be paid to the gatekeeper,

the community was questioning the service of the company itself with regard to 1) the erratic and insufficient distribution of meat during the hunting season; and 2) the lack of fair distribution of donor goods, that were usually left with the gatekeeper by passing travellers, missionaries and others. The community's hunting rights had been greatly curtailed when the Botswana government sold rights to the company whose clientele was 'the big white trophy hunter', for whom members of the community tracked. Part of the concession agreement was that hunters could keep the heads as trophies, but the carcases were to be equitably distributed to three villages dotting a huge area. The logistics (huge distances, 4x4 tracks in deep sand, scarcity of fuel, etc.) made regular deliveries almost impossible. These observations were discussed with the company, which agreed to the bartering of clothes for camping rights. Thus, where one paradigm might see a victimology in what might be interpreted as 'hand-outs', another identifies agency and resistance in the nature of the exchange.

2   The whole paragraph is a précis of a note sent me by William Ellis after the conference.

3   Ellis intentionally uses 'bushmen' with a small b (see article, this volume). Small b bushman is always a simulacrum. San/ding the research in the title refers to Ouma !Una's comments that she is San/d, not San, an imposed politically correct and pejorative term preferred by the politicians who impose identity on, and categorise, people who resist by reifying 'Bushmen' as a term of resistance (see Tomaselli 2007: 56).

References

Douglas, S. and J. Law. 1997. Beating about the Bush(man): reflection on 'Miscast: negotiating Khoisan history and material culture.' *Visual Anthropology* 10(1): 85–108.

Fabian, J. 1979. Rule and process: thoughts on ethnography as communication. *Philosophy of the Social Sciences* 9(1): 1–26.

Fabian, J. 1983. *Time and the Other*. Columbia: Columbia University Press.

Glynn, P. 2013. *What Dawid knew: a journey with the Kruipers*. Johannesburg: Picador.

Gordon, R. 1990. People of the Great Sandface: People of the great white lie. *Commission of Visual Anthology Review* (Spring): 30–34.

Isaacson, R. 2001. *The healing land*. London: Fourth Estate.

Jackson, S. and S. Robins. 1999. Miscast: the place of the museum in negotiating the Bushman past and present. *Critical Arts* 13(1): 69–101.

Lange, M.E., L.M. Jansen, R.C. Fisher, K.G. Tomaselli and D. Morris. 2013. *Engraved landscapes. Biesje Poort: many voices*. Gordon's Bay: Tormentoso.

Masilela, N. 1987. The white South African writer in our national situation. *Matatu* 3(4): 48–75.

Mikalsen, O. 2008. Development communication and the paradox of choice: imposition and dictatorship in comparing Sámi and San Bushmen experiences of cultural autonomy. *Critical Arts* 22(2): 295–332.

Myburgh, P. 2013. *The Bushman winter has come: the true story of the last band of |Gwike Bushmen on the Great Sandface*. London: Penguin.

Nicholls, B. 2008. Apartheid cinema and indigenous image rights: the 'Bushman myth' in Jamie Uys's *The Gods Must be Crazy. scrutiny2* 13(1): 20–32.

Rouch, J. 1988. Our totemic ancestors and crazed maters. In Cinematographic theory and new dimensions in ethnographic film, *Senri Ethnological Studies* No. 24, ed. P. Hockings and Y. Omori. Osaka: National Museum of Ethnography.

Ruby, J. 1977. The image mirrored: reflexivity and the documentary film. *Journal of the University Film Association* 29(1): 104–111.

Sætre, M. 2003. The bushmen and the Others. *Current writing: Text and Reception in Southern Africa* 15(3): 118–134.

Sienaert, E. 1988. Perspectives on and from oral testimony: Piet Draghoender's lament. *Mosaic* 21(3): 227–241.

Tomaselli, K.G. 1992. Myths, racism and opportunism: contemporary film and TV representations of the San. In *Film as ethnography*, ed. I.P. Crawford and D. Turton, 205–222. London: Manchester University Press.

Tomaselli, K.G. 1993. The post-apartheid era: the San as bridge between past and future. In *Eyes across the water* II, ed. R.M. Boonzajer Flaes and D. Harper, 81–90. Amsterdam: Het Spinhuis.

Tomaselli, K.G. 1997. Orality, rhythmography and visual representation. *Visual Anthropology* 9(1): 93–116.

Tomaselli, K.G., ed. 2007. *Writing in the San/d: autoethnography amongst indigenous southern Africans*. New York: Altamira Press.

Wynberg, R., D. Schroeder and R. Chennels. 2009. *Indigenous peoples, consent and benefit sharing: lessons from the San-Hoodia case*. London and New York: Springer.

Filmography

Myburgh, P.J. 1985. *People of the Great Sandface*. Anglia TV. 120 mins.

Saetre, M. 2002. *I Am, You Are?* VHS, DVD. (Ngwatle). 40 mins.

Index

INDEX

For Product Safety Concerns and Information please contact our EU
representative GPSR@taylorandfrancis.com Taylor & Francis Verlag GmbH,
Kaufingerstraße 24, 80331 München, Germany

Batch number: 08153807

Printed by Printforce, the Netherlands